thomson ● com

changing the way the world learns

To get extra value from this book for no additional cost, go to:

http://www.thomson.com/wadsworth.html

thomson.com is the World Wide Web site for Wadsworth/ITP and is your direct source to dozens of on-line resources. *thomson.com* helps you find out about supplements, experiment with demonstration software, search for a job, and send e-mail to many of our authors. You can even preview new publications and exciting new technologies.

thomson.com: *It's where you'll find us in the future.*

The Religious Life in History Series
CHARLES HALLISEY, *Series Editor*

The Chinese Way in Religion

SECOND EDITION

Jordan Paper
York University

Lawrence G. Thompson, Emeritus
University of Southern California

Wadsworth Publishing Company
I(T)P® *An International Thomson Publishing Company*

Belmont, CA • Albany, NY • Bonn • Boston • Cincinnati • Detroit • Johannesburg • London • Madrid
Melbourne • Mexico City • New York • Paris • Singapore • Tokyo • Toronto • Washington

Religion Editor: Peter Adams
Assistant Editor: Kerri Abdinoor
Editorial Assistant: Kelly Bush
Marketing Manager: Dave Garrison
Print Buyer: Stacey Weinberger
Permissions Editor: Robert Kauser

Copy Editor: Lauren Root
Cover Designer: Gary Head
Cover Photo: Victoria & Albert Museum,
   London/Art Resource, NY
Compositor: R&S Book Composition
Printer: R. R. Donnelley & Sons

The cover illustration is of the *fêng* (phoenix) on a tapestry. The *fêng* represents female spiritual energies and is often paired with the *lung* (dragon), representing male spiritual energies, which appears on the cover of the complementary volume to this one, *Chinese Religion: An Introduction*. Together they represent the intertwining of the numinous in its interrelated male and female aspects.

Printed in the United States of America
1 2 3 4 5 6 7 8 9 10

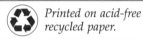 *Printed on acid-free recycled paper.*

For more information, contact Wadsworth Publishing Company, 10 Davis Drive, Belmont, CA 94002, or electronically at http://www.thomson.com/wadsworth.html

International Thomson Publishing Europe
Berkshire House 168-173
High Holborn
London, WC1V 7AA, England

International Thomson Editores
Campos Eliseos 385, Piso 7
Col. Palanco
11560 México D.F. México

Thomas Nelson Australia
102 Dodds Street
South Melbourne 3205
Victoria, Australia

International Thomson Publishing Asia
221 Henderson Road
=05-10 Henderson Building
Singapore 0315

Nelson Canada
1120 Birchmount Road
Scarborough, Ontario
Canada M1K 5G4

International Thomson Publishing Japan
Hirakawacho Kyowa Building, 3F
2-2-1-Hirakawacho
Chiyoda-ku, Tokyo 102, Japan

International Thomson Publishing GmbH
Königswinterer Strasse 418
53227 Bonn, Germany

International Thomson Publishing
Southern Africa
Building 18, Constantia Park
240 Old Pretoria Road
Halfway House, 1685 South Africa

Library of Congress Cataloging-in-Publication Data

The Chinese way in religion/Jordan Paper, Laurence G. Thompson.—
   2nd ed.
      p.   cm.—(The Religious life of man)
   Includes bibliographical references.
   ISBN 0-534-53735-9
   1. China—Religion.   I. Paper, Jordan.   II. Thompson, Laurence G.
BL1802.T52   1997
299'.51—dc21   97-12647

Contents

Foreword

The Religious Life in History series introduces the richness and diversity of religious thought, practice, experience, and institutions as they are found in living traditions throughout the world.

Some of the religious traditions included in the Religious Life in History series are defined by geography and cultural arenas, while others are defined by their development across cultural and geographic boundaries. In all cases, however, the introductions seek to take full account of the variety within each tradition while keeping in sight the traits and patterns that encourage both scholars and members of various religious communities to distinguish a particular religious tradition from others around it. Moreover, as a set of introductions to quite different religious traditions, the series naturally invites comparison between different ways of being religious and encourages critical reflection on religion as a human phenomenon more generally. Thus, in addition to containing volumes on different religious traditions, the series also includes a core text on the study of religion, which is intended to aid the kinds of comparative inquiry and critical reflection that the series fosters through its introductions to religion in particular cultural and historical contexts.

The basic texts in the Religious Life in History series all provide narrative descriptions of a religious tradition, but each also approaches its subject with an interpretive orientation appropriate to its focus. Some traditions lend themselves more to developmental, others to more topical, studies. This lack of single interpretive stance in the series is itself instructive. It reflects the interpretive choices made by the different authors, choices informed by a deep knowledge of the languages and cultures associated with the religious tradition in question. It also displays the methodological pluralism that characterizes the contemporary study of religion. But perhaps most importantly, it can serve as a useful reminder that what is considered religiously important in one context may not be so in another; indeed, what is viewed as religious in one culture may not be so regarded elsewhere.

Many of the basic texts in the series have a complementary anthology of reading selections. These include translations of texts used by the participants of a tradition, descriptions of practices and practitioners' experiences, and brief interpretive studies of phenomena important in a given tradition. In addition, all of the basic texts present a list of materials for further readings, including translations and more in-depth examinations of specific topics.

The Religious Life in History series was founded more than two decades ago by Frederick J. Streng. While Streng was editor of the series, continuous efforts were made to update the scholarship and to make the presentation of material more effective in each volume. These efforts will continue in the future through the publication of revised editions as well as with the addition of new volumes to the series. But the aim of the series has remained the same since its beginning: As Frederick Streng said, we hope that readers will find these volumes "introductory" in the most significant sense—as introductions to new perspectives for understanding themselves and others.

Charles Hallisey
Series Editor

Preface

In this reader, as in our *Chinese Religion: An Introduction,* we have proceeded from the conviction that Chinese religion may most fruitfully be studied as an expression of Chinese culture. We have sought primarily to provide descriptions and analyses that would illustrate this functioning of religion in the culture.

The defect of our approach is some slighting of the textual materials, and this has indeed caused us some uneasiness. So far as the works of the Confucian Canon and the philosophers are concerned, the abundance of available translations may enable the reader to compensate for what is not provided here. The most conspicuous omission in our anthology is that of Buddhist texts. Our problem here was the difficulty of selecting any few pages that would be basic, representative, and intelligible without an inappropriately elaborate apparatus of notes. In the end we settled for more pages of other sorts of materials and hope that available studies and translations may supplement them.

In any case, the lament of the anthologists (and their critics) must inevitably be that there is so much valuable material left out. They can only hope that they will not be taken to task as well for what they have put in. So far as that is concerned, we have aspired to present a multifaceted image of Chinese religion from earliest antiquity to the present day. Although we have used the same theoretical schema as in our *Introduction,* we have not followed the same order of treatment. We have here proceeded in a roughly historical line, with compromises effected here and there. Thus, for example, the selections from the Confucian *Analects* have been placed under Religion of the State instead of under the Ancient Native Tradition because the prominence of Confucius *in religion* seems most evident in the State cult.

An anthology is by definition the work of many hands, and it is a pleasurable obligation to express our gratitude to the many scholars (and their publishers) who herein illumine our subject. Special appreciation is due the colleagues who read and commented upon the manuscript, professors Spencer J. Palmer, Brigham Young University, and Willard Johnson, California State University, Long Beach. Professor Frederick J. Streng, editor of the series of which this volume is a part, has again placed us under heavy obligation, with his stimulating suggestions, encouragement, and stubborn refusal to accept anything but the best solution to every problem. Had it been feasible to incorporate every sound idea offered by each of these colleagues, this would indeed have been an ideal book; for the imperfect book that it is, in fact, they bear no responsibility.

Laurence G. Thompson
University of Southern California

Preface to the Second Edition

A quarter-century has passed since the first edition of *The Chinese Way in Religion* was prepared, and *Chinese Religion: An Introduction* is now in its fifth edition. The study of Chinese religion has advanced considerably since this work first appeared, and a large number of important studies of Chinese religion have since been published. Twenty-five years ago, the study of Chinese religion was still in its infancy, and most scholars concerned with the study of modern Chinese religion were anthropologists and sociologists, whereas scholars writing on traditional Chinese religion were trained in philosophy or intellectual history. Since that time, the field of Chinese religion as an aspect of the history of religions (comparative religion) has burgeoned, and the then radical approach of considering Chinese religion in the singular has to a degree become normative. This new edition had dropped some readings tangential to the study of Chinese religion and added a number of studies written since the first edition.

The changes in the structure of *Chinese Religion* have created a chasm with *The Chinese Way in Religion* for classroom purposes, since it was difficult to coordinate the two complementary volumes. In this new edition, the structure is identical with the new (fifth) edition of *Chinese Religion*. Each chapter of this volume of readings corresponds to the chapter of the same number in the introductory textbook.

I consider it a privilege to be afforded the opportunity to revise the pioneering work of Laurence Thompson. While the revisions continue, the spirit of the original edition, undoubtedly, some of the new choices reflect my own research concerns.

Jordan Paper
York University

A Note on Pronunciation

The romantization of Chinese words in this edition continues the Wade-Giles system utilized in *Chinese Religion: An Introduction*, except where the original excerpted articles or books utilized a different mode. The Pin-yin system is now becoming standard and will be found in the selections by Kenneth Dean, Terry Kleeman, and Jordan Paper (selections from *The Spirits Are Drunk* and the *Journal of Chinese Religions* only). It is hoped that this will not cause undue confusion.

Copyrights and Acknowledgments

pp. 89–106 reprinted by permission of the author and publisher from Chung-yuan Chang, "An Introduction to Taoist Yoga" in *The Review of Religion*, Vol. XX (Chicago, © 1956; pp. 131–148. Parts of the article later appeared in *Creativity and Taoism* by Chung-yuan Chang.

pp. 103–106 reprinted by permission of the author and publisher from Michael Saso, *The Teachings of the Taoist Master Chuang*, Yale University Press (New Haven), © 1978; pp. 198–203.

pp. 107–114 reprinted by permission of the author from John Lagerway, *Taoist Ritual in Chinese Society and History*, Macmillan Publishing Company (New York), © 1987; pp. 216–228.

pp. 123–127 reprinted by permission of the author and publisher from Rodney L. Taylor, *The Religious Dimensions of Confucianism*, State University of New York Press (Albany), © 1990; pp. 60–64.

pp. 137–146 *Ennin's Diary—The Record of a Pilgrimage in Search of the Law*, translated from the Chinese by Edwin O. Reischauer, copyright 1955, The Ronald Press Company (New York); pp. 61–63, 71–73, 217–218, 222–225, 231–234, 300–302, 321–322, 330–332, 341–342, 347–348, 361–362, 373, 382, 391–392, 214–215, 271–272.

pp. 146–153 reprinted by permission of the publisher, from Ferdinand D. Lessing, *Yung-Ho-Kung*, The Sino-Swedish Expedition Publications, Vol. 18 (Stockholm), copyright 1942; pp. 15–35, condensed.

pp. 154–156 reprinted by permission of the author and publishers, from John Blofeld, *The Wheel of Life*, Rider and Co. (London), © 1959; pp. 87–90.

pp. 156–160 reprinted by permission of The University of Chicago Press from "Diary of a Chinese Buddhist Nun: T'ze Kuang" translated by Y. Y. Tzu, in *The Journal of Religion*, Vol. VII, Nos. 5–6, October 1927, copyright 1927; pp. 612–618.

pp. 174–182, 196–198 reprinted by permission of the author and publisher from Jordan Paper, *The Spirits are Drunk: Comparative Approaches to Chinese Religion*, State University of New York Press, © 1995; pp. 159–162, 247–259.

pp. 183–190 reprinted by permission of the author from Michael Saso, *Blue Dragon, White Tiger: Taoist Rites of Passage*, The Taoist Center (Washington, D.C.), distributed by University of Hawaii Press (Honolulu), © 1990; pp. 165–174.

pp. 200–203 reprinted by permission of the publisher from Kenneth Dean, *Taoist Ritual and Popular Cults of Southeast China*, Princeton University Press (Princeton), © 1993; pp. 64–67, 69.

pp. 204–206 reprinted by permission of the authors from Jordan Paper and Li Chuang Paper, "Matrifocal Rituals in Parilineal Chinese Religion: The Variability of Patriarchality," *International Journal of Comparative Religion and Philosophy* 1/2 (Toronto), © 1995; pp. 27–39.

pp. 207–216 reprinted by permission of the author from Jordan Paper, "Mediums and Modernity: The Institutionalization of Ecstatic Religious Functionaries in Taiwan," *Journal of Chinese Religions* 25, © 1996; pp. 105–129.

Table of Chinese Religious History

(Ruling dynasties)   (Major religious events and characteristics)

I. FORMATION OF NATIVE TRADITION

Hsia (?–?1751 B.C.)
(not yet confirmed by archaeology)

Shang (?1751–?1111)   Oracle bones; ancestor worship already
(last centuries also called Yin)   dominant; worship of spirits of natural
                                                phenomena

Chou (?1123–221)   Feudal polity; *Shih Ching, Shu Ching, Yi*
722–481, "Spring and Autumn"   *Ching;* Confucius (551–479); *Ch'un Ch'iu*
(period covered by *Ch'un Ch'iu*)   and commentaries; ?Lao Tzu (*Tao Te*
403–221, "Warring States"   *Ching*). Formative Age of Philosophy:
(feudal system destroyed)   Mo Tzu (480–390), Meng Tzu (Mencius)
                                                (390–305), Chuang Tzu (365–290), Hsün
                                                Tzu (340–245), *et al.; Analects, Chung*
                                                Yung, Ta Hsüeh, Li texts, *Hsiao Ching*

Ch'in (221–206)   First Emperor establishes totalitarian
(First Emperor unifies China)   dictatorship, attempts thought control
                                                by book burning; rise of "religious
                                                Taoism"

II. INTRODUCTION, ASSIMILATION, AND DOMINANCE OF BUDDHISM

Former Han (206 B.C.–A.D. 9)   Imperial polity finally established; first
                                                great expansionist empire; Confucian-
                                                ism becomes state orthodoxy; scholars
                                                concentrate on texts of Confucian canon;
                                                state university founded to teach this
Later Han (A.D. 23–220)   canon; great age of credulity and super-
                                                stition; religious Taoism flourishes;
                                                Buddhism enters China and begins
                                                missionary work.

Three Kingdoms (220–265)   Rise of Neo-Taoist philosophy
(China partitioned)

Tsin (265–420)   Neo-Taoism and Buddhism eclipse
                                                Confucianism; Ko Hung (*Pao P'u Tzu*)
                                                (253–333?)

China partitioned between Southern   Buddhism flourishes
(Chinese) and Northern (non-Chinese)
Dynasties (420–589)

Sui (589–618)
(China united under Chinese rule)

T'ang (618–907)   China the world's greatest civilization;
                                                Buddhism reaches zenith of its
                                                influence, and then its temporal
                                                prosperity destroyed by State (845); first
                                                stirrings of Confucian renascence

III. RENAISSANCE OF NATIVE TRADITION:
DOMINANCE OF NEO-CONFUCIANISM

Five Dynasties (907–960)
(brief period of disunion)

(Northern) Sung (960–1127)	Chinese high culture attains its peak; rise of Neo-Confucian philosophy to reassert ancient native tradition against Buddhism
Second partition of China, between Southern Sung (Chinese) and Kin (non-Chinese) (1127–1280)	Continuation of cultural brilliance despite political weakness; Chu Hsi (1130–1200) greatest Neo-Confucian philosopher, whose interpretation of the canon was orthodox until 20th century
Yuan (1280–1368) (all of China under Mongol rule)	Europe gets its first, glamorous impression of Cathay from book of Marco Polo (in China 1275–1292)
Ming (1368–1644) (last Chinese dynasty)	Neo-Confucian orthodoxy dominant; beginning of unbroken contact with Europe: Matteo Ricci, S.J., reaches Peking (1600), followed by hundreds of Catholic missionaries
Ch'ing (1644–1911) (all of China under Manchu rule)	Neo-Confucian orthodoxy strait-jackets Chinese thought; "Rites Controversy"; decline of Catholic missions and proscription of missionary work; Protestant missions begin (1800); China's invasion by Western world (19th and 20th centuries)

IV. DISRUPTION OF TRADITION BY WESTERN IMPACT

Republic of China (confined since 1949 to Taiwan, *i.e.*, Formosa) (1912 to date) People's Republic of China (Communist-controlled mainland) (1949 to date)	Collapse of imperial polity; disruption of tradition

Data on dynasties much simplified. Dates for Hsia and Shang follow Tung, Tso-pin, *Chung-kuo Nien-li Chien-p'u* (Taipei: Yee Wen Publishing Co., 1960); dates of Chou philosophers follow Ch'ien, Mu, *Hsien-Ch'in Chu-tzu Chi-nien* (Hong Kong: University of Hong Kong Press, rev. ed. 1956), Vol. II, final chart.

The Chinese Way in Religion

CHAPTER 1

The Early Chinese Worldview

AN EARLY CLAN ORIGIN MYTH

The earliest Chinese texts are oracular inscriptions on ox scapulae and tortoise plastrons, which are brief and enigmatic. Several texts from the early Chou period nearly three thousand years in age have survived that inform us about early Chinese religious understanding and practice. The *Shih* (*Scripture of Odes*) and the *Shu* (*Scripture of Documents*), from which the following readings were taken, remained extant because they became the foundation texts of the *Ching* (*Canon of the Literati*),[1] along with the *Yi* (*Scripture of Change:* a divination manual that served as the basis for later philosophically oriented appendixes).[2] Reconstructed in the early Han dynasty following the Ch'in dynasty destruction of books, the *Ching* became the basis for the civil service examination system, the only door to both wealth and prestige until the present century.

The songs and odes collected in the *Shih* include those depicting the elite clan sacrifices[3] and recounting clan origin myths that may have been sung at the sacrifices, but we cannot know this for certain. Chinese origin myths did not focus on the creation of the world and humans as is normative to the Bible but rather were concerned with the origin of the aristocratic clans, an orientation found in many religious traditions; for example, in the native traditions of the Americas and in central African cultures.

Ode no. 245 (of the 305 odes) conflates the mythic origin of sacrifice, indeed of human culture, and the origin of the Chou ruling clan. This clan traced its origin to a more-than-human spirit, as did the myths of virtually all the ruling clans, from the earlier Shang dynasty to the last, the Manchu Ch'ing dynasty. The Ode begins with the impregnation of a human woman through spiritual means by a spirit being, often with bird connotations—the argument has been made by some scholars that the footprint was a bird's, that of a partially bird-bodied spirit—as was the case with the

---

[1]See *Chinese Religion: An Introduction*, Appendix I.

[2]See *Chinese Religion*, Chapter 2.

[3]For an example, see *Chinese Religion*, p. 42.

Shang and the Ch'ing. The child that ensues from this impregnation endures trials similar to those of the Greek Hercules. On maturity, he founds agriculture; hence, his title, Lord of Millet. With the produce from agriculture and husbandry, he institutes the sacrifices, the means for the living to communicate with superhuman powers, the dead of the clan. The following translation by the editor (J.P.) is based on but differs in major respects from that of Bernhard Karlgren (*The Book of Odes*).[4]

The one who first gave birth to our people [clan],
She was Chiang Yüan.
How did she birth the people?
She gave *yin* and *hsi* sacrifices
That she would no longer be barren.
She stepped in the big toe of Ti's [Power's] footprint.
She became radiant; she was enlarged;
She was blessed, and so she became pregnant.
It came about quickly that she gave birth, that she nurtured.
And so there was Hou Chi [Lord Millet].

She fulfilled her months,
and her first-born came forth.
There was no bursting, no rending,
No injury, no harm.
Manifesting the divine nature of it,
Did Shang Ti [Power on High, the totality of the ancestral spirits] not give
  her ease,
Did it not enjoy (her) sacrifices!
She bore her child with ease.

They laid him in a narrow lane;
The oxen and sheep nurtured him between their legs.
They laid him in a forest on the plain;
He was found by the woodcutters of the plain.
They laid him on cold ice;
Birds covered and protected him.
Then the birds went away,
And Hou Chi began to wail.
It carried far; it was strong—
His voice was that loud.

Then he crawled,
Then he was able to walk, to stand firmly.
He sought food for his mouth;
He planted (the soil) with large beans;
The beans waved (in the wind).
The cultivated grain had plenty of ears;
The hemp [for clothes] and grain (grew) thickly.
The gourd stems bore ample fruit.

---

[4]Stockholm: Museum of Far Eastern Antiquities, 1950, pp. 200–202.

Hou Chi's husbandry
Followed the method of assisting (the plants).
He cleared away the wild grass;
He sowed it with the yellow riches;
It grew evenly and luxuriantly.
It was thick; it was tall;
It flowered and set ears;
It became firm and good;
It had ripe ears; it had solid kernels.
Then he built his house in T'ai.

He sent down the fine cereals.
There was black millet, the double-kerneled;
Millet with red sprouts, with white sprouts.
He extended the black millet and the double-kerneled;
He reaped it, he took it by hectares;
He extended the millet with red sprouts and with white.
He carried it on his shoulder; he carried it on his back;
He brought it home and initiated the sacrifice.

Our sacrifice, what is it like?
Some pound (the grain), some bale it out,
Some sift it, some tread it.
We wash it and soak it;
We steam it through and through.
We plan (the sacrifice), we think it through.
We gather southernwood, we offer fat;
We take rams to sacrifice to the spirits of the road;
We roast, we broil,
In order to begin the coming year.

We fill the *tou* [stemmed] vessels,
The *tou* and the *teng* vessels.
As soon as the fragrance ascends,
Shang Di serenely enjoys it.
The far-reaching fragrance is truly good.
Hou Chi initiated the sacrifice,
And the people have given no offense
Nor cause for regret to the present day.

EARLY INTERACTION WITH THE SPIRIT REALM

The *Shu,* only parts of which are actually of pre-Han dynasty date, contains records of speeches and other events pertaining to the ruling Chou clan that date to approximately three thousand years ago. In the following excerpt, the model minister from the standpoint of later Confucian ethics, the Duke of Chou (Chou Kung), prays for the recovery from illness of his elder brother, the King. It is this act among others, even if apocryphal, that led later theorists to view the Duke of Chou as exemplifying the ideal of human relationships: between son and father (the Duke of Chou is sacrificing to his dead father and more distant relatives, who function as deities), between younger brother and elder brother (the Duke puts the welfare of his older brother before his own), and between minister and ruler (the Duke, who served as a major minister in the government, offers his life to save that of his sovereign). In this excerpt, we receive a clear depiction of the concept of prayer, of communication with powerful superhuman forces, in early China. We also can note, even at this early time, of the importance of writing in Chinese religion. All major communications between the literate aristocracy and the numinous though spoken, were also in writing. The writing itself had a sacred aura and was to be carefully kept and reverenced. In the following passage, the ubiquitousness of divination in aristocratic life and government is made manifest. The translation below, by Bernhard Karlgren (*The Book of Documents,* pp. 35–36), has been slightly edited.

SHU: "THE METAL-BOUND COFFER"

After the victory over the Shang, in the second year, the king fell ill and was not happy. The two princes (Shao Kung and T'ai Kung) said: "We shall for the king solemnly take tortoise oracle."[5] Chou Kung said: "One cannot distress our former kings." The prince then proffered himself. He made three altars on the same arena. He made an altar on the southern side, facing north. Chou Kung took his place there. He held upright a *pi* jade disc and he grasped a *kuei* [jade] tessera. And so he addressed T'ai Wang, Wang Ki and Wen Wang.[6] The scribe then put on tablets the prayer, saying: "Your chief descendant So-and-so has met with an epidemic sickness and is violently ill. If you three kings really owe a great son to Heaven (i.e., if he must die), then substitute me. Tan [his personal name], for So-and-so's person. I am good and compliant, clever and capable; I have much talent and much skill. I can serve the Spirits. Your principle descendant does not, like me, Tan, have much talent and much skill; he cannot serve the spirits. But he has been appointed in the Sovereign's hall, extensively to possess the four quarters and thereby be able firmly to establish your descendants on Earth here below. Of the people of the four quarters, there are none who do not revere and fear him. Oh, do not let fall the precious mandate [fate to reign] sent down by Heaven, then our former kings will also forever have a reliance and resort (i.e., sacrifices to sustain them). Now I will announce the inquiry to the great tortoise. If you grant me my wish (that the king may recover), I will with the *pi* jade disc and the *kuei* tessera return and wait for your order (to be called away by death). If you do not grant me my wish, I will shut up the jade disc and the tessera (i.e., function no more as an officiant in sacrifices)." Then he divined with the three tortoises [i.e., three times]; all in the same way were auspicious. He opened the bamboo tubes (receptacles for writing slips) and looked at the documents [seemingly referring to divination by the *Yi*]; they likewise indicated that this was auspicious. The prince said (to the king): "According to the content (of the oracle), the king will suffer no harm." (The king said:) "I, the little child,[7] anew have obtained an

---

[5]Pyroscapulamancy, the use of which has a circumpolar distribution, uses the plastron of a tortoise or the scapula of a herbivore. (J.P.)

[6]The founding ancestors of the Chou royal house, the last being Chou Kung's deceased father and that of the king. (J.P.)

[7]Self-referent term used by rulers. (J.P.)

appointment from the three kings (i.e., a new spell of life): for a distant end I shall plan; what I now expect is that they will care about me, the One Person."[8] When the prince had returned, he placed the tablets in the metal-bound coffer. The next day the king got better [but the Duke of Chou did not die]. . . .

EARLY COSMOLOGY AND RELIGION
ACCORDING TO HAN SCHOLARS

Aside from the three texts mentioned above, as well as a few texts from the later part of the Chou period, the material we have on the early Chinese religious understanding is based on a synthesis of Han dynasty scholarship. The Hans scholars were attempting to reconstruct the beliefs and practices of a past from which they were separated by a gulf whose bridge had been burned by the First Emperor of Ch'in.

We wish now to give some idea of this sort of reconstruction, which will not only reveal what the Han scholars conceived ancient civilization to have been like, but equally important, the sort of thinking that was characteristic of the new age of Han itself. Or at least this sort of thinking was characteristic of the intellectual level of Han society. It may serve as representative of the religious outlook of the literati just before the Native Tradition was engaged by the very different thought of Buddhism.

The material to follow is from a book called *Po Hu T'ung: The Comprehensive Discussions in the White Tiger Hall,* E. J. Brill (Leiden, 2 vols., 1949 and 1952), by Tjan Tjoe Som [Tseng Chu-sen]. The "comprehensive discussions" of the title refer to a council of scholars on the Classics called by the Later Han Emperor Hsiao-chang in C.E. 79 to consider and render authoritative exegeses of various uncertain points in the Scriptures. We give first a few words of explanation by the author, and then some selections from his translations of various parts of the *Po Hu T'ung* text itself. We have condensed and edited the excerpts.

Like many precontemporary translations, the following was made before an interest in precisely translating technical philosophical terms, as well as an awareness of inaccurate androcentric use of language, had developed. Accordingly, where you find the word "man," you should understand the Chinese intent is "humans." The use of "God" is problematic. A better word would have been "Spirit" or "Deity," for the term "God" is gendered and obscures the fact that the "Deity of Earth," for example, is female, whereas the complementary "Deity of Heaven [Sky]" is male. Finally, the term translated as "Five Elements" is now almost universally translated as "Five Agents," to avoid a Hellenistic reading of the Chinese term.

PO HU T'UNG

[The *Po Hu T'ung*] gives us an idea of the way in which the Classics were interpreted in the Han period. We have often heard of the combination of Classical

---

[8]Title frequently used by rulers. (J.P.)

(*ching*) and Apocryphal (*wei*) Books, of the *ching* being the warp and the *wei* being the woof, the former constituting the outer, the latter the inner study; nowhere else can we find such a clear and comprehensive illustration of this curious method of interpretation as in the *Po hu t'ung*.

It gives us an idea of the cosmology of the Han, that curious blending of naturalism and ethics, in which such great emphasis was laid on correct ritual behavior, and in which the King figured as the living link and mediator between the world in Heaven and everything under Heaven. Even if the *Po hu t'ung* is unsatisfactory in its descriptions of details, probably no other text presents so complete a picture of this cosmology as a system. . . . (pp. 175f)

(Concerning the Apocryphal Books (*wei*) mentioned above): It would . . . not be too far wrong to assume that the contents of the *wei* on the whole were already current during the second century B.C., but that they did not take the shape of the written documents with their bizarre titles until later, while at the same time new elements, especially historical allusions, were introduced.[9]

In the process of amalgamation of the diverse beliefs into one universal system during the Former Han, the *wei* with their cosmological speculations and their classifications provided the background against which the scholars tried to understand and explain the Classics. On the whole the Classics did not provide a systematic and organic world-conception. . . . All the same we must assume that in general the Schools, including the Confucians, were arguing and disputing with each other against the background of the same world-conception, though we do not exactly know what it was. When in the Han Confucianism was made the official creed the situation changed. Political unity having been established, a new world-conception had to be found, corresponding with that unity, and not or not sufficiently furnished by the Classics. The *wei* united the beliefs current in the Han, many elements of which had been handed down from non-Confucian Schools of pre-Han times. They became complements to the Classics indeed, and not only interpretations of the Classical texts, which, somehow, despite their ambiguous wording, did not bear stretching beyond a certain degree of elasticity. Thus on the one hand the *wei* 'popularized' the Classics by proving that they did not conflict with the prevailing beliefs, on the other hand these beliefs were 'authorized' by enlisting the support of the Classics. . . . (p. 118)

The Five Deities

What is meant by the Five Deities (*wu-ssu*)? They are the outer door, the inner door, the well, the hearth, and the impluvium.[10] Why are they worshipped? Because they are the places where men dwell, by which they go in and out, and where they drink and eat. Therefore they are worshipped as spirits. How do we know that the Five Deities are called outer door, inner door, well, hearth, and impluvium? The "Yüeh ling" (a chapter of *Li Chi*) says: "[In spring] they sacrifice to

---

[9]Readers desiring a thorough treatment of this subject should see Fung Yu-lan, translated from Chinese by Derk Bodde, *A History of Chinese Philosophy* (Princeton Univ., vol. 2, 1953), chap 3 (L.G.T.)

[10]So rendered by our translator. The term literally means "the central place where the rainwater drops down from the roof." However, it is usually understood as indicating the middle of the room or hall. (L.G.T.)

the inner door, [in summer] to the hearth, [in the middle of the year] to the impluvium, [in autumn] to the outer door, and [in winter] to the well."

Why is it that only [those with the rank of] great officer and higher have the right to sacrifice [to the Five Deities]? A common officer has a lowly position and a meagre remuneration, [so] he only sacrifices to his ancestors. The *Li* says: "The Son of Heaven sacrifices to Heaven and Earth, the Feudal Lords sacrifice to the mountains and rivers, the Ministers and great officers to the Five Deities, the common officers sacrifice to their ancestors." (Another text says:) . . . "There should be no presuming to resume any sacrifice which has been abolished [by proper authority], nor to abolish any which has been so established. A sacrifice which it is not proper to offer, and which yet is offered, is called a licentious sacrifice. A licentious sacrifice brings no blessing."

Why are the Five Deities successively sacrificed to in the course of the year? They follow [the succession of] the Five Elements. . . . (pp. 376f)

The Gods of the Earth and of the Millet (she chi)

Why is it that the King has a God of the Earth and of the Millet? [They are the gods whom he can ask] for prosperity for the benefit of all under Heaven, and whom he can thank for their works. Without land man would not [be able to] eat. Land [,however,] is wide and extensive, and cannot be worshipped everywhere. The species of grain are too numerous, and cannot be sacrificed to one by one. Therefore a tumulus of earth is erected for an altar of the God of the Earth in order to make manifest the holder of the earth. Millet is the most important of the species of grain. Therefore an altar of the God of Millet is erected, to which sacrifices are made. The use of millet is most general because it has absorbed the equi-balanced and harmonious influences of the yin and the yang. Therefore it is considered the principal [of the species of grain].[11]

Why are there two sacrifices [to the Gods of the Earth and of the Millet] in a year? In spring [the sacrifice] means a request [for prosperity], in autumn it means a thanksgiving [for the received boon]. . . .

Why is it that the King and the Feudal Lords each have two altars of the God of the Earth? Both are Lords holding land. Therefore a text says: "The King has two altars of the God of the Earth; he erects one altar for all under Heaven, called the 'Great Altar of the God of the Earth' *t'ai-shê*, and another for himself, called the 'King's Altar of the God of the Earth' *wang-shê*. (Similarly the Feudal Lords.) To the Great Altar thanks are offered for its works on behalf of all under Heaven. To the King's Altar thanks are offered for its works on behalf of the capital. The Great Altar is more honourable than the King's Altar. . . .

Why must the King and the Feudal Lords have a Warning God of the Earth? (*chieh-shê*, the God of Earth of a vanquished State) To remind that there is preservation and loss, and to indicate that those who do well will succeed and those who do evil will fail. Therefore a text says: "Of the God of the Earth of a vanquished state the upper part is covered, and round the lower part a palisade is built." Another text says: "The God of the Earth of a vanquished state is roofed in." It indicates that it is separated from [the influences of] Heaven and Earth. . . . The *Li* says:

---

[11]For the archaic myth in which "Lord Millet" is portrayed as the ancestor of the Chou, see the *Shih Ching* poem in the preceding (L.G.T.).

"The Gods of the Earth and of the Millet of a vanquished state must be used as a screen for the ancestral temple." It means that they are treated contemptuously.

Why is the altar of the Gods of the Earth and of the Millet outside the middle and inside the outer gate [of the palace]? To honour [the gods] and yet to be near to them. They are [treated in] the same [way] as the ancestors. . . . A text says: "To the right there is the altar of the Gods of the Earth and of the Millet, to the left there is the ancestral temple."

Why is it that the altar of the God of the Earth has no roof? To keep it in contact with the fluids of Heaven and Earth. Therefore a text says: "The Great Altar of the Son of Heaven must [be open to] receive the hoarfrost, the dew, the wind, and the rain, so that it can be in contact with the fluids of Heaven and Earth." Why is there a tree on the altar of the Gods of the Earth and of the Millet? That it may [thereby] be honoured and recognized. [Thus] the people may see it from afar and worship it. [The tree is] also the expression of [the god's beneficent] capacities. . . .

Why does the King sacrifice in person to the Gods of the Earth and of the Millet? The God of the Earth is the spirit of the earth. The earth produces the ten thousand things, and is the host of all under Heaven. Out of reverence for it [the King] therefore sacrifices in person.

What is the size of the altar? A text says: "The altar of the Gods of the Earth and of the Millet of the Son of Heaven is fifty feet wide [on each side], that of the Feudal Lords is one half thereof." What is its colour? A text says: "The Son of Heaven has a Great Altar; it is green on the east, red on the south, white on the west, black on the north. The top is covered with yellow earth. Thus, when [the Son of Heaven] is going to enfeoff a Feudal Lord [with a territory] in the east, he takes [a clod of] green earth [from his altar], wraps it in a white *mao* [leaf, and gives it to him]. For each [Feudal Lord receiving a fief the Son of Heaven] takes [earth] from the [corresponding] side [of his altar], with which [the Feudal Lord constructs the mound for his [own altar of the] God of the Earth. . . .

Is music used at the sacrifice to the Gods of the Earth and of the Millet? The text says: "Music [the instruments of which are] executed in metal and stone, finding its expression in tunes and notes, and used in the ancestral temple and at the altar of the Gods of the Earth and of the Millet." (pp. 379–386)

The Five Elements

What is meant by the 'Five Elements' *wu-hsing*? Metal, wood, water, fire, and earth. The word *hsing* (which is a verb) is used to bring out the meaning that [in accordance] with Heaven the fluids have been 'put into motion' *hsing*. Earth aids Heaven as the wife serves her husband, and the Minister serves his Lord. . . .

Water has its position in the northern quarter. The north is [the place] where the yin-fluid lies beneath the Yellow Sources, having as its task the nourishment of the ten thousand things. 'Water' *shui* means *chun* 'level.' It nourishes the things equally, possessing the propensity of always being level.

Wood [has its position] in the eastern quarter. The east is [the place] where the yang-fluid begins to move, and the ten thousand things begin their life. 'Wood' *mu* means *cho* 'to knock'; the yang-fluid moves and jumps, knocking against the earth to break out.

Fire [has its position] in the southern quarter. The south is [the place] where the yang is superior, and the ten thousand things hang down their [luxuriant] branches. 'Fire' *huo* means *wei-sui* 'to follow as a result'; it means that the ten thousand things have fully unfurled themselves. *Huo* also means *hua* 'to change'; the yang-fluid holding sway, the ten thousand things transform themselves and change.

Metal [has its position] in the western quarter. The west is [the place] where the yin begins to rise, and [the development of] the ten thousand things is called to a stop. 'Metal' *chin* means *chin* 'to stop.'

Earth [has its position] in the center. The center is [occupied by] the earth. The earth has as its task to bring forth the ten thousand things. 'Earth' *t'u* means *t'u* 'to bring forth.' . . . (pp. 429f)

Why is it that the Five Elements alternate their 'kingship'? Because they engender each other in succession, so that [each of them has] an end and a beginning. Wood engenders fire, fire engenders earth, earth engenders metal, metal engenders water, water engenders wood. . . . It is said that each of the Five Elements by its nature is either the yin or the yang. Since wood engenders fire, why is it that [fire] repays it by consuming its mother? The reply is: Metal conquers wood, and fire on behalf of wood wishes to destroy metal; [but] metal is hard and strong difficult to smelt, therefore [wood,] the mother, sacrificing its own body, comes to the aid of fire to burn metal. . . .

Why is it that wood is 'king' for seventy-two days? Earth is 'king' during the four last months of the season, each time for eighteen days; together [with each of the other four elements it governs] for ninety days, which makes one season. [Each of the four elements together with earth is] 'king' for ninety days. . . . (pp. 437–439)

The Five Elements having a constant existence, why does fire suddenly disappear? Water is the elder yin; [it represents] punishment, therefore it is constantly existent. Metal is the younger yin, wood the younger yang; their fluids are weak and admit of no change; therefore they are also constantly existent. Fire is the elder yang, infinitesimal and fine, a representation of the Lord of men, representing him as honoured and constantly hidden, as the Son of Heaven abides in the confines of the nine double [walls], guarded by his subjects. [As fire is] concealed in wood, [so the Lord of men] reposes in consideration for others. Wood grows of its own nature, metal requires [the force of] man to be taken out and shaped because the yin, being lowly, cannot of itself take shape. . . .

Why is it that Heaven is light within and dark without, whereas man is light without and dark within? It means that Heaven and man exercise their influence by their desire to supplement each other. . . . (pp. 440f)

[Here follows an interesting series explaining the way nature gives the pattern for human social behavior; we give only a few examples]:

According to what pattern does the son succeed after the death of his father? He patterns himself after wood, which, terminating [its rule, is succeeded by] fire [taking up] 'kingship.'

According to what pattern does the son obey his father, the Minister obey his Lord, and the wife obey her husband? They pattern themselves after Earth, which obeys Heaven.

According to what pattern does the King bestow his favours first on his relatives and close associates, and afterwards on the distant? He patterns himself on the rain from Heaven, from which the highest [parts of the earth] first receive [the benefit].

According to what pattern does the son wear mourning for his parents? He patterns himself on wood, which withers in the absence of water.

According to what pattern does the mourning last three years? It patterns itself after [the fact that there is] one intercalary month in three years, by which the Way of Heaven is terminated. (pp. 442–445)

District Archery Contests

Why does the Son of Heaven in person practice archery? To aid the yang-fluid in stimulating the ten thousand things. In spring the yang-fluid is small and weak, and it is to be feared that the [ten thousand] things, meeting obstructions, will not be able to come out by their own strength. Now in archery [the arrow proceeds] from the inside to the outside, it pierces and enters the solid and hard [target, thus] resembling the bringing forth of [nascent] things. Therefore by means of archery they are stimulated [to come out]. (p. 474)

Calamities and Extraordinary Events

Why does Heaven [send down] calamities and [cause] extraordinary events? It is to warn the Lord of men and make him conscious of his deeds, so that he may wish to repent his faults, attend to his spiritual power, and exercise deeper solicitude. A text says: "When the conduct [of the Son of Heaven] shows shortcomings, and his passion goes against Heaven, it will provoke calamities to come down as a warning to men." (p. 489)

When the sun is eclipsed, why must it be rescued? Because the yin is encroaching upon the yang. A drum is beaten and a victim is sacrificed to the God of the Earth. This god is the personification of the assembled yin [-forces]. It is tied with a red cord, and a drum is beaten to attack it; [thus] with [the help of] the yang the yin is reproved. Therefore the *Ch'un Ch'iu* says: "[In the sixth month, the first day of the moon] the sun was eclipsed. Drums were beaten and victims offered to the God of the Earth." (The translator notes that while one commentator suggests that "the god is first reproved by the beating of the drum, and afterwards treated with ceremony by the offering of victims," two of the classical commentaries—which themselves attained scriptural status—hold that "the use of victims is against the rites.") (p. 491)

Divination with the Milfoil and the Tortoise-shell

From the Son of Heaven down to the common officer every one has to practise divination with the milfoil [stalks] and the tortoise-shell because in important matters where decisions have to be taken on dubious points one must show that one is not going to act of one's own accord. The *Shang shu* (*Shu Ching*) says: "If thou hast doubts about any great matter consult with thy Minister, consult with the common people, consult the tortoise-shell and the milfoil." (Another text says:) "To determine [the issues for] good or evil [of all events] in all under Heaven, to make all under Heaven full of strenuous endeavors, there are no [agencies] better than divination with the milfoil or the tortoise-shell." . . .

Why is it that from among the number of dry plants and hard bony material only the milfoil and the tortoise-shell are used [for divination]? They are the longest-living things between Heaven and Earth, therefore they are consulted. . . .

Why is it that at the divination with the milfoil the drawing of the figures must take place in the ancestral temple? Because, observing the rules attached to one's status, one applies for wisdom to the most exalted. Therefore [the stalks are] consulted through the medium of the ancestors.

What is the place [taken by the divinator] to divine an [auspicious] time? [The divinator] takes his place in the west, and faces east; this is his position at the divination with the milfoil. During the divination he turns to the west, after it he turns back, and faces east. His standing in the east and his facing the west when he is consulting the stalks [as, when he is consulting the tortoise-shell,] means that the younger [east] consults the elder [west].

With a cap of white deer-skin and white silk nether-garments gathered at the waist, [thus the divinator] applies [for advice] to the plain material [constituted by the milfoil and the tortoise-shell]. . . .

Why are the tortoise-shell and the stalks buried after they have been used up? Out of reverence, to avoid that the things which have been honoured should be polluted by men. (pp. 522–526)

Heaven and Earth

What does *t'ien* 'Heaven' mean? *T'ien* means *chên* 'to govern.' Resting on high, [Heaven] regulates [all that is] below it, governing on behalf of man. Earth is created out of the primeval fluid, and is the ancestor of the ten thousand things. *Ti* 'Earth' means *shih* 'to spend,' *ti* 'to examine.' Responding [to Heaven] it spends [its nourishing powers] and brings about transformations; it investigates and examines unerringly; reverencing the beginning it honors the end; therefore it is called *ti*.

The ten thousand things contain the capacity of mutation and change. In the very beginning there was first the Great Origin (*t'ai-ch'u*), then came the Great Beginning (*t'ai-shih*); when the assuming of form was completed it was called the Great Simplicity (*t'ai-su*). It was [still] chaotic, undivided, invisible, inaudible. Then it divided, and after the clear and the muddy were separated the infinitesimal and sparkling [elements] emerged and dispersed, and the multitudes of things were endowed with life.

The infinitesimal [elements] became the Three Luminary Bodies and the Five Elements. The Five Elements produced the emotions and instincts; the emotions and instincts produced harmony and equilibrium; harmony and equilibrium produced intelligence and understanding; intelligence and understanding produced the spiritual power [proceeding from the possession] of the Way; this again produced cultural refinement. . . . (pp. 591f)

CHAPTER 2

Prescientific Theory
and Religious Practice

USE OF THE *YI CHING*

The *Tso Chuan* is a long and detailed history of feudal China from 722 to 481 B.C., in particular as that history concerns the State of Lu. It is the text we must consider in conjunction with *Shu, Shih,* and *Yi,* as we attempt to find evidence of the beliefs and practices in early China. The translation is by James Legge, *The Chinese Classics,* vol. 5, p.103.

Two divinatory practices were standard at the courts of the feudal states in archaic times. One was by the tortoise shell and the other by the stalks of the milfoil plant. We give now one of the instances recorded in *Tso Chuan* of divination by the stalks, which clearly shows the oracular use of the *Yi Ching* in Ch'un Ch'iu times:

Duke Li of Ch'en . . . begat Ching-chung, during whose boyhood there came one of the historiographers of Chou to see the marquis of Ch'en, having with him the *Chou Yi.* The marquis made him consult it by the milfoil on the future of the boy when he found the diagram Kuan (☷☴), and then by the change of manipulation, the diagram P'i (☷☰). "Here," he said, "is the deliverance;"—'We behold the light of the State. This is auspicious for one to be the king's guest. (See the *Yi* on the fourth line, counting from the bottom, of the diagram Kuan).' Shall this boy in his generation possess the State of Ch'en? Or if he do not possess this State, does it mean that he shall possess another? Or is the thing foretold not of his own person, but of his descendants? The light is far off, and its brightness appears reflected from something else. K'un (☷) represents the earth; Sun (☴), the top part of the diagram Kuan, wind; Ch'ien (☰), heaven; Sun becoming Ch'ien over earth [as in the diagram P'i], represents mountains. Thus the boy has all the treasures of mountains, and is shone on by the light of heaven:—he will dwell above the earth. Hence it is said, 'We behold the light of the State. This is auspicious for him to be the king's guest.' A king's guest fills the royal courtyard with the display of all the productions of his State, and the offerings of gems and silks,—all excellent things of heaven and earth; hence it is said—'It is auspicious for him to be the king's guest.'

"But there is still that word—'behold,' and therefore I say the thing perhaps is to be hereafter. And the wind moves and appears upon the earth;—therefore I say it is to be perhaps in another State. If it be in another State, it must be in that of the Chiang;—for the Chiang are the descendants of the Grand-mountain (legendary emperor Yao's chief minister). But the mountains stand up as it were the mates of heaven. There cannot be two things equally great; as Ch'en decays, this boy will flourish."

USE OF *FÊNG-SHUI*

Our second selection in this chapter is an article by Jack Potter, entitled "Wind, Water, Bones and Souls: The Religious World of the Cantonese Peasant," which we reproduce in extenso from the *Journal of Oriental Studies* (University of Hong Kong), VIII, 1 (Jan. 1970), pp. 139–153. It brings together the several most important ingredients of the peasant religion and further shows that the yang force that fêngshui endeavors to utilize is in fact the universally found principle of *mana*. Research for this study was carried on by the author during 1961–63 in the village of Ping Shan in the New Territories of Hong Kong. (The Cantonese terms used in this paper are romanized following the Chao system of Cantonese romanization. Yuen-ren Chao, *Cantonese Primer* [Cambridge, Mass.: Harvard University Press, 1947]. We omit the Chinese characters appearing in the original paper.)

Much has been written about Chinese peasant religion, but there have been few attempts to show how these diverse 'superstitions' (as they are sometimes called) function as a meaningful system in the lives of Chinese peasants.[1] In this paper I present an interpretation of the religious and magical beliefs of the villagers of Ping Shan, a Cantonese lineage in Hong Kong's New Territories.[2] I attempt to show how their basic social values and supernaturalistic beliefs and practices interrelate to form a meaningful and fairly consistent worldview and philosophy of life. The intense drive for success and security in this world, the mainspring of a dynamic and highly competitive society, was intimately related to the villagers' view of their place in the universe and their relations with the superhuman forces and beings which inhabited this universe.[3] If the villager was able to bind these supernatural forces to his will, or enlist the aid of supernatural

---

[1]Notable exceptions are the works by J. J. M. De Groot, *The Religious System of China*, 6 vols. (Leiden: E. J. Brill, 1892–1910); Francis L. K. Hsu, *Under the Ancestors' Shadow* (New York: Columbia University Press, 1948), and C. K. Yang. The interpretation of Chinese religion given here, although based on different data, is similar to the one given by De Groot.

[2]The field research on which this article is based was carried out in Ping Shan, a Chinese lineage in Hong Kong's New Territories, from August 1961 through January 1963. The Ping Shan lineage is made up of eight villages centered on an ancestral hall dedicated to the lineage founder. The Tangs of Ping Shan have inhabited this area since the twelfth century, and although many changes have taken place in village culture over the past fifty years since their incorporation into the British Colony of Hong Kong, enough of the old beliefs still remain to allow a reconstruction of these major features of their belief systems.

[3]Unlike many peasant societies that have a worldview characterized by what Professor George M. Foster, in 'Peasant Society and the Image of Limited Good', *American Anthropologist*, 67:193–315 (1965), has called the Image of Limited Good, the Cantonese and Chinese peasants in general exhibited an intensive achievement orientation. I do not mean to imply that the Image of Limited Good model is entirely inapplicable, because many aspects of Chinese peasant life do correspond with this model.

beings, it was possible to achieve a long life, success and fortune. If he did not deal with these forces and beings in a proper fashion, thus alienating or disturbing them, and if he did not receive their aid in his worldly affairs, life could be a continuous series of disasters and failures. Those ordinary persons who simply 'lived along' with average success had achieved a kind of neutrality in their relations with the supernatural world. They succeeded in passing through life without incurring the ill effects that would have resulted if they had alienated or disturbed the supernaturals, but they had not obtained supernatural aid; their mediocrity was mute testimony to this failure.

From the villager's point of view, all success was the result of luck or fortune, and all failure—including death, the ultimate failure—was due to bad luck and ill fortune. That everyone would exert maximum effort to succeed was taken for granted; but success in this world could not be assured by hard work and effort alone. For no matter how hard one tried one could not be assured of success unless one was lucky, and one was lucky only if [one] could utilize supernatural power in [one's] worldly affairs. Consequently, most religious and magical action was an attempt to avoid the unlucky supernatural elements of the universe and to control or enlist the aid of supernatural forces and beings that could bring one luck.

In a sense, one's fate was sealed by the concatenation of astrological influences present at birth and noted in a person's 'eight characters,'[4] but in spite of this the Cantonese peasant attempted to overcome cruel fate by enlisting supernatural aid. The Cantonese peasant's *weltanschauung* was not a fatalistic one, except in complete failure, nor was it an optimistic one, except as seen from the pinnacle of success. The universe was essentially a stage on which human beings, impersonal supernatural power, and supernatural beings interacted in a constant drama of life and death, success and failure. A person's fortunes were determined by how he fared in this complicated drama of life.

A belief that the universe contains as its essence an impersonal supernatural power lies at the base of the villager's cosmology and plays an important role in his religious and magical beliefs. According to several of the more educated and sophisticated villagers, the *hey shae,* a kind of primordial energy, is the vital animating principle of the universe. The villagers sometimes called it *dey mat,* or 'pulse of the earth,' and conceived of it as flowing or pulsating through the land configurations that form the earth's surface. This primordial energy has two manifestations: *yang* (Cantonese *yeung*) the bright and active male principle; and *yin* (Cantonese *iam*), the dark and passive female principle. The *yin* and *yang* are not two separate substances; they are simply two aspects of the *hey shae.* In a sense, the *yin* is merely the absence of *yang,* and vice versa. An analogy can be drawn with electricity: the universe has two 'poles'; the positive or *yang* pole, and the negative *yin* pole. The *hey shae* is manifested in the *yin* and *yang* which in turn give rise to the five elements: gold, water, fire, wood, and earth. These elements, in various combinations and permutations, make up all things in the phenomenal universe.

Allied to this conception of the *hey shae,* are the pervasive beliefs and practices centering around *fung shui,* literally 'wind and water,' which is the Chinese term for the set of geomantic influences that lie at the core of their magical sys-

---

[4]The eight characters denote the exact time of a person's birth. They are important in that they are believed to hold the key to a person's fate in life.

tem.[5] The essence of this idea is that the configurations of land forms and bodies of water on the face of the earth direct the flow of the *hey shae* and that this has great implications for the fate of the world's human inhabitants. When discussed in the context of *fung shui* this primordial energy is sometimes called *lung hey* or 'dragon vapors.' *Fung shui, dey mat, lung hey,* and *hey shae* are all terms used by the villagers to refer to this fundamental and all-pervasive supernatural power.

Fung shui is the source of all luck and efficacy. A successful man, family, or lineage is successful because they have 'good *fung shui*'; if they are not successful, it is because they have 'bad *fung shui.*' *Fung shui* can be a beneficial force if properly handled, but it can also be an extremely dangerous and destructive force if improperly dealt with. If one gets too large a dose of *fung shui* it may cause disease or even death, not only for an individual family, but an entire village or an entire lineage group. Handling *fung shui* is like dealing with a high voltage electric current; the benefit one receives from its power is directly proportional to the technical skill employed. The occult pseudoscience of *fung shui* has been developed over the centuries by the Chinese into what is undoubtedly one of the most complicated magical systems in history. Since ordinary villagers could not hope to understand the finer points of the science, practised and experienced experts were usually consulted in important *fung shui* matters. These specialists, called *fung shui sin shaang* or '*fung shui* teachers,' were common in the rural areas of China and were frequently consulted by the villagers. The *fung shui sin shaang* learned their trade by reading the ancient texts on the subject written to train professional practitioners and interested scholarly amateurs and by serving as apprentices of a recognized specialist.

It is difficult to convey the extent to which the thoughts and actions of the villagers of Ping Shan revolve around *fung shui* matters. Almost all important actions, whether they be individual or collective, must be adjusted to and guided by the *fung shui* influences that might affect or be affected by these actions. In the New Territories, and probably in Kwangtung Province as a whole, entire villages were set up according to *fung shui* prescriptions to ensure the prosperity and safety of future generations. Villages had to be constructed at the foot of a hill if possible so that the *fung shui* could flow gradually from the higher mountains along the crests of smaller hills to concentrate on the village. Village sites had to have bodies of water standing in front of them to balance the flow of *fung shui* coming down from the mountains. The height of village houses, the plan and layout of the village, the shape of house roofs—even the maximum size that the village could safely attain—were all theoretically governed by *fung shui* requirements. Since villages required special groves of *fung shui* trees as a curtain at the rear of the village, some villages had to postpone construction for several years

[5]Maurice Freedman (in chapter 5) of his *Chinese Lineage and Society: Fukien and Kwangtung* (London: Athlone Press, 1966) has discussed *fung shui* in much more detail. The description he gives there of geomantic beliefs in the New Territories tallies in most important respects with the description given here. And I refer the reader to this book for an interesting analysis from a somewhat different point of view and a good bibliography on the subject. However, as is apparent from what I have written in this paper, I do not completely agree with Freedman's statement (p. 124) that *fung shui* is not like most of the rest of Chinese religion; there is no reliance on the will of a deity; there are no gods to serve or placate. I agree that *fung shui* is not like *some* other elements of Chinese religion; but I would tend to emphasize the interrelationship between *fung shui* and the rest. I would stress that *fung shui* is governed by some of the basic ideas that are found elsewhere in Chinese religion and magic.

to allow the *fung shui* trees to reach a proper height! The exterior and interior construction of village houses, including the exact size and location of doors and the direction in which they were to open, were determined by *fung shui*. *Fung shui* is so important that even today quarrels frequently occur in the village over such seemingly innocent matters as opening up a new window in a village house. If the neighboring household should suffer illness or misfortune it would definitely be blamed on the *fung shui* disturbances created by the new window. Even a man's face can be said to have good or bad *fung shui*. Some of the villagers in the New Territories even go so far as to grow sizeable handle-bar mustaches during certain periods of their lives because a *fung shui* specialist told them that their luck and money would flow away from them during these years if protective measures were not taken.

The flow of invisible *fung shui* currents follows the pull of gravity like water and these ethereal currents that flow through the mystical environment of the Cantonese peasant are even more difficult to control than streams or rivers. To obtain maximum benefit from a *fung shui* current it must be captured and restrained in exactly the proper amount. If the concentration of the 'dragon vapors' upon a house, a village, or an ancestral grave is too powerful it may lead to the death or impoverishment of the people involved; if it is too weak the inhabitants will at best have only mediocre luck. To contain the flow of magical power and to ward off unpropitious currents, retaining walls are erected in front of buildings, villages and ancestral halls.

It is a cardinal rule of the science of *fung shui* that moving bodies of water can conduct *fung shui* power rapidly away from a given site. For this reason, a good *fung shui* site must never be so situated as to see water flowing away from it. Water is needed to balance the power of the *hey shae* flowing down to concentrate on the site, but it must be standing or flowing inward towards the location. If a locality has bodies of water flowing away from it sometimes remedial steps can be taken. In Ping Shan an entire village and a large pagoda were constructed as a retaining wall to prevent the *fung shui* of the main villages and the central ancestral halls of the lineage from being swept out to sea by a river that once flowed by the front of the village.

Fung shui requirements vary for different structures. What might be proper *fung shui* for an entire village or a large ancestral temple might be terribly destructive if concentrated upon a single ancestral tomb. There is a proper balance of *fung shui* for individual houses, for whole villages, for ancestral halls, for ancestral tombs and for temples. *Fung shui* is an exact science, like Newtonian physics, and the traditional prescriptions for different purposes are set down to the smallest detail. A difference of a few feet in the location of a grave or a difference of a few inches in the height of an ancestral tomb might spell the difference between success and fortune for entire generations of descendants. Even apparently minor matters like the digging of a village well might be so disturbing to the flow of the village *fung shui* as to kill everyone in the village. The villagers of Ping Shan claim that numerous people who once dwelt at the rear of their village died off because the Hong Kong government erected a police station on the hill behind their village which cut off their flow of *fung shui*.

The officers of the New Territories Administration are continually beset with difficulties concerning *fung shui* matters because the construction of a road or the erection of a new building inevitably harms the *fung shui* of nearby villages and results in interminable litigation by the villagers who demand compensation for the damage done to their *fung shui*. Most roads in the New Territories have a serpentine quality that is due more to *fung shui* requirements than to bad engineering. Everything in the lives of the villagers, then, from the construction of a village latrine to the determination of the direction in which bridal sedan chairs were placed was determined according to *fung shui* criteria.

However, the principal way that *fung shui* affected the lives and fortunes of the villagers was not so much through the propitious location of houses and temples as it was through the ancestral cult, one of the other important pillars of Chinese peasant religion. The family ancestral spirits enshrined on household altars were the foci of the family ancestral cult. More distant lineage ancestors of earlier generations, enshrined in central and branch ancestral halls, were the foci of lineage and lineage subsegments. Family ancestors were worshipped daily, on the major holidays throughout the year, and especially during the Ching Ming grave-cleaning ceremony in the spring. More distant ancestors of the lineage were worshipped in ancestral hall rites twice yearly, in the spring and fall, and the tombs of lineage ancestors located in the surrounding hills and mountains were worshipped collectively by groups of descendants during a period of several weeks in the autumn of each year.

In ancestral rites the descendants honored their ancestors and furnished them with food, drink, and money that they could use in the nether world of hell. Ancestral spirits of the family who went back for only a few generations were remembered as individual personalities and were basically benevolent beings who watched over and protected their immediate descendants. Lineage ancestors seated in the ancestral halls and tombs were for the most part not remembered as individual personalities. Ancestors this far removed were regarded almost as deities. Villagers frequently referred to more distant ancestors by the term *poosat* (Mandarin *pu-sa*), the general term used to refer to temple deities of Buddhist or Taoist origin. Family ancestors were also sometimes called *kwae* the term used to refer to the malicious spirits from hell, indicating that even they could be malevolent if not properly treated and cared for.

An important element in the ancestral cult of Kwangtung Province and other areas of South China is the elaborate and peculiar burial practices and cult of the dead that is distinctive of this region. Cantonese funerals are similar to those found in other parts of China but the Cantonese have an additional set of practices associated with the dead that is more elaborate than those found elsewhere. The usual practice of the villagers of Ping Shan is to first bury the body in a wooden coffin on a special burial hill near the village. Then after a period of from five to ten years has elapsed the coffin is disinterred and the skeletal bones of the ancestor are ritually washed. The remains are then placed in a ceramic funerary vessel, about two feet high and one foot in diameter, called a *kam taap*. These ceramic pots are then placed in neutral *fung shui* spots on the hillsides in the vicinity of the village.

Even the *kam taap* were theoretically only temporary resting places for the ancestral bones. The ideal was to finally bury them in one of the elaborate circular masonry and brick tombs that were the preferred final resting places for the villagers' ancestral spirits. However, for most ancestral spirits, the ceramic funerary vessels were the final resting places because only families of some means could afford the expense of hiring a *fung shui* specialist to undertake the sometimes lengthy process of locating a tomb site in the surrounding mountains which had excellent *fung shui*. The fee of the *fung shui* specialist was high, the tomb site would be expensive if it was a good one, and the expense of constructing an elaborate tomb was out of the question for most village families. Consequently, most *kam taap* were left permanently exposed on the hillside where they were worshipped every spring by the immediate descendants of the enclosed ancestral spirit. After a few generations, however, most of the *kam taap* were lost and the ancestral spirits they contained would be forever forgotten. The *kam taap* might be overgrown with vegetation or they might be kicked open by a stray buffalo and the bones scattered. Even if the *kam taap* were not lost or broken the descendants would after a period of time discontinue the yearly worshipping and grave cleaning ceremony because only seldom was ancestral property attached to a *kam taap* burial and the villagers soon ignored a burial that had no property attached to pay for the worshipping expenses and to purchase roast pork to be divided among the male descendants. Most ancestral spirits ceased to be important as a focus for collective worship after a few generations if they were not buried in a permanent tomb.

It was only the wealthier villagers who were able to achieve a real immortality. Their families had sufficient wealth to transfer their ancestral spirits to a permanent tomb endowed with property where descendants could worship down through the generations. Furthermore, they were able to locate the tomb on an excellent *fung shui* spot that would ensure succeeding generations of continuing fame and prosperity.

The transfer of the *kam taap* to a permanent tomb was a lengthy and critical process that had to be undertaken with extreme care. After the *fung shui* specialist had located a burial plot with promising *fung shui*, the family would purchase the site and under the direction of the *fung shui* teacher proceed to build a tomb whose size and shape exactly fitted the *fung shui* of the site. The *fung shui sin shaang* took special care to trace out the flow of the magical currents in the surrounding countryside so that he could locate the tomb on the exact spot where the lucky influences were concentrated. The grave was ideally surrounded by two enclosing spurs of hills on the right and left side of the grave, called the 'green dragon' and the 'white tiger' respectively, which held the tomb in their protective embrace. Water should be visible flowing in towards the tomb and the winds should be neither too strong nor too mild. The villagers described a good grave site as being 'comfortable' for the ancestor buried there. The *kam taap* containing the ancestral bones was buried a few feet below the ground at the rear of the semicircular tomb, facing outward through the arms of the grave and the encircling hills. Above and to the rear of the *kam taap* was placed the tombstone on which was carved the birth and death day of the deceased and any special honors he may have achieved during lifetime, such as passing the imperial examinations or serving as an official.

Every detail of the tomb's construction and the arrangements for transferring the *kam taap* to the tomb were planned with painstaking care. The direction in which the ancestral bones faced outward from the tomb and the depth at which the *kam taap* was buried were determined with precision by the specialist. The direction in which the ancestral skull faced from the tomb was important because on this depended, among other things, which of his sons and their lines of descent would receive most benefit from the *fung shui* of the grave. If the entombed ancestor faced in one direction the line stemming from the eldest son might prosper; if it faced in another direction the second son's line would prosper, and so on. Often the situation was made even more complicated because one direction might bring them increased numbers, while a third direction might ensure that certain descendants would pass the imperial examinations and become high officials. Since the consequences of each direction were explained in detail by the *fung shui* specialist before the burial, sons often quarrelled over the position in which the *kam taap* was to be placed in the tomb. The depth of the burial and the exact moment when the *kam taap* was lowered into the grave were also important because if the timing was not exactly suited to the grave's *fung shui* the entire effect might be lost.

So strong was the belief in the importance of *fung shui* that even the entombment might not be permanent if the family of the entombed person ran into a period of bad luck. The quality of a grave's *fung shui* was often tested several years after burial by digging up the *kam taap* and examining the condition and color of the skeletal remains. If the bones were golden in colour this showed that the *fung shui* of the grave was good; however, if the bones were found to be black, this showed that the *fung shui* was bad and they might be removed and buried in a different location. If a set of brothers had differential success in the years following the burial of their father the unsuccessful sons would suspect that the *fung shui* of the grave would doom them to poverty while promoting the success of their brothers. In this case quarrels and even violence might ensue, with some of the brothers wanting to move the bones and others opposing their efforts.

The system of logic behind *fung shui* beliefs was self-fulfilling. If a group was successful then the *fung shui* of their graves must be good; if the descendants were not successful, then the grave must be a bad one. As an added prop to the system, it was believed that certain graves were good for only certain periods of time, thus explaining any marked changes in the fortunes of a group. This elaborate pseudo-science was perfectly consistent, given certain assumptions, and could never be disproved. The *fung shui* specialist could always think up some reason why his predictions did not work out and in any case the effects were only noticeable over generations, long after the specialist had died. The system was remarkably persistent because it did give *some* explanation for the differential success of family lines in a society which encouraged achievement and yet could award only limited amounts of wealth, prestige and power. After all, there had to be some explanation for the fact that some branches of a lineage over the centuries increased in numbers and produced officials and wealthy merchants, while other branches of the lineage ended up as a few families of poor tenant farmers.

One important effect of the system was that a person's or a family's success did not necessarily imply the inferiority of other less successful members of the village community because in the last analysis success could be attributed to the impersonal whims of fate or the character of one's ancestral tombs. This was especially important in a community as tightly knit as a Chinese lineage where envy and jealousy might seriously damage the solidarity of the community. The Chinese lineage rested upon an ideology which held that all lineage members were brothers and a fiction which held that all were social equals. The magical and impersonal explanation for differential success furnished by the *fung shui* system softened to some extent the effects of great social differentiation which was a feature of many communities. In functional terms, *fung shui* plays somewhat the same role in Chinese villages that the civil-religious hierarchy plays in the village communities of Latin America. Both mechanisms help to maintain the solidarity of the village community; one by eliminating wealth differences and the other by attributing such differences to impersonal fate.[6]

The extreme care taken in this lengthy and costly process of burial, reburial, and entombment gives some indication of the importance attached to *fung shui* by the villagers. So much care was taken because a man's fortunes and those of his descendants were believed to be largely determined by the character of his and his lineage's ancestral graves. If the *fung shui* of the graves was good, then all or part of the descendants would become wealthy, achieve high official position, increase in numbers—or all of these things. On the other hand, ancestral graves with neutral or poor *fung shui* might lead to the impoverishment or even the physical extinction of a line of descent.

In addition to the complicated magical system of *fung shui* the Cantonese peasant had a well-developed system of beliefs involving anthropomorphic supernatural beings. The world of the villager was inhabited by myriads of gods, ghosts and devils who profoundly affected his life on earth. The supernaturals were endless in their variety but, in the eyes of the villagers fell into a limited number of functional categories defined on the basis of how they affected human fortunes.

The first category consisted of the *zan* and *poosat* which included ancestral spirits and other deities of Buddhist, Taoist or Confucian origin. The *zan* and *poosat* were basically benevolent beings from whom the villagers could expect aid in the form of magical power or supernatural intervention. The second category of supernaturals was the *kwae,* malevolent spirits which were to be propitiated and avoided if at all possible. The *kwae* caused directly or indirectly all misfortune, failure, illness and death in the world.

As might be expected, supernatural beings also participated in the fundamental dualism of Chinese cosmology. The *zan* and *poosat* embodied the *yang* principle and were spoken of as 'bright' and 'lucky' beings. The *kwae* embodied the *yin* principle and were dim and unlucky creatures from the world of the shades who returned to earth to haunt and torment humans. This dualism is also found in the closely related cosmological beliefs of the villagers, whose universe was divided into three layers: (1) the lower *yin* world of hell and purgatory; (2) the upper *yang* world of heaven; and (3) the phenomenal world of earthly existence in which supernaturals from the other two layers interacted with living humans.

These three sections of the universe are closely interrelated to form one unitary system. Living humans after death become *kwae* and go to be judged by the ten judges of hell. Those persons who had lived moral lives passed through hell and entered heaven where they waited to be born again as bugs or men, depending upon the character of their previous life on earth. Those persons who died unnatural or unfulfilled deaths—such as being executed or murdered, committing suicide, or dying in childbirth—and those persons who committed evil deeds during their lifetime, spent more time in hell, where they underwent hideous and unmerciful torture. The poor souls in purgatory became the *kwae* that returned at night to torment human beings and cause them misfortune and death. Another

---

[6]Cf. G. Foster, p. 305, and Eric R. Wolf, *Sons of the Shaking Earth* (Chicago: University of Chicago Press, 1959), p. 216.

important source of *kwae* were those persons who died without male descendants to worship them and provide them with the food, clothing, and money necessary for life in hell. These people also became hungry, wandering ghosts who preyed upon hapless humans and forced them to give them sustenance.

The *zan* and *poosat* were, like the *kwae,* basically human in character and origin, whether they were ancestral spirits or Buddhist and Taoist temple deities. Many deities enshrined in local temples were famous men who accomplished such great deeds that they were deified after death. In many cases, the only difference between ordinary mortals and deities was that the deities had been men of extraordinary ability and power.

This basic kinship between deities and men can also be illustrated by a curious practice that the villagers have of referring to particularly successful men as *shang poosat,* usually translated as 'living buddha.' This, however, is not an accurate translation of the term because it implies too close an association with Buddhism and idols. *Poosat* is the term used to refer generally to any powerful benevolent deity, whether it be an ancestral spirit or the Buddhist deity *Koon Iam,* the Goddess of Mercy. The use of this term to refer to successful men signifies that living men, if they command enough magical power, can approach the status of deities. It also implies that such men are treated much like deities; they are persons to whom one shows deference in the hope of receiving a favor; and they are men with whom one likes to associate in the hope that some of their luck will, literally, 'rub off.'

Supernatural beings play an important role in the religious life of the villagers. Each year there is a complex ceremonial calendar in which worship at local shrines and household altars plays an important part. Deities and ancestral spirits are worshiped in the hope that these supernatural beings may help the villagers to get rich and have a healthy and secure life. The propitiation of the *kwae* has an equally important place, with several major festivals designed to bribe them with offerings and force them to leave the village. The central conception on all religious worship is to obtain power and help from benevolent supernatural beings and to ward off the attacks of the *kwae.*

At this point, to complete the system of thought, it is necessary to introduce the villagers' beliefs concerning human souls and to relate these beliefs to other parts of the system. All villagers agree that a person has ten souls: three *wan* and seven *p'aak.* The villagers are no more certain about the exact nature of all these souls than are most Christians about their similar belief and were unable to explain clearly just what happened to these multiple souls after death. Some of the more sophisticated villagers suggested that the seven *p'aak* souls represented the animal senses of the body (the seven bodily orifices) and disappeared at death, whereas the three *wan* souls were aspects of one major soul called the *ling wan* which after death went to heaven or hell. The villagers also spoke of a person as having one major soul, the *ling wan.* However much puzzlement and disagreement there was about the significance of these multiple souls and what happened to them after death, all agreed that a person's fortunes in this life were closely related to the quality of his *ling wan.*

In the view of the villagers, a person's soul represented his life force and vital spirit. Illness was commonly believed to be caused by the temporary loss of one's soul, and death was believed to result from the permanent separation of the soul from the body.

The state of a person's soul was said to be either lucky or unlucky, bright or dim. A person with a bright soul was lucky and succeeded in everything he attempted. Since a person with a luminous soul was imbued with the *yang* principle, the *kwae* shrank back from him in fear and were unable to cause him harm. Most villagers were afraid to wander out at night because this was the time when the *kwae* returned from hell. But persons with bright souls could wander out at night unafraid since the *kwae* were repelled by his soul-light. A person with a bright soul-light had in effect captured a portion of the vital *yang* spirit of the universe and could use it to accomplish anything he wished. The *kwae* were almost as much afraid of him as they were of the powerful temple deities who were imbued with even more power.

On the other hand, a person whose soul-light was dim was an unlucky person who failed in almost everything he attempted. His family were continuously beset by the *kwae* which resulted in sickness, poverty, and even death. Instead of repelling the *kwae*, people with dim soul-lights actually attracted *kwae* to them. They had to feel their way carefully and cautiously through life and had to employ every magical means available to guard against the incursions of the ghosts and devils. But, even with all these precautions, the most they could hope for would be to achieve an ordinary existence with a minimum amount of security; they could never become successful or powerful people.

Fung shui, the cult of the dead, the belief in supernatural beings, and the conception of souls—all key elements of the Cantonese peasant's religious and magical beliefs—are not simply disconnected superstitions. On the contrary, they are mutually interdependent elements in a meaningful view of the universe and man's place in this universe. Furthermore, the villagers' supernaturalistic beliefs and practices are intimately related to their cultural values and to their cosmological and philosophical beliefs.

The basic goals of the villagers were the pursuit of wealth, power and prestige. The pursuit of these goals took place within a universe that was basically divided into two opposing impersonal forces: the *yin* and the *yang*. Everything in the universe, at any given point in time, was affected by its mode of interaction with these two ultimate forces.

The villagers' beliefs concerning the *yang* principle are by no means unique for they are based on a concept similar to that of *mana*, an idea which plays an important role in many religious systems of the world. *Mana*, as conceived by the peoples of the Pacific and by various American Indian tribes (although here it is called by different names), is an impersonal supernatural power that is the source of all efficacy in the world. A man is successful because he possesses *mana*: a warrior is a great warrior because he has obtained 'power.' In Durkheim's theory of religion the belief in an all pervasive supernatural power is the essence of the sacred and is the basic and original element in all religious systems.[7] The Cantonese peasant's conception of a basic supernatural power which is the driving force of the universe, whether it be called *yang*, *hey shae*, *fung shui*, or 'luck,' is basically the same as the belief in *mana* held by other people of the world.

---

[7]Cf. Emile Durkheim, *The Elementary Forms of the Religious Life*, trans. J. W. Swain (Glencoe: The Free Press, 1954), chapter 6.

The *mana* principle underlies the entire Cantonese system of religion and magic. The pseudo-science of *fung shui* is merely one involved method of capturing *mana*. Most ritual practice involving deities and ancestors were attempts to obtain power from these beings. Supernatural beings were more powerful than humans principally because they control more *mana* than ordinary humans. A lucky person was lucky because he possessed *mana*, and the amount of *mana* possessed was evidenced by the brightness of his soul. *Kwae* were dangerous because they were dim creatures who stole the vital power of human beings.

The elaborate cult of the dead involving ancestral bones and *fung shui* was merely another important method of capturing magical power for the use of living descendants. Two aspects of the ancestral cult make this clear. First, a person must actually participate in the yearly ancestral sacrifices at the tombs of his ancestors to receive benefit from the grave's *fung shui*. Second, among the most important ritual paraphernalia used in the ancestral sacrifices are the roast pigs placed on the altar as offerings. This ritual pork is divided among all male descendants present at the sacrifices, with equal shares given to each man present. The ritual pork is not an ordinary offering because once it has been placed before the ancestors it takes on a sacred, magical quality and is believed to be especially lucky. All Chinese like to eat pork from a good grave and sometimes even nonlineage members are offered some as a prized gift. What is even more revealing, bits of this sacrificial pork are pressed into the mouths of small children who are too young to eat solid food.

The significance of these practices, I believe, can be interpreted as follows. The ancestral bones located in a good *fung shui* site receive the full force of the *fung shui* or *mana*, that pulsates through the earth's surface. If the *fung shui* is potent, the ancestral bones turn a bright yellow color and are considered extremely efficacious. The yellow coloring of the bones result from the *mana* infused into them, the same *mana* that lights a lucky person's soul. During the ancestral sacrifices the magical power of the ancestral bones is transmitted to the sacrificial pork; and this is why the pork is considered lucky. When consumed by the members of the kinship group, this magical power is absorbed by the souls of the members of the group. If the *fung shui* is really good, great quantities of *mana* will be absorbed by the descendants, their soul-light will be bright, and they will be successful in every aspect of their lives. Most importantly, such lucky persons will then give birth to sons at propitious times, ensuring that they have good 'eight characters.' And so the explanation runs full circle and the system is complete. Wind, water, bones, and souls all fit together in one fairly consistent system of religion and magic that enables us to understand many aspects of Cantonese culture.

As is evident in this paper, however, Cantonese peasant culture exhibits several contradictory themes; and not all elements of the villagers' belief system can be understood by using this cognitive model. If all success is due to fate, then the logical behavioral consequences of such a belief would be a fatalistic acceptance and resignation to fate. This is certainly not the prevailing attitude of the Cantonese who exhibit a strong motivation and drive for achievement. There is then a contradictory theme in Cantonese culture which holds that effort and ability are necessary for success and that all is not left to fate. I do not think that this is at all unusual for I suspect that few cultures are so well-integrated that all elements can be subsumed under one model. Most cultures are a complex of different cognitive models that interrelate in complex fashion are often mutually contradictory.

The contradictions in Cantonese culture are no more inconsistent than the Calvinistic ethic which held that a person's fate is predetermined but that the only way one could know whether he was among the saved was his success in doing God's will in his calling on this earth.

There is at least one other important cognitive model in Cantonese culture which fits into neither of the models discussed above and that is the Buddhist idea that a person's fate is based upon the morality of his actions in life. This Buddhist theme is different from both the fatalistic system of magic and the achievement orientation of the villagers. They represent three different aspects of the villagers' world view that are contradictory to the analyst but apparently do not worry the people who act in this system, who easily jump from one cognitive map to the other in different life situations. A complete account of the values and world view of the Cantonese peasants would include all three of these different cognitive models with some account of how they intersect in the lives of the villagers. In this paper I have outlined only one of these basic systems which allows us to understand a great deal of what goes on in the culture.

LITERATI SPIRIT MEDIUMS

Contrary to Eurocentric values found in many Western depictions of Chinese religion, elite religious practices did not markedly differ from those of the nonelite. Mediumistic practices (spirit possession) were not limited to the uneducated. It is most likely that the Incorporator of the Dead (*shi*) was possessed by the primary ancestral spirit recipient during the sacrifices in early times. The sacrificial rituals were mediated by the Incorporator of the Dead, usually a grandson or granddaughter-in-law (depending on sex) of the primary recipient of the specific sacrifice. Once possessed, it is the ancestor who eats the food and drinks the wine and speaks pronouncements to those gathered. By the T'ang dynasty, this office of the sacrificial rituals had disappeared.[8]

Around the time this practice faded away, we find the literati, the elite following the full implementation of the civil service system, taking part in mediumistic rituals in which they allow their bodies to be taken over by spirits to write messages to humans, a practice that continues to the present day (see Chapter 12). Excepting cosmic deities as Sky (Heaven) and Earth, which are not known to be involved in possession, all of the spirits and deities were once human. Most important, of course, are the ancestral spirits. Next come the effective deities, those that can ameliorate human problems. Through possessing cooperative humans, often the literati or those educated in the Taoist tradition, they can address the human condition in writing. Throughout the centuries an enormous number of books have been written by these spirits (*shanshu*). Some of these volumes describe, after Buddhist influence, the temporary heavens and hells (purgatories). Other admonish humans to live a good life. Some are the autobiographies of deities. In these respects, Chinese religion is unique.

---

[8]For details on the Incorporator of the Dead and the description in the Scriptures on Ritual of the methods used to elicit possession trance, see Jordan Paper, *The Spirits Are Drunk: Comparative Approaches to Chinese Religion* (Albany: State University of New York Press, 1995), (pp. 111–115. For an example of mention in the *Shih*, see *Chinese Religion*, p. 42 (where *shi* is translated as "Personator of the ancestors").

Wen-ch'ang (Wenchang) is one of the most important Chinese deities, sacrificed to by Chinese emperors for over two millennia. The patron deity of literature, he is invariably found in Confucian temples and the spirit patron of students studying for the civil service examinations. From the Sung dynasty on, he has written of the many facets of his lives, in which he has different names, through possessed literati. The following excerpts are from Terry Kleeman's translations, including his commentaries, of the first of these dating to 1181, the *Book of Transformations (A God's Own Tale: The Book of Transformations of Wenchang, the Divine Lord of Zitong,* pp. 99–101, 107–111). (Technical notes have been deleted.)

Spirit Marriage

Finding a mate cannot be left to chance,
Meetings in this life are the result of karmic affinities.
Her mind and body did not decompose, as if waiting for me,
Reliving the events of a dream, how can it be coincidence?
Once there was an heir to carry on my enterprise
Suddenly her fragrant soul was sealed again within the deepest springs.[9]
Abruptly cut off in my prime from the relations of man and woman,
The sentiment of all was to praise me as a born transcendent.

As a youth I was by nature quiet and seldom hit it off with others. As I grew older, and passed the age of capping, I still had no spouse. It was not just that no worthy matchmaker appeared. I also was not really interested in pursuing a mate. Previously, when my mother was suffering her illness, she regretted never having seen her grandchildren, and it troubled me that I was acting unfilially. One night I dreamed that I came to a forest at the foot of a mountain, where a solitary tomb towered. Beside it there was a gate, and within a beautifully adorned young woman sat. She looked at me and said, "Are you not Zhang Shanxun?" I was surprised to be referred to by my name,[10] and asked her reason for doing so. She said, "You and I live so close we can hear the other's chickens and dogs. I am from the Zhong family. Once my uncle met with your family to discuss your good qualities, because he considered that you were fond of learning and esteemed propriety, like a gentleman of old. He argued for giving me to you in marriage, but my father criticized this plan because of your unattractive appearance. I, however, had already come to admire you wholeheartedly. Later I was promised to Zhong.[11] Zhong was the son of a rich family, but had made no reputation for himself. I was humiliated, and for this reason became ill and died. It has been three years now. I have come here for your sake. Why do you not think of a way to deal with this situation?" I awoke with a start.

A month later I had the same dream again. So when I had a free day I went for a stroll with my friend Yi Jiancheng, seeking out secluded spots. Suddenly we

---

[9]These are the famous Yellow Springs, abode of the dead in archaic Chinese cosmology.

[10]In ancient China it was taboo to use the name of one's direct ancestor, and impolite to use the name of someone living in general except in relations of the closest intimacy.

[11]The given name Anru here means "the content wimp." Several of the names in this story have meanings, perhaps reflecting the allegorical nature of the tale (see the Commentary). The family name of the young woman, Zhong, is the personal name of the god in a later incarnation. The surname and given name of his friend, Yi Jiancheng, might be translated "deportment steadfastly complete."

found ourselves at a place identical to that in the dream. I had just told my friend this, and we were both wondering at the similarity, when someone emerged from the tomb and called me "husband." It was the person I had seen in my dream. It turned out that Yi was a maternal uncle of the woman. He ran to tell her parents to bring her back home, and in the end we were married.

COMMENTARY

Zhang Shanxun's encounter with his deceased bride-to-be shows that the power of Fate transcends even death and offers a further proof of Zhang's true divine identity. But the tale also reflects a custom of performing spirit marriages that was in existence in the Song and survives today both in China and in the Chinese diaspora.

When a daughter dies before marriage, this is considered a great tragedy, both because the girl will have no descendants to sustain her in the other world and because the force of her sexuality remains pent-up and unvented. The souls of dead virgins are credited with such power that sometimes they are able to climb the ladder of divinity, passing from frightening unquiet ghost to local goddess to national deity, as the patron saint of seafarers, Mazu, did during the Song. To protect themselves from the rancor of these unfortunate spirits, families arrange a marriage for the girl, either with the dead son of a neighbor or with a living individual willing to take responsibility for her. The groom may be selected in a number of ways, but in at least one modern example, recorded by David Jordan, he was visited in a dream by the spirit of the dead girl, just as in this episode. By accepting such a match the god encourages others to agree to such disagreeable but necessary arrangements.

Such beliefs were already prevalent during the Song. The Southern Song author Kang Yuzhi (fl. 1131), in his recollections of life under the Northern Song titled *A Record of Yesterday's Dreams* (*Zuomenglu*), records the custom of arranging ghost marriages between young men and women who had died before marriage. A special "ghost matchmaker" was employed and divinations were performed on the appropriateness of the match; the bride was often supplied with a symbolic dowry. During the wedding ceremony the spectral bride and groom showed their approval by causing banners to shake. Sometimes a teacher who had passed on was also designated to continue the education of the young man, presumably in preparation for a career in the divine bureaucracy. It is said that after the ceremony the bride or groom would appear in the dreams of their new relatives. If all these procedures were not followed properly, one of the newlyweds might visit misfortune upon the living.

In this chapter the Divine Lord also goes out of his way to point out his lack of interest in sex. As a clan god of the Zhangs and as a provider of progeny the god of Zitong was expected to have a large and extended family. One structure found in his temple-complex, the Family Blessings Tower, celebrated this aspect of his identity; there his image was surrounded by those of his parents, sons, grandsons, and great-grandsons. But fertility must not be confused with debauchery. The Divine Lord affirms his sacred nature, and sets a good example for the householder, by transcending sexual desire without rejecting the sexual relations necessary to maintain the family.

Subduing the Epidemic

The death of both my parents was due to an epidemic.
I suffered and grieved with a resentment at this injustice that cut to the bone.
As long as they lived their loving support never faltered,
On diverging paths in the worlds of light and darkness, I could not give vent to
  my fury.
Divine troops seized the fiends and appeared in a bright light,
The perfected being who transmitted the rite and register had come in a
  dream.
My brush alit and wrote a charm, saving the people from ailments.
How could I permit the five demons to tarry for even a moment?

When both my parents died from an epidemic, they caught this misery in summer, and suffered all the more. Every time I thought of the cruelty of the epidemic demons, my hatred for them cut to the bones. But the worlds of light and darkness are on different paths, and I could not revenge myself on them no matter how I tried. Once in desperation I compared this to the time I had diverted the stream at the banks of their grave; then I had in fact relied on the power of the Perfected Scripture of the Great Grotto and the golden statue. So I chanted the scripture and worshiped the statue even more fervently, until I should receive supernatural aid in controlling the epidemic demons. After three years I suddenly dreamed that the golden statue I worshiped spoke to me, saying, "You have memorized the True Scripture of the Great Grotto thoroughly, but you have never seen the Rite and the Talisman of the Great Grotto. Now I will bestow these upon you, that you may master the evil devils. Thus not only may you achieve your original purpose, but also aid Heaven in promoting moral transformation and assist the state in saving the populace." He took from his sleeve two books. I bowed one hundred times and accepted them. When I awoke the books were before my pillow. One was titled *Register of the Great Grotto*, the other *Rite of the Great Grotto*. I opened the register and began reading. When I reached the line "Ten thousand heavenly cavaliers and armored troops are placed under your command," suddenly there was wind and thunder and daylight turned to night. Countless figures in golden armor and vermillion sashes were arrayed before me. They bowed and asked for my orders. Three men holding red banners in the midst of the troops first addressed me, saying, "We wish to hear your commands." I was flustered, but found myself saying in a sharp voice, "I command you to subdue the epidemic demons. All the members of a certain household in this village are suffering from the epidemic. Go there and drive them forth to me." When I had finished speaking one of the banner-bearers led a hundred-odd men into the house, and in a moment had captured the demons. He pushed five men forward. One wore a tiger skin, another a cock's crown, a third had the face of a dog, a fourth the face of a crow, the fifth the head of a donkey. They held feathered placards, representing fire and water, axes and chisels. I rebuked them angrily, and was about to destroy their forms, when they pleaded, "We, your disciples, are born from the seasonal cycle and take form from seasonal breaths. There are certain districts in which we roam and certain people whom we afflict. Those who have a heavy accumulation of other worldly offenses are visited with disaster; death comes to those whose heavenly lifespan is at an end. We certainly do not dare to

act on our own initiative. If Your Perfected Honor would deign to treat us with
indulgence, we will henceforth observe your restrictions. If when we are spreading epidemics we see your honor's charm, we shall not dare to enter there." I
thereupon instructed them in accordance with the ritual and they left. Whenever
anyone in the neighborhood came down with the epidemic I gave them a talisman and performed a ritual on their behalf. All recovered completely.

COMMENTARY

The rising population density and increasing inter-regional trade that were characteristic of the Song facilitated the spread of communicable diseases. By the
twelfth century epidemics occurred on the average once every five years. They
must have been particularly severe in Sichuan, which was at the time among the
most densely populated regions of China, and the phenomenal drop in population during the late Song and early Yuan has been attributed to the ravages of
epidemics.

In this episode the Divine Lord of Zitong confronts the demons thought to
spread these epidemics. Since at least Han times epidemic diseases have been attributed to demonic influence, and the great *nuo* exorcism performed at the end
of each year was intended to drive off such malefic spirits. Early sources name
three such spirits, sons of the legendary emperor Zhuanxu. The Ming dynasty
1476 Soushen ji relates that the Five Emissaries of the Epidemic appeared to Emperor Wendi of the Sui (r. 581–604). The ensuing epidemic left many dead, and
when Emperor Wendi was told that there was no way to control these spirits, he
enfeoffed them as generals and established a shrine to them. A scripture from the
Yuan or Ming, *209 Zhengyi wensi bidu shendeng yi,* consists of a ritual to propitiate
five epidemic spirits in which each is named and associated with one of the cardinal directions. In modern Taiwan, epidemic gods are a prime focus of worship,
though usually they are found in a group of twelve.

Gods or demons of the epidemic have an important but ambiguous position
in Daoism. They are originally evil demons who had to be subjugated or propitiated. But they are also powerful gods, who control the fates of many, and who
have their function in the ordained workings of the world. The Divine Lord faces
just this dilemma. Having acquired certain powers through the bestowal of two
magic scriptures, he wants only to revenge himself upon the epidemic spirits for
having caused the death of his parents. But the spirits point out that they only attack those who are destined to die, either due to moral transgressions or because
they have reached the end of their natural lifespan. Demons also are agents of
Heaven. The Divine Lord contents himself with an agreement by which they will
defer to his authority, when such is made manifest through the posting of one of
his talismans. No doubt the Zitong cult at this time was actively writing such talismans and bestowing them on adherents of the cult in return for donations. The
passage from the *Register of the Great Grotto* cited in this episode probably is a
paraphrase of a line in the *Precious Register,* which reads "Ten thousand cavaliers,
armored troops and divine emissaries are placed under your command."

We should note also the transformation the Divine Lord goes through when
he begins to give orders to his divine soldiers. Although in his conscious waking
mind he does not know how to address these divine figures, a deeper layer of his

being asserts itself, and he naturally assumes the authority that is his in his true identity as a celestial deity. A similar awakening occurs in a later incarnation, in chapter 72. In Chinese legend and folklore divine beings who assume human form often are unaware of their true identity until some crisis or other event stimulates their memory.

CHAPTER 3

The Family:
Kindred and Ancestors

A MANUAL ON FAMILY RITUALS

The Canon of the Literati contains three scriptures on ritual, aspects of which were probably already anachronistic when they were put together from earlier materials in the early Han period. By the Sung dynasty, it was felt that new iterations of the sacrificial ritual procedures were needed. Among those written, the one by Chu Hsi (1130–1200), whose interpretations of the *Canon of the Literati* later became a government-sanctioned orthodoxy, withstood the test of time. Not only was it highly influential in China into the twentieth century, but it also influenced the religious practices of Korea, Japan, and Vietnam. The following translation of the section on the offering hall is by Patricia Buckley Ebrey (*Chu Hsi's* Family Rituals: *A Twelfth-Century Chinese Manual for the Performance of Cappings, Weddings, Funerals, and Ancestral Rites*, pp. 6–20—the notes have been slightly condensed).

The Offering Hall

This section originally was part of the chapter on sacrificial rites. Now I have purposely placed it here, making it the first subject, because its contents form the heart of "repaying one's roots and returning to the beginning,"[1] the essence of "honoring ancestors and respecting agnatic kin,"[2] the true means of preserving status responsibilities in the family, and the foundation for establishing a heritage and transmitting it to later generations. My arrangement will let the reader sense that what is placed first is the most important.[3] This chapter provides the basis

---

[1] Allusion to *Li-chi*, "Chiao t'e-hsing" 25:20b, 26:7a.

[2] Allusion to *Li-chi*, "Ta chuan" 34:10b, 13a.

[3] In this chapter the more routine activities in the offering hall are described. Chu Hsi retains a chapter on sacrificial rites, however, that is largely devoted to the four seasonal sacrifices based on classical prescriptions. Most of the activities described in the present chapter have only loose classical precedents.

for understanding the fine points in the later chapters concerning movements and postures, for walking here and there, getting up and down, going in and out, and facing various directions.

The ancient system of ancestral shrines (*miao*) does not appear in the classics.[4] Moreover, there are elements of it not permitted to the lower ranks of today's gentlemen (*shih*) and commoners.[5] Therefore, I have specially named the room the "offering hall" and extensively adapted customary rituals in formulating its procedures.[6]

- When a man of virtue (*chün-tzu*) plans to build a house, his first task is always to set up an offering hall to the east of the main room of his house.[7]

In setting up the offering hall use a room three *chien* wide.[8] In front of the altars is the inner door and in front of it the two staircases, each with three steps. The one on the east is called the ceremonial stairs, the one on the west the western stairs. Depending on how much space is available, below the steps should be a covered area, large enough for all the family members to stand in rows. On the east there should be a closet for books, clothes, and sacrificial vessels inherited from the ancestors, and a spirit pantry.[9] Have the wall go around them and add an outer door, which should normally be kept bolted.

If the family is poor and its space cramped, set up a one-*chien*-wide offering hall, without the closet and pantry. As substitutes, cases may be put at the base of the east and west walls. In the western one store the inherited books and clothes and in the eastern one the sacrificial vessels.

The main room refers to the front hall. When space is limited [and there is no front hall], it is also acceptable to make the offering hall to the east of the reception room.

---

[4]Why Chu Hsi would say this is not clear. See the "Wang-chih" and "Chi-fa" sections of the *Li-chi* 12:13b–21b; 46:8a–b. Generally speaking, in the classics the number of ancestral shrines (*miao*) was governed by rank; for instance, great officers (*ta-fu*) could have three shrines at which they could make offerings to their three ascendant ancestors. The "Wang-chih" passage says that gentlemen (*shih*) could have one shrine and commoners none; the "Chi-fa" passage divides gentlemen into three levels, the highest of which could have two shrines, for offerings to their fathers and grandfathers, the highest of which could have two shrines, for offerings to their fathers and grandfathers, the middle with one shrine for their fathers, and the "commoner gentlemen" with no shrines.

[5]In the Sung only high-ranking officials were permitted to construct *chia miao*.

[6]Chu Hsi was the first one to use the term "offering hall" (*tz'u-t'ang*) for the place within a home where sacrifices to ancestors were offered. Ssu-ma Kuang had called it an "image hall" (*ying-t'ang*), a term Chu Hsi also used in referring to other people's halls. *Ying-t'ang* was also used by Ch'eng I, who, however, objected to the use of images (portraits). Chu Hsi probably adopted *tz'u-t'ang*, a term used earlier for temples dedicated to sages or worthies, to avoid the term image. Images, or portraits, however, never lost their popularity. T'ang To said they should be brought out at major sacrifices, and Hsü Ch'ien-hsüeh argued that they were no more uncanonical than many other accepted practices.

[7]In the seventeenth century Sun Ch'i-feng stressed that those whose resources were inadequate could simply sweep a room and set out the ancestral tablets there. A separate building was not necessary.

[8]A *chien* was a unit used to measure the size of rooms, being the space between two pillars.

[9]The commentator in the 1732 ed. said the spirit pantry held the dishes used for the spirits.

As a general rule, the house with the offering hall should remain in the possession of the descent-line heir[10] generation after generation, and not be subject to partition.[11]

Here and throughout this book, in organizing the room, no matter which direction it actually faces, treat the front as south, the rear as north, the left as east, and the right as west.[12]

- Make four altars to hold the spirit tablets of the ancestors.

Inside the offering hall, near the north end, have a stand for the four altars. Inside each altar, put a table.[13] In the case of a great line, or a lesser line that is heir to a great-great-grandfather,[14] the great-great-grandfather is furthest to the west, with the great-grandfather next to him, the grandfather next, and the father last. A lesser-line succeeding to a great-grandfather does not presume to sacrifice to a great-great-grandfather, and so leaves the westernmost of the altars empty. Likewise, a lesser-line heir to a grandfather does not presume to sacrifice to a great-grandfather, and so leaves the two western altars empty; and a lesser-line heir to a father does not presume to sacrifice to the grandfather, and so leaves the three western altars empty. If a great line has a gap in its generations, a western altar is also left empty, as in a lesser line.[15]

The spirit tablets are all stored in a case and placed on the table, the front to the south. Hang a short curtain in front of each altar. In front of these altars, set up an incense table in the center of the room, with incense burners and incense boxes on it.[16] Set up another, similar incense table in the space between the staircases.

Anyone who is not the eldest main-line son does not presume to sacrifice to his father.[17] After a younger brother dies, his sons and grandsons, if they live with the eldest brother, will set up an offering hall for him in their private apartment, adding new altars each generation.[18] When they leave and set up a separate res-

---

[10]The descent-line heir (*tsung-tzu*) is the eldest son, generally in a line of eldest sons.

[11]That is, division among brothers when the family property is divided.

[12]That is, as though one was in the room with one's back to the altars looking out toward the steps and courtyard.

[13]ARCLIC (1:3b) rewrote this to mean that each altar is put on a table, which makes more sense than the original. Illustrations also make this assumption.

[14]A great line (*ta-tsung*) is the line of eldest sons continuing indefinitely from a founding ancestor. A lesser line is the line of eldest sons going back no more than five generations. Great lines and lesser lines continually spin off new lesser lines, founded by younger sons.

[15]The gaps in generations probably refer to cases where information about an ancestor had been lost, much more likely in a great line than a short lesser line.

[16]Burning incense was not a part of classical rites but seems to have entered Chinese ancestral rites through imitation of Buddhist worship ceremonies. Burning incense was a standard element of all worship activities by Sung times.

[17]"Main-line" sons are sons of the legal wife. Thus, sons of concubines, even if older than sons of the wife, do not take charge of the sacrifices to their father. Nor do younger sons of the wife. Ssu-ma Kuang defended allowing younger sons to perform sacrifices since through official service they often were scattered about the country. In a letter Chu Hsi wrote that in such cases they could perform a modified rite without tablets but with a paper list of ancestors.

[18]Chu Hsi offered another solution to large complex families in YI, 90:2316. The most senior descent-line heir would sacrifice to his ancestors the first day in the offering hall, then the second day the heir of the younger uncle (or younger great uncle) would offer sacrifices in the hall, and so on, all using the hall, but on different days.

idence, they will set up a full offering hall. If the younger son lives separately during his own lifetime, he can set up a study where he lives, on the model of an offering hall. After his death, his descendants can turn it into an offering hall.

- Collateral relatives who died without descendants may have associated offerings made to them there according to their generational seniority.

Associate a great uncle and his wife with the great-great-grandfather. Associate an uncle and his wife with the great-grandfather. Associate one's wife, a brother, or a brother's wife with one's grandfather. Associate one's son or nephew with one's father.[19] All these tablets should face west. The tablet cases for them should be like the standard ones. If a nephew's father later sets up an offering hall, his tablet should be moved there.

Master Ch'eng [I] said that when children die so young that there is no mourning for them, no sacrifices are made either. When they die in early youth, sacrifices are performed only during the lifetime of their parents. When they die in middle youth, mourning continues through the lifetime of their brothers. When they die in late youth, mourning continues through the lifetime of their fraternal nephews. When adults die without heirs, sacrifices are made through the lifetime of their brothers' grandsons. These rules were all created on the basis of moral principles.[20]

- Establish sacrificial fields.

On first erecting an offering hall, calculate the size of the current fields and for each altar set aside one part in twenty as sacrificial fields. When "kinship is exhausted"[21] for any ancestor, convert the specified land into grave fields.[22] Later on, do the same for each regular or associated ancestor. The descent-line heir manages the property to supply the expenses of the sacrifices.

If earlier generations did not set aside any fields, then gather the descendants together at the grave site, calculate the size of their total land, and take a share. The descendants should write an agreement and inform the authorities. Neither mortgaging nor sale of the sacrificial fields is allowed.

- Prepare sacrificial utensils.

Suitable numbers of benches, mats, armrests, tables, wash basins, braziers, and dishes for wine and food should be prepared and stored in the closet. They

---

[19]The pattern here is to associate each person with the main-line ancestor two generations senior to him or her. As implied here, there were separate tablets for wives which were placed next to the tablets of their husbands. In the classics only the first wife had a tablet at the main altar next to her husband, and Ch'eng I retained the principle that only one wife's tablet could be matched to the husband's though he allowed that this could be a second wife (taken after the first wife died) if she were the mother of the heir. Chu Hsi held similar views in the 1170s but later disagreed, preferring the T'ang practice of allowing the tablet of any full wife (i.e., still excluding concubines).

[20]I.e., they are not given in the classics.

[21]That is, after four generations, when the ancestor is no closer than great-great-great-grandfather to anyone still alive.

[22]These fields are not grave sites, but crop fields whose income is dedicated to supporting the rituals performed at graves.

should be kept locked up and not used for other purposes. In the absence of a closet they may be kept in a case. Those that cannot be stored may be lined up along the inside of the outer gate.

- Early each morning the presiding man enters the outer gate to look in.[23]

The presiding man here is the descent-line heir who is in charge of the sacrifices of this hall. When he looks in in the morning he wears the long garment, burns incense, and bows twice.

- All comings and goings must be reported.

When the presiding man and presiding woman are about to go some place, before departing they enter the outer door of the offering hall and perform the "respectful look." They do the same on returning. After they return from staying away overnight, they burn incense and bow twice. When they will go far or will stay away more than ten days, before leaving they bow twice, burn incense, and report, "So and so is about to go to such a place and presumes to report it," then repeat the double bow. They do the same on their return, except they say, "Today A returned from such a place and presumes to appear here. If they are gone for a month, they open the inner doors, bow twice at the bottom of the stairs, then ascend the ceremonial staircase and burn incense. When their report is completed, they bow twice, go down, resume their earlier places, and bow twice again. Other family members do the same but do not open the inner door.

Here and elsewhere in this book the following conventions are followed. The presiding woman is the wife of the presiding man.[24] Only the presiding man uses the ceremonial steps to go up and down; the presiding woman and other people, even seniors, use the western steps.[25] For bowing, men bow two times and women four times, in either case called a double bow. This is also the practice when men and women bow to each other.

- On New Year's Day, the solstice, and each new and full moon, make a visit.[26]

A day before New Year, the solstice, and the new or full moons, wash, sweep, and practice purification for a night.[27] The next morning get up at dawn, open the door [of the offering hall], roll up the curtains [in front of the altar], and set a large dish of fresh fruit on the table in front of each altar. Put a tea cup, a tray, and a wine cup and saucer by each place. In front of the box of spirit tablets, set a bundle of reeds. Pile some sand in front of the incense table. Place another table above the ceremonial steps. On it place a wine decanter, a cup and saucer, and a

---

[23]That is, he does not climb the steps or enter the inner doors. Chu Hsi is said to have made daily visits of this sort.

[24]Except for the funeral rituals, when she is the widow of the deceased, if surviving.

[25]There are exceptions in the wedding rites.

[26]The solstice in question was the winter solstice. The phrase "new and full moon" could also have been translated "first and fifteenth of each month" since the Chinese used true lunar months.

[27]According to the *Li-chi*, "Chi-t'ung" 49:4b–5a: the purification aimed at purifying one's thoughts to be ready to perform the sacrifice.

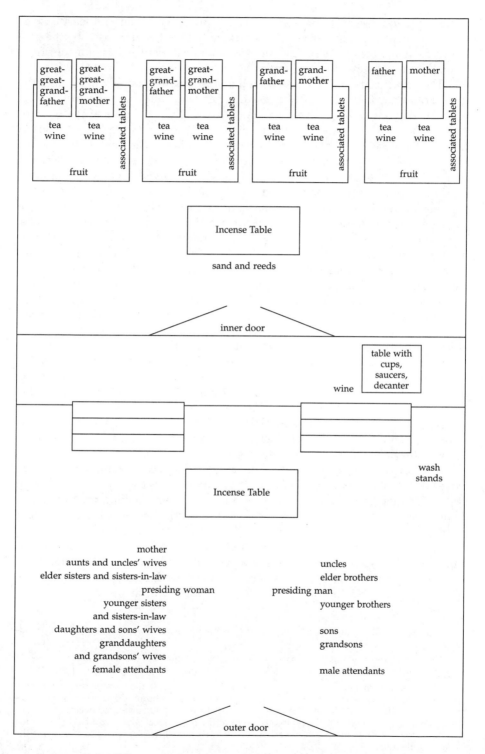

Layout of the Offering Hall for Visits

wine bottle to its west. Two wash basins and towels go at the southeast base of the ceremonial steps. The basin with a rack on the west is to be used by the presiding man and his relatives. The one without a rack on the east is for the attendants. The towels are all in the north.[28]

The participants, in full attire, from the presiding man on down, all enter the gate and take up their places. The presiding man faces north at the base of the ceremonial staircase. The presiding woman faces north at the base of the western steps. When the presiding man's mother is alive, she assumes a special place in front of the presiding woman. If the presiding man has uncles or elder brothers,[29] they stand to his right, slightly in front of him, in rows in order of rank with the most senior at the west end. When there are uncles' wives, aunts, wives of elder brothers, or elder sisters, they stand to the left and slightly in front of the presiding woman, in rows in order of rank with the most senior at the east end. The younger brothers are on the presiding man's right, slightly behind him. Sons, grandsons, and male attendants are in back of the presiding man in rows in order of rank with the most senior at the western end. The wives of the presiding man's younger brothers and his younger sisters are slightly behind the wife, to her left. The wives of sons and grandsons, daughters, and female attendants are to the rear of the presiding woman in rows with the most senior at the eastern end.[30]

When everyone is in place, the presiding man washes his hands, dries them, goes up the stairs, and inserts his official plaque. He opens the tablet case, takes the spirit tablets of his ancestors, and puts them in front of the case. The presiding woman washes, dries, goes up the stairs, and takes the spirit tablets of the ancestresses and sets them to the east of the men's tablets. Next they take out the associated tablets in the same way. An order is given to the eldest son and his wife or the eldest daughter[31] to wash, dry, and come up. Starting with the lowest-ranking ones, they set out the associated tablets one by one, in the way described above. When this is completed, everyone from the presiding woman down returns to his or her place on the lower level.

The presiding man proceeds to the front of the incense table where he invokes the spirits, inserts his plaque, burns incense, bows twice, and steps back a little. The attendants then wash, dry, and come up. After taking the top off the wine jar and filling the decanter, one attendant carries the decanter to the right of the presiding man and another takes the cup and saucer to the left of the presiding man. The presiding man kneels, followed by both attendants. The presiding man takes the decanter, pours the wine, and hands the decanter back. Then he takes the cup and saucer, the saucer in his left hand, the cup in his right. After he pours the wine out in libation on top of the reeds, he then hands the cup

---

[28]These attendants are family servants or possibly younger brothers or sons of the presiding man.

[29]Elder brothers would presumably be sons of concubines. Or the term might be loosely used for cousins older in age but whose father was younger than the presiding man's father.

[30]To visualize this more simply, all the women are on the west and men on the east. Except for the presiding man and woman, they are all in rows by generation, the most senior generation closest to the altars. Within each row, the men and women are arranged according to age (or husband's age), the oldest closest to the center of the room. Chang Tsai said having the men on the east and women on the west was based on "human feelings," so presumably it was the custom of the time.

[31]If the eldest son is not yet married.

and saucer to an attendant. After taking out his official plaque, he prostrates himself. On rising, he retreats slightly before bowing twice, then goes down the stairs and back to his place. At this point he greets the spirit by bowing twice with all those in line. Then the presiding man goes up the steps, inserts his official plaque, takes the decanter, and pours wine, first for the principal ancestor, then for the associated ones. Next he orders his eldest son to pour for all the lower-ranking associated ones.

The presiding woman comes up and takes the tea whisk.[32] An attendant follows her with the bottle of hot water. They pour the tea, following the steps given above. As in the prior case, she orders the senior daughter-in-law or the eldest daughter to continue. The sons, wives, and attendants leave first, returning to their places below. The presiding man takes out his official plaque. He and the presiding woman stand in front of the incense table on the east and west, respectively.[33] After bowing twice they go back down to their places. With all those in line they take their leave of the spirit with two bows.[34] With that they leave the hall.

At the winter solstice, make a sacrifice to the first ancestor, carrying out the ritual as given above.

On the day of the full moon, everything is as in the previous ceremony except for these changes: wine is not set out, nor are the tablets taken out; the presiding man pours the tea, his eldest son assisting him; the son goes down first and the presiding man, standing to the south of the incense table, bows twice, then comes down.

According to the *Ritual*, "when the father-in-law has died the mother-in-law retires,"[35] so the presiding man's mother does not take part in the sacrifice. It is also said, "A younger son does not make sacrifices."[36] Therefore, today sacrifices are managed by the appropriate descent-line heir and his wife, who act as presiding man and presiding woman.[37] When he has a mother, uncle, uncle's wife, elder brother, or elder brother's wife, then special places are reserved for them in the front, as described above.

Here and elsewhere in this book, "in full attire" means that those in office wear a scarf-cap,[38] official robes, a belt, boots, and hold official plaques.[39] *Chinshih* degree-holders wear scarf-caps, scholar's robes,[40] and belts. Unemployed gentlemen wear scarf-caps, black robes, and belts. Those without official status

---

[32]For making whipped tea.

[33]T'ang To incorporated the popular practice of burning paper money here.

[34]The commentator in the 1732 edition noted that the text should add here that the tablets are put back in the case.

[35]From *Li-chi*, "Nei-tse" 27:11a.

[36]From *Li-chi*, "Ch'ü–li" 5:19b; 12:11a.

[37]That is, if possible they are performed by the descent-line heir of a great-great-grandfather; if not possible, then by the descent-line heir of a great-grandfather, and so on.

[38]"Scarf-caps" were standard male headgear, derived originally from scarfs wrapped around the head and tied at the back. By Sung times they were fully fashioned hats with two vestigial ties extending from the left and right sides.

[39]These oblong plaques were a part of official insignia since ancient times. In the Sung they were to be made of wood or ivory, depending on rank.

[40]*Chin-shih* were those qualified for office by passing the civil service examination given once every three years in the capital.

all wear hats, robes, and belts. Those unable to manage all of this may wear the long garment or light robes. Those with office may also wear hats and so on, but this is not full attire. Wives wear headdresses, large dresses, and long skirts. Unmarried daughters wear hats and jackets. Concubines wear headdresses and jackets.

- On the customary festivals, make offerings of seasonal foods.

The festivals are those locally observed, such as Clear and Bright, cold food, double five, Middle Origin, and double nine. The foods offered are the local specialties enjoyed at those festivals, like rice dumplings. They are presented on a large plate accompanied by vegetables and fruit, with the same sort of ceremony as at New Year, the solstice, and new moons.

- When an event occurs, make a report.[41]

Follow the same ceremonial as at New Year, the solstice, and new moons, but stop after presenting tea and wine and bowing twice. After the presiding woman goes back down to her place, the presiding man stands to the south of the incense table. The liturgist[42] takes the board and stands to the left of the presiding man, where he kneels to read it. When finished, he rises. The presiding man bows twice, and goes back down to his place. The rest is the same.

To report appointment to office, the prayer board reads:

On the first day of this month of this year, year-cycle, your filial son A, of such office, presumes to announce clearly to his honor, his late such-type relative, of such office, title, and appellation and his late such-type relative [wife of the former] of such title and family name, that on such day of such month he has had conferred on him such post. Due to the teachings of his ancestors, he now enjoys rank and salary. For the benefits he has received, he is overcome by gratitude and admiration. Earnestly, with wine and fruit, he extends this devout report.[43]

To report a dismissal or demotion, say one was "dismissed from such a post, that having discarded the ancestral teachings, one is in trepidation and uneasy. Earnestly, . . ." If the person concerned is one's son or younger brother, then say, "A's such-type relative. . . ."

To report a posthumous title, make the report only to the altar of the spirit receiving the honor.[44] Set an incense table in front of the altar and another table to the east. Set out clean water, powder, a cup, brush, inkstone, ink, and pen on it. The rest is the same, except the prayer board reads:

---

[41]Making reports of these sorts in an offering hall does not seem to have been the common practice in Chu Hsi's time. He is quoted as saying that most people made reports at the ancestors' graves.

[42]This would not be a professional priest, but a relative, such as a younger brother or son, who reads or chants prayers and reports to the ancestors.

[43]This form gives the minimum that should be said, with the formal polite language to be used.

[44]Officials could petition for posthumous titles for their deceased parents and grandparents, the rank of the title depending on their own official rank.

On such day of such month we received an edict conferring on our late such-type relative such office and on our late such-type relative [his wife] such a title. A, due to the instruction he received from his ancestors, holds a position at court beyond what he deserves. Through the grace of the sovereign, this honor has been conferred. A's salary came too late to support his parent, which leaves him unable to choke back his tears. Earnestly, . . .

If the title was conferred because of a particular achievement, write a separate explanation of it. When the report is complete, bow twice. The presiding man advances to take the spirit tablet and put it on the table. The attendant scrubs off the old characters and smears over the tablet with the powder. After letting it dry, someone good at calligraphy is told to reinscribe the tablet with the newly conferred office and title. The recessed center is not changed. Use the wash water to wash the walls of the offering hall. The presiding man takes the tablet and puts it where it was, then returns to his place. The rest of the ceremony is the same as the others.

When the first main-line son of the presiding man is born, he is presented when he is a full month old.[45] The ceremony is like the one above, but no liturgist is used. The presiding man stands in front of the incense table and reports:

A's wife, of B surname, on such day of such month, bore a son named C. We presume to present him.

When the report is over, he stands to the southeast of the incense table and faces south. The presiding woman with the child in her arms comes forward to stand in the space between the steps and bow twice. The presiding man comes down to resume his place. The rest of the ceremony is the same.

For the reports at cappings and weddings, see their respective chapters [2 and 3].

Here and elsewhere in this book, for the prayer board, use a board a foot long and five inches wide. Write the words on a piece of paper and paste it on the board. After it has been used, tear off [the paper] and burn it. The opening and closing of the prayers are all like the first example above, except that to address a late great-great-grandfather or grandmother, one refers to oneself as a filial great-great-grandson; to address a late great-grandfather or great-grandmother, one refers to oneself as a filial great-grandson; to address a late grandfather or grandmother, one calls oneself a filial grandson; and to address a late father or mother, one calls oneself a filial son. One uses any offices, titles, and appellations the ancestor had. If he had none, one uses the number of his generational seniority while alive before the term "his honor."[46] For an ancestress, one uses "madame of such family name." Generally, in referring to oneself, say "filial" only if one is the descent-line heir.

---

[45]In this text, only the birth of the eldest son is reported. This son will one day be a descent-line heir, and so his birth is of particular interest to the ancestors since he will serve them. However, some ceremonial observance of the first-month birthday for all children was a common custom of the period. T'ang allowed this ceremony for the birth of any son.

[46]That is, if he was the twenty-third boy in the generation according to age, he would have been called "23" while alive and after death can be called "His honor 23."

For the prayers at reports of events, there should be a single board for all four generations. The terms of reference should be based on the earliest ancestor.[47] Reports are addressed only to principal ancestors, not to associated ones. Set out both tea and wine.

- Should there be flood, fire, robbers, or bandits, the first thing to save is the offering hall. Move the spirit tablets and inherited manuscripts, then the sacrificial utensils.[48] Only afterward take the family's valuables. As one generation succeeds another, reinscribe the spirit tablets and move them to their new places.

For the ceremonies for reinscribing and moving the tablets, see the section on the second sacrifice of good fortune in the chapter on funerals [4, 20]. In the family of a great descent line, when the kinship of the first ancestor is exhausted, his tablet is stored at his grave, and the great descent line manages his grave field in order to offer the grave sacrifice, once each year leading the agnates to make a sacrifice there.[49] This does not change though a hundred generations go by. When ancestors from the second generation on down have their kinship exhausted, or in ordinary lesser descent line families when the great-great-grandfather has his kinship exhausted, then the tablet is removed and buried. The ancestor's grave fields are managed in rotation by the various units, who once each year lead the descendants to make a sacrifice.[50] This also does not change though a hundred generations go by.

FROM THE PAST TO THE PRESENT

The following description of the household shrine and the Seventh Moon festival in the ancestral cult is taken from the notable study by anthropologist Francis L. K. Hsu, *Under the Ancestors' Shadow* (New York: Columbia University Press, 1948), pp. 182–191. This book was based upon the author's field investigations, during 1941 to 1943, of the "small semirural community" of West Town in the far southwestern province of Yunnan.

Each household has a family shrine. The shrine is situated in the central portion of the second floor of the west wing of the home. It is installed on the ground

---

[47]I.e., whether one calls oneself a son, grandson, etc.

[48]Some authors argue that these must have included genealogies, as Chu Hsi's plan for descent-line organization implies genealogical knowledge.

[49]Yang Fu says that since this tablet is "stored," not "buried," great descent lines must have a second offering hall at the first ancestor's grave. Whether or not Yang Fu is reading Chu Hsi correctly, this belief conformed well to the practices of descent groups of the thirteenth century.

[50]"Units" (*wei*) here is a vague term, which may refer to households or to collateral lines. The latter, however, is usually referred to as *fang*, branches of a descent group. Managing sacrificial fields by rotation was indeed a common custom. Note that earlier, under "Establish sacrificial fields," the descent-line heir was said to manage the sacrificial fields, and rotation was not mentioned.

floor only when the house is a one-story structure. Occasionally the shrine is for ancestors only, but more often it houses a number of popular gods.

Ancestors are represented in such a shrine either on a large scroll or on separate tablets. The scroll is a large sheet of mounted paper containing names, sex, and titles of the ancestors who are (theoretically) within *wu fu,* or five degrees of mourning . . . [but] this rule is not always observed. On the scroll of a poor and illiterate Ch family only a small number of the ancestors were represented, because "the old scroll was destroyed by fire and these are the only ones we can remember." On the scroll of a Y family many ancestors beyond the five degrees were represented, because they "have not had another scroll made yet." The tablets are made of wood, but if there is no time to have one made, a paper one will be substituted.

The popular gods in all family shrines are three: *Kuan Kung* [often called *Kuan Ti*] (the warrior from Three Kingdoms), Confucius, and one or more Buddhas. A fourth popular figure is the Goddess of Mercy or Fertility.[51] As a rule these gods are represented by images. In addition, there are often other spiritual figures in family shrines which the family members cannot identify. In at least one shrine there was a large tablet for Confucius as well as his supposed image. Before the shrine is an offering table, on which there are two incense burners, one for ancestors and one for the gods, two candlesticks, and a flower vase or two. At the foot of the table are two round straw cushions for the kneeling worshiper.

Incense is offered in each burner daily, usually by a woman of the house. This act is performed every morning just before breakfast. There is no offering of food except on occasions of marriage, birth, division of the family, and during the ancestor festival.

The festival occurs around the fifteenth of the Seventh Moon, but in effect it begins on the first of the month and ends on the sixteenth. On the first of the month the portion of the house containing the shrine is cleared of nonessential articles and cleaned. Offerings of the following items are made: fruit, preserves, candies, two or more bowls containing fragrant wood, some lotus or other flowers in the vase, and a number of dishes or bowls of cooked food. Red candles are inserted in the candlesticks. A new cloth, as well as a front cover, is placed on the offering table. If the tablets are encased, their covers are removed. The offerings and arrangements may be made by both men and women. The offerings may be replaced with fresh ones from time to time throughout the fifteen days.

If the family can afford it, as many West Town families can, one or more priests are invited to read scriptures and perform certain rituals before the shrine during this period. Such priests may be hired for one day or for several days, depending on how much the family is willing to spend. The greater the number of priests and the longer they are utilized, the more beneficial it will be for the dead and for the living. If only one priest is hired, he sits on a stool at the right of the offering table. His equipment consists of a wooden "fish," a pair of cymbals, many volumes of scriptures, the family's complete genealogical record, as well as the names and birthdays of all its living members. These data are written on a long folder of yellow paper. The priest recites the scriptures and performs all the pertinent rites continuously for the entire period of his employment, stopping only for meals and opium, but uninterrupted by the family's work on the shrine.

---

[51]Kuan-yin, presumably. (L.G.T.)

The function of the priest in connection with the dead ancestors was clear to all informants: to report the names of the dead to superior deities and to uplift them by scripture reading so that they will be able to proceed to the Western Heaven of Happiness as soon as possible. The reason for a complete list of the names of the family's living members is not clear to all. Some insist that it is to bless the living; others say that it will make the dead happier by showing them what worthy descendants they have. . . .

Some time during the first thirteen days of the month a married daughter makes a visit to her parents' home. She takes with her the following gifts: a number of loaves of sweetened bread; two or three pounds of pork; pears or other fruit; and a number of bags filled with ingots made of paper for members of the parents' family who have died within the last twelve months. She will be entertained at a specially prepared meal upon her arrival. She presents these gifts to her parents, pays proper ritual homage before the family shrine, and is supposed to remain for three days. In practice, however, most married daughters have to leave sooner because of the pressure of work in their husbands' households. After a woman has died, her daughter-in-law makes this visit on her behalf. When the latter has also died, then the grand-daughter-in-law will make the visit. Informants agreed that this ceremonial relationship was always kept up for several generations. Every married woman must return to the home of her husband before the fourteenth of the Seventh Moon for the big ceremony.

If a member of the family has died within a year of the Seventh Moon, the family will make a special offering and ritual homage to the recently deceased. This occasion always includes the burning of a quantity of ingots made of paper and sealed in bags, each inscribed with the names of the recipients and their immediate descendants. This ritual is generally designated as *shu* (burn) *hsin* (new) *pao* (bags).

If there has been no death within the last twelve months, the family worship takes place on the afternoon of the fourteenth. The service is performed in one of two ways, depending upon family habits. Members of the several branches of the household can perform the worship together, with joint offerings of food, wine, and incense, or they can perform it separately, with individual offerings. The dishes offered on this occasion are all elaborately prepared and contain chicken, pork, fish, and vegetables. Each dish is topped with a flower design. If the household worships as one unit, all dishes, together with at least six bowls of rice, six cups of wine, and six pairs of chopsticks are laid on the offering table in advance. Members of the household then kowtow one after the other before the altar. Generally men kowtow first, followed by women and children. But this rule is not rigidly kept. . . .

If several branches of the household perform the ceremony separately, each branch will use its own offering trays. One tray contains six or eight bowls of chicken, meat, fish, etc., and a second tray contains two bowls of rice, two pairs of chopsticks, and two cups of wine. These trays are presented at the shrine by one or two male members of the branch, followed immediately by the other members. They kowtow before the altar, the elder before the younger, and men before women. The usual number of kowtows appears to be four, but often individual members perform this obeisance five, nine, or even more times. Various branches of the household may come into the shrine room with their trays at approximately the same time, or representatives of one branch may arrive before those of another have completed the ritual. Indeed, the whole second floor of the wing may be crowded and noisy.

The atmosphere among the worshipers on this occasion appears to be greatly influenced by whether or not the male members of the family or household are scholarly. If some of them are, the atmosphere is more serious than otherwise. In all cases the West Town worshipers seem to be much less serious than the families in North China which I observed before 1937 on such occasions. . . .

When the offerings and homage at the family altar terminates, the same dishes are taken by a male member of the household (or branch of the household) to the clan temple. There the food is briefly offered at the main altar, and the male who delivers it kowtows a number of times. After this, the offering food is taken back to the house, and all members of the household come together to feast on it. If it is not enough for everyone, more food will be added until all are satisfied. Male and female members of the household eat at the same table.

During the day incense sticks are inserted at numerous places in the family home: on the lintels of all portals, special parts of the walls, and in many sections of the courtyard. During the ceremony at the family altar practically equal amounts of homage are given to ancestors and to the gods beside them. In some families the offering dishes are placed between the two groups. In others, identical offerings are placed before each group. In some families, all kowtows are intended to be shared by both; in others, all members prostrate themselves twice, once before each group.

After the meal, the *shu pao* (burning the bags) ceremony begins. Each bag contains a quantity of silver ingots and bears the name of a male ancestor and his wife, of the descendants who are providing the bag for them, and the date on which this is burned, together with a brief plea entreating the ancestors to accept it.

In general it is the custom to provide one bag for every direct male ancestor of the lineage (whether he is in the family shrine or not) and his wife or wives. By the word "direct" I refer to those deceased members, however remote, who are lineal ancestors of the person who is providing the bags. In other words, they are father, father's father, father's father's father, etc., not father's brother, father's father's brother, etc. Most families keep a list or a separate book containing the names of those ancestors who figure largely on this occasion. If first and second cousins live in the same household, each will thus provide for his own parents and grandparents until they come to a common ancestor. For the recently deceased, the number of bags per ancestor is at least doubled and may be much larger and more elaborately decorated. Each bag is burned with some coats and trousers cut out of paper.

In very rich families, music may accompany the ritual homage before the family altar as well as the *shu pao* ceremony, but this is unusual. A big container with some ashes and a bit of fire is placed in the middle of the courtyard just outside the west wing of the house. A young member of the household then kneels on a straw cushion beside the container, facing the west wing. The rest of the household may be sitting or standing around him. All the bags are heaped beside the kneeler. He first picks up the bag for the most ancient lineal ancestor, reads slowly everything that is written on it, and then puts it on the fire. As he does so, another member will throw on the same fire one or two suits of the paper coats and trousers. This procedure is repeated with all the bags, and in many cases it may take one or two hours to complete the ceremony. After all bags are burned, the ashes are poured into a stream which finally carries them into the lake.[52]

Shortly after the household ceremony and sometimes while it is still going on, the worship in the clan temples begins. Families who have no clan temples omit this ceremony; those who have them never fail to perform it. Although this is more formal than the worship at the family altar, the degree of formality varies from clan to clan. I watched such ceremonies in five temples in the years 1942 and 1943 and have had several informants describe for me the ceremonies in four others. The more elaborate and formal ceremony appears to have taken place in Y temple.

In 1943 the clan was represented by one or two male members from each household, totaling about 140 individuals. Two men were elected in advance each year from among the senior and more active members of the clan to act as treasurers as well as general managers of the ceremony. With the help of junior members of the clan they had the temple cleaned before the occasion, the altars decorated, and the kitchens made ready for use. A team of volunteer cooks who prepared a number of special offering dishes was chosen from among the clan members. In the temple a pair of big candles was lighted on the table before the center altar. The tables before the side altars held incense burners, but no candlesticks. Large numbers of lighted incense sticks were inserted in each burner.

As soon as the hired bugler and drummer arrived, the ceremony was begun. All male individuals present, including those who had cooking and other duties to perform, stood in six or seven rows of about twenty each facing the main altar in the hall. Without regard for wealth, power, or learning, the rows were arranged in order of seniority with regard to generation and age. The older men of the senior generation came first, followed by the younger ones of the same generation, and then the older men of the succeeding generation. One member stood aside and acted as master of ceremonies. After giving an order for the rows to be formed and another order for them to kneel down, the master of ceremonies knelt down too and proceeded to read aloud from a document written on yellow paper. This was a general report about the clan and its prosperity. It was called Piao and contained the names of all living male descendants of the clan. The names were included by order of seniority in generation and age, as in the formation of the rows. After the reading, the document was burned. While it was being burned, the master of ceremonies gave orders for the kneeling congregation to kowtow: once, twice, thrice, and a fourth time. He then shouted "Stand up," and pronounced the completion of the ceremony.

Musicians played during the ceremony, except for the period when the general report was being read aloud. As soon as the ceremony was completed, five bags of paper ingots were burned to the ancestors. One large bag with some special decoration was marked for the "very first ancestor" (the ancestor of origin). The other four were marked for "all ancestors of all generations." All five bags were provided by "all descendants of the Y clan." After this event the company sat down at various tables to eat a hearty meal. The seating was also more or less in accordance with seniority of generation and age.

---

[52]Burning carries the messages and the gifts to the spiritual realm as the smoke disappears into the atmosphere. The ashes are disposed of carefully. (L.G.T.)

In sharp contrast to the lack of formality at household altars, generally the temple ceremony calls for the wearing of one's best clothes. Most of the elders wore the ceremonial short coat on top of their gowns. The atmosphere during the entire proceeding was very solemn. There was no joking, laughter, or unnecessary noise or movement. . . .

. . . The ceremony at lesser ancestral temples, such as those of Ch clan and a Y clan, was performed without the accompaniment of music, but with much solemnity. . . .

FUNERAL RITES IN TAIWAN

Death in the Chinese society means becoming an ancestor. As the ancestral cult is central in this society, so the rites connected with death and its aftermath are the most protracted and serious of all Chinese religious practices. The rituals (*li*) were written into elaborately detailed codes before the beginning of the Christian era, and those codes have been in force down to the twentieth century. While there are variants on the rituals at different times and places, and in accordance with the social and economic status of the family, in essentials they conform to the prescriptions in the sacred Li texts.

What follows is an outline of the funeral rites in Taiwan as they would ideally be carried out by the Hoklo Taiwanese (i.e., those Chinese natives of the island province whose ancestral homes were in the mainland province of Fukien, across the Strait of Taiwan). Readers interested in studying a much more detailed account, with extensive interpretive commentary, should consult J. J. M. de Groot, *The Religious System of China*, Vol. I (Leyden, 1892; reprinted in Taipei, 1964).[53]

(1) *Moving the bedding.* The time of death of all males and females who are of middle age and above, married, and have posterity, is called "the end of long life." When death seems imminent, the dying person is moved into the main hall (the room where guests are entertained), where upon two long trestles are placed boards, covered with a mat. For males this deathbed is placed on the left side, and for females on the right side of the hall. However, if there are those of the older generation still living in the household, then they do not "move the bedding," or else they only move it to a side wing of the main hall. In the case of minors who die untimely, they do not "move the bedding."

The icons of the household deities, including the soul-tablets of the ancestors, which are enshrined in the main hall of every home, are covered to avoid contamination from the evil influences of death.

---

[53]Our summary is taken principally from Ts'ao Chia-yi, "Taiwan chih sang-tsang (Taiwanese funerals), in *Taiwan Wen Shian* (a quarterly journal), IX, 4, Dec. 1958, pp. 61–66. This is supplemented by information from two articles by Ho Lien-k'uei: "Sang-tsang" (funerals), in *Taiwan Feng-t'u Chih* (Taiwanese Life and Customs), Taipei, 1956, pp. 80–84; and same title in *Taiwansheng T'ung-chih Kao* (Draft Local History of Taiwan), Taipei, 1955, *chüan* 2, pp. 28f. We have also utilized Ch'en Han-kuang, "Taiwan Fu-lao-jen chin-chi chih tiao-ch'a" (Taboo among the Fukienese in Taiwan), in *Taiwan Wen Shian*, XIII, 2, June 1962, 24–38; and Wang Chin-lien, "Tai-wan-ti sang-su" (Taiwanese funeral customs), in *Ibid.*, VI, 3, Sept. 1955, pp. 57–60.

When breath ceases the pillow is replaced by a stone or with "Hades paper" (paper stamped to resemble banknotes, negotiable in purgatory), and the body is covered with the "water bedding" (a coverlet red on top—red is auspicious—and white on the bottom—white is the color of death).

Below the feet of the dead one is placed "rice at the tips of the feet": the rice is heaped up in the bowl to overflowing, in the shape of a pointed hilltop; on it is placed an egg and a chopstick. An oil lamp is lighted and kept alight day and night. It is said that these prevent the soul from starving or from losing its way on the road to purgatory through the *yin* region. In addition, Hades paper, "money to buy the way" from the malicious devils along this road, is burned on behalf of the deceased.

The entire household let their hair go unkempt, kneel, and wail.

The rice bowl of the deceased is broken. A paper figure of a boy and a girl are placed one on either side of the corpse, with incense sticks; these are called "slave spirits."

(2) *Guarding the bedding*. It is believed that if a cat should jump over the corpse prior to its coffining, it will surely rise up as a vampire. Therefore the family members guard against this very strictly. The sons and grandsons sleep beside the corpse at night. This act "exhibits the utmost filiality" and "prevents untoward happenings."

(3) *Sending over the small sedan chair*. A small sedan chair is made from paper and filled with Hades paper money. This is burned before the corpse. The purpose is to inform Heaven of the death.

(4) *The fingertip money*. When a person realizes his death is near he will keep some coins on his person. (This is according to Ts'ao; but according to Ho, it is the family members who put 120 coins in the sleeve of the deceased.) The sleeve is shaken and the coins caused to drop out into a wooden rice measure. This is called "releasing the fingertip money." The family head then divides these coins among all the family members, each of whom strings his or hers together (the old Chinese "coppers" had a hole in the center). The idea is that these will enrich the survivors. Some of the clothing and personal effects of the deceased will also be distributed among the close family members; the idea here is similar, and also includes the thought that the dead will not be forgotten.

(5) *The washing of the corpse*. All the family don mourning garments. The "filial son" (eldest son of the deceased) takes an earthenware basin to a stream (or it may be taken for him by a Taoist priest), throws in some coins, scoops up some water, wails, and returns. This is called "begging water" or "buying water." With this water the corpse is washed by family members: if a male, by sons and grandsons; if a female, by the daughters-in-law.

(6) *Announcing the death*. Since everything connected with funerals is white, this is called "announcing the white" and white cards are sent to relatives and friends. When making an oral announcement the word death is not used; the messenger says, "drink a cup of water for me," and immediately leaves the home of relative or friend without looking back.

(7) *Wailing in the street*. When the close female relatives are coming to condole, as they approach the house they must wail, using certain sorrowful words.

(8) *Meeting the "outside family" guests* (those to which a family is related by marriage). A table is set before the gate of the bereaved house, covered with a

cloth, and set with candlesticks and incense brazier holding unlit sticks of incense. The filial males kneel there and greet the relatives from the wife's family and the uncles, who lift one corner of the tablecloth and enter the house.

(9) *The "buriers."* Prior to the coffining only the closest relatives and friends come to condole; they are called "buriers." After addressing some words of condolence to the chief mourner, these will light a pair of incense sticks (two sticks are used in almost every funeral rite), kneel by the corpse, and wail. The filial son and daughter (his wife) kneel and wail also, in appreciation for the buriers' condolences.

(10) *Setting up the soul-silk.* Prior to the making of a permanent soul-tablet one is made of paper, about a foot high and three inches thick, in the shape of a blunt-tipped sword. On this are written the surname, tabu personal name, and public appellation of the deceased, together with his rank, posthumous name, the year, month, and day of death. This is placed before the deceased for his soul to receive the prayers of the survivors. Buddhist and Taoist priests are asked to set up this "soul-silk."

(11) *Paying respects.* The relatives and friends present elegiac scrolls (pairs of vertical paper scrolls with appropriate sentiments in matched words); or packages wrapped in white paper containing such items as white candles, Hades money, certain pastries, incense sticks; or rolls of brocade material; or money to help defray the funeral expenses. These are arranged before the corpse, with labels on them saying "with respect," or "funeral articles."

(12) *Putting on the grave-jackets.* The grave-jacket is called "longevity jacket," or "old person's jacket." They are mostly prepared after the age of fifty, in expectation of death. They are made of white material, their number varying with age and wealth, from three (for the young) to seven (for the middle-aged) to eleven or more (for the aged). Nine, however, are never worn, as the word for nine sounds in the local dialect like the word for dog.

The grave-jackets are not directly put on the corpse. The filial son first puts a "coolie hat" on his own head. Around the top of the hat is an encircling bamboo fillet into which are inserted two small, red candles. He seats himself on a bamboo stool which is set on a winnowing basket outside the house. The idea is thus expressed that the deceased will never "wear" the pure sky over his head, nor will his feet ever again tread the pure earth. The filial son holds his arms outstretched, with a piece of hemp rope across his shoulders, and an old woman who is considered to have led a blessed life puts the grave-jackets on him inside out. He is fed with "longevity noodles." The grave-jackets are transferred from the son to the corpse by slipping them off of either end of the rope; the coolie hat is hung up on the rooftop by means of a bamboo pole. After the filial son has climbed down from the bamboo stool, he kicks it behind him and re-enters the house without a backward look. The grave-jackets have no buttons, and those of the males are in the style of the Han dynasty.

(13) *Meeting the coffin.* When the empty coffin nears the house, a peck and two pints of rice are pressed onto the cover of it to "repress" the evil influences of the coffin. The filial son and daughter welcome the coffin, kneeling and saluting it, burning paper Hades money. They wail, and follow the coffin into the house.

(14) *Opening up the soul-road.* Soul masses are said by Buddhist and Taoist priests so that the soul will not go astray on its journey to purgatory.

(15) *Taking leave of life*. After the washing and garbing with the grave clothes, the mouth of the corpse is filled with rice, a table is set with "twelve dishes" (six vegetable and six meat), and the Buddhist and Taoist priests chant. Putting the rice into the corpse's mouth is called "taking leave of life."

(16) *Filling the corpse's mouth*. In addition to rice, jade or jewels may be put in, so that their precious influences may serve to protect him if he is attacked by demons.

Ho mentions another custom at this point: Every family member takes hold with one hand of a long, hempen rope, one end of which is attached to the sleeve of the dead person. They then ask the augur (who has come to select an auspicious time for the coffining) to cut off the portion held by each; whereupon each person wraps up his portion in a sheet of silver Hades money and burns it. This is called "cutting off lots," and represents the idea of separation from the soul of the deceased.

(17) *Encoffining*. The bottom of the coffin is fitted with a board in which are carved seven holes in the form of the seven stars of the constellation Great Bear. Over this is placed some Hades money. The corpse is put into the coffin, being provided with paper hat and boots. The sides of the coffin are further stuffed with more Hades money to prevent the body from shifting about.

Should the deceased be a young person who has not been married he must also be provided in the coffin with a cooked egg, a stone, and salted beans.[54] Some wood ashes are sprinkled in the bottom, which will protect the deceased from enemies. The outside relatives are asked to observe the coffining (to ensure that there will be no later lawsuits over any irregularities), and the coffin is nailed shut. Any persons whose zodiacal birth-animal is opposed to that of the deceased will avoid this moment as unlucky. Everyone is also careful not to let his tears or his shadow enter the coffin as it is being closed, lest this endanger his own health and luck. The coffin should be placed with its head to the south and foot to the north, orientation of the hall permitting.

(18) *Striking the tub*. The interval elapsing between the encoffining and the burial will vary according to the circumstances of the family. In poor families it will not be more than one to three days, while in wealthy families it may be several months or even several years. During this interval the outside wood is oiled every few days by people from the coffin shop to make it more waterproof and airtight; this is called "striking the tub."

(19) *Taking out the coffin*. The coffin is taken out to the roadside where it is the object of the sacrifice of a pig's head and other viands. The place in the main hall where it had been resting is sprinkled with salt and rice to dissipate the evil influences. After taking the coffin outside, five or seven bowls of white rice are placed on it, with a single chopstick stuck therein. The women accompany the coffin in their mourning garb, wailing.

(20) *Offering sacrifice*. Two kinsmen from the outside family lead in the formal sacrifice to the departing coffin's inmate: Incense is burned, the mourners drop to their knees and kowtow (letting the forehead touch the ground) thrice; rise and repeat the kneeling and kowtowing; hasten forward to make a libation of wine, pouring the wine into a pan full of sand which sits in front of the spirit

---

[54]Symbols respectively of rebirth, transformation, and sprouting.

table; again kneel and kowtow, at the same time wailing. Needless to say the filial sons also accompany them. After the outside relatives, it is the turn of the family members and friends. During all of this ceremony there is a continual accompaniment of music from the funeral band.

(21) *Circumambulating the coffin and sealing it.* Upon the conclusion of these sacrifices the filial son and his wife, led by Buddhist and Taoist priests, circumambulate the coffin thrice, wailing. The purpose is to indicate that they cannot bear to part from its inhabitant. Then the coffin is sealed by someone from the outside family, this nailing down being accompanied by auspicious sayings which by puns augur well for the family in such matters as sons and wealth.

(22) *Thanking the guests (i.e. the outside family).* When the procession has gone down one or two streets the coffin is halted, and the guests are thanked for their trouble in coming from afar. The guests thereupon bow to the coffin and take their leave. The procession goes on to the cemetery.

(23) *The funeral procession.* This is commonly called "going to the hill." On the day of the burial all the relatives and friends gather. In the morning the Buddhist and Taoist priests start their chanting and worshiping. The elaborateness of the procession of course varies according to the financial means of the family; here is how a full-fledged parade would be arranged:

First comes what is called "the deity who clears the road." This a paper and bamboo figure of a man, in whose hollow interior are hung the innards of a pig. He is borne by a rabble of beggars and "Lohan-feet"—riff-raff who make a living by this sort of thing—until the grave is reached, at which time they must make off with the pig innards, fleeing without a backward look lest they be struck dead by the spirits.

Then comes a five-colored banner, followed by two pairs of lanterns, bearing the name of the deceased on one side, and the words "a hundred sons, a thousand grandsons" on the other. The characters are written in red on the first lanterns and in blue on the second. After the lanterns there comes a "straw dragon" made from rice straw, whose head emits smoke as it is set afire. Hades money is scattered along the way to distract evil spirits.

Musicians come next, striking a big drum and a gong, and playing on the *la-pa* (a Central Asian trumpet). They are followed by sons and daughters of the deceased who carry red silk "spirit banners," while grandsons and granddaughters carry yellow silk banners.

Then come white parasols, signifying death, and two palanquins each carried by four men; on the first there is a large incense brazier, and on the second there is a drum. Behind the palanquins there are borne elegaic scrolls supplied by relatives and friends on which are written such sentiments as "Riding the crane he returns to the West"; or "Now he is an ancient."

More palanquins now appear, on which ride girls dressed up as "the twenty-four paragons of filiality." Behind these there comes a paper sedan chair in which are pasted paper figures of the deceased attended by four mourners of his nephews' generation. The chair is followed by baskets of flowers and by animals which are simulated in paper or sometimes consist of live pigeons who would fly back by themselves when released at the grave.

A most important member of the procession is the sedan chair for the soul. It is carried by four mourners of the deceased's nephews' generation. In it are a rice peck-measure, the "soul silk," and a pair of "soul sedan chair lanterns." When the burial is finished the eldest grandson rides home in this chair, carrying the peck-measure and the soul silk.

This chair is followed by Buddhist and Taoist priests, who in turn precede the coffin itself. The coffin is covered with a more or less elaborately embroidered cloth. The coffin of a poor person will be carried by four men; the common coffin will require eight to sixteen men; while the coffin of a family of wealth with many relatives may use thirty-two to sixty-four pallbearers. The "filial son," wearing sackcloth and grass sandals, walks behind the coffin, weeping. His eldest son carries a soul flag which is like a small mandala. Then follow the other sons, carrying small white paper lanterns in one hand and a mourning staff in the other (this is about a foot long, made of bramble or bamboo tipped with a bit of red cloth or hemp). After the sons come the close relatives of the deceased, all dressed in mourning.

The end of the procession is brought up by the rest of the mourners, friends and relatives, who in the old days would wear white mourning bands on their heads, and in later days wear the bands on their left arms. In Japanese times (1895–1945) they would wear paper badges below the breast.

(24) *Opening up the grave*. Prior to the funeral the eldest son has, in consultation with an augur, selected the gravesite. There, incense and candles are lit, and gold Hades paper money is burned in sacrifice to the earth gods—the "god of the hill" and the "local earth god." (There are two kinds of mock paper money: the gold is for the *shên*, or beneficent deities, and the silver for the *kuei*, or maleficent spirits.) These sacrifices are to pray for their protection of the deceased. They are called "the opening [of the grave] omens." The actual construction is called "opening up the grave."

(25) *Putting [the coffin] in the grave*. When the coffin reaches the cemetery, the "soul-silk" or spirit tablet, which has of course accompanied it during the funeral procession, is placed upon the altar which stands in front of the tombstone. The funeral pennants are stuck into the ground to either side of the grave, and sacrificial meat and wine is set before it. The coffin is put down in front of the grave and the filial son on its left, the filial daughter-in-law on its right, pay their last respects and wail. When the coffin is lowered into the pit, all must avoid standing close enough for their shadows to be trapped as the dirt and stones are piled over it. During this time there is a continuous music from the funeral band, and the Buddhist and Taoist priests chant.

The filial son again sacrifices to the local earth god, and then, bearing the spirit-tablet, kneels in front of the grave, where some dignitary (according to one source this would be the head of the clan) has been invited to "dot the *chu*" (i.e. with a brush dipped in vermilion ink, to place the final dot on the character *chu*, which signifies that the tablet is now the actual residence of the soul of the deceased). The spirit tablet is then set on a rice measure in front of the grave, where it receives the libation of the one who has dotted the *chu*, accompanied by the burning of incense, kneeling of all parties, and the din of music from the band. Led by the Buddhist and Taoist priests the funeral party circumambulates the grave, wailing, and then they return home.

The spirit-table is borne by the eldest grandson,[55] seated in the sedan chair. The route taken on the return must be exactly the same as that going to the ceme-

---

[55]This is a vestige of one feature of the ancient rites which has not survived: the personator. At sacrifices to the deceased the grandson would sit silently as the representative of his

tery, in order that the soul shall not lose its way. Some earth from the grave is carried home in an incense brazier and put on the spirit table. The soul-silk is put in back of this. The Buddhist and Taoist priests again burn incense and Hades money and chant sutras.

(26) *Thanking Earth.* Three or seven days after the burial the filial son and other close relatives go to the cemetery to sacrifice. This is called "thanking Earth," or "paying off the [lime] ashes," or "completing the tomb." After performing a sacrifice a venerable person is asked to "scatter the five grains"; besides the grains he also scatters small nails and copper coins. The filial son and daughter-in-law pick these up in their mourning garments and carry them home. They will give wealth and sons (through punning correspondence with the Chinese words). The daughter of the deceased should leave money for the gravediggers and musicians on top of the grave.

(27) *Settling the spirit.* The soul-silk is placed on a sackcloth-covered table at the side of the main hall. With it on the table there are incense, candlesticks, and a spirit-table lamp; there are also a male and a female figure made out of paper. The male holds a water pipe (Chinese version of the hooka) and the female holds a tea tray and teacup. Sacrificial meats and wine are provided. Buddhist and Taoist priests are asked to chant sutras and burn incense, and to settle the soul in its place, while the filial son and other family members kneel and wail during the sacrifice. This is commonly called "settling the spirit." After this the seven weeks sacrifices commence.

(28) *Sacrificing by weeks.* The days following the death are divided into seven periods of seven days each—although after the first week the periods are actually shortened to six days, on the theory that "time passes quickly for the dead." Some say that after seven days the dead return to inspect, and so they are thus sacrificed to. During the first week the filial son and his wife sacrifice; during the third week the filial daughter sacrifices; during the fifth week the filial grandson and granddaughter sacrifice.

These sacrifices are all accompanied by the "sounds of clashing cymbals" (i.e. the services of Buddhist and Taoist priests). During the sacrificial periods rice and side dishes are offered morning and evening to the spirit of the deceased. When the women sacrifice they wail. The sacrifice is called "filial rice" or "proffered rice." After the seven weeks are over there is the "sending of rice": A bag of rice about five inches long by three inches wide, and a small bundle of firewood are placed on the spirit-table (i.e., the altar on which the temporary soul-silk stands).

(29) *Riding the horse to seek forgiveness of sins.* During the first, third, and fifth week sacrifices, Buddhist and Taoist priests are called in to say soul masses, which is vulgarly called "making good karma." There are "three-mornings" services (i.e. beginning one morning and terminating on the third morning) and "noon-night" services (beginning at noon and terminating the same day at midnight).

The ritual called "sending off the horse [to seek] forgiveness" is as follows: A paper horse and paper official are made and set on a stand in an open place

---

grandfather to receive the sacrifices. It is an obvious symbolization of the continuity of the family line, the grandson actually conceived as the "reincarnation" of the ancestor in the generation before his father. This alternation of generations was further symbolized in the alternation of tablets on the shelves of the ancestral temple. It is thus not merely the natural affection between the old and young which accounts for the special closeness of grandparents and grandchildren in China, as contrasted with the formal distance maintained between father and son.

atop a long bench, underneath which is placed a charcoal brazier with live coals in it. The priests rapidly circumambulate this bench, and then ask the village head or a schoolmaster to read a document begging Heaven for forgiveness of the sins committed by the deceased; this person will be attired in a long gown and riding jacket (of the old style). The opening section of the document he reads has the following lines (the original is in verse):

> With both hands I accept a document,
> Not knowing what is contained in it.
> Before the hall of the forgiving-official I open my mouth to read it.
> The spark of light of this soul penetrates the nine [realms of] sunya
> (emptiness).

The closing section has the following lines:

> Before the reading of the opening of this prayer for forgiveness had been
> completed
> The sins and enmities of the deceased's soul had been forgiven.
> the sons and daughters will carry on their filial conduct forever,
> Protect the sons and grandsons and give them all blessings and long life.

After the reading of this document the priests again circumambulate the table swiftly, and then they burn the "forgiveness official," the "forgiveness horse," and the "forgiveness petition" together. Following this ceremony the priests perform on their musical instruments.

Then before daybreak there is the dedication to the deceased of the numerous replicas made with paper—houses, furniture, everything he will need in the nether world; plus such deities as the god of the hill and the local earth god, and "the twenty-four paragons of filiality"—which are also transmuted into the etherial dimension by burning.

(30) *Expelling the spirit.* This ceremony takes place at one of several intervals after the death: either on the last day of the seven weeks; on the hundredth day; on the first death anniversary; or on the second death anniversary. Again Buddhist and Taoist priests are called in to chant scriptures, and then they perform the rite of burning the soul-silk (this is now replaced by the permanent wooden tablet), and getting rid of the altar on which it has been standing. The altar-table is thrown outside the house by the roadside. When this is done there must be men made up to resemble dragons and tigers, called "dragon and tiger fighters"; otherwise the men who move the altar-table, and the bereaved family will suffer from the evil spirits. Also, anyone carelessly stepping on the oil which was in the lamp on the altar-table will get sick, so the children are taught not to walk on the side of the road where it was thrown. On this occasion wealthy people again have a service held "to make good karma."

(31) *The soul-tablet.* The permanent wooden tablet is inscribed like the soul-silk and placed in the main hall on the altar beside the other ancestral tablets. A pinch of the ashes from the incense brazier on the altar-table of the recently deceased is put into the brazier before these ancestral tablets, this commonly called "joining the braziers." Those who are unable to ask Buddhist and Taoist priests to perform this rite will usually do it themselves on New Year's Eve.

(32) *The tombstone.* On this is carved the date and tabu personal name of the deceased. According to one source the number of characters in an inscription must correspond to the five characters "birth, old age, sickness, death, suffering," which is of course the Buddhist summary of existence; the native Chinese attitude shows up in the same requirement, which goes on to specify that the words "sickness," "death," and "suffering" are themselves tabu.

(33) *Hanging up filiality.* The death is made known by special announcements pasted on the gate posts. Special cards of thanks are later sent to all the relatives within the five degrees of mourning, thanking them for their condolences.

(34) *Avoidance of certain days for funerals.* Certain double dates according to the Chinese calendar, and conflicting horoscopic days must be avoided or bad luck will follow; hence an expert is consulted to decide on auspicious times and days.

(35) *Changing the burial.* Those who believe in the theories of *feng-shui* (geomancy) or heed the words of Buddhist and Taoist priests and soothsayers, call the burial of the corpse the "unlucky burial," and the burial of the bones the "lucky burial."

In eleven or twelve years, or as early as five or six years after the original burial, on an auspicious day, they will offer sacrifices, and have the workmen who specialize in such matters open the tomb and break open the coffin. The bones will be removed and washed and dried in the sun. Then they will be properly arranged and placed in a "golden peck-measure"—an earthenware jar about three feet high and one foot in diameter. This is temporarily stored in the grave pit, or else in a small shrine called "temple of Yu Ying Kung" (collective name for spirits bereft of their due sacrifices), or "repository of all good [spirits]"; such temples usually being on a hillside or in the cemetery by the roadside. A small red marker is fastened to the little temples saying "ask and ye shall receive" (*yu ying* literally meaning the latter), or "repository of all good [spirits]." Afterwards the bones are reburied in another place selected as auspicious by the *feng-shui* expert.

(36) *Beckoning-the-soul burial.* In the case of those whose corpses cannot be found for burial, such as those who have been killed in war or died by drowning, it was formerly the practice to make a silver tablet five inches long by three inches wide, to inscribe on it the name of the deceased, the filial son to dot the *chu* with blood from his finger, and to bury this tablet inside of a "golden peck-measure."

CHAPTER 4

The Community:
Gods and Temples

MATSU—AN IMPORTANT COMMUNITY DEITY

Of the numerous deities that have throughout history been prominent in Chinese religion, few have been thoroughly studied by modern scholars. Yet the nature of the religious beliefs and practices of the folk and the communities can only be understood if these cults are analyzed. In the following essay we present information about one cult, which is particularly useful for our purposes for several reasons: First, it was officially sanctioned by the imperial government and hence may illustrate one aspect of the State religion; second, it was an immensely popular cult and not merely kept up by official support; third, it was primarily concerned with protection of seafarers, and thus its deity may serve as an example of an occupational or "professional" tutelary god; fourth, it demonstrates how people become gods in China; and fifth, it continues to be a vital part of present-day religion over a wide area of China.

Matsu or Matsu-p'o is a Fukienese localism, an affectionate family term something like "Granny." The goddess thus familiarly called by the people is formally known as the Holy Mother in Heaven (*t'ien-shang sheng-mu*), and holds the high titles of Imperial Concubine of Heaven (*t'ien-fei*) or Imperial Consort of Heaven (*t'ien-hou*). A deity prominent for centuries particularly in the southern coastal provinces, Matsu is in Taiwan today second in popularity among Taiwanese only to Kuan-yin. The religious census of 1960 states that she is the chief deity of 383 temples throughout the island province.[1]

While above all the protectress of those who must venture upon the waters, her spiritual power was more generalized to include broader protective and merciful functions. She is not only the patroness of sailors, but long ago became a universally worshiped deity who was included in the official cults as early as the reign of the Mongol Emperor Kublai Khan (during the 1280s).

---

[1]L. G. Thompson, "Notes on Religious Trends in Taiwan," *Monumenta Serica*, XXIII, 1964.

It is in Taiwan today that we are able to get our clearest look at this cult, so we shall advert especially to that case. First we may mention briefly examples of her prominence elsewhere. In a book published in 1865, the missionary Justus Doolittle remarked that the image of this deity would always be found as patron in the local guildhalls of out-of-town businessmen visiting Foochow.[2] According to John Shryock, the only provincial and trade guide-hall mentioned in the Local History of Huai-ning, an important city of Anhui province, is that of Fukien, which is entered as the T'ien-hou Temple.[3] C. K. Yang mentions "the large variety of accounts [about Matsu] given in inscriptions of temple steles found in local gazetters . . ." and states that "there were temples dedicated to this goddess in all coastal provinces as well as in localities along major navigable rivers." Yang explains that "the high percentage of official cults among temples of craft and trade deities is due to the official status of the large number of temples along the southern coast dedicated to T'ien-hou . . ."[4] Col. Valentine R. Burkhardt, in his fascinating volumes of personal observations concerning the beliefs and practices of the Hong Kong Chinese, has much to say about the cult of the Queen of Heaven. For example, among "the Boat People, the birthday of the Queen of Heaven . . . is the most important of their religious festivals." He states that "the temples to the Queen of Heaven are by far the most numerous in the Colony . . . So great is her popularity that twenty-four temples in the Colony are dedicated to her."[5]

Her close resemblance to the popularized Buddhist deity Kuan-yin has been noted by many writers, and Reginald Johnston, in his description of P'u-t'o-shan, the island center of Kuan-yin's cult, has pointed out that shrines to Matsu are found there as well.[6]

Matsu is popular in geographical designations. There is a small group of islands off the Fukien coast bearing the name. The capital town of the P'eng-hu islands (Pescadores) was called Ma-kung, or Matsu's Temple. An old temple to Matsu is one of the sights of Macau, and it seems that the very name of Macau was derived by the Portuguese from this temple.[7] There is a temple to Matsu even in San Francisco's Chinatown. It is especially interesting to note that in the initiation ceremonies of the Triad Society (T'ien-ti Hui, or Hung League), most prominent of the secret societies in modern and recent times, Matsu appears several times. There is for instance the description of the "ferryboat for the valiant Hungs," where she stands on the stern of the vessel and Kuan-yin stands in the hold. In fact, according to Ward and Stirling, an earlier name of this secret society was "The Family of the Queen of Heaven."[8]

---

[2]Justus Doolittle, *Social Life of the Chinese*, New York, 1865, I, p. 262.

[3]J. K. Shryock, *The Temples of Anking and Their Cults*, Paris, 1931, p. 26.

[4]C. K. Yang, *Religion in Chinese Society*, Univ. Calif., 1961, pp. 72f; 147.

[5]V. R. Burkhardt, *Chinese Creeds and Customs*, Hong Kong, 3 vols.: Vol. I (1953), p. 13; Vol. III (1958), pp. 110 and 154.

[6]R. F. Johnston, *Buddhist China*, London, 1913, p. 268.

[7]See, for example, Ping-ti Ho, *The Ladder of Success in Imperial China*, Columbia Univ., 1962, p. 196; Søren Egerod, "A note on the origin of the name of Macao," *T'oung Pao*, 47 (1959), pp. 63–66.

[8]J. S. M. Ward and W. G. Stirling, *The Hung Society or the Society of Heaven and Earth*, London, 1925, Vol. I, pp. 79ff; Gustave Schlegel, *Thian Ti Hwui. The Hung League or Heaven-Earth League*, Batavia, 1866, pp. 70; 108f; 131.

Turning now to Taiwan and a few examples of the substance of the cult, we find the first historical evidence only with the late arrival of Chinese rule over the island—the conquest of the Dutch by Cheng Ch'eng-kung (known in Western writings as Koxinga) in 1662. Cheng believed his victory was aided by the supernatural intervention of Matsu, and so he had her temple at Luerhmen (the port for the capital town of Taiwan, now Tainan City) renovated and supplied with a new image and other furnishings.[9]

Cheng Ch'eng-kung was a loyalist in the cause of the Ming dynasty, which was toppled by the Manchu invaders who founded the last dynasty called Ch'ing. He took Taiwan because the Manchu forces had made the mainland untenable and he needed a base. Twenty-one years later the Ch'ing government was ready to attack Taiwan, and now Matsu showed her impartiality: Several stories of her aid to the Ch'ing forces have been preserved in written sources. She was observed bearing a banner and urging on the Ch'ing warriors during the battle for P'eng-hu. Credit for the victory was due to the inspiration this sight gave to the hard-pressed attackers. Again, when the victors landed in the almost waterless Pescadores, Matsu caused a small well to produce enough water for all of them. These miracles were not totally unexpected, however, as the Ch'ing admiral had before the invasion dispatched several officials from the Board of Rites to burn incense, make offerings, and pray for aid before the image of Matsu in her home temple on the island of Meichou; following which, the admiral himself had made a pilgrimage to her shrine. It may be that the goddess was finally persuaded of his sincerity and the justness of his cause when, upon seeing that the living quarters of the attendant monks were not in good repair, he generously donated 200 taels of gold to rectify this situation.[10] It was in gratitude for Matsu's help in the Ch'ing victory that she was by Imperial decree raised in rank from Imperial Concubine to Imperial Consort of Heaven.

More typical perhaps of incidents in which Matsu protects mariners is the story of the return of a ship bearing the captured Taiwanese rebel Lin Shuang-wen to Amoy in 1787. When the vessel arrived at Ta-tan Men, a tiny island in midstream of the entranceway to the great bay, it was already dusk. The skipper wanted to anchor and wait for daylight to go on in, but having spent four days at sea the official in charge was impatient to reach Amoy, which could already be seen in the distance. He gave the order to proceed. A gale had started to blow, the junk began to list, and soon it was so dark they could not see where they were going. The crew were in a panic. Two anchors were dropped, but they would not hold. When all seemed lost they suddenly saw a gleaming light ahead, and the cry went up, "Matsu has come!" The light moved as if someone were guiding them through the rocks in a small boat, and indeed, by following its guidance, they finally entered the harbor safely. This was all the more extraordinary in that for a vessel to enter Ta-tan Men in the dark was unheard of, because of the menace of rocks.[11]

---

[9]See especially Lin Heng-tao, "Lu-erh-men t'ien-hou-kung chen-wei lun-chan chih chieh-chüeh" (the upshot of the dispute over the genuineness of the T'ien-hou Temple at Lu-erh-men), in *Taiwan Feng-wu*, XI, 5 (May 1961), 3–5.

[10]Story as in *T'ien-fei Hsien-sheng Lu (A Record of Miracles of the Holy Mother in Heaven)* (TWTK No. 77), Taipei, 1960, pp. 44f.

[11]Story as in *ibid.*, pp. 71f.

It is said that there are three temples in Taiwan today where Matsu's spiritual power is generally recognized as most potent: One is in P'eng-hu, one at a town called Pei-kang, and one at a place called Kuan-tu near the hot springs resort of Pei-t'ou, outside of Taipei. The tale of the founding of the Kuan-tu Temple may serve as an example of the continuing credibility of Matsu's powers.[12]

According to this story, the image of Matsu at the Kuan-tu Temple was once the protective icon aboard a large junk. The vessel was caught in a typhoon and sunk in the Taiwan Strait, and the image floated into the bay at the mouth of the Tan-shui River. The people of the villages in the vicinity pulled it out of the water and set it up in a certain temple. After several days had passed, Matsu appeared in a dream to one of the local men and asked him to see to the construction of her temple. She told him she had already selected the site, and instructed him that wood from a certain hill was to be used for the building.

The next day the image was gone from the temple where it had been deposited, and it was found at the place in Kuan-tu where the temple now stands only after four days of searching by the villagers. This naturally convinced the people that Matsu had indeed chosen her own place of residence, and they subscribed funds for construction of the temple. The man who had had the dream went to the hill as directed and asked the landowner for the lumber. To his surprise the landowner replied that he was a man of his word, and fully intended to honor the contract which had already been made the day before with a mysterious young woman. Upon being informed that this was obviously the goddess herself, the landowner immediately donated all the necessary lumber.

It was estimated that three days would be required for workmen to cut down the trees. To their amazement, however, that very evening a storm uprooted the trees and even chopped them into boards, then hurled them down the hill to the site of the temple. The news of Matsu's miracles spread far and wide, and in a short while several thousand believers had assembled at the spot to participate in the work of construction. This of course made the work go faster, but created a shortage of food. However, this crisis was overcome when the resident monks discovered behind the rising building a small cave, from which cooked rice was flowing. The amount produced was exactly enough for the workers. Needless to say this made it easy for the temple to be completed in record time.

The story is completed with the addition of a parable involving the well-known mythical theme of the inexhaustible food supply. One greedy fellow tried to get more out of the miraculous rice-producing hole so that he could sell it for a profit. In the dead of night he stole out to the spot and began digging to enlarge the opening. The result of course was that the flow of rice ceased entirely, which everyone realized was Matsu's punishment for his greed.

These stories illustrate the beliefs of the cult, and we may next turn to the question of its historical origin and evolution. This question does not much concern her devotees, whose faith is securely anchored in reports of such miracles. They may commonly have heard a biography of the goddess that goes something like this:

She was born in the small island of Mei-chou, which is off the coast of Fukien province. She was the sixth daughter of a petty official named Lin. She was born

---

[12]Story as in Hsieh Chin-hsuan, "Shen-mi ti Kuan-tu Ma-tsu" (The mysterious Matsu of Kuan-tu), *Taiwan Feng-wu*, IV, 3 (Feb. 1954), pp. 15f.

at the beginning of the Sung dynasty (about A.D. 960). She was of course a remarkably intelligent, pious, and studious girl, devoted to religious practices. One day, seated at her loom, she fell into a trance in which she saw three ships carrying her father and two elder brothers. The ships were storm-tossed and about to founder. She took her father's ship into her mouth, and seized her brothers' ships with either hand, dragging them toward the safety of the shore. Unfortunately her mother called to her just at the critical moment, and as she roused and answered her, the ship with her father aboard fell from her mouth, and he was lost. This turned out to be not just a nightmare, but an actual miracle, when her brothers returned in a few days to tell of their narrow escape and the sad fate of their father. The girl refused to marry (very remarkable behavior in the Chinese society). She spent her short life in continuing service to her mother (the most commendable behavior) and in perfecting her religious powers. At the age of twenty-eight she was transformed into a spiritual being. After that time she was seen very often by those in danger on the sea, and became famous as their savior.[13]

The journal of a well-educated merchant who paid a visit to Taiwan at the end of the 17th century attests that belief in the goddess was not confined to the simple folk, but was generally accepted:

> Matsu is the most puissant of the deities of the seas . . . Whenever a junk is in danger, if they pray to her she will answer their prayers. Often her spirit soldiers will be seen guarding them, or the goddess herself will come to save them. Her miracles are too numerous to recount. In the middle of the ocean, when wind and rain obscure [everything], when the night is black as ink, at the tip of the mast there appears the light of the goddess, manifesting her divine help. Or in the vessel there will suddenly shine forth a glowing fire like the gleam of a lamp, which will rise up the mast and then be extinguished. The mariners say this is the fire of Matsu, and if it leaves, [the ship] will inevitably meet with disaster—a prophecy which is always strangely fulfilled. In the vessel they store a "Matsu staff," and whenever a great fish or sea monster tries to come near the ship they fend it off with the Matsu staff. . . .

After giving a sketch of the traditional biography, and some particulars about later miracles, the author continues:

> Up to the present time when the women of the Lin clan in Meichou are going out to their fields, they simply place their children in the temple saying, "Auntie, watch them carefully!" They are commonly gone all day, but the children don't cry or get hungry, nor do they go beyond the threshold of the temple. When the women return in the evening each finds her own children and takes them home.[14] It seems that the goddess loves the children of her clansmen.

---

[13]See, for example, Chuang Te, "Ma-tsu shih-shih yü T'ai-wan ti hsin-feng" (The history of Matsu and the religious beliefs in Taiwan), *Taiwan Feng-wu*, VIII, 2 (June 1957), pp. 5–16. J. J. M. de Groot already gave the common version in *Les Fêtes Annuellement Célébrées à Emoui (Amoy)*, Paris, 1886, Vol. I, pp. 260–267.

[14]Yü Yung-ho, "Hai-shang chi-lüeh" (Brief account of [journeying] on the sea), in his *P'i-hai Chi Yu (Small Sea Travel Journal)*, TWTK No. 44, Taipei, 1959, pp. 59f.

Careful scholarly examination of the Matsu legend in its several variants had not been undertaken until as recently as the 1950s, when a Taiwanese named Li Hsien-chang began publishing his findings in several Japanese journals. From a meticulous examination of the extant historical sources, Mr. Li has shown clearly how the legend built up through gradual accretions, as later writers added details to the materials they found in earlier documents. If the film is run in reverse, so to speak, we come to the earliest stage, and the four simple facts—or apparent facts—which are all that the Sung sources can tell us: (1) that Matsu was from Mei-chou; (2) that she was a daughter in the Lin family; (3) that she was versed in fortune-telling; (4) that after she died she was worshiped. The rest of the story, so much more interesting and detailed as we come to Yuan and Ming and Ch'ing writings, is, so far as can be discovered from documentary evidence, entirely an embroidering of these four facts.[15] Of course there must be adequate reasons why the cult should have arisen in the first place, but these reasons must remain conjectural in view of the lack of any further historically attested facts.[16]

A note may be added concerning the attendants of the goddess. In her temples one will find two subordinate figures (aside from any other notable deities who may have been invited to share the temple with Matsu), whose names are Thousand-league Eyes (Ch'ien-li Yen) and Favoring Wind Ears (Shun-feng Erh). With slight variations, their images will conform to the following description: Both are standing, to left and right of Matsu, in attitudes respectively of looking and listening afar. As one writer puts it, "they seem strange but not fierce, martial but not frightening." One shades his eyes with one hand, the other has a hand to an ear, to indicate their functions. They have short beards or no beards. They wear earrings, bracelets, and ankle bracelets. Their colored jackets are perhaps blown open to reveal the chest. They have red feet. They may hold weapons or be empty-handed. Eyes has a green face and body; Ears has a red face and body. Their faces may be decorated here and there with gold.[17]

Although they look like "barbarians"—perhaps barbarian seamen—they are in fact derived from ancient mythology, and may be traced through many centuries of transmogrifications. The latest, as in the case of so many of the characters in the modern Chinese pantheon, is the version to be found in the famous *Canonization of the Gods*, a work of the Ming dynasty which is a melange of myths concerning the struggle between the last, wicked ruler of the Shang dynasty and the founder of the Chou.[18] In any case, these figures are appropriate symbols for two powers essential to the miracle-working capacity of Matsu: the ability to see across the seas and to hear how the winds are blowing.

---

[15]See Chinese translations of Li's work in *Taiwan Feng-wu*, seven articles published between Dec. 1960 and Dec. 1963.

[16]The first major study of the subject is now available in a Western language: Bodo Wiethoff, "Der Staatliche Ma-tsu Kult," *Deutsche Morgenländische Gesellschaft Zeitschrift* (Wiesbaden), 116, 2 (1966), pp. 311–357.

[17]Chang Ching-ch'iao, "Ch'ien-li yen ho shun-feng erh" (Thousand-league Eyes and Favoring Wind Ears), *Taiwan Feng-wu*, V, 8/9 (Aug. 1955), 43f.

[18]One should consult Liu Ts'un-yan, *Buddhist and Taoist Influences on Chinese Novels, Vol I: The Authorship of the Feng Shen Yen I*, Wiesbaden, 1962.

RELIGION IN RURAL COMMUNITIES

Experienced students of China have always recognized the danger of attempting to generalize in descriptions of the land and its cultures. It may be permissible to make one grand generalization: The Han culture—that of the "Chinese Chinese" as against the numerous ethnically distinct groups that have historically been included within the political boundaries of China—is basically homogeneous, with many greater and lesser variants. The homogeneity is the result of a similar economic basis in intensive agriculture; a single language (although modified by extreme dialectical variations); a single writing system based upon meaning rather than sound, thus enabling the classical writings of ancient times to be fairly intelligible to all literate persons; a common system of cosmology and ethics; and other factors. Not the least important of these shared cultural factors is the assemblage of religious beliefs and practices. The existence of the local variations makes it difficult to give a sample in our readings that will not be misleadingly parochial—especially when we are dealing with religion in the community. As is quickly discovered from reading community studies of different places in China, the details of religious conditions are as diverse as every other aspect of community life. What follows, therefore, must be taken merely as suggestive. We have brought together observations from several authors who have studied communities in widely separated areas of China, and at different times, and whose personal points of view are quite disparate.

Our first selection comes from one of the earliest avowed attempts at a "sociological study" of Chinese villages, *Village Life in China* (Fleming H. Revell Co. New York, Chicago, Toronto 1899) by the Protestant missionary, Arthur H. Smith. While this work would hardly pass muster today as a piece of objective scholarship, one can extract some useful information from it. We take a few passages from chapter 9, on "Village temples and religious societies," pp. 136–140.

The process by which the inconceivably great numbers of Chinese temples came to be is not without an interest of its own. When a few individuals wish to build a temple, they call the headmen of the village, in whose charge by long custom are all the public matters of the town, and the enterprise is put in their care. It is usual to make an assessment on the land for funds; this is not necessarily a fixed sum for each acre, but is more likely to be graded according to the amount of land each owns, the poor being perhaps altogether exempt, or very lightly taxed, and the rich paying much more heavily. When the money is all collected by the managers, the building begins under their direction. If the temple is to be a large one, costing several hundred taels, in addition to this preliminary tax, a subscription book is opened, and sent to all the neighboring villages, and sometimes to all within a wide radius, the begging being often done by some priest of persuasive powers, dragging a chain, or having his cheeks pierced with spikes, or in some way bearing the appearance of fulfilling a vow . . . Lists of contributions are kept in the larger temples, and the donors are expected to receive the worth of their money, through seeing their names posted in a conspicuous place, as subscribers of a certain sum. . . .

It is seldom safe to generalize in regard to anything in China, but if there is one thing in regard to which a generalization would seem to be more safe than another, it would be the universality of temples in every village throughout the empire. Yet it is an undoubted fact that there are, even in China, great numbers of villages which have no temple at all. This is true of all those which are inhabited exclusively by Mohammedans, who never take any part in the construction of such edifices . . . The most ordinary explanation of a comparatively rare phenomenon of a village without a temple, is that the hamlet is a small one and cannot afford the expense . . . In the very unusual cases where a village is without one, it is not because they have no use for the gods; for in such instances the villagers frequently go to the temples of the next village and "borrow their light," just as a poor peasant who cannot afford to keep an animal to do his plowing may get the loan of a donkey in planting time, from a neighbor who is better off.

The two temples which are most likely to be found, though all others be wanting, are those of the local god [*t'u-ti*], and of the god of war [Kuan-ti]. The latter has been made much of by the present dynasty, and greatly promoted in the pantheon. The former is regarded as a kind of constable in the next world, and he is to be informed promptly on the death of an adult, that he may report to the city god ("Ch'eng Huang"), who in turn reports to Yen Wang, the Chinese Pluto. In case a village has no temple to the T'u-ti, or local god, news of the death is conveyed to him by wailing at the crossing of two streets, where he is supposed to be in ambush.

Tens of thousands of villages are content with these two temples, which are regarded as almost indispensable. If the village is a large one, divided into several sections transacting their public business independently of one another, there may be several temples to the same divinity. It is a common saying, illustrative of Chinese notions on this topic, that the local god at one end of the village has nothing to do with the affairs of the other end of the village.

When the temple has been built, if the managers have been prudent, they are not unlikely to have collected much more than they will use in the building. The surplus is used partly in giving a theatrical exhibition, to which all donors are invited—which is the only public way in which their virtue can be acknowledged—but mainly in the purchase of land, the income of which shall support the temple priest. In this way, a temple once built is in a manner endowed, and becomes self-supporting. The managers select some one of the donors, and appoint him a sort of president of the board of trustees (called a *shan chu*, or "master of virtue"), and he is the person with whom the managers take account for the rent and use of land. . . .

The temples most popular in one region may be precisely those which are rarely seen in another, but next to those already named perhaps the most frequently honoured divinities are the Goddess of Mercy (*Kuan Yin P'u Sa*), some variety of the manifold goddess known as "Mother" (*Niang Niang*), and Buddha. . . .

It is impossible to arrive at any exact conclusions on the subject, but it is probable that the actual cost of the temples, in almost any region of China, would be found to form a heavy percentage of the income of the people in the district.

The Rev. Smith wrote mostly from his years of residence in Shantung province; our next author, also a missionary but in addition a professional sociologist with the more objective standards of a later generation, writes about a village in the southern province of Kwangtung. Daniel H. Kulp's *Country Life in South China* (Teachers College, Columbia University, 1925; reprinted in Taipei, 1966) is a milestone in scientific community studies in China. From the chapter on "Religion and the spiritual community" (pp. 284–314) we extract the summary section entitled "Religious attitudes."

Sufficient data have been presented to show that religion colors every aspect of life in Phenix Village. The living person must constantly be alert if he would refrain from injuring or offending the hosts of spirits all about him. He consumes much time and money in constant effort to maintain a harmonious participation in his plurality of communities: the living, the departed ancestral spirits, and the spirits of nature that work their will through the operation of natural forces. Each of these communities [is] equally real. Out of all his religious practices he wins satisfaction for his wish for security and achieves a sense of solidarity with his folk, natural, human, living, departed, present or historical. To break with these communities, to refuse to conform to the customary demands made upon one by the mystical members of the communities was a thing unheard of until the introduction of Christianity and modern science.

Thus all matters, projects, plans, behavior of every kind are measured by community norms first founded in favor of the family, its head, and back of all, its spiritual head or departed ancestor. What these norms are and how they grew up can be seen in the ancestral worship and in the filial duties of everyday life. The wise sayings of a powerful and learned *chia-chang* [defined earlier by author as the head of a particular kin-group—moiety or branch-family], after his death, are repeated and transmitted from generation to generation, providing fixed norms and schematized behavior patterns for the living. Out of the mystical assumptions of the living, the sanctions of the dead become powerful means of control of the conduct of the living. Attention centers on ancestors and not descendants; the look of the community is backward and not forward in any mundane sense; continuity, conservatism, traditionalism, institutionalism, familism are the great societal values. The individual person is of value only as he, while living, enhances and defends these values. Human prosperity is worth while only as it makes possible the happiness of the spirits, who, in turn, can produce human prosperity. There is an interaction between the human and the spiritual that creates a fundamental interdependence of the two and places religion at the center of all familist practice.

That these attitudes are based on error makes no difference sociologically. They motivate behavior and illustrate how in human conduct the notions that people hold in their minds about themselves and the roles they play in various groups are the real and immediate determiners of action. The man participating in ancestral worship is constantly projecting himself into the future world; he sees himself in the situations and conditions that he believes his departed ancestors are now in; he also sees himself in relation to the living descendants who later will be called upon to worship him; the guaranteeing of that status in the future life is his central problem. Out of this objective has developed the whole complex of familicentrism. That is why religion is not individual and personal religion so much as it is collective and group religion. Individuals pray not for themselves but for their families.

The culture complex of religion in Phenix Village is made up of attitudes, values and practices of all the various religious systems to be found in China. Until Christianity was introduced, there was no sectarianism whatever in the village. The same person followed animistic practices, spiritist seances, Buddhist adherence, Taoist customs and Confucian standards; but the important thing to note is that there was no sectarian adherents who marked themselves off from other religious groups and refused to follow certain practices as not belonging to their religion. The essence of sectarianism is the refusal to compromise. Strictly speaking, the sects exist but not in any practical way in Phenix Village. There is no Buddhist, nor Taoist, nor Confucian temple. For the laity, then, religion is a mingling of the practices of all these religions together with the familist religion of ancestral worship.

Lacking the knowledge to criticize any of the religions, the ordinary person frankly believes whatever religious faiths he encounters. The scholars of the village are skeptic about Buddhism and Taoism but they do not interfere with the people in following Buddhist or Taoist practices. The scholars are advocates of Confucianism. They keep quoting Confucius or his disciple Mencius until gradually the norms of conduct that the great sage enunciated seep down to the last man or woman in the village. So it is that the people believe in animism and worship the spirits of objects of nature. They have strong faith in the Buddhas, for they practice Buddhist customs and contribute money to erect Buddhist temples; they follow Taosim, for they call upon the Taoist priest of the region to perform ceremonies for the dead, use Taoist charms for protection against demons, and on certain days observe vegetarian diets.[19] Lastly, they proudly refer to the teachings of Confucius as moral standards for familist practice and close every debate by quotations from his classics as to what is proper.

We further quote from the same chapter the paragraph labeled "Village philosophy":

Part of the philosophy of the people of Phenix Village has been illustrated by their notions of religion and ancestor worship. Briefly, opinion is shaped and action undertaken according to whether they will please the gods they worship or glorify their ancestors. Fate rules all. The people do not entirely subscribe to a laissez-faire social policy for they think that collective action in worship and ceremony will either control the gods and so their own future well-being or ameliorate their condition by changing the mood of the gods. They constantly alternate from fatalistic laissez-faire-ism to a practical magic. They manipulate charms, mutter formulas, spread mystic characters to the wind, wear amulets and in all sorts of ways try to control their environment to meet their wishes, as best they can. But when all their effort, individual and collective, fails, when floods come in spite of prayers and death carries off their kin, worship notwithstanding, then they acquiesce and call it *Ming* or Fate.

Our third selection is from the field report of Bernard Gallin, an anthropologist who spent sixteen months during 1957–58 in a village of west-central Taiwan. His book is entitled *Hsin Hsing, Taiwan. A Chinese Village in Change* (University of California, 1966); this selection comes from pages 248–256.

---

[19]Vegetarianism is usually considered a Buddhist, rather than a Taoist, custom. (L.G.T.)

The lunar calendar forms the base for the schedule of calendrical rituals—the *pai-pai* [religious worship festivals] which are celebrated by the whole village on set days. One such important rite is the *pai-pai* for unworshiped, anonymous ancestors. Such forgotten and neglected ancestors wander about the countryside looking for sustenance, becoming negative powers or harmful spirits (*kuei*) which often make trouble for people. Although they are regarded as demons, the Taiwanese follow universal custom and refer to them euphemistically, calling them good brothers (*hao hsiung-ti*) to avoid antagonizing them.

Pai-pai for the good brothers are held regularly on the second and sixteenth of each lunar month by all the villagers of the area. On these dates each household worships individually, but outside of its house since "one does not invite negative powers or spirits into the *kung t'ing* [main room]." The sacrifices for this occasion are usually quite simple and consist of vegetable soups and perhaps some cut-up pork and/or fish. . . .

The villagers also tend the spirits of other unknown people.

In addition, the villagers also worship spirits of the unknown dead which have been confined for long periods of time or even permanently to the underworld for having led immoral lives. During the seventh lunar month these spirits are released and permitted to journey to the surface, where they roam about for the entire month. At this time they must be offered sustenance. The villagers refer to them as good brothers also, but unlike the good brothers worshiped on the second and sixteenth of each lunar month, these good brothers are "criminal" good brothers.

Until a few years ago each community in the Hsin Hsing area and the city of Lukang worshiped them with large *pai-pai* held throughout the month made it possible for the people in one place to invite people from elsewhere to share in their feast. . . . [The sacrifices] are offered not only to the good brothers but also to an underworld god known as P'u Tu Kung who watches over the good brothers. The villagers call this occasion, the fifteenth of the seventh month, Chung Yuan.

The most frequent *pai-pai* which villagers define as calendrical are the four which are held independently by all village families on the same days of each lunar month. On the first and fifteenth, all the gods and their soldiers and horses are worshiped. On the second and sixteenth days of each month, as mentioned above, offerings are made to the good brothers. . . .

One of the most important family holidays of the year is celebrated in winter in the first lunar month—the Chinese New Year. . . . The New Year's celebration actually begins on the twenty-fourth day of the twelfth month, when the villagers send the gods off to heaven. They burn incense and a special paper money called *chia ma* and shoot off firecrackers. The paper money bears a picture of a horse which symbolizes the horse on which the gods ride to heaven. The families sacrifice fruit and cake at a very simple ceremony.

On New Year's Eve the villagers worship their ancestors in the *kung t'ing*. . . . The next day the worship of the ancestors begins anew and is repeated daily until the third day of the first month. On these three days the villagers also worship the three brother gods (San Chieh Kung),[20] and many of them, including men, young women, and children, spend their time gambling during the period of rest from work.

---

[20]T'ien Kuan, god of heaven; Ti Kuan, god of earth; Shui Kuan, god of waters. (L.G.T.)

The fourth day of the first month is called Chieh Shen or "welcome the gods." On this day the gods who went to heaven come back to earth. The villagers offer sacrifices and burn incense and paper money to welcome them back.

The ninth day of the first month is the birthday of T'ien Kung, the highest of the gods. Although the villagers consider him a vegetarian, they nevertheless sacrifice pork, duck, and chicken in addition to vegetable dishes and cakes, explaining that T'ien Kung eats only the vegetables, but his friends and the other gods eat the meats.

The fifteenth day of the first month, called Shang Yuan or "the first full moon of the New Year," is the occasion for worship of all the gods and ancestors with sacrifices of meat, vegetables, incense, and paper money by each individual family.

Late in the second month or early in the third is Ch'ing Ming Chieh, "one hundred days after Tung Chieh" (the winter solstice). On this day, village families go to the cemetery to clean and sweep the graves and worship their ancestors. If a family has built a new house, married a son, or produced a baby boy during the year, they will hold a special ceremonial and offer many sacrifices at the grave site. In addition, for three years following the death of a member of the family, a special ceremonial takes place at which the female members of the family wail as they did at the funeral. . . .

The twenty-third day of the third month is the birthday of the goddess Matsu [for details concerning her cult, see the separate article by Thompson]. . . . Each year many people from far-off villages and even cities travel to Lukang in long processions by hired trucks, bicycles, pedicabs, sedan chairs, and on foot to worship Matsu on her birthday. Some Hsin Hsing villagers also go to Lukang to worship Matsu on this day, but most worship her at home because they are too busy to travel to Lukang. However, Lukang is considered a very exciting place when it is filled with tens of thousands of people who have come to worship Matsu, and many villagers, especially young people and women, go there in the evening to watch the festivities.

In addition to the recognition which is accorded Matsu on her birthday, for at least the last forty years Hsin Hsing and eleven other villages in the area have held a joint procession each year to worship Matsu some weeks after her birthday. . . . On the day of the procession, the villagers assigned to carry the sedan chairs assemble at a prearranged spot to begin the circuit through the twelve villages. A large statue of Matsu, borrowed for the occasion from her temple in Lukang, is carried in a big sedan chair by several villagers. As the procession passes through the village, the residents worship the goddess, and a local shaman invites her to eat. Village teams of performers accompany the procession. They dance, give exhibitions of traditional boxing and sword play, act out little incidents or excerpts from traditional Taiwanese operas or stories, or do a dragon dance in which a large, green paper dragon is carried over the heads of many men who weave in and out to simulate his sinuous movements. The whole occasion is extremely gay and entertaining and, it is felt, most rewarding. Many food offerings to the goddess are displayed in each village along the route. They are provided by each village family and are eaten at dinner in the evening, after the Matsu procession has passed. . . .

The twenty-fourth day of the fourth month is the birthday of the Hsin Hsing village god, Ta Shih Kung. Those villagers who have been working elsewhere normally come home for this *pai-pai,* and even some of the members of village families whose business or work has required them to move to the city return for this day and stay overnight or several days with relatives in the village. The main reason for this influx is that the celebration is one of the gayest and most festive of all those held during the year.

All families worship Ta Shih Kung in a joint *pai-pai* held in the courtyard of one of the largest *tsu* [clan] houses in the village. A shaman is present to exorcise any devils that may be near and to invite the god to eat the sacrificed food, the best the villagers have all year. Guests are invited from all over the area to join in the festivities, and for weeks or even months in advance the villagers issue invitations to relatives and friends.... The entertainment includes not only the good food and the contact with different people, but also a puppet show performed by a professional group hired from a city. The puppet show is based on stories from dynastic history and is a source of delight to the villagers and their guests... The carnival atmosphere of the occasion is augmented by the presence of vendors of food, sweets, sugarcane, and betel nut who come from Lukang and surrounding villages to sell their wares.

The puppet show and other communal expenses of the *pai-pai* are paid for with money collected from each village family by the pot master for Ta Shih Kung and his assistants, who also arrange for the show. Each village household is assessed an amount calculated on the basis of land operated (whether owned or rented) and the number of people in the household. The families of village shamans are not required to contribute any money on such occasions....

During the fifth and sixth months, the busy agricultural season, there are no important village *pai-pai* other than the usual four to worship the gods, their soldiers and horses, and the Good Brothers. Most festive holidays and calendrical rites fall in months when the farmers are not busy with agricultural chores....

The fifteenth day of the eighth month is the birthday of T'u Ti Kung, the Earth God. On this day the villagers hold a *pai-pai* at his temple which is located on the road in front of the village. Each village family worships individually with sacrifices of pork, vegetable dishes, and moon cakes. No guests are invited to dinner on this occasion....

In the ninth month there are no special *pai-pai*, but around the middle of the tenth month, the village has one of its largest joint *pai-pai* of the year on the occasion called *tso p'ing-an* [literally, "making peace"]. By the time of this *pai-pai*, the farmers have harvested their rice, and at the ceremonial worship of T'ien Kung, his soldiers, and many lesser gods, they think T'ien Kung for giving them a good crop and "peaceful days." The ceremony is held in the courtyard of one of the largest village *tsu* houses, and a shaman invites the gods to partake of the sacrifices. Huge amounts of paper money are offered to the god....

Each village in the area arranges to hold its *tso p'ing-an pai-pai* on a different day. Thus, for a period of almost two weeks, the villagers busy themselves with visits to relatives and friends to help them celebrate their *tso p'ing-an* festival. Hsin Hsing village alone entertains hundreds of guests on this occasion....

Some time during the first half of the eleventh month, the villagers celebrate Tung Chieh. Each family worships its ancestors in the *kung t'ing* with steamed round dough cakes and other simple sacrifices. Some families also worship at the village Earth God temple, and others go to the Matsu temple in Lukang.

The sixteenth day of the twelfth month is called Wei Ya and is the last day of the year on which the Good Brothers are worshiped by each family. On this day the villagers also go to the Earth God temple to ask T'u Ti Kung to protect their livestock. The average family does not have guests to dinner, but landlords are supposed to invite their hired men to eat on this occasion. . . .

By the twenty-fourth day of the twelfth moon, as already indicated, the villagers begin to prepare for the New Year's celebration by sending the gods off to heaven. . . .

Most clearly classifiable as noncyclic rites of passage (crisis rites) are those associated with life-cycle events . . . such as the ceremonies held at a birth, on a boy's sixteenth birthday, upon marriage, and at death. Though they are rites of passage, they function also as rites of intensification, since they draw together family and *tsu* groups, including relatives and friends from the surrounding area, and often large segments of the village.

Functioning similarly are the times when a villager is seriously ill or when young men are being sent off for military service. While both situations are of immediate concern only to a particular family, the entire village may be requested to participate in a *pai-pai* and offer its prayers and sacrifices for the well-being of each person thus endangered. In case of a serious illness, the patient's family requests the villagers' participation by sounding a gong at dawn on the day on which the *pai-pai* is to be held. It would be rare for any village family (no matter what its relationship with the sponsoring family) to be unwilling to participate.

Still another noncyclic *pai-pai* which clearly functions as a rite of intensification rather than a rite of passage occurs when a god from some distant place comes to the village for an unscheduled visit. The villagers may be notified of the impending visit by a local god speaking through a shaman while he is in a trance. On the day of the announced visit, the entire village holds a joint *pai-pai* to welcome and worship the god. The occasion may become a regular *pai-pai* event as a result of the shaman's earlier announcement and may eventually become a part of the village's regular cyclic calendar of rituals.

PILGRIMAGES

The connection between mountains and religion is a very old and universal one. Mountains are one of the most imposing of natural phenomena, which the premodern mind invariably saw as living, divine powers. In China five mountains have since antiquity been singled out as "sacred peaks" of more than local fame: Sung Kao in the Center, T'ai Shan (Shan means mountain) in the East, Heng Shan in the South, Hua Shan in the West, and Heng (a different word in Chinese) Shan in the North. Besides these there is of course any number of mountains with sacred connections, such as O-mei Shan in Ssuchuan province, and Wu-t'ai Shan in Shansi, famous centers of Buddhist pilgrimage. Of the five sacred mountains of the ancient Native Tradition, T'ai Shan is by far the most important, its cult dating back as far as the Shang dynasty, and continuing to modern times. As one of the vital cults of both popular and official religion, enduring through the entire span of Chinese history, it will obviously be of great interest in the study of Chinese religion. It has been the subject of a lengthy monograph by the noted French Sinologist Edouard Chavannes, and it is from this work, *Le T'ai Chan: Essai de Monographie d'un Culte*

Chinois (Paris, 1910; reprinted in Taipei, 1970), that we translate the following material. It is taken from the first chapter, "The Cult of T'ai Shan" (pp. 3–43). (L.G.T.)

Mountains, in China, are divinities. They are considered to be natural forces that act in a conscious manner and who can, in consequence, be rendered favorable by sacrifices and touched by prayers. But these divinities are of diverse importance: Some are small, local genie whose authority is only exercised in a small territory; others are majestic sovereigns who hold immense regions in dependence. The most celebrated are five in number. . . . Among these five mountains, there is one yet more renowned than the others; this is T'ai Shan or the Peak of the East. . . .

T'ai Shan, which raises its heavy silhouette just to the north of the prefectural capital of T'ai-an-fu, is not a very imposing mountain; its altitude is in fact only 1545 meters above sea level. It is, however, the highest mountain in eastern China, and thus is considered to govern all the surrounding heights and to preside over the East. . . .

Folklore also informs us that the mountains are the habitat of personages who are endowed with marvelous faculties; fairies and gnomes frolic there. In China, under the influence of Taoism, these genies of the mountains have been conceived to be men freed from all the fetters which hinder our existence and cut it short. These are the immortals, the blessed ones among whom one will be able to take nourishment from marvelous utensils of jade, and who give one ambrosia to drink, as it is said in the inscriptions of three Han [dynasty] mirrors.

But the mountain is not only the place where celestial deities and immortals appear; it is itself a divinity. (Beginning with the Chou and coming to Ming times—fourteenth century—T'ai Shan has been given official ranks and titles by various emperors.) The general attributes of a divine mountain are of two sorts: On the one hand, indeed, it presses by its bulk on all the surrounding territory and is the principle of its stability; it is the regulator which prevents the soil from moving and the rivers from overflowing; it prevents earthquakes and floods. On the other hand clouds accumulate around the summit which seems to produce them and which merits the Homeric epithet, "assembler of clouds"; the divine mountain has then under its orders the fecund clouds which shed fertility upon the world and cause it to bring forth harvests.

Numerous prayers of the Ming period show us that T'ai Shan is indeed invoked by virtue of these two attributes. In the spring, it is begged to favor the growth of the grain; in autumn, thanks are offered for the harvest which it has protected. It is asked to help men by its invisible and powerful action which distributes rain and clear weather in the right proportions and which permits the nutritious plants to attain their maturity. In case of drought, it is very natural that it should be addressed, for "to see to it that the rain comes to the worker at the right time is the secret task for which it has the responsibility." Thus, when the rains are awaited, the [budding] ears of grain stud the fields like stars, and the peasants begin to fear famine, the sovereign of men has recourse to the majestic Peak which can and should put an end to this misfortune. In the same way, in case of earthquake or flood, prayers appropriate to the circumstances recall to T'ai Shan its functions as ruler of the whole region and ask it to restore order.

In texts which are of interest for the history of Chinese religion, one will notice the relations which are supposed to exist between the emperor and the god of T'ai Shan. Whenever there is trouble in the world, the emperor begins by accusing himself of lack of virtue. It is, in fact, a leading idea in the religious psychology of the Chinese, that, on the one hand, physical calamities have as their first cause moral faults, and, on the other hand, the sovereign is responsible for the sins of all men, for, if he governed well, all the people would act properly. However, at the same time that he confessed his offenses, the emperor reminded the god of T'ai Shan that he also was not safe from reproach. If sacrifices are offered to him and if he is loaded with honors, it is because his protection is counted upon. By betraying the confidence that has been placed in him, he ceases to merit the regard that has been evinced for him.

No doubt, the god of T'ai Shan is not the cause of the misfortunes which have befallen the people; but, as he has as his duty to collaborate with Heaven for the prosperity of living beings, it is reprehensible when he does not promptly remedy the scourges that have been pointed out to him. "If it is by my faults that I have drawn down calamities," said an emperor to him in 1455, "assuredly I do not decline the personal responsibility; but, for the turning of misfortune to good fortune it is truly you, oh god, who has the duty to apply yourself to it. If a fault has been committed and you do not perform a commendable act, you will be as guilty as I. If, on the contrary, you transform misfortune into good fortune, who will be able to equal your merit?" The same emperor said in 1452, on the occasion of a flood of the Yellow River, "Whose is the responsibility? Assuredly, it is due to my lack of virtue; but you, oh god, how could you alone be exculpated? You should so act that, when the waters flow, this is beneficial, an advantage and not a torment to the people; then you and I will have acquitted ourselves of our respective duties; towards Heaven we will have no fault; towards the people we will have nothing to be ashamed of."

Thus, the emperor and the god of T'ai Shan appear to be like two high dignitaries, almost equal in rank, who have been designated by Heaven to assure the welfare of the people, the one by his sage government which establishes harmony and virtue among men, the other by his regulative influence which maintains good order in the physical world. Moreover, both are accountable for their acts to Heaven, which has invested them with their functions, and to the people, who look to them for their prosperity. By the constant cooperation of a moral power which is the Emperor with the powers of nature such as the god of T'ai Shan, droughts, earthquakes, and floods would be avoided and the people would be happy.

The god of T'ai Shan is also invoked in other cases where his intervention appears less easily explicable at first sight. We find, indeed, in the Ming era prayers, some announcements to this divinity of the imminent departure of the imperial armies for some remote military expedition. The sovereign first takes the precaution of declaring that he knows the gravity of all warlike enterprise. He enumerates the grievances which oblige him to have recourse to arms, despite his repugnance to using coercive means. Having thus justified his decision, he indicates that his troops will abandon their families to brave the perils and the fatigues of a long road; he supplicates the divinity to so act that the soldiers will be free from pestilential emanations which could decimate them, and asks him to permit all the men to return safe and sound to their hearths.

The question arises as to why T'ai Shan should be brought into the case on such occasions; how is it that this local god, who presides in the east, can act at a distance to safeguard the armies which are going to chastise rebels in Kwangsi or Tonkin? The answer is furnished by the clause which ends these prayers: "As I do not dare to address myself inconsiderately to the Emperor on high," we read in one of these pieces, "it is you, oh god, who are willing to take this request into consideration for transmittal to him on my behalf." In another, it is said: "I ardently hope that you, oh god, will transmit and forward to the Emperor on high (my request)." Or again: "I hope eagerly that you, oh god, will take into consideration my sincerity and that you will inform the Emperor on high of that." Thus, in all these cases, the god of T'ai Shan is not asked to perform acts which are beyond his jurisdiction; he simply plays the role of intermediary between the sovereign of men and the supreme divinity, the Emperor on high, who alone is qualified to preside over the general direction of the universe. As this supreme divinity is too distant and too majestic for one to dare to address him directly, one asks a subordinate divinity to intercede with him. T'ai Shan is moreover well chosen to fulfill this task since his height brings him near to heaven.

The religious attributes enumerated thus far are common to the god of T'ai Shan and to the other mountain divinities of China . . . But there are other attributes which pertain only to T'ai Shan; it is these that we shall now study.

T'ai Shan is the Peak of the East. It presides in this capacity over the East, that is to say, over the origin of all life. Like the sun, all existence commences in the East. The *yang* principle, which makes the sap rise in green plants, is concentrated in the Peak of the East from which emanate vivifying influences. In 1532, when an emperor prays to have a son, he addresses himself to T'ai Shan because this mountain is the inexhaustible source of births.

At the same time that T'ai Shan carries in its womb all future existences it is, as a logical consequence, the receptacle to which lives return when they have come to an end. As early as the first two centuries of our era it was a widespread belief in China that, when men die, their souls return to T'ai Shan. In the popular literature one finds a whole series of stories which inform us about a sort of Elysian Fields where the dead continue to speak and act as they did in life. There they intrigue for official position, and the recommendations of influential personages are very useful—it is another subterranean China which spreads out under the sacred mountain.

Since T'ai Shan creates lives and takes in the dead, it has therefore been concluded that it governs the longer or shorter duration of human existence. It joins in itself the attributes of the Three Fates, giving, sustaining, and terminating life. Thus one prays to it for the prolongation of one's days, as for example in the case of a certain Hsu Chun (circa A.D. 100) who, being gravely ill, turns to T'ai Shan to ask for life. A poet of the third century of our era writes with melancholy: "My life is declining; I have a rendezvous with the Eastern Peak."

Tradition localizes precisely the place where the souls of the dead are assembled at the foot of T'ai Shan: It is on a small hill, called Hao-li Shan, which is about two kilometers to the southeast of the town of T'ai-an-fu. In the immediate vicinity of this hill there was celebrated in bygone times the solemn sacrifice *shan,* addressed to the earth, and that is why the kingdom of the dead which is in the earth is located there. A temple has stood here for more than a thousand years. Today, it is more popular than ever. When one visits it, one is immediately struck by the innumerable funeral steles which form long rows as in a cemetery. These steles have been erected by families or by village communities to mark the spot where their dead ancestors have been reunited.

In the temple of Hao-li, which is comprised of several very magnificent buildings, one sees, just as in the principal temples consecrated elsewhere to the god of T'ai Shan, a series of seventy-five chambers arranged all along the walls of an interior court. These are so many tribunals in which the trials of the infernos are represented by means of mud statues. The cult of T'ai Shan seems to us here, then, to be associated with the rewards and above all with the punishments of the other world. This poses a problem in religious history: Until this point, indeed, the god of T'ai Shan has appeared to us to be a divinity of nature. In that he governed the rains and the stability of the soil, that he was the principle of life and death, he was only concerned with the natural phenomena which did not involve any moral element. This is moreover the reason for which his cult is a Taoist cult, for Taoism is principally a nature religion, to the contrary of Buddhism which is above all a moral religion. Throughout the whole extent of the Chinese empire, it is the Taoist priests who officiate in the sanctuaries of divinities symbolizing the forces of nature. If this is so, how is it that in the cult of T'ai Shan there enters the moral idea that souls are punished or rewarded in the other world according to their good or bad deeds?

It is perfectly certain that this idea is not inherent in the cult, and that it was introduced only by the T'ang period, the seventh or eighth century of our era. One can explain this intrusion as an influence of Buddhism on Taoism. In Buddhism the idea of retribution for deeds is early and essential. It is, one can say, the very basis of this religion which neglects nature entirely in favor of ethics. Now Buddhism, an ethical religion imported from India into China, was there implanted by the side of Taoism, a nature religion of purely Chinese origin. Coexisting thus, the two systems have over a long time reacted with each other. Taoism has then borrowed from Buddhism its ethical theory of punishments and rewards and has copied its infernos exactly from those of Buddhism. Having made this addition to its religious foundations, it has then sought for some cults to which to attach it. It has found two: One is that of the *Ch'eng-huang,* the god who presides over the wall of the town and who is the magistrate charged with judging the conduct of the citizens; the other is the cult of T'ai Shan by which this divinity presides over the souls of the dead. That is why one finds in China representations of the tortures of hell in two sorts of Taoist temples, the one being those of the god of the city (*Ch'eng-huang miao*), the others being those of T'ai Shan (*Tung-yüeh miao*). This also explains why, in these two sorts of temples, one often perceives, suspended above one of the doors or against a wall, an enormous abacus. The presence of this calculating machine signifies that the divinity of the place has for his mission to keep the accounts of human actions and to balance up the good and the evil.

We omit here the author's study of the imperial sacrifices called *feng* and *shan*, which were at several times in history—from 110 B.C.E. to C.E. 1008—held on T'ai Shan.

The cult of T'ai Shan, as we have studied it to this point, is the official cult; the documents of which we have availed ourselves in order to set forth its diverse aspects derived for the most part from the imperial administration. It remains to indicate what it has become in popular practice.

The cult of T'ai Shan is one of the most widely spread in China. In every town of any importance, one finds a temple of T'ai Shan which is called either the temple of the Eastern Peak (*tung-yüeh miao*), the temple of He who is equal with Heaven (*t'ien ch'i miao*), or finally, "traveling palace of T'ai Shan" (*T'ai Shan hsing kung*). In these buildings, a multitude of votive tablets eulogize the divinity in four-character [inscriptions]. Some recall his names:

> The Peak, the ancestor, the *T'ai*, the *Tai*.

Others liken his influence or his height to those of Heaven:

> His saintly virtue equals Heaven.
> His height reaches to Heaven.
> The Peak of the mountain matches Heaven.

Others again recall that T'ai Shan is the principle of all existence, that he sustains life by his beneficent action, finally that he is the master of life and death:

> To all beings he gives life.
> His authority governs the mechanism of life.
> His bounty extends to living people.
> His bounty is lavished upon the multitude of the living.
> The depth of his grace is a second creation.
> He shows as on the palm of his hand life and death.

but the largest number of these tablets allude to the judicial functions of T'ai Shan who controls rewards and punishments in the world of the dead:

> He judges without partiality.
> All is reflected in the mirror of *T'ai*.
> Here it is hard to cheat.
> He terrifies those who are far, he affrights those who are near.
> His divine power rewards and punishes.
> He does good to the good, he does evil to the evil.
> He gives good fortune to the good, he sends calamity to the wicked.
> The wicked do not endure.
> When he glances down, it is frightening.
> It is difficult to escape his penetrating gaze.

Certainly it is this role as judge of hell that is now in the popular imagination the essential role of the god of T'ai Shan. The seventy-five courts of justice which, in the Temples of the Eastern Peak, display along the walls of the principal court the frightful torments reserved for wicked men after their death, are well calculated to strike sinners with religious terror. This is why multitudes flock to the temples where the clever monks promise them that with some money and much incense they will get into the good graces of the terrible arbiter of their destinies beyond the tomb.

However, an attentive observer will not be slow to realize that in certain temples of the Eastern Peak the god of T'ai Shan is not alone in drawing homage to himself. I recall that, when I was visiting the *Tung yüeh miao* in Peking, which is outside the most northerly of the two eastern gates, my attention was attracted by some women who were betaking themselves to the temple in a strange manner. Scarcely had they taken three steps than they prostrated themselves at full length on the dusty road in the midst of the hubbub of chairs, wheelbarrows, mules and donkeys which crowded the way. They stood up to take three more steps and then make the same prostration. Now, the destination of their painful route was *not* the principal hall in which the god of T'ai Shan was enthroned; they were headed towards other sanctuaries occupied by female divinities. We have now to investigate the goddesses who are the object of such ardent devotion.

The most important among them is one called *Pi hsia yuan chün*. The term *pi hsia* designated the colored clouds which herald the dawn. As for the term *yuan chün*, it is a title that the Taoists give to female divinities. It is thus that *Hsiu Wen-ying*, goddess of lightning, is called by them *Hsiu yuan chün. Pi hsia yuan chün* is then the princess of the colored clouds: She is the goddess of the dawn and is considered to be the daughter of T'ai Shan, god of the East. This cult is not very old. It seems to have begun with the discovery on the summit of T'ai Shan, in the year A.D. 1008, of a large stone statue. The emperor Chen-tsung immediately had a replica made in jade which was placed near the pool where the first statue had been found; the pool was after that known as "the pool of the jade woman." The idol soon attracted numerous worshipers; the sanctuary consecrated to her was continually enlarged and it has become today the most magnificent of the temples that cover the summit of T'ai Shan. It was above all during the Ming era that the cult of the goddess flourished. It became, in the north of China, the equivalent of the cult of Kuan-yin in the provinces of the south. They were not satisfied to assign her a subordinate place among the temples of the Eastern Peak, but they erected special buildings for her. . . . In our day, one finds in the north of China a great number of temples devoted to the princess of the colored clouds; they are called *niang niang miao*, "Temple of the Lady," or *Pi hsia yuan chün hsing kung*, "Traveling palace of the princess of the colored clouds," or in abbreviated form, *Pi hsia kung*.

. . . Most often she is accompanied by two other goddesses: One holds in her hands an emblematic eye; she is the lady of good eyesight (*yen ching niang niang* or *yen kuang nai nai*) who prevents eye diseases. The other is the lady who gives babies (*sung tzu niang niang* or *sun tzu nai nai*). . . . In the various temples that I have visited, the statues of these two acolytes were covered with votive offerings, eyes made of cardboard and dolls of plaster, which attested to the fact that multitudes of women had received help from the good goddesses, healers of the bad eyes of infancy and guarantors of fertility.

But the three goddesses are not always alone and one finds them sometimes accompanied by six other ladies who are like fairies that protect motherhood. The first favors gestation; the second makes delivery easy for a woman; the third makes the child normal; the fourth prevents the fatal smallpox of infancy; the fifth opens the intelligence of the newlyborn; the sixth governs the mother's lactation. . . .

This group of *Pi hsia yuan chün* and her acolytes, which plays a great role in the religious life of the women of northern China is, in our day, the center of attraction of the cult localized on T'ai Shan. It is towards them that the crowds of worshipers press who, during the first four months of each year, hasten to the sacred mountain on pilgrimage. All religions are explicable by psychology and are but the crystalizations of human feelings. So it often happens that after man has produced a god in his own image, woman in her turn creates a divinity which better satisfies her aspirations. This is what has happened here, and by the side of T'ai Shan who is a god useful to men, the good goddesses have appeared because the women have desired them with all the ardent faith of their maternal hearts.

Pi hsia yuan chün and her cortege are not the only divinities who have been associated with T'ai Shan. If we visit the great temple *Tai miao* in the town of T'ai-an-fu we will note, beyond the edifice in which the god of T'ai Shan is enthroned and that where *Pi hsia yuan chün* is worshiped, a hall dedicated to the spouse of T'ai Shan. Another is dedicated to three brothers of whom the eldest is named *Mao Ying,* still another is dedicated to *Ping-ling,* who is the third son of T'ai Shan, yet another is dedicated to a little-known personage who bears the military title of *t'ai-wei.* And finally there are the seventy-five courts of justice each of which has its own president. All these divinities and some others besides are enumerated as forming the court of the god of T'ai Shan in a Taoist treatise entitled "The true book of the discourse pronounced by the venerable god *Yuan shih* on the subject of the Eastern Peak who delivers from evil and acquits from sins." . . .

T'ai Shan with its pantheon of gods and goddesses succors not only the thousands of pilgrims who each year come to visit the holy mountain. It is not even absolutely necessary, in order to assure the deity's good will, that one should go to one of the temples which has been raised to him in each town of northern China. One can obtain his aid in an efficacious and constant manner by having recourse to amulets which are impregnated with his supernatural energy. The traveler who journeys through northern China often has occasion to remark the stones which, encased in a wall, or set up at the entrance to an alley or opposite the gate of a house, show the inscription *T'ai Shan shih kan tang.* This phrase signifies that "the stone of T'ai Shan is able to cope," which is to say that it can oppose the evil spirits who try to work mischief in the home or to penetrate into the street. The stones which have this magical power are not always from T'ai Shan except metaphorically, for they are made, according to the locality, from the most diverse rocks. They prove, nevertheless, the power that is attributed to T'ai Shan in warding off demons. Another way of having constantly at one's disposal the protective force of T'ai Shan consists in tracing its image according to certain mysterious rules, which makes a sovereign charm against all evil. To tell the truth I have never come across the diagram of T'ai Shan by itself; but one often sees engraved in stone, modeled in bronze, or painted on porcelain the "Tableau of the true form of the five Peaks," which shows the conventional images of the five mountains among whose number T'ai Shan is found. By carrying this marvelous talisman on oneself one can brave the greatest perils without fear.

Aside from the important communal aspects of neighborhood and village temples, communities, as well as individuals, may take part in pilgrimages. Sometimes these will be primarily groups of women, sometimes clans within a village, and sometimes whole villages will periodically travel on a pilgrimage to a sacred site, often a mountain.

The official understanding and the popular one of sacred sites can differ considerably. For example, as described by Chavannes, the Deity of T'ai Shan is male, but mountains in and of themselves in the Chinese worldview are female. At the complementary altar compounds honoring Sky and Earth phenomena in Beijing, the male Sky altars are devoted to celestial phenomena, the female Earth altars to mountains and waters. Pilgrimages to T'ai Shan continue in importance. In 1986, on the communist holiday of May Day, over 50,000 Chinese ascended the mountain, according to the local newspaper. While not all were pilgrims, many were making offerings at the various temples on the way to the summit. At the top, the temple to the Deity of T'ai Shan had long since fell into disrepair and had been cleared away. Unless one had access to old Chinese guidebooks, one would not be aware that a cleared area was once the site of the temple. Next to it, the temple to Pi Hsia Yüan Chun is in good repair and flooded with worshipers. She is a fertility deity to whom one can pray for male progeny, essential for the maintenance of family. For ordinary Chinese, the Deity of T'ai Shan is of far less importance. It was interesting to note the number of young honeymoon couples at the mountain. How many were aware of Pi Hsia Yüan Chun's primary sacred role was not ascertained.

A number of temples to Kuan Yin are also pilgrimage sites, especially on her birthday, and particularly in Chechiang Province. Again, the primary purpose of these popular pilgrimages is to pray for sons. A third deity important for this purpose is Nü-wa. The following description of a contemporary pilgrimage during the Jen-tsu Festival is from the doctoral dissertation of Yang Li-hui at the Center for Chinese Folklore of Beijing Normal University. The excerpt has been translated and edited by the editor (J.P.).

Near the beginning of the lunar year, in celebration of Fu Hsi's birthday, there is a month-long Jen-tsu (Ancestors of Humans) Festival at the T'ai-hao (Fu-hsi) Mausoleum in Huai-yang, Honan Province. The county contains the archeological remnants of China's oldest city, which are contiguous with the mythic past. This ancient city is understood to be the capital of Fu-hsi's mythic kingdom. The Ancestors of Humans refers to the paired deities, the male Fu-hsi and the female Nü-wa. Prior to the destruction of the Cultural Revolution, among the many temples at the T'ai-hao complex, there were several to Fu-hsi and one to Nü-wa. As of 1993, the three temples to Fu-hsi, but not the one to Nü-wa, had been reconstructed.

Before the Han period, the two deities had independent myths. Among her achievements, Nü-wa brought the yellow earth [the color of the north China plain's loess soil] together and created humans; and she also patched the vault of the heavens by melting and melding five-colored stones. As the Supreme Matchmaker, she presides over marriages. Fu-hsi is one of the three Sage Emperors or culture-heroes, inventing, among other cultural developments, the fishing net and creating the Eight Trigrams. Brother and sister, in Han myths, Nü-wa and Fu-hsi married after a deluge to continue the human species. They are portrayed with human upper bodies and serpent lower bodies, their lower parts intertwined. Among Chinese there is still some discomfort with their incestuous relationship.

The Festival draws tens of thousands of pilgrims daily from provinces near and far. Others may come to worship on the first or fifteenth of any lunar month. Most are women, and many stay for the full month of the celebration. They are there to reverence their ultimate ancestors and to pray for children. Many of the pilgrims travel together in Hsiang-hui (Pilgrim Societies) led by a woman; the members are considered sisters and brothers to each other. Women are usually supported by their husbands and their families in making these trips, for they benefit the family as a whole. Images of Nü-wa, as well as those of Kuan-yin, are likely to be on the pilgrim's family altars along with the ancestral tablets.

Among the many customs specific to the festivals are songs to Nü-wa that women learn in dreams, and fertility dances that are passed on matrilineally. These dances elicit ecstasy and lead to possession by the goddess.

A major industry of the area is the manufacture of clay figurines called Ni-ni-kou (mud dogs), which relate to relevant myths. They are of diverse shapes, including, for example, one of a simian figure with a human face and a large vulva painted on its abdomen. The figures recall Nü-wa's creation of humans from earth. Among the many rituals associated with these images is that of soaking them in water and drinking the liquid as a medicine. After a monetary donation, clay figures in the form of children may be displayed before Nü-wa's statue. A red string is tied around their necks, and the images are then hidden in the worshipers' clothes. The worshipers will talk to the images on the journey home but to no one else. On reaching home, they place the images under the mattress. If a child is born within three years, it is attributed to Nü-wa, and thanksgiving offerings are made accordingly.

Although the temple to Nü-wa had yet to be rebuilt as of in 1993, its former site was crowded with people praying for children, and the wall remnants had been blackened by the smoke of burning incense. In a cornerstone to one of the rebuilt temples was a round hole four centimeters in diameter. Called the Tsu-sui Yao (Pit for Descendants), it undoubtedly represented Nü-wa's vagina. The hole was black from the tens of thousands of women who have touched it to gain children.

Hence, although Fu-hsi is the apparent dominant deity of the Jen-tsu Festival, the most important customs all relate to Nü-wa and are oriented toward worship of the pudenda and reproductive power. And this is far from a modern phenomenon, for the Jen-tsu Festival accords in timing with the Sang-Ssu Festival of the distant past. In the *Li-chi* and *Chou-li* [two of the three Scriptures on Ritual], a Gathering in the Second Month of Spring is described, in which offerings are made to the Supreme Matchmaker and otherwise illicit erotic behavior between males and females is tolerated, a ritual certain to increase fertility.

As at T'ai Shan, the patriarchal aspect of Chinese culture over time may have merged Nü–wa with Fu-hsi and made the male deity officially dominant, but the people know to whom offerings are due. Women especially understand who really gave birth to humans and to whom they should pray for children.[21]

---

[21]The material on the Jen-tsu Festival is taken from Jordan Paper, *Through the Earth Darkly: Female Spirituality in Comparative Perspective* (New York: Continuum, 1997).

CHAPTER 5

The State: Emperor and Officials

IMPERIAL WORSHIP

The religious rituals of the Imperial Court might be considered as the paradigm for the State religion as a whole. In each administrative center of the vast empire the official in charge would have to see to it that the prescribed temples and altars were set up and that the prescribed services—sacrifices in honor of State-recognized deities—were held there during the year. The temples and altars were in general small versions of the great establishments at the capital, and the local official was the small counterpart of the Emperor. However, the Emperor did not personally act as officiant in many ceremonies, his dignity of course not permitting that he should humble himself in the worship of the most exalted deities. These were Heaven, Earth, the Imperial Ancestors, and the Gods of Land and Grain.

We give here the vivid descriptions of Joseph Edkins (*Religion in China,* Boston, 2nd edition, 1878, Chapter 2: "Imperial Worship," pp. 18–38). It was written in the mid-nineteenth century, when these services were still being carried on and when the vast, symbolic complex of temples and altars in Peking was in actual use and not merely an architectural museum. We give this material at considerable length, because it includes much that is of general application in the study of Chinese religion, We have edited the text as necessary.

I. The imperial worship of China is ancient, elaborate, and solemn. At the establishment of each new line of emperors fresh regulations in regard to sacrifices are enjoined, but it is usual to follow old precedents to a very large extent. . . .

The chief center of the religious solemnities embraced in the imperial worship is the altar of Heaven. This is in the outer city of Peking, and is distant two miles from the palace. There are two altars, the southern, which is called Yüan-ch'iu, or "round hillock," and the northern, which has upon it a lofty temple, called Chi Nien Tien, "temple for prayers for (a fruitful) year."

Beside special occasions, such as the establishment of a dynasty, the conclusion of a successful military campaign, or the accession of an emperor, there are three regular services in each year. They are at the winter solstice, and the beginning of spring, and at the summer solstice. The first and last of these are performed on the southern altar, the second at the northern.

The spectacle is most imposing. The Emperor proceeds the evening before, drawn by an elephant, and accompanied by grandees, princes, and attendants, to the number of about two thousand. He passes several hours of the night within the park of the altar of Heaven, in a structure called Chai Kung, or Palace of Fasting, which corresponds to the "Lodge for passing the night while upon the road," mentioned in the classical work *Chou Li*. Here the emperor prepares himself by quiet thought for the sacrifice. He spends the time in silence; and, to remind him of the duty of serious meditation, a copper man fifteen inches high, attired as a Taoist priest, is carried in the procession, and placed before him on his right, as he sits in the fasting-hall. The image bears in its hand a tablet inscribed, "Fast for three days." It is intended to assist the Emperor to keep his thoughts fixed.. The idea is, that if there be not pious thoughts in his mind, the spirits of the unseen will not come to the sacrifice. The three fingers of the left hand of the image are placed over the mouth, to teach silence to the monarch of three hundred millions of people while he prepares himself for the ceremony.

The altar of Heaven consists of three marble terraces, circular, and ascended by twenty-seven steps. The uppermost of the three terraces is paved with eighty-one stones, arranged in circles. It is on a round stone in the centre of these circles that the Emperor kneels. Odd (i.e. *Yang*) numbers only are used, and especially multiples of three and nine, in the structure of this altar.

As the visitor stands on this terrace, he sees on the north the chapel for preserving the tablets, beyond it a semicircular wall, and farther still the buildings connected with the north altar and temple. This temple is ninety-nine Chinese feet in height, and has a triple roof, with blue tiles. Both altars are ascended by four flights of steps, towards the four cardinal points. Behind the visitor, a stone's throw from the altar on the south-east, is the furnace for the burnt-sacrifice, in which a bullock is consumed to ashes. On the south-west are three lofty lantern poles, the light from which is very conspicuous in the darkness of the winter night at the solstice, when the kneeling crowd, headed by the Emperor, is engaged on the successive terraces of the altar and the marble pavement below in performing the prostrations appointed in this the most solemn act of Chinese worship.

The two altars, with the park, three miles in circuit, which surrounds them, date from A.D. 1421, when the third emperor of the Ming dynasty left Nanking, and made Peking the capital. . . .

The upper terrace of the great south altar is 220 feet in diameter, and nine feet high; the second 105 feet in diameter, and eight feet high; the third and lowest is fifty-nine feet in diameter, and eight feet one inch in height. The entire height, then, it twenty-five feet two inches, but the base is already raised five feet by a gradual ascent. The low encircling wall is roofed with blue tiles.

In place of the green porcelain furnace on the south-east for the burnt sacrifice, there was anciently an altar on the south called T'ai T'an. The word *t'an*, "altar," shows that in the time of the *Li Chi*, one of the classics [compiled probably during the second century B.C.], which uses this term in describing it, it was an altar, and not a furnace.

The altar on which the Emperor kneels, and where the written prayer is burned, corresponds to the Jewish altar of incense. The furnace, or rather the altar, which it now represents, corresponds to the Jewish altar of burnt-offering. The furnace is nine feet high and seven feet wide, and is placed outside the low inner wall which surrounds the altar. . . . Outside of the furnace is the outer wall, distant 150 feet from the inner. Beside it is the pit for burying the hair and blood of the victims, a ceremony instituted apparently with the idea that it would be possible in this way to convey the sacrifice to the spirits of the earth, just as the smoke and flame of the burnt-offering convey the sacrifice to the spirits of heaven.

It is impossible here to avoid seeing a striking resemblance to the Roman sacrifices which contained the burial ceremony, with a similar idea attached to it, in their worship of the terrestrial divinities. . . .

The animals are slaughtered on the east side of the altar, everything appertaining to the kitchen requiring to be upon the east side. They consist of cows, sheep, hares, deer, and pigs. Horses were formerly used, but not now. The house where these animals are kept is on the north-west of the altar, near the hall in which the musicians and dancers who take part in the sacrificial ceremonies meet to practice for these occasions.

The idea of a sacrifice is that of a banquet; and when a sacrifice is performed to the supreme spirit of Heaven, the honour paid is believed by the Chinese to be increased by inviting other guests. The emperors of China invite their ancestors to sit at the banquet with Shang Ti, the supreme ruler. A father is to be honored as heaven, and a mother as earth. In no way could more perfect reverence be shown than in placing a father's tablet on the altar with that of Shang Ti. Yet, at the same time, another idea is present: The Emperor desires, in fulfillment of the duty of filial piety, to pay the greatest possible honor to his parent. . . . On the upper terrace of the altar the tablet of Shang Ti, inscribed "Huang T'ien, Shang Ti," is placed, facing south, immediately in front of the kneeling Emperor. The tablets of the Emperor's ancestors are arranged in two rows, facing east and west. Offerings are placed before each tablet.

Large and small millet, panicled millet and rice, are boiled as if for domestic use. Beef and pork in slices, with and without condiments, are presented in the form of soup. Salt fish, pickled fish, pickled slices of hare and of deer, pickled onions, bamboo shoots, pickled parsley and celery, pickled port and vermicelli, come next. The condiments used in making the dishes are sesamum oil, soy, salt, pepper, anise, seed, and onions.

The fruits offered are such as chestnuts, sisuphus plums, water chestnuts, and walnuts.

Wheat flour and buckwheat flour are made into balls, with sugar in the middle, and afterwards stamped so as to become flat cakes.

Three cups of *chiu*[1] are placed in front. Next comes a bowl of soup. Then follow eight rows of basins, making twenty-eight in all. They consist of fruit, basins of rice and other cereals boiled, pastry, and various dishes.

Jade stone and silk offerings intended to be burnt are placed behind these twenty-eight dishes. Then there is a whole heifer, with a brazier on each side for burning the offerings.

Behind the heifer are placed the five worshipping implements of Buddhism, namely, an urn, two candelabra, and two flower jars. Behind these are more candelabra, and the table in the south-west corner at which the Emperor reads the prayer.

---

[1]Author's note explains this is "either distilled or not distilled. It is the Mongol and Turkish *arahi* and *arrack*, and the Japanese *sake*. The number three is expressive of honor. The same mode of showing respect is employed in the sacrifices to the Earth spirit and to the Emperor's ancestors."

On the second terrace, on the east side, the tablet of the sun is placed, and also that of the Great Bear, the five planets, the twenty-eight constellations, and one for all the stars. On the west side is placed the tablet of the moon spirit, with those of the clouds, rain, wind, and thunder. . . .

Twelve pieces of blue silk are burned in honor of Shang Ti, and three of white in honor of the emperors. Seventeen pieces of silk, yellow, blue, red, black, and white, are burned in honor of the spirits of the heavenly bodies, and wind and rain.

Several kinds of incense are used. All are composed of fragrant woods ground to sawdust, and then made up into bundles of sticks or pastilles of various shapes.

The Emperor is the high-priest, who acts personally or by deputy in all the public sacrifices performed for the sake of obtaining rain or securing freedom from calamities. His position then is like that of the patriarchs in the religion of Genesis. He combines the offices of chief magistrate and high-priest. The particulars of his duty as priest of the people are such as offering prayer for a good year, presenting the offerings, and worshiping. Besides these, he previously inspects the animals in their sheds when living, and afterwards when slain and made ready for the sacrifice.

On proceeding to the robing-tent, he washes his hands and puts on sacrificial robes. He then, guided by the directors of the ceremonies, mounts the altar and stands near the kneeling cushion, while all the princes and nobles take their places on the steps and terraces of the altar or on the stone pavement below. When told to kneel, he kneels. When told to light incense and place it in the urns, he does so. When led to the tablets of his ancestors and told to kneel before each and kindle incense sticks, he does all this. He is afterwards led back to the chief tablet, and there he performs the ceremony of the three prostrations and nine knockings of the head (kowtow). In this he is immediately imitated by the attendant worshipers in their various positions.

The music, which has been in course of performance by the appointed 234 musicians, stops. The Emperor is led to the table on which are placed the offerings of jade and silk which are to be burned. Here he kneels, having the heifer behind, offers the jade and silk, and rises. The officers whose duty it is to sing here interpose with a song descriptive of the presentation of the bowls of food. Other officers bring up these bowls, together with hot broth, which last they sprinkle three times on the body of the heifer. Meantime the Emperor is standing on the east side of his tent. More music is now performed, the piece being called "The song of universal peace." Upon this follows the performance of the ceremony of presenting the bowls of food before the various tablets by the Emperor. Then the first cup of wine is presented, the Emperor officiating. Appropriate music is performed.

The officer in charge of the prayer places it on the table intended for this use, and it is there read by the Emperor. It is, at the sacrifice in February, couched in such terms as the following:

"I, thy subject, by hereditary succession son of heaven, having received from above the gracious decree to nourish and console the inhabitants of all regions, think with sympathy of all men, earnestly desirous of their prosperity.

"At present looking to the approach of the day *Hsin* and the spring ploughing, which is about to take place, I earnestly look up, hoping for merciful protection. I bring my subjects and servants with offerings of food in abundance, a reverential sacrifice to Shang Ti. Humbly I pray for thy downward glance, and may rain be granted for the production of all sorts of grain and the success of all agricultural labours."

The remainder of the prayer is an encomium upon the deceased emperors worshiped on the same occasion.

After reading this prayer, the Emperor takes it to the table for silk offerings and the jade scepter. Here, kneeling, he places it in a casket with the silk, and then makes some more prostrations.

The second presentation of the cup of wine now takes place, and after it the third, the Emperor officiating. The music here takes the name "The song of excellent peace," and "The song of harmonious peace."

The band of musicians on the pavement below, numerous as it is, is no larger than that of the dancers, who move in a slow step through several figures. When the songs are ended, a single voice is heard on the upper terrace of the altar chanting the words, "Give the cup of blessing and the meat of blessing." In response, the officer in charge of the cushion advances and kneels, spreading the cushion. Other officers present the cup of blessing and the meat of blessing to the Emperor, who partakes of the wine and returns them. The Emperor then again prostrates himself, and knocks his forehead three times against the ground, and then nine times more to represent his thankful reception of the wine and meat. The assemblage of princes and nobles all imitate their lord once more at this point. An officer calls, "Remove the viands." The musicians play a piece suitable to this action, and another called the "Song of glorious peace."

The spirit of Heaven is now escorted home again to the tablet chapel on the north of the altar.

The crier then chants the words, "Carry away the prayer, the incense, the silk, and the viands, and let them be reverently taken to the T'ai T'an. . . . The crier calls, "Look at the burning." The proper music is played, and the Emperor proceeds to the spot set apart as most suitable for observing the burning. The officers upon this take the tablet on which the prayer is written, the worshiping tablet, the incense, the silk, and the viands to the green furnace, within which they are placed and burned. At the same time the silk, incense, and viands offered to the tablets of the emperors are taken to the large braziers prepared for them, and there burned.

The ceremonies here terminate, and the Emperor returns to the palace.

The spirit of the worship may be partly judged of from the hours at which it is performed. At the south altar it must be at midnight, because that is the hour called *Tzu*. Tzu is the first of the twelve hours, and was applied to the eleventh month, or December. The sun is at Tzu when he passes the winter solstice. The day was divided into twelve parts, because there are twelve lunations in a year. It was natural to begin counting the months from the time when the sun was at the lowest point. The time of the solsticial sacrifice of winter should be regulated on the principle that the hour Tzu is on this account most suitable.

When the spring sacrifice takes place near the beginning of the year, the time chosen at present is the first glimmering of the dawn. But formerly midnight was the hour.

The sun is worshiped at the Sun altar at four o'clock in the morning, and the moon on the Moon altar at ten in the evening. . . .

II. The character of the Chinese imperial worship at the Earth altar is substantially the same as at the altar of Heaven, except that instead of the worship of star gods and the sun and moon we have that of the spirits of mountains, rivers, and seas. . . .

There are two terraces to the altar. One is sixty feet square, and six feet two inches high. The other is 106 feet square, and six feet high. Only even (i.e., *Yin*) numbers are made use of in the construction of the altar. Yellow tiles are employed in roofing the walls. The steps on each of the four side are eight in number. A ditch surrounds the altar. It is 494 feet four inches long, eight feet six inches deep, and six feet wide.

Between the altar and the ditch is a wall six feet high, and two feet thick, and within it are four open gateways. Outside of the north gateway, a little to the westward, is the pit for burying the prayer and silk, which are offered to the Spirit of Earth. Beside it is the spot where the silk offered to the spirits of the emperors worshiped at the same time is burned.

On the upper terrace, when the sacrifice takes place, are arranged the tablet of the spirit of Earth facing north, and those of the emperors facing east and west.

On the lower terrace fourteen Chinese and Manchurian mountains are represented by fourteen tablets, and the seas and rivers of China each by four tablets. Half of the mountains, seas, and rivers occupy the east terrace, and half the west. The seas are simply north, south, east, and west. The mountains and rivers are worshiped by their names, and they are selected on account of their size and sacredness.

In the sacrifice to Earth, the burial of the prayer and the silk, it is to be noted, takes place at a spot on the north-west. The tablet, according to the present arrangement, faces to the north, and the spirit, therefore, has the ceremony in sight. The west is, as being on the left hand, the position of honor. The Emperor, after the presentation of the three cups of wine, is directed to proceed to a certain station on the altar where he can conveniently observe the process of burying, which here corresponds to the burning of the prayer and silk in the sacrifice to the spirit of Heaven.

The prayer is as follows: "I, thy subject, son of heaven by hereditary succession, dare to announce to Hou T'u, the imperial spirit of Earth, that the time of the summer solstice has arrived, that all living things enjoy the blessings of sustenance, and depend for it upon thy efficient aid. Thou art placed with imperial Heaven in the sacrifices which are now presented, consisting of jade, silk, the chief animals used for food, with various viands abundantly supplied." . . .

The spirit of Earth is the only spirit beside the spirit of Heaven to whom in prayer the Emperor styles himself a "subject."

The colour of the jade presented is yellow. The prayer is written on a yellow tablet. The twenty-eight dishes, the three cups of wine, and the solitary bowl of soup are the same as at the temple of Heaven. The gold lamps are wanting, as also the gold censers, one pair of the candelabra, and the flower-vases.

The designation Shang Ti is applied to the spirit of Heaven only. . . .

The musical instruments are the same for the spirit of Earth as for the spirit of Heaven, viz., two kinds of stringed instruments, two kinds of flutes, etc.—sixty-four in all; but the bell is gilt for the sake of having it yellow. The two hundred and four musicians and dancers, instead of blue, wear black robes embroidered with figures in gold. Blue, on the other hand, is the color used in the worship of Heaven.[2] . . .

When the emperor sends an officer to perform his duties at the sacrifice, the details are much less complex. . . . The same omissions occur if the Emperor's son is deputed to perform the ceremonies. These omissions clearly show that a priestly character is attributed to the Emperor by virtue of his office.

The presentation of food and wine to the spirits who are worshiped indicates that the Chinese idea of a sacrifice to the supreme spirit of Heaven and of Earth is that of a banquet. There is no trace of any other idea. . . .

III. The imperial worship of ancestors constitutes one of the most important portions of the official worship.

The imperial Temple of Ancestors is on the south-east of the Wu Men, or chief gate of the palace. It is called T'ai Miao, the "great temple," and is divided into three principal *tien* or halls, and several smaller. The front *tien* is used for the common sacrifice to all ancestors at the end of the year. The middle *tien* contains the most important tablets, each in its shrine. Emperors and empresses are placed in pairs. . . . All face to the south. . . . The sacrifices on the first day of the first month in each of the four seasons are offered in this hall. . . .

The times for sacrifice are not only the first of every third month and at the end of the year, but whenever great events occur. The Emperor, when informed that the time has come for inspecting the prayer, proceeds to the Pao Ho Tien or Ch'ung Ho Tien, both of them state halls in the palace. The prayer, written on a yellow tablet, is presented and approved.

The sacrifices are offered in the middle and back halls of the ancestral temple at the same time, in order that all the imperial ancestors, remote as well as near, may enjoy them. . . . The dishes are the same as those used in the sacrifices to the spirits of Heaven and Earth. They are placed before the Emperor and Empress in common. . . . The prayer is read from a table on the south-west, chosen because it is the point of greatest humility, the east being the position of honor. An officer reads the prayer upon his knees, in the name of the Emperor. The prayer states the Emperor's descent as son, grandson, etc., as the case may be. Then follows his proper name, which is not permitted to be written or pronounced by any of his subjects. The prayer proceeds to say: "I dare announce to my ancestor that I have with care, on this first month of spring (or any other of the four seasons), provided sacrificial animals, silk, wine, and various dishes, as an expression of my unforgetting thoughtfulness, and humbly beg the acceptance of the offerings." The prayer contains the titles of all the deceased emperors and empresses prayed to. . . .

Six poems are sung, each to a different melody. Some of the names of these airs are the same as those used at the sacrifices at the altar of Heaven. . . . Here follows a specimen: "Ah! my imperial ancestors have been able to become guests with supreme heaven. Their meritorious acts in war and peace are published in all regions. I, their filial descendant, have received the decree of heaven, and my

---

[2]Author's note: Yellow and brown are both expressed by *huang*. The earth color here meant is the light brown of the soil in North China, but black is the color of the north. The altar of Earth is the "north altar," Pei T'an.

thought is to carry out the aims of those who preceded me, thus ensuring the gift of long prosperity for thousands and tens of thousands of years." This is sung when the Emperor presents the silk. . . .

The Emperor must not call himself "your subject." He must say "your filial descendant, the Emperor."

This ceremony being so burdensome as to entail on the Emperor the necessity of kneeling sixteen times, and knocking the forehead thirty-six times against the ground, is an indication of the importance attached to filial piety, and to the character of the Emperor as an example of virtue to all his subjects. . . .

Another ancestral temple of the emperors is within the palace. It is called the Fêng Hsien Tien, and is in the eastern portion of the palace. Besides this there is the temple at the tomb of each emperor.

IV. A very important branch of the imperial worship is the sacrifices to the gods of land and grain. The altars to these spirits are on the right hand of the palace gate. Their position corresponds to that of the Temple of Ancestors.

The altar of the spirit of land, Shê, consists of two terraces, both ascended by flights of three steps. The upper terrace is covered with earth of five colours. Yellow occupies the middle, blue the east, red the south, white the west, and black the north.

On the south-west of the altar is a spot for burying the victims. The tablet to the god of land, Shê, is on the terrace on the east. That to the god of grain, Chi, is on the west. Both face north. There are two tablets occupying the position of guests, Hsia T'u, called Kou Lung, looks west, and Hou Chi east. The last of these was superintendent of husbandry to the [mythical] Emperor Yao; the first was officer of Huang Ti [also a mythical emperor]. They represent, it may be safely said, the founders or chief promoters of Chinese agriculture.

The worship takes place in the middle months of spring and autumn, and on occasion of important events when announcements are to be made to them.

The sacrifices are the same as in the worship of ancestors and of the temple of Earth, as regards the twenty-eight dishes, but a bullock, pig, and sheep are all offered, and the jade and silk to be burned are placed beyond the three animals. . . .

ELITE FEMALE RITUALS AND RITUAL RULES

Joseph Edkins being a male, he would, of course, not have been present in the inner, female quarters of the palace when rituals were carried out. At the same time, given his culture and time, it would not have occurred to him that complementary rituals were being carried out by the women of the palace while the emperor was carrying out his own. The following study of female rituals in the palace and among the elite is excerpted from the editor's *Through the Earth Darkly: Female Spirituality in Comparative Perspective*.

Three ritual texts were edited into their extant form during the Han dynasty, approximately two thousand years ago and became part of the Five, later Thirteen, Classics, the basis of elite education for the civil service examinations. These texts are the *Li-chi*, which focuses on the rituals of royalty; the *Yi-li*, which provides the rituals of the ordinary aristocrats; and the *Chou-li*, which is a descriptive list, probably idealistic, of all the offices of the preceding historical period. As we shall see in the concluding section, there was strict separation of the sexes in elite culture, including education. Males were to teach males; females to teach females. Hence, these texts were written by males for males, and only tangentially refer to exclusively female rituals, but have a more complete account of those rituals in which males and females took part. We have no extant records of female teachings with regard to ritual practices.

While these texts include elements that were already anachronistic at the time they were finally edited and romanticize an ideal past, they undoubtedly include much of the practices of the day. These ritual practices continued with little change in regard to those aspects that will be discussed in this section, for but minor changes can be found in Chu Hsi's *Family Rituals* of the Sung dynasty, a thousand years later.

Female Rituals: Hairpinning Ceremony

Aside from childbirth rituals, which are not discussed in the ritual texts, as they were not carried out by males, the only gender-specific rituals were those that denoted the transition from childhood to adulthood. Much has been made in Western writings on Chinese religion that only elite males had such a ritual: the Capping Ceremony. Yet the *Li-chi*, in several places, mentions the parallel female Hairpinning Ceremony that seems to have slipped unnoticed by these scholars (including myself until I did this research). Clearly, a particular hairpin, which the text mentions need not be worn with informal dress, was the female equivalent of the adult male formal cap. For both males and females, this ritual of status transition took place at the age of twenty (the Chinese mode of age counting is one to two years more than the Western one, depending on when in the year the person is born). However, in one place the text gives the age of fifteen for females, and the ceremony is to take place whenever a young woman was betrothed if she had not reached the age of twenty. The ritual was conducted by the principal wife of the household, but no details are provided as they are for the equivalent male ritual.

Mixed-Gender Rituals: Sacrifices

Chinese religion focuses on sacrificial rituals, sacrifices primarily directed toward the dead of the family, including mortuary rites. The Chinese focus on balance, particularly gender balance, requires equal participation of males and females in these sacrifices. This was so important that it was the theoretical purpose of marriage, at least from the standpoint of religion. In the *Li-chi*, we find the following passage:

> Confucius said: [In a discussion of funerals.] The head of the clan [the eldest son on the death of the clan head], even if seventy years of age, must not be without a principal wife [to carry out the rituals]."

A prince on asking for a consort from another prince is to make the request as follows:

I request the ruler's elegant daughter to share my poor state, to serve in the ancestral temple and at the Altar to Soil and Grain.

The passage goes on to elucidate the sacrificial duties of husband and wife, constantly alternating their respective preparation for and activity in the sacrificial rites.

According to the *Li-chi*, the essential gender balance of the sacrificial cele-
brants models cosmic patterns:

> The celestial movements provide teachings . . . [At the sacrifices,] the ruler is at
> [the top] of the steps [of the eastern hall]; the principal wife is at the [most west-
> ern] chamber. The Great Brightness (Sun) comes up in the east; the Moon comes
> up in the west. This is the differentiation of Yin and Yang and the principle of
> husband and wife. The ruler [facing west] offers wine in a vessel decorated with
> an elephant (a symbol of male fecundity: thunderstorm), the wife [facing] east of-
> fers wine in a vessel [decorated with clouds and mountains] (female symbol:
> earth). The rituals proceed with mutuality above [the stairs] and the musicians
> respond to each other below [the sacrificial hall]. Thus, harmony is achieved.

Throughout the descriptions of the details of the sacrificial rituals, male and
female activities are balanced and reciprocal. For some rituals, the ruler and his
consort, together with clan members and their wives and the higher officials and
their wives carry out the various procedures in the sacrificial hall or at various
altars. For other rituals, the ruler, etc., is in the clan ancestral temple, which is just
outside the palace, while his consort is carrying out similar rituals in the inner
chamber, modeling the practice and theory that males concern themselves with
outer affairs, that is matters outside of the household, while females concern
themselves with inner, the household, affairs.

The *Yi-li* text, which is written in more mundane prose and concerned with
the details of the practices of the ordinary elite, confirms that the above were not
just theoretical ideals. In describing the different sacrifices, in every case, there
are parallel offerings by the wife of each celebrant with the same ritual. And when
the wife pours wine for the celebrant to drink, the husband then pours wine for
his wife to drink.

This text also clarifies the banquet that follows the ancestral sacrifices, where
the living of the family eat the sacrificial food and drink the wine after the spirits have taken their fill. Western scholars have read the sacrificial odes of the earlier *Shih* (Odes) to the effect that only the men took part in this feasting and
drinking. The *Yi-li* makes clear that while the clansmen and their guests feasted
in the outer hall, their wives were feasting in the inner, female, chambers.

In examining Chu Hsi's *Family Rituals* of a thousand years later,[3] we find little change in the overall understanding of gender roles in sacrificial rituals. Both
in the offering hall and at the grave site, males and females place themselves respectively to the east and the west. Rituals are presided over by the appropriate
male and his wife, who each perform virtually the same rituals. One interesting
change is due to the influence of Buddhism, aspects of which by this time were
amalgamated into Chinese religion. As Buddhists avoided alcoholic beverages,
tea became a popular drink. In the Sung dynasty sacrifices, we find men offering

---

[3]See Chapter 3. (J. P.)

wine and women offering tea. Spirit tablets continue for both female and male ancestors to five generations, and women handle the spirit tablets of females as men do for males.

Ritual Roles

The two most important roles in the sacrificial rituals are the person offering the sacrifice, the Descendant, and the person who is possessed by the ancestral spirit to whom the sacrifice is offered and drinks the wine and eats the food, the Incorporator of the Dead, who was, for all intents and purposes at the time of the sacrifice, the honored dead. Since these ritual texts are written by and for males, the Descendant and the Incorporator of the Dead, when gender is mentioned, are almost always referred to as male. Fortunately, there is one passage in the *Li-chi*, which, in describing how a female is to receive a gift from a ruler, also provides the behavior she is to use when serving as an Incorporator of the Dead, as well as the circumstances in which she would be in this ritual role.

The strict separation of the sexes required that an elite individual of one gender would not be possessed by an ancestor of the opposite gender, nor would a person of one gender be the chief celebrant in the sacrifice to a female ancestor. When an ancestral sacrifice was to be held, the son of the deceased male or the daughter-in-law of the deceased female, with a specialist in divination, divined the appropriate day for the fast. During the preparations leading up to the sacrifice, including extended fasting and meditation, the Descendant, with other members of the family, divined which grandson or granddaughter-in-law should become the Incorporator of the Dead. During the sacrifice, one can but assume that as the wife supported the husband in his role of Descendant, so the husband supported his wife when she took on the role of Descendant.

There are other situations, mentioned in the *Li-chi*, in which a female would preside at sacrificial rituals. If there were no son, an unmarried female would preside at the funeral and subsequent sacrifices of her mother or father. Also it must be noted that the ritual of the ruler ploughing the first furrow in the spring at the altar to the First Agriculturist was paralleled by the ruler's wife carrying out a spinning ritual at the altar to the First Sericulturist. Again, as this is a female ritual, no details are provided.

The *Chou-li*, in listing the duties of the many officials, also mentions female offices. In this regard, it must be understood that the king, and later the emperor, had multiple wives. In Chinese culture, because of the ideology of gender balance, there can be but one wife that is the equal of her husband, who is termed here, the principal wife. Multiple wives were essential to a ruler for two reasons: to ensure a son for the patrilineal succession and to cement various political alliances the arose during a reign. Based on their natal families status, these wives are termed wives of the second rank, of the third rank, and concubines. The later were also members of the family into which they entered and had their tablets on death placed with the female ancestors of the family. (The one female emperor during the T'ang dynasty—eighth century—had a harem of male concubines.)

All of these wives had official and ritual roles, and the following descriptions directly follow the *Chou-li* text. Wives of the second rank were to oversee the concubines with regard to their education, etc. They assisted in the sacrifices, with details provided in the text. When visitors are received, they accompany the

Queen or Empress (the wife of the first rank, the principal wife). During grand funeral ceremonies, they again accompany and assist the Empress.

Wives of the third rank are in charge of the preparation for sacrifices, funerals, and receiving visitors. They are in charge of the palace's female staff, and for the visitations required by the funerals of ministers and other high officials. The royal concubines aid the wives of the third rank in the preparations for sacrifices.

The palace staff included female ritual specialists to assist the above in carrying out their duties. These women seem to have been shamans and/or mediums, as they also functioned as exorcists to rid the inner chambers of any evil emanations and to drive away calamities, and they were to be able to spiritually create a felicitous atmosphere.

Government officials included female mediums. They were in charge of removing negative influences. In times of drought, they called down rain with special ritual dances. When the Queen made a visit of condolence, they walked in front of her with a male ritual specialist. When there was a great calamity, they chanted, cried, and supplicated the spirits. From other texts, we know that mediums were predominantly female and had important government roles, which continued to the end of the first millennium of the common era.

CHAPTER 6

Three Ways of Ultimate Transformation: (1) Taoist Tradition

AN INTRODUCTION TO TAOIST YOGA

The primary goal of "religious Taoism" was the prolongation of life, or even immortality. To accomplish this, the Taoist Adepts used various techniques: most important, respiratory, sexual, dietary, and alchemical. The latter was closely similar to, and very likely the ultimate source of, the alchemy of the European middle ages; but its interest was in production of an elixir of immortality rather than in the riches to be won by transmuting base metal into gold. No doubt in China, as in the West, the experiments of the alchemists were directly responsible for many discoveries in prescientific chemistry and pharmacology. The dietary, sexual and respiratory techniques have continued to the present time to be central practices of serious seekers of long life or immortality. As for the sexual techniques, the reader may consult the translation of a modern text, the *Hsing Ming Fa Chüeh Ming Chih,* or *Secrets of Cultivating Essential Nature and Eternal Life,* provided by Lu K'uan-yü (Charles Luk), in his *Taoist Yoga: Alchemy and Immortality* (London, 1970). It is more than possible that the Tantric practices of attaining salvation through sexual congress, as found in both Hinduism and Indian Buddhism, may derive from the ancient Taoist disciplines of China.[1]

Here we give a comprehensive account of the most basic of the Taoist techniques, yogic breathing. The author of this article, Chung-yuan Chang, is a leading authority on the subjects of Taoism and Ch'an (Zen) and the relationships between the two. "An Introduction to Taoist Yoga" was published in the *Review of Religion,* XX (1956), pp. 131–148.[2]

I. It is a general impression that Yoga as practiced in China is of Indian origin and was brought in with Buddhism, but when we examine the works of Lao Tzu and Chuang Tzu, we find they contain both the basic philosophy of Yoga and

---

[1]For discussion of this matter, see R. H. van Gulik, *Sexual Life in Ancient China* (Leiden, 1961), Appendix I, "Indian and Chinese Sexual Mysticism."

[2]A considerably modified version of this material was later published by the author in his book *Creativity and Taoism* (New York, The Julian Press, 1963, chapter 4).

adumbrations of its techniques. Yoga, as the Indian philosophers interpreted it, was a Way of abstract meditation and transcendental wisdom, "these two means being just like two bullocks tied to the yoke of a cart and leading to a destination."[3] Of course this partnership was a commonplace in Taoist thinking many centuries before the introduction of Buddhism from India. Particularly do we find the Yoga emphasis on breathing exercises well suggested in the writings of Taoist founders. An examination of the writings of Lao Tzu and Chuang Tzu in any detail gives ample credence to this contention. References to the three basic elements of Indian Yoga—abstract meditation, transcendental wisdom, and breathing techniques—are clearly and unmistakably set forth.

If we look, for example, at the thought in Chapter XVI of the *Tao Te Ching*[4] we can see how the theory of Yoga was well developed in China by the time of Lao Tzu.

> Devote yourself to the utmost Void:
> Contemplate earnestly in Quietness.
> All things are together in action,
> But I look into their nonaction.
> For things are continuously moving, restless,
> Yet each is proceeding back to its origin.
> Proceeding back to the origin means quietness.
> To be in quietness is to see "Being-for-itself."
> "Being-for-itself" is the all-changing-changeless.
> To understand the all-changing-changeless is to be enlightened.
> Failure to understand leads to absurdity and disaster.
> The all-changing-changeless is all-embracing.
> To embrace all is to be selfless.
> To be selfless is to be all-pervading.
> To be all-pervading is to be transcendent.
> To be transcendent is to attain *Tao*.
> To have attained *Tao* is to be long-lasting.
> When he loses himself among all these the Man of *Tao* does not cease to exist.

In this chapter Lao Tzu looks into the two aspects of things—subjectively into his own Self and objectively into all other things—and he awakens into a new consciousness. One's mind is always in action, but Lao Tzu keeps his mind in the extreme quietude of nonaction. In nonaction his mind sees its own nature and becomes being for itself. This being for itself, or Self Nature, is part of the universe. It interfuses with other things, with the nature of the "ten thousand things." Because this interfusion is all-pervading and all-embracing, the subject is included in the object and the object in the subject. Therefore Lao Tzu speaks of the selfless. When one is selfless, in the Taoist sense, he is in the realm of Non-Being or Void.

---

[3]S. Radhakrishnan, ed., *History of Philosophy Eastern and Western* (London, 1952), p. 180.

[4]The *Tao Te Ching* is most difficult to translate, and, to do it complete justice, the translator should have experienced spiritually the concepts of the author, as well as understanding them intellectually. The writer of this paper, in the preparation of this translation, has tried to convey the meaning through his own experience.

On the other hand, all objects, all things, are seen first as objects in action, growing and flourishing. But when one looks into their origins, their roots, one sees their non-action. The flow is from movement to quietude. Objects themselves fade into the Non-Being or Void. When subject and object have both entered the realm of Non-Being we have abstract meditation—one of the basic requisites of Yoga. When the individual achieves this point in the practice of Yoga and is conscious of the realm of Non-Being, he has entered the region of transcendental wisdom. "To be transcendent is to attain *Tao*."

We also find references to meditative breathing in the *Tao Te Ching*. In Chapter X we read:

> Can you concentrate on your breathing to reach harmony
>   And become as an innocent babe?
> Can you clean the Dark Mirror within yourself
>   And make it of perfect purity? . . .
> Can you enter and leave the realm of Non-Being
>   And leave nothing to be retained there?

To achieve the Void, Lao Tzu himself recommends breathing exercises. To be sure, none of the details of such exercises are set forth, but that such techniques existed and were familiar to Lao Tzu we can hardly doubt. In the works of Chuang Tzu these ideas are developed in greater detail. Chuang Tzu, for example, describes the "fasting mind" in his Chapter IV. Here also he speaks of concentration, breathing, and the concept of enlightenment in some detail:

> Concentrate on your meditation. Do not listen with your ear but listen with your mind—not with your mind, but with your breath. Let hearing stop with the ear, the mind stop with its pictures. To concentrate on breathing is to prepare the emptiness for receiving things—the *Tao*. It is because *Tao* abides only in emptiness. This emptiness is the fasting mind. . . .
>   Look at emptiness! In the chamber of emptiness there is produced light. The feeling of gaiety lives in repose. It not only permeates this repose but extends outward even while one is sitting still. Let the eye and the ear turn their communication within but eliminate all consciousness from without. The spirits and gods will dwell in this emptiness, as will the inner man (the Real Self). This is the way of transforming all things. . . .[5]

These notions of concentration and light are further explained in Chapter XXIII: "When one has reached extreme repose one gives forth a heavenly light. One who has developed this heavenly light sees his inner man (Real Self). Only through such cultivation can man reach eternity."

In these two quotations we can make out clearly the three important points of Yoga, i.e., breathing to enforce the process of abstract meditation toward the attainment of "extreme repose," or emptiness; from emptiness, or repose, one comes to enlightenment, sees the Real Self, and is associated and interfused with the universal forces of the gods and the spirits. This is the process of self-transformation leading to a highly integrated personality.

---

[5]This and subsequent translations from Chuang Tzu are by the author of this paper.

Although Chuang Tzu emphasized the method of breathing (the perfect man breathes "from the heels"), he was opposed to those who used breathing techniques to achieve longevity, without any understanding of the philosophy underlying the techniques. In an interesting passage he criticizes these men:

> Men who blow and breathe noisily, and inhale and exhale silently, in order to release the old air and obtain new air, who hibernate like bears and stretch their necks like birds—these men are simply striving for longevity. Such scholars indulge in breathing exercises in order to develop their physiques, wishing to live as long as Peng Tzu. They are given over to such practices (Chapter XV).

But breathing exercises were more than this, more than mere hygienic aids. Ideally, they were an aid to attaining spiritual self-recognition, to becoming one with the universe and its natural forces. It was essential to understand the philosophy behind the technique. In the Confucian canon, too, as, for example, in the works of Hsun Tzu (*ca.* 198–*ca.* 238 B.C.), we frequently find a critical attitude toward those scholars who practice breathing exercises merely as an aid to longevity or physical well-being. Mencius (371?–289? B.C.) recognized a relationship between breathing and the personality, although he does not go into any detail, preferring to keep his discourse on a purely philosophical level.

We can look outside purely philosophical and speculative writing for confirmation of the early existence of some concepts of meditative breathing in China. We find, for example, a famous poem by Ch'ü Yüan (d. *ca.* 288 B.C.), entitled "Wandering in the Distance," which suggests a close connection between the concept of *Tao* and breathing exercises as an aid to its attainment. The poem, freely translated, reads:

> Eat six kinds of air and drink pure dew in order to preserve the purity of the soul. Breathe in the essence of the air and breathe the foul air out. The *Tao* can be received but it cannot be taught. The *Tao* is small and without content, and yet it is large without limit. Do not confuse your soul—it will be spontaneous. Concentrate on the breath and *Tao* will remain with you in the middle of the night.[6]

Moreover, when Buddhism was introduced into China, during the third and fourth centuries A.D., most Buddhist philosophers used Chuang Tzu to interpret Buddhism. We have, for example, the Buddhist monk Hui-yüan (334–416). When he attempted to explain the Buddhist theory of reality, he was obliged to resort to the teachings of Chuang Tzu to make his teachings intelligible. The practice of turning to Lao Tzu or Chuang Tzu to interpret Buddha became so widespread that the term *ko yi*, or "method of analogy," became the accepted description of this species of inter-religious influence.

Tao-an (312–385), in his introduction to the *Sutra on Breathing,* used typical "method of analogy" techniques in explaining Indian meditative breathing to the Chinese. Note the great use of Taoist terminology in the following passage:

> The breathing technique known as Anāpāna refers to the inhaling and exhaling the breath. *Tao* and *Tê* rest in all places, there is no place that they are not to be found. Anāpāna is the use of breathing to achieve inward integration. There are four med-

---

[6]From the *Ch'u Tz'u* ("Collection of the Poetry of Ch'ü yuan, Sung Yu, and Others"), Author's translation.

itation techniques which make use of the functions of the body. Through breathing exercises we pass through the six stages toward integration. Bodily exercises lead through four stages toward concentration. These steps consist of taking away and taking away until we have reached the point of complete non-activity. The stages consist of forgetting and forgetting until we have done away with all desire. By non-activity we come into accord with things. By non-desire comes harmony in our affairs. By being in accord with things we can see into their nature. Through harmony in our affairs we can accomplish our missions. Accomplishing our mission, we make all *that is* consider itself as the *other*. Seeing into the nature of things, we cause the whole world to forget the self. Thus we eliminate the other and we eliminate the self. This is to achieve integration into the One.[7]

This quotation of Tao-an ostensibly describes Buddhist Yoga, but it describes very closely the Taoist concept of the achievement of non-being. It is not merely a matter of borrowed terminology. The goal of Oneness is a mutual goal of the Buddhist yogi and the Taoist meditative breathing practitioner. Methods of achieving the goal, as the Buddhist put it, by "taking away and taking away" and by "forgetting and forgetting" are the classic Taoist roads toward Enlightenment. They are the well-known methods of *wu wei* (non-activity) and *wu yü* (non-desire). It is not merely a coincidence or a matter of convenience that the Buddhists turned to the Taoist classics when they sought to interpret their teachings to the Chinese. These teachings, in no greatly different form, were already familiar to the Taoist.

II. From what we have said above it would seem that Buddhist Yoga and Taoist Yoga were very similar. Indeed, this is true, in the sense that the goals of both are one and the same. But the similarity does not go all the way. The systems of the two Yogas are quite different in many respects. The Taoist system of meditative breathing was a product of its native ground. We have not merely the works of Lao Tzu and Chuang Tzu, but many other roots. There is, for example, the well known *I Ching* ("Book of Changes") and the widely prevalent theories of the Five Elements and the Yin-Yang Schools, as well as the works of the Chinese alchemists, numerologists, and diviners. Above all, there were the Chinese cosmological theories and the macrocosmic-microcosmic view of man as the universe contained in the individual.

The fundamental, or in any event the earliest, text of the Taoist Yoga, or meditative breathing school, is the third century *Chou Yi T'san-t'ung-ch'i* ("Synthesis and Agreement with the Chou Changes"), the work of Wei Pe-yang. It is a difficult and complicated work, dealing in the arcane and the alchemical, but it is worthy of study for those who wish to understand the foundations of Chinese Yoga. It deals with all of the theories mentioned above as contributing to the meditative breathing school—from abstruse cosmological speculation to alchemical practices and number and word magic.

First, let us look at the macrocosmic-microcosmic theory which serves as the basis of Chinese Yoga. The classic work on this subject is known as the *Huai-nan-tzu*,[8] dating from the second century B.C. This work discusses the position of man in the universe. We read:

What is spiritual is received from the Heaven while the body and its material form are derived from the earth. We say: "From the One came the Two. The Two

---

[7]*Tripitaka*, Lv, 43. Author's translation.

[8]Ch. VII. Author's translation.

evolved into the Three and the Three into all things. All things hold up *yin* and clasp *yang*." It is the harmony of the spirits of *yin* and *yang* on which all harmony depends. It is said, "At one month the embryo is formed; at two months it has skin; in the third and fourth month tissue and shape evolve; in the fifth muscle; in the sixth bone; in the seventh physical completion; in the eighth movement; in the ninth activity; and in the tenth birth." The body being completed, the internal organs have their form. . . . The senses are the outward, and the internal organs the inward regulators . . . each has its fixed rules. The roundness of the head is like the Heavens; the firmness of the foot is like the earth. . . .

Heaven has four seasons, five elements, nine divisions, three hundred and sixty days. Similarly, man has four limbs, five internal organs, nine orifices, and three hundred and sixty joints. Heaven has wind, rain, cold, heat; man, similarly, has joy, anger, taking, giving. . . . Man forms a trinity with Heaven and Earth, and his mind is the master. . . . In the sun there is a bird standing on three legs, and in the moon a toad with three legs. . . .

Thus, man is a microcosmic universe. This idea occurs frequently, indeed constantly, in Taoism, and the meditative breathing school proved no exception in using this concept for its own purposes. Through meditative breathing, man achieved the natural integration with the universe that was destined for him and foreshadowed in so many ways, according to early Taoist theory.

In early Chou times a system of eight trigrams (solid and broken lines) and sixty-four hexagrams, supposedly simulating the cracks in tortoise shell, were developed for use in prophetic rituals. Gradually these trigrams and hexagrams took on complicated symbolic meanings. The nature of these meanings is propounded in the famous *I Ching*. Arbitrary numerical categories were established and assigned fixed symbols. These symbols were picked up and used by the founders of Chinese Yoga. Let us look at a few examples of this categorizing impulse as it is displayed in the *I Ching* and note the parallels in typical Yoga theory.

The four primary trigrams, as set forth in the *I Ching*, are *chen, li, tui,* and *k'an*. These are correlated with the four seasons and the four directions, as well as with arbitrarily derived numbers. The yogi took these categories, for example, and assigned them to the internal organs, such as heart, kidney, liver, and lung. Thereon was built an elaborate relationship with the *I Ching* categories of south, north, east, and west, the four seasons, and other corresponding categories.

FOUR BASIC TRIGRAMS AND THEIR MEANING IN I-CHING

Trigram	Direction	Season	Number
chen	east	spring	8
li	south	summer	7
tui	west	autumn	9
k'an	north	winter	6

APPLICATION TO THE SYSTEM OF YOGA

Five Elements	Inner Organs	Animal	Five Greatnesses	Constant Virtue
wood	liver	blue dragon	great beginning	love
fire	heart	red bird	great change	propriety
	(mercury)			
metal	lung	white tiger	great simplicity	righteousness
water	kidney	black turtle	great origin	wisdom
	(lead)			
earth	spleen		great ultimate	faith

In *Synthesis and Agreement* the four directions also are used to denote four of the elements and four appropriate animals. East is associated with wood, west with metal, north with water, and south with fire. East is the blue dragon or the liver; west, the white tiger or the lung; south, the red bird or the heart; and north is the black turtle or the kidney. From the *I Ching* we learn that the *chen* trigram suggests the idea of movement. From *chen* the circulation through other trigrams, *li, tui,* and *k'an* sets forth. Thus, in its Appendix V, we read:

> All things issue forth in *chen*, which is East. . . . *Li* suggests the brightness where all things come to see each other. This trigram represents the South. . . . *Tui* is the West and Autumn, the season in which all things are moving by their joy. We say, "*Tui* refers to the spirit of joy." . . . *K'an* refers to water. It is the trigram of the north, where all things return to rest and comfort. We say, "Rest and comfort indicate *K'an*".[9]

Man's breath, according to the Taoist yogi, circulates among the inner organs, even as movement and quietude complete its circulation among the four trigrams, and as the ether of the world circulates among the four seasons and the four directions. The breath is the unifying principle which makes a Oneness of the microcosm of the body. Generally, however, the yogi prefers the category five to that of four. The fifth category represents a unifying principle in the center of the other four. The Taoists correlate the fifth category with the spleen, or earth. This is the storage place of all the energies and source of supply of vital force to all the other organs.

In an apocryphal addition to the *I Ching* known as the *Yi-wei Ch'ien-tso-tu* ("Apocryphal Treatise on the 'Change'") commented on by Cheng Hsüan as early as the second century, we find a metaphysical category of four which was later picked up by the Taoist yogi. The relevant passage in the *Yi-wei Ch'ien-tso-tu*[10] reads as follows:

> In olden times the Sages worked upon the principles of *yin* and *yang* to determine the principles of growth and decline and began *ch'ien* and *k'un* to encompass the fundamentals of Heaven and Earth. But that which has form is produced of the

---

[9] Author's translation.

[10] I, 7–9. Author's translation.

formless. Whence came *ch'ien* and *k'un*? In answer we may say that first there was the Great Principle of Change, then the Great Beginning, then the Great Origin, and then the Great Simplicity.

The yogi has, typically, added a fifth (spleen-earth) category. This is the Great Ultimate, the unifying whole.

The Confucian element in Chinese Yoga appears in the adoption of the five constant virtues of love, righteousness, propriety, wisdom, and good faith. East is love, west is righteousness, south is propriety, north is wisdom, and the central category is good faith.

The various threads of earlier Chinese theory (the Yin-Yang School, conventional Taoism, the Five Elements School, the *I Ching*, numerological theories, etc.) were first brought together as components of the new Chinese school of meditative breathing in the *Synthesis and Agreement*, the work which we have mentioned above as the basic classic of the school. As to the value of the word-magic involved, we will not attempt to make any comment here, but limit ourselves to descriptive commentary rather than symbolic interpretation. That the symbolism is a rich and complex one, will be obvious, I believe, even from the very simple suggestion of some of its aspects which I have outlined here.

Why, then, since we have spent some time indicating the four (or five) elements which go into the Taoist-Yogi concept of the microcosm of the inner man or Real Self—why, the initiate to Chinese Yoga may ask, do we commonly find merely two internal elements suggested as polar aspects of the internal unity? Symbolic word-play of this sort is, of course, subject to endless variation. This instance is a relatively logical one. The five internal elements combine, by the force of the central, unifying principal, into one. The four outer elements form two pairs which become the polar focuses. East and south combine, and west and north combine. The dragon, that is, goes toward the fire, and the tiger goes to the water. Here we have the two centers: fire, represented by the Trigram *li*, and water, represented by Trigram *k'an*. The former is the symbol of the heart, the latter of the kidney. According to the Taoist Yogi, the unification of *li* and *k'an* or the heart and the kidney is called the "small circulation" of breathing technique. Centered here is one of the important functions of Taoist Yoga. The theory of the "small circulation" breathing, arbitrarily correlated with the various categories of season, element, direction, ethical principles, animals, with their appropriate trigrams, patently displays the influences we have named above of indigenous Chinese speculation—Confucian ethics, Taoist cosmological views, and the lesser magical theories of the alchemical and divinatory practitioners.

For the Taoist yogi, in addition to the "small circulation," there is the idea of the "grand circulation." This grand circulation commences at the tip of the spine and moves upward along the spine to the head, forward and downward through the face and ventral surface back to the tip of the spine. One portion of this movement is, of course, rising, the other falling. The rising movement is known as the *yang* movement, the falling movement is known as the *yin* movement. *Yin* and *yang*, of course, are the basic polar dichotomies of Chinese thinking, representing the pairing of positive and negative, masculine and feminine, ascending and descending, etc. This rising and falling movement is symbolically paralleled with the waxing and waning of the seasons of the year. The influential Yin and Yang

School of Chinese thinking and the *I Ching* combine to bring a characteristic contribution to *Taoist Yoga*.

In the *I Ching* we find an arrangement of twelve hexagrams to represent the circular movement of *yin* and *yang* and, at the same time, to indicate the movement of the seasons. *Yin* is represented in the diagram below by a broken line (— —) and *yang* (——) by a solid line.

Hexagram	䷗	䷒	䷊	䷡	䷪	䷀
Name	fu	lin	t'ai	ta-chuang	kuai	ch'ien
Month	11th	12th	1st	2nd	3rd	4th
Hexagram	䷫	䷠	䷋	䷋	䷓	䷁
Name	kou	tun	fou	kuan	po	k'un
Month	5th	6th	7th	8th	9th	10th

In the upper row we see that the influence of *yang*, the unbroken line at the bottom of each hexagram, beginning at *fu*, steadily increases in succeeding symbols until, in the last hexagram (*ch'ien*), it is complete and all the lines are *yang*. At the same time there is a decrease in the influence of *yin*, represented by the broken line.

The second row illustrates exactly the reverse situation. Here we have a decreasing *yang* and an increasing *yin*, until, in the last hexagram, there is only *yin*, represented by the broken line. Scholars of the Yin-Yang School identified the twelve hexagrams with the twelve months of the year, beginning, as shown in the diagram, with *fu* as the eleventh month, when *yang* begins its influence, and ending with *k'un*, the tenth month, when *yang* begins its influence, and ending with *k'un*, the tenth month, when *yin* reaches its point of complete dominance. Here we have a graphic representative of the fluctuating influence of *yin* and *yang* during the course of a year.

This whole symbolic *Gestalt* was taken over by the Taoist yogi, who adapted the increasing and decreasing influence of *yin* and *yang* to their concept of the circulation of the breath around the body. Since *yang* symbolizes a rising movement, the yogi takes the hexagram *fu* as the starting point of the grand circulation at the tip of the spine. The following hexagrams are assigned positions along the spine upward through the various stages to *ch'ien* at the top of the head. Thus does the *yang* influence rise to its peak at the apex of the grand circulation. When the breath descends through the face, chest, and ventral surface back to the tip of the spine the influence of *yin* waxes. Corresponding hexagrams are placed along the downward course, indicating that the *yin* element is increasing. At the last stage, *k'un*, the *yin* element reaches its utmost influence and the circulation returns to its starting point.

For the Chinese yogi this circulation of the "breath" throughout the body is divided into two "courses." The rising circulation, from the tip of the spine to the top of the head ((or, more precisely, to the upper lip) is known as the *To Mu*, or Controlled Course. The descending circulation, from the head (from the lower lip) to the tip of the spine, is known as the *Jen Mu*, or Involuntary Course. These concepts are purely imaginative, of course, but the yogi visualizes it as the supposed path of the circulation of breath. This circulation of the "breath" may be better described as a circulation of a heat current, which is felt by the practitioner. The upward movement is also known as the movement of *yang* and the downward movement as the movement of *yin*. When the practitioner is able to complete this circulation, it means that a complete cycle of *yin* and *yang* has been achieved. This completed cycle is considered the attainment of *Tao*.

We can see from this brief description of the "grand circulation" breathing exercises that they were deeply influenced by the Yin-Yang School and by the ideas in the *I Ching*. In short, we see that the theory of the small circulation and the grand circulation breathing (the basis of Taoist Yoga) can, in large measure, be traced back to the influence of the Taoist and Confucian classics and other native Chinese sources—the work of the numerologists, alchemists, and others.

III. The objective that the Yogi holds before himself in his exercises is the complete elimination of thought. Rather, he tries to "get behind" his thoughts, i.e., transcend himself by looking into the storage house of the unconscious, where he sees his Real Self. If one understands the philosophy of Taoism and is "enlightened" to the Real Self there is no need of the system of Yoga. But most people cannot attain enlightenment through sudden revelation, and they need a technique to help them eliminate the floating thoughts which obscure their true vision. The one important technique is that of concentration. According to Taoist Yoga one picks a spot, such as the *Ming Tang*, or the Hall of Light, the spot between the eyes, and bends his concentration upon it to attain the vision of the heavenly light. Concentration upon a particular spot rules out other thoughts, and the mind is opened and the light shines within. However, the concentration-spot need not be the *Ming-Tang*. It may be various other parts of the body (the tip of the nose, the navel, the tip of the spine) or other outside objects. Usually the spot is that between the eyes, or, more commonly, just below the navel. The spot below the navel is known as the *Ch'i Hai*, or Sea of Breath. *Ch'i Hai* is the most important center and is known as the Regular Red Field. It is the lowest of the three Red Fields supposed to lie within the body. The other two, the Middle Red Field and the Higher Red Field, are in the region of the heart and the center of the brain. The Higher Red Field is located in the middle of the nine sections, or "courts" of the brain, and is known as the Mud Pill Court. Between the Middle Red Field andthe Lower Red Field is the *Huang Ting*, or Yellow Court, in the region of the navel. This is the source of life (the umbilicus). "Mercury" from the heart above and "lead" from the *Ch'i Hai* below combine here to create the elixir of life. *Huang Ting* is the storage house of this elixir.

There are numerous dorsal centers in addition to the internal centers mentioned above. Three are the most important. They are *Wei-lu*, the tip of the spine, the beginning of the Controlled Course which sends the heat current upward and the end of the Involuntary Course by which the heat current descends to its beginning. The point behind the kidney on either side of the spine are the centers called the *Chia Chi* ("beside the spine"). In the neck is a third center known as the House of Wind (*Feng fu*). This is the last gate through which the upward heat current passes moving to the Higher Red Field. The accompanying diagrams[11] indicate the centers, seen from the front and the back.

---

[11]The two pictorial diagrams reproduced here are from the *Hsing Ming Ch'ih Kuei* ("meaning of Nature and Destiny") mentioned later in the text. These pictures from the original work were published in a later edition (1669), in the Princeton University Library.

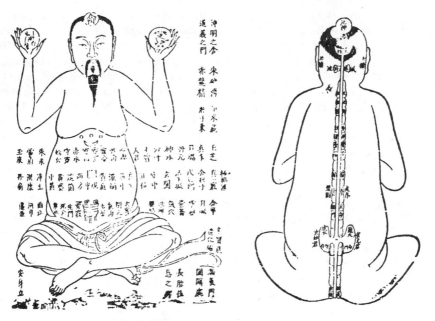

DIAGRAM I (Left): FRONT VIEW. The practitioner of Yoga sitting in a characteristic position. On the abdomen are indicated the positions of the Middle Red Field (new moon and three stars), the Yellow Court (square), and the Lower Red Field (cauldron). The Upper Red Field is located in the head. In the right hand is a Moon, symbolized, as is common in Chinese mythology, by a rabbit. In the left hand is the Sun, symbolized by the three-legged bird mentioned in the *Huai-nan-tzu*. The sun and moon are brought symbolically into a unity within the Yogin. The three rows of Chinese characters beneath the Middle Red Field, the Yellow Court, and the Lower Red Field are a variety of synonomous names for these centers. The Middle Red Field, for example, is also known as Spiritual Gate, Sea of Nature, Stream of the Heart, Heavenly Prince, Jade Mushroom, Red Mercury, etc., some twenty-four synonyms in all for the Middle Red Field alone. The Yellow Court is also known as the Old Grandmother, the Mysterious Gate, the Empty Middle, etc. The Lower Red Field, symbolized by a crucible, or cauldron, for melting and transmuting lead, is also known as the Sea of Breath, Earth Cauldron, Gate of Life, Flower Pool, Genuine Lead, etc. Around the figure are quotations from Taoist texts, recondite and mystical in character. Typically they read: "The House of the Spirit is the Door of Righteousness."

DIAGRAM II (Right): REAR VIEW. This diagram illustrates the important "centers" of the ascending, or Controlled Course, of the grand circulation. These centers are located along the spine. The lowest, at the tip of the spine is *Wei Lu*, the "Gate of the Tail." Another important center, located half-way up the spine and in the region of the kidneys, is *Chia Chi* ("beside the spine"). It is the center for transmitting the upward and downward breath currents. A third center is located in the head, and is known as *Yuan Shen* ("Primordial Spirit"). It is the seat of Nirvana (the Upper Red Field in the front view). Alternative names are: Heavenly Valley, The Jade Mountain, and many others. Also indicated on the diagram are the subsidiary centers in the genital region (between *Wei Lu* and *Chia Chi*, and known variously as The Dark First Prince, the Mysterious Prince, etc.) and in the neck (The Jade Pillow Gate, Heavenly Pillar, etc.).Details of these centers and their significance vary from authority to authority.

A brief comparison of Taoist Yoga "centers" with those characteristically used in Tantric Yoga may be of interest to those more familiar with the Indian system. Edward Conze[12] points out that there are four main internal centers in Indian Tantric Yoga practice: in the region of the navel, in the heart, in the neck, and in the head. The corresponding centers in Chinese Yoga are easily discernible in the accompanying diagrams. Sir John Woodroffe, in his *The Serpent Power*,[13] identifies six centers: "Inside the Meru, or spinal column, are the six main centres of Tattvik operations . . . Muladhara, Svadhishthana, Manipura, Anahata, Vishuddha, and Ajna." The first is the tip of the spine, the second is the genital region, the third the navel, the fourth the heart, the fifth in the throat, and the sixth between the eyes. All, indeed, have obvious Taoist Yoga counterparts easily between the eyes. All, indeed, have obvious Taoist Yoga counterparts easily definable in the accompanying diagrams. The question arises, which influenced which? Conze points out that Tantric Yoga was not organized until the fifth or sixth century.[14] It is most interesting that the *Synthesis and Agreement*, published in the third century and the basis of Chinese Yoga, nowhere mentions Indian practices. Even the *Wu Chen P'ien* ("Enlightenment of Truth"), published about 1095, has references to what we know as Indian Yoga, but only in the slightest and most allusive fashion. Later works indicate a familiarity on the part of the authors with Indian practices. The excellent but little known *Hsing Ming Ch'ih Kuei* ("Meaning of Nature and Destiny"), by an unknown author,[15] published in the sixteenth century, shows a complete knowledge of Indian Yoga and has a picture of Lao Tzu, Confucius, and Buddha sitting together in meditation—with Buddha in the central position. Much evidence suggests that Chinese Yoga developed along a highly independent course in the early centuries of its existence, as well as having independent roots in Chinese culture. Possibly Tibetan texts unavailable to the author or further light from Indian sources can better clarify this point.

A rather more detailed word on breathing techniques is probably necessary for a rounded understanding of Chinese Yoga. Taoist meditative theory emphasizes light, rhythmic breathing—so light that "a feather will not stir before the breath." This is known as *t'ai hsi* breathing, or "breathing of the embryo." When one inhales, the air is sent to the bottom of the lungs, even lower, as if to breathe with the abdomen. The Lower Red Field beneath the navel, the "Sea of Breath," is supplied with this air. When one exhales, the diaphragm rises and the abdomen pulls in. This is the contrary of ordinary "chest" breathing. In practice, breaths are counted for training purposes, but as the technique is perfected this is dropped. One feels that one is not breathing at all.

By this concept breath can circulate anywhere throughout the body—typically in the great circulation through the spine to the top of the head and down the front. Actually air, of course, cannot go through bone and flesh. It is,

---

[12]*Buddhism: Its Essence and Development* (New York, 1951), p. 198.

[13]Published under the pseudonym Arthur Avalon (London, 1919).

[14]Conze, *op. cit.*, p. 176.

[15]The pictures reproduced by Richard Wilhelm, in *The Secret of the Golden Flower* (London, 1947), pp. 29, 41, 51, 63, were taken from this work. The "Inner Process" chart, published by Erwin Rousselle, "Seelische Fuhrung im Lebenden Taoism," *Eranos Jahrbuch 1933* (Zürich, 1934), Tafel 1, p. 150, is taken from a Taoist temple picture, and deviates in a number of important points from the classical texts.

rather, a heat current, moving upward and downward. Even the idea of the "heat current" is not a very convincing one to the Western reader, but the writer was told on good scientific authority that concentration upon the blood vessels can make a measurable difference in the temperature of the spot. The Chinese yogin can send a heat current in a circular pattern around the navel which stimulates the practitioner in a short period into a trancelike state.

The writer has tried to present information on the Taoist system of Yoga. It is to be hoped that the phenomenon will be scientifically investigated some day on a truly objective basis which will enable the indifferent or the unsympathetic to form unbiased judgments of the theory and its practice.

IV. A concrete example of the practice of Chinese Yoga may serve as a fitting conclusion.

There is an interesting and authentic story[16] of a student who actually achieved Enlightenment through an interesting discipline under his master. In the Ming Dynasty (about the sixteenth century) there was a student who sought Enlightenment. One day he passed by a cave on a mountain top and saw a Taoist Master practicing meditation. He went up to him and made a bow, but the Master ignored his politeness. The student realized immediately that the Master must have achieved the highest stage. Immediately he sat down opposite him and practiced meditation. After a time the Master got up to make some tea. When the tea was ready the Master took a cup for himself and then put the cup back and resumed his meditation. The visitor came up, took a cup of tea and returned the cup the same as the Master had. Neither of them uttered a single word. In the evening the Master got up and prepared his dinner. When it was ready he took a bowl and ate. The visitor came forward and took a bowl and ate with him. After dinner they both sat back again. In the middle of the night the Master got up and took a stroll around the mountain pass. His guest did the same thing, both of them returning to their original places. The next day was very much the same. They meditated together, shared their simple meals in silence. After seven days the Master spoke, saying: "Sir, where do you come from?" The man replied, "The South." The next question was, "What makes you come here?" The man said, "To see you." "My face is just like this," the Master said. "There is nothing particular there." "I have already recognized that well," the man replied. The Master explained that during his stay of thirty years in his cave he had never met such a congenial companion. The man stayed with him and learned from him. One night as the disciple walked along the mountain path he felt a sudden lightning circulating within him. There was a roar of thunder in the top of his head. The mountain, the mountain stream, the world, and his very self all vanished. This experience lasted "for about the time it would take for five inches of incense to burn." After that he felt that he was an entirely different man and that he was purified by his own light. The student was told that even this light must be put aside. His Master, indeed, had experienced it frequently over the course of thirty years and had learned to pay no attention to it.

This story exemplifies the path through meditative breathing toward the final achievement, the Enlightenment. The quiescence of the student and the master symbolizes the need for meditation and clearing the mind of all thought. Those

---

[16]Quoted from *Cheng Chung-yin* in his "Random Notes" section of the periodical, *Chia Hsün* ("Message of Enlightenment"), Shanghai, VIII (August 1954), 10.

who look inward may suddenly even forget that they are looking. This is when the body and the heart are completely freed and all entanglements disappear. Greetings from guests are ignored, distinctions of name disappear, the face of the master disappears, even the purpose of meditation itself is forgotten. When one has advanced this far one's heart is empty, the essence of one's nature is manifest, and the light of consciousness transforms itself into the light of essence.

Taoist Yoga[17] is a product of Chinese culture. If we wish to evaluate it in a socio-cultural context we must know something of its origins. Philosophically we must look back to Lao Tzu and Chuang Tzu. But Lao Tzu and Chuang Tzu were philosophers in a true sense and not magic theorists. They suggested the possibility of Yoga-like practices as an aid to attaining spiritual enlightenment, but they did not attempt to elaborate techniques or build up fanciful symbolisms. This work was chiefly the product of far lesser minds, who gave themselves over unthinkingly to the pursuit of vain and nonspiritual ends. That they accomplished something in the field of spiritual experience seems undeniable to the author, but it must be admitted that much of their work was the mere product of "medieval" alchemical hopes. It was an attempt at "scientific" explanation of phenomena without adequate scientific basis for judging, and it inevitably flew off into the excesses that are apt to be the chief pitfall of abstract speculation.

As to the value of Yoga practices, the author is personally convinced, not, however, in any proselytizing sense. The point of Yoga is the attainment of *Tao*. The value of Yoga is entirely as a means to an end; if *Tao* can be attained by other means, all well and good. Yoga can be put aside as an unnecessary aid. If it helps the individual in his effort to understand himself and see somewhat more clearly his relationship to the universe around him, then it serves the end of any spiritual exercise—self-realization.

TEACHINGS CONCERNING THE MEDITATIONS OF UNION

Beginning in the 1960s, several Western scholars became associated with Taoist priests in Taiwan; a few were adopted into the families of these hereditary priests and were ordained. What has become apparent from these associations is that the Taoist texts are esoteric treatises; that is, they do not in and of themselves present a comprehensive and comprehendible understanding of Taoist traditions. The texts were to be studied with Taoist masters through the long process of initiation. It is due to the dedicated work of these scholars that those outside of China now have, to a limited degree, an entrée into the meaning of these texts and into Taoist religious understanding. As an example, a small part of Michael Saso's book on *The Teachings of the Taoist Master Chuang* (pp. 198–203) has been excerpted to elucidate the concept of mystic union (technical references have been deleted).

---

[17]The word Yoga is not generally used by the modern Chinese, who refer, rather, to "quiet sitting" or meditative breathing. The term, however, was early introduced into Chinese, through Buddhist texts, such as Yogācāryabhūmi-śāstra, the work of Asaṅga (fourth century A.D.) in India and translated by Hsüan-tsang (596–664), in the transliterated form as *yü chia*. This expression is not now in wide use. In this paper the author has used the word Yoga as being most generally familiar to Western readers.

The disciples of Master Chuang were . . . ranked according to their ability to perform interior meditation. There were three kinds of disciples who flocked to Chuang's ritual performances and listened to his discourses in the front room of the busy Hsinchu residence. The first group were the retainers and the musicians, who came simply to earn a few extra Taiwanese dollars as drummers, flutists, violinists, and cymbal players. These men were minor Taoists in their own right and could on occasion fill in as acolyte or even read one of the lengthy canons of merit and repentance. But they were never ordained and were not given the secrets of ritual meditation. The second group of disciples were the Taoists who belonged by family descent to the Cheng-i Tz'u-t'an, the fraternity of Taoist brethren of Hsinchu City and other parts of north Taiwan. Descendants of the famous Taoists who had flocked to Lin ju-mei's center for studies in the late Ch'ing period, these men were professional Blackhead or orthodox Taoists ordained to the lowest San-wu Tu-kung, the grade six "Surveyor of Merits." They knew and followed the meditations outlined below by Master Chuang.

The last and highest circle of Chuang's disciples were his sons, A-him and A-ga, who were destined to become masters after the retirement of their father. To this elite circle I was sometimes admitted, not as a rival in the profession of public ritual but as a scholar interested in sources of Chuang's teachings. My questions, as related in chapter 3, provoked A-him and A-ga to deeper study, a result that made Chuang quite happy. Many of the esoteric doctrines, which Chuang had hidden even from his sons, were found in my borrowed copy of the printed Taoist Canon. This made my attendance at the lessons appreciated by both A-him and A-ga. It was clear, however, that we were given only a fraction of the total knowledge of Master Chuang. It was required of the older son, A-him, to study some twenty years, from his eleventh to his thirtieth birthday, before even being considered for ordination. For this event, mastery of the meditations of union with the Tao were required.

Teachings Concerning the Meditations of Union (The Ling-pao Five Talismans)

The discourses of Chuang on the Tao of the Right always began with a lengthy lesson on "basic doctrines," the so-called Pen-wen. These evening sessions were very long and boring and my first reaction was to try to escape them. Since there was no way of avoiding the lecture if I was to obtain the esoteric oral teachings that always came at the very end, I soon learned to take copious notes of Chuang's discourses. My efforts were rewarded when I realized, by comparing the notes with canonical texts, that Chuang's long monologues paralleled passages in the early Taoist Canon. I soon learned that canonical passages could be substituted for Chuang's lessons and brought the Canon for him to read instead. According to the teachings of Master Chuang, the progress from the many spirits of the cosmos to the meditation of union with the Tao went according to well-ordered stages. Thus, one began with the ritual called "Inviting the spirits," when all of the benevolent rulers of the cosmos were summoned. From the initial ritual, the adept passed through a gradual refinement, reducing the number to nine, five, and three spirits, until finally only one spirit was present in the microcosm. On the evening set aside to speak of the five spirits who rule the five elements, Chuang commented on the following canonical passages:

> Primordial Heavenly Worthy spoke,
> To the five elder emperors,
> The crowd of great holy ones of the ten heavens,
> All of the assembled lords of the transcendent ultimate (Wu-chi),
> With their wives, who were gathered together,
> In the realm of red brightness,
> Sitting in a fragrant garden,
> Under a fragrant mulberry tree.

The cosmos was described in Chuang's meditation as being in darkness, that is, generation was not yet accomplished. In the period before Lung-han (before primordial gestation), the *Ling-pao Five Talismans* (the same given to Yü the Great to control the floods), were described as initiating the process of light, life, and generation:

> A bright-five-colored light penetrated the abyss,
> In the five directions.
> Suddenly in the heavens there appeared writings,
> In the shape of characters, each ten feet square.
> They appeared quite naturally,
> Generated by the Tao,
> Above the mysterious void.
> In the very center of the five rays of light
> Were carved wen writings.
> These sparkled and glittered in a dazzling manner,
> Their light penetrated outwards in the eight directions;
> A subtle, vital light, spreading out like the spokes of a wheel.
> The light was so bright that one could not look directly at it.
> The mind was befuddled by the light.

In the canonical text, the *Ling-pao Five Talismans* are described as a wheel of five lights, the source of primordial breath, hub of the eight trigrams and the eight directions. They resonate through nature with a harmonious melody:

> The heavenly writings, jade characters,
> Flew off and disappeared into the primordial breath
> Of the mysterious void,
> Where they congealed and became Ling-wen,
> "Writings which bear spirit and life" (ling-pao chen-wen).
> Joined to the eight trigrams, they became harmonious tones.
> Joined to the five talismans, they became chang charms.
> From possessing them, the primordial state
> Called Lung-han was formed.[18]
> The visible world was generated.
> The workings of water and fire,

---

[18]"Lung-han" is the esoteric term for the state of primordial chaos, or Hun-tun; thus the period of gestation from the transcendent Tao to the T'ai-chi is seen to be completed in five stages, presaging the Ling-pao five talismans, and ritually enacted in the Su-ch'i.

Life and death,
The myriad kalpas, and
The light of primordial yang were initiated.
The two principles, yin and yang
Used them to carve out the three realms.
The holy sages mounted them,
To attain to union with the transcendent.
The five sacred peaks hold them,
And are thereby filled with spiritual power.
All things by possessing them have life breath (ch'i).
The nation which possesses them is at peace.
The Ling-pao five writs
Are the middle way of generation,
The root of heaven and the way of earth,
Deriving from the (Tao) of Wu-wei.
He who holds them will not die.
He who honors them will have eternal life.
He who holds them in feudal oath[19]
Will see the realized immortals descend.
They who practise and perfect them
Become immortal spirits;
Passing over the struggle of death, they
Enter into eternal life.

The five writs are also called "great Sanskrit secret mudras," a term used since the early sixth century alluding to the fact that the five talismans were drawn in "bird-like" esoteric symbols which resembled the foreign Sanskrit words coming from India.[20] The *Ling-pao Five Talismans,* therefore, are seen as five lights issuing from the eternal transcendent Tao before the gestation of Primordial Heavenly Worthy; that is, they helped to form the immanent Tao, or Hun-tun, the stage of primordial chaos which was the beginning of cosmic gestation. The five writs order all of nature (li tzu-jan) and are the source of life breath (ch'i).They allow the Taoist adept to cross over from the state of a mortal man into immortality or hsien-hood. They assist the dead to cross over from the realm of stygian darkness into eternal life. In a passage from the sixth-century Canon, intoned by Master Chuang from my borrowed manual, the *Ling-pao Five Talismans* are described in their present-day role in Taoist ritual:

The Ling-pao true writs
Were generated before Primordial Heavenly Worthy,
In the center of the void abyss,
Before heaven and earth's roots.
Before sun and moon gave off their light,
In the dark and murky transcendent ancester (Tao),
They produced Hun-tun, yin and yang.
Because of them the great yang, the sun was made;

---

[19]Thus a feudal treaty is made between the Taoist and the heavenly worthies, using the five talismans as symbol of enfeoffment.

[20]The talismanic writings of the fang-shih seem to have preceded the coming of Buddhist sutras and sanskrit from India; the Taoists of the north-south period claimed a Taoist origin even to the Buddhist teachings.

Because of them the spirit chart (*Ho-t'u*) was formed.[21]
The primordial originator alchemically refined them
In the abyss of the yang palace;
Formed them in the palace of flowing fire.
As they were formed, they sent off rays of red light.
Thus they were called ch'ih-wen, bright red writs;
Again they were called Ch'ih-shu Ling-t'u
The red script spirit chart.[22]
Thus the myriad emperors were able to have audience with the Tao,
To fly up and stride in the void of emptiness,
To travel in the heavenly realms,
While burning incense and scattering flowers,
They chanted the sacred spirit writs.
It was at this time that the heavens sent down the
Twelve mysterious regulators (twelve stems),
And the earth responded with the twenty-four rules.[23]

The heavens hold the five writs as feudal treasures,
And thereby rule all that is above.
The earth guards them as a secret,
Thereby causing peace to reign.
The five ancient emperors hold them in their hands,
Thus causing stability and proper order in nature.
The three sources (sun, moon, and stars) are sustained by them,
Thus maintaining celestial light.
The highest holy ones worship them,
And are thereby realized.[24]
The five sacred peaks obey them,
Thereby attaining spiritual power.
The emperor (son of heaven) holds them,
And thereby rules the nation.
The nation that possesses them attains the Great Peace (T'ai-ping).

AN EXORCIST RITUAL

Similar to the previous elucidation of meditative practice and understanding, the association of scholars with Taoist priests has also led to a more complete understanding of Taoist public rituals. A common cause for people to seek the help of a priest for an exorcism ritual is to assist the deceased members of the family in reaching a comfortable afterlife. The following full discussion from John Langerway's *Taoist Ritual in Chinese Society and History* (pp. 216–28—slightly condensed), is rich in detailing the complexities and the nuances of an exorcism ritual.

---

[21]This phrase and the following (note 22) are to be identified, in Chuang's interpretation, with the *Ho-t'u*, or the *Ling-pao Five Talisman* form.

[22]Another term for the *Ho-t'u*, or the *Ling-pao Five Talismans*.

[23]The twenty-four solar interstices, which correspond to the twenty-four registers of the Meng-wei or Cheng-i-sect teachings; see TT, vol. 878, *Cheng-i Meng-wei Lu*.

[24]The term means "union with the Tao." Thus the chen-jen means the man who has realized union through the Ling-pao ritual meditation.

It covers the purposes of the ritual, the relationship between Taoist priest and mediums, and the relationship between the inner and outer (the esoteric and exoteric) aspects of the ritual.

The Attack on Hell, as its name suggests, is an exorcistic ritual. It is a ritual performed by a priest whose attributes are military rather than civil. Before actually attacking the "fortress of hell" and releasing the soul of the dead, the priest wraps a red bandana around his black cap, takes up a buffalo horn, and blows on it to summon the soldiers of the Five Camps. Such military rituals are normally beneath the dignity of a civil official, whose proper role is the "worship of the Way" (*feng-tao*), and it is only by popular demand, according to Master Ch'en, that the high priest consents to do it himself.

That it is indeed a popular ritual, in both senses of the term, may be seen in a variety of ways. There is, first of all, the fact that it is frequently performed in the Taoist temples called Temple of the Eastern Peak and whose activities contain many features of popular religion. Even more revealing is the fact that the actual destruction of hell, whether performed in the Temple of the Eastern Peak or elsewhere, is often the work of mediums. At the decisive moment they burst into the closed family circle and either tear the fortress to pieces with their bare hands or smash it with a "divination chair." (This is a small chair held by two persons, one of whom, a medium in trance, writes "characters" with one of the chair's legs on a surface of wood or stone at the behest of a divinity who has come to "sit" in the chair and answer questions put to him. Sometimes the action of the chairbearers is a purely parallel one to the main ritual. They simply stand to one side, in front of another table, swinging the chair to and fro throughout the ritual and writing with one of its legs from time to time. This writing action becomes increasingly frenzied and sustained during and immediately after the destruction, as their role in such cases is less to perform the act of destroying the fortress than it is to "verify" that the priest's destruction has been successful. It goes without saying that the Taoist high priest considers such doubling and such verification superfluous and views it with disdain.

A third indication of the popular character of the Attack is its use of theatrical dialogue, as in the Dispatch of the Pardon. Like that ritual, therefore, the Attack is already in and of itself a double ritual, even when no mediums at all are involved, with half of it turned heavenward and half of it earthward. . . .

If the ritual is popular because it is theatrical, it is also theatrical because it is popular. In it, the whole family crouches in a tight semi-circle around the paper fortress, and everyone reaches out a hand to help shake it at appropriate moments. In other words, the ritual is popular because it involves the family members directly in a way none of the other rituals do. Spectators otherwise, now they become participants. The Attack on Hell, therefore, when it is performed, is without question the emotional highpoint of the Ritual of Merit. If the stunts of the Pardon-dispatch often lead to laughter, the tense drama of shaking the fortress often leads to tears. Clearly, to the participating family members, the Attack on Hell involves not only the soul's rescue from hell but also its departure from their midst. It is the moment when they most directly confront *their* loss and the necessity of achieving their own detachment from the deceased.

The necessity of this leave-taking is the real source of the tension that manifests itself in the Attack. An exorcism, its essential purpose is to ensure that the deceased *not* return to haunt the family. In principle, it is performed, therefore, only in the case of an "untoward death" (*wang-ssu*), that is, a death which is likely to produce, not an ancestor who will watch over the family's fortunes but a "vengeful ghost" who will trouble them. . . .

Although the Attack no longer seems to be reserved exclusively for untoward deaths—the principal deceased in the ritual we have been describing had died of natural causes at the age of sixty-two—its exorcistic character is unquestionably more obvious in such cases. In the case of Ritual of Merit observed in 1981, for example, held after the death by accident of an adolescent girl, the fortress was destroyed by the chair-wielding mediums, who then, as it were, chased the family members with the image of the deceased girl into the shop where she had lived and worked. Once inside, the family slammed shut the metal shutters that protect the shop at night, while the two barefoot men continued to swing the chair in front of the closed shop for a good half-hour, building regularly to a furious pitch that ended with their battering the shutters with the chair. The Taoist priest, who had to wait for the chair-bearers to finish before they could do the ritual Crossing the Bridge and go home, watched this spectacle with increasingly open disgust and impatience. They in fact tried unsuccessfully to stop it several times. The mediums simply went on swinging and battering, as if trying to recapture the soul they had just enabled to escape. It is worth noting that similar conflict between the regular Taoist priests and the mediums often occurs in the context of the invitation of the equally dangerous gods of pestilence (*wang-yeh*).There, too, after a relatively brief and dignified Taoist ritual, the mediums repeat the invitation at far greater length and with considerable show of violence. It would seem to be the presence of the demonic—the terrestrial—that provokes such ritual doubling.

The particular ritual observed began with everyone on the altar, facing south. The family members went directly outside and turned around to face north while Master Ch'en, in his black *hai-ch'ing* robe, placed incense on the main tables and then came to sing the introit before the Table of the Three Realms:

> To transcend the difficulties of the Three Realms and
> Obtain release from the five sufferings of the earth-prisons,
> All turn to the scriptures of the Most High and,
> Mediating purely, make obeissance.

The introit is followed by the Ritual of Merit formula for the purification of the altar, and then the priest sprays the fortress with symbol-water and blows his exorcist's horn. He then "opens to the light" the figures inside and outside the fortress, using the blood of a cock's comb. He sets fire to some "old money," waves it all around the fortress, blows on his horn, and pours symbol-water through it.

The triple sequence of invocations and libations that follows is entirely inaudible because of ferocious percussion and horns. Each segment of the sequence consists of a presentation of incense, accompanied by blasts on the buffalo horn, followed by an invocation, a recited passage, a song announcing the libation, and then a libation. The divinities invoked are the usual supreme divinities, plus the various heavenly worthies, divine judges, and soul-catchers of the Merit Ritual, much like the Invocation. The first recited passage—a pastiche of lines from

Lao-tzu—concerns the cosmic workings of the Great Way (heaven), the second is a prayer for the "compassion of its Great Power" (earth), and the third gives a summary description of the ritual (man). . . .

Before turning to the theatrical half of the Attack, we have to consider two other ritual acts that occur in the first half. The first is the lighting of a single candle on the table in front of the priest at the end of the first invocation and recitation. Perhaps this candle stands for the "divine light [of the Way] which carries out its transformations"; it would certainly come as no surprise should candlelight be used to "enlighten" the benighted souls in the underworld. . . .

The master "expresses his sincerity" by reciting a poem, then "hands the symbol-candle to the keeper of the lamps on his left" and goes again before the Heavenly Worthy to ask for the "document staff," which, after reciting another poem, he "hands to the keeper of incense on his right." The ritual master has thus an instrument of life on the one hand and an instrument of death on the other. Put another way, half of him is civil, the other half military, and the relationship between the two is just what it is in the Attack ritual: first the civil (celestial), then the military (terrestrial). The Taoist, even when waging a "holy war" on the "citadel of brass," is in the first place a civil official. He knows how to perform the external spectacle; he prefers to perform the internal ritual.

The second ritual act in the first part of the Attack occurs at the conclusion. When the priest has finished the triple sequence of invocations and libations, he reads the memorial, then repeats the entire list of divinities once more, this time to thank-dismiss them, and finally he burns the memorial. This first half of the Attack is thus a complete ritual in and of itself, including even a message-dispatch. The same is true of Lin T'ien-jen's Destruction of Hell ritual, in which a traditional Lamp-lighting ritual (*kuan-teng*) is completed before the Destruction of Hell begins. The Lamp-lighting is composed of the request for the candle and the staff, a recitation addressed to the Savior from Distress, the lighting of the lamps of the nine hells, a series of three invocations, each preceded by a presentation of incense, the burning of several symbols for the destruction of hell, the dispatch of an announcement, and the recitation of *The Scripture of Salvation from Distress*. The similarity of structure to this part of the Attack is striking, to say the least.

Now we begin the description of the ritual theater. The priest starts by spraying symbol-water toward the south and toward the north; then he lights a paper cone and uses it to purify a long, pronged staff and the fly-whisk. He drops the burning "old money" and steps over it. Then, as in a theater, he introduces himself by singing a verse:

> I recall that day when I was wandering in the mountains,
> I saw the tears flowing from the eyes of all mortals.
> A student of the Way on Dragon-Tiger Mountain,
> I swore my heart would not rest until I had achieved the Way.

He carries on in ordinary speech:

> I am none other than the Real Man of Marvelous Movement Who Saves from Distress. I come from the Mountain of the Great Net [Ta-lo, the supreme heaven beyond the Three Realms]. I have come down from my mountain this evening for no other reason than that my host has asked me to his home to invite the Three Pure Ones, ancestors of the Way, to recite the litanies of confession and

compassion and to reimburse the treasury of the underworld. The merit of the confessions has been achieved, the pardon has been proclaimed, and I have received the directives of the ancestors of the Way to come to the fortress to save the soul of so-and-so.

The text indicates that at this point the officiant may "sing whatever he wishes" (such as "Mu-lien Saves His Mother," in the ritual we observed), Master Ch'en walked as he sang, leaning on his pilgrim's staff. This symbolizes the trip to hell, and therefore at the end of the song the priest says:

I hear before me very distinctly the sound of drum and gongs. This must be the Gate of the Demons in the fortress of the underworld. I'll hide to one side and see what hour they are announcing.

There is a great burst of percussion, which ends with a series of drumbeats and blows to the gong announcing that it is midnight. This leads the Real Man to sing another song:

The first watch has been drummed,
The drum has been beat in the bell tower . . .
Man lives a bare hundred years,
A hundred years that pass like a distant dream.
Begin to practice early;
Do not wait until it is too late.

The Real Man then goes to the gate, shakes his staff at it, and calls on the demon general in charge that night to open up. Again there is a sound of percussion, and again the priest sings:

The Demon Gate before the Hall of Yama opens:
Cangues and chains are lined up on either side.

"This is the place of judgment," he adds, "where each person gets his just deserts."
At this point a new protagonist, the guardian of hell's gate, enters the scene. According to Master Ch'en, this role may be played either by the drummer—as in the ritual observed—or by an acolyte with a buffalo-head mask. He also begins by announcing himself:

I have received King Yama's instructions to guard the Demon Gate. A little devil has just come in and reported that the soul of someone who has died is knocking loudly at our gate. As it is an auspicious day and the night is clear, it must be a good man or a faithful woman from the world of the living who wishes to pass through my gate.

The clerk summons the little devil, and the orchestra plays music suitable as for an audience with the Real Man.

The Real Man calls impatiently, "Hurry and open up."
"Who's knocking so loud on my door at this hour?" the demon wants to know.
"It's me, the Real Man of Marvelous Movement from the Mountain of the Great Net."

"Why isn't the Real Man on his mountain studying the Way, reciting scriptures, picking medicinal plants, and subliming the elixir?"

The priest explains that he as come "with directives from the ancestors of the Way" to save so-and-so. Sorry to bother you. Hurry and open up."

"So the Real Man wants to enter the gate?"

"Precisely."

"That's easy enough."

"Then open up."

"Just let me ask the Real Man whether he brought any money or any precious gifts for us devils when he came down from his mountain?"

"That's no way to talk."

"How so?"

"I'm a student of the Way. I eat what others give me. I've come all alone ten thousand miles. How could I carry any money or gifts for you?"

"You really have nothing?"

"Nothing."

"Then forget it."

"I'll forget it. Just open up!"

"Has the Real Man never heard the words of men of old?"

"Say on."

"From of old there is an eight-character saying about the way to open the mandarin's gate: 'No money, don't come; with money, it's open.' If you've no money, you may as well be off." The demon laughs.

The demon has no need to tell him all this, replies the Real Man, "I knew it before you said it."

"Knew what?"

"That all your talk is just to get some money."

The demon asks why else he should be losing sleep and exposing himself to the cold.

"Well, if it's money you want, my host has given me some paper money to bring along. Wait while I burn some paper money for you demons." The priest lights a paper cone and throws it at the drummer. The demons ask where the money has been burnt, and the priest replies, "At the foot of the Drum Tower." The demon doesn't want to leave his post to get it. Besides, paper money is as worthless in the underworld as it is in the land of the living; he wants "copper cash." What about all the paper money burned on Ch'ing-ming, or in the middle of the seventh month, asks the Real Man. "Where does it all go?" The demon responds that Yama often sends "little devils into the world of the living to spy on sinners," and they need copper cash for such trips because merchants don't accept paper money. The Real Man repeats all that in the form of a question, and the demon replies, "Precisely."

"I haven't a single copper cash."

"Then forget it."

"I'll forget it. Just open up!"

"Real Man, are you aware that we judge the living and the dead according to their deeds here at the Demon Gate?" This judgment, he goes on to explain, is based on two books, one for those who have lived out their span of life, another for those who have not.

"How does your great King Yama judge someone who has done good and whose years are not yet up, but he comes before the Demon Gate by mistake?"

"Someone who has done good and whose years are not yet up?"

"Just so."

"Our great king looks in the Record of Life to see whether this person, while he was alive, worshiped the Three Treasures, was a filial child to his parents, helped build bridges and roads, took delight in good deeds, and loved alms-giving. If so, our great king sends a golden lad and a jade lass to bring him back to the other world. Such is the Great Book of Life."

"And what about the bad man, how do you clerks of Yama judge such a one when he dies and comes to the Demon Gate?" (According to Master Ch'en, the orchestra should produce a "whistling" sound here to imitate the sound made by demons.)

"Our great king sees from the Register of Death that this person, while he was alive, did not respect the Three Treasures, was disobedient to his parents, twitted his elder brother and beat his wife, killed, committed arson, and did every imaginable kind of evil deed. When he sees this, the great King Yama sends the bullheaded general with a pitchfork and the horseheaded general with chains to hail him into the eighteen prisons of Feng-tu. . . . such is the Great Book of Death."

"So you here at the Demon Gate urge people to do good, do you?"

"That's right."

"Good?"

"Good gets a good reward."

"Bad?"

"Bad gets a bad return. Sooner or later, everyone gets what he has coming."

"But you demons don't pay back everyone."

"That's because their time hasn't come, it's not because we here at Demon Gate don't repay good and evil."

"You say it's that their time hasn't come, not that you at Demon Gate don't judge and repay good and evil?"

"Just so."

"Now that you devils have discussed good and evil so clearly, open the gate so I can go through."

"The Real man has heard that the two great Registers of Life and Death are important here. What is important to you who study the Way?"

"For us students of the Way, when we leave home, it's the texts and teachings of the scriptures which are most important."

"Wonderful!" The demon laughs.

"Wonderful? Don't talk that demon talk!"

"No, that was a joyous 'wonderful!' from the heart. Real Man, sing us a snatch from one of those fine scriptures from the Mountain of the Jade Capital in the Great Net that saves the souls of the deceased, and when we've heard it loud and clear, we'll let the Real man through."

"Can demons listen to scripture?"

"Even among brigands one finds bodhisattvas, so why shouldn't demons be able to listen to scripture?"

The priest tells the little devil to spread flowers and light incense and candles if he really wants to hear a song. When he has finished singing the song, he calls on the demon once more to open up, which at last the demon does. The priest says, "We fray a path with clasped hands between life and death. We do a somersault and leap through the Demon Gate" (this somersault is not actually done, unlike the Pardon ritual). Then he sings, "The road from the Demon Gate goes right through to the Yellow Springs. I see the road is lined on both sides by the flags of the demonic host. I hear the sound of drums and gongs. It is terrifying. I must not be afraid."

(This song, according to Master Ch'en, is punctuated by the name of the god of music, sung as a refrain. Thus music presides over the passage into hell here, as laughter and clowning did in the Pardon ritual.)

After the song, the Taoist may go on to describe the horrors he encounters in hell: sinners in stocks, heads split open, pools of blood on the ground. "This is the fiery road through the Yellow Springs. It's no place for a student of the Way to linger. I had better burn some paper money." Once again he demands that the Demon Gate be opened, and once again the demon asks who's disturbing the peace at such an unearthly hour. The priest identifies himself anew and repeats the name of the person he has come to save.

"The Real Man is late."

"What do you mean, late?"

"When Yama mounted his throne, you had not yet come. You arrived just as Yama was leaving his hall. There's nothing to be done."

"Look, demon, I've come a long ways over great mountain ranges. What do you mean, there's nothing to be done because I'm late?"

"Real Man, when Yama mounted his throne, I went with him, and when he left the hall, so did I. If I let one soul go, I will be held accountable. I dare not take any such initiative."

"Demon, the proverb has it that even a heart of iron softens [if it's beaten long enough]."

"When one word doesn't hit the mark, a thousand are of no use."

"Demon, do you see the staff I have in my hand?—It's the precious defense given me by order of the ancestors of the Way. On the left it controls dragons, on the right it tames tigers. One thrust, and heaven is clear; two thrusts, and earth is potent; three thrusts, and stocks are smashed and iron locks opened."

"I don't believe you."

"Acolyte, beat the drum of the law three times and have Hsü Chia summon forth the divine soldiers of the Five Camps to smash the fortress."

Hsü Chia is Lao-tzu's (Lord Lao's) disciple and patron saint of the "redhead" Taoists in southern Taiwan. At this point therefore, the officiant, after rattling his pronged staff menacingly in front of the fortress, comes back in front of the Table of the Three Realms, wraps a red bandana around his black cap and trusses up his sleeves: he has become an exorcist.

He begins by summoning the agents "attached to the symbols" (*chih-fu*) of the Three Realms (Three Offices). Blowing on his buffalo horn and lighting in succession three rolled cones of "old money," he drops them in the center, then to his right, and to his left. Paper money is burned in front of the fortress. The chairbearers, who have been swinging the chair throughout off to one side, come now in front of the fortress and swing the chair back and forth violently. At the same time, and with equal violence, the family members shake the fortress, and there is furious clanging of gongs as one by one the priest lights, lets burn, and drops in the four corners and in the center five paper cones to summon the soldiers of the Five Camps. Then he sprays a mouthful of symbol-water at the fortress and makes the same ram gesture he made at the end of the Sealing of the Altar. "Acolyte," he says, "beat the drum of the law three more times, and I'll smash the fortress." The mourners shake the fortress and call to the soul, "Come get your money, come wash." The Real Man lights the paper cones stuck on the prongs of his staff and stabs the fortress.

In the ritual observed, Master Ch'en, holding the soul-banner, now reinvites the various divinities and makes a final prayer for the soul's salvation. Then the envelope which has marked the "seat" of the Savior from Distress is burned, together with some paper money. To instructions from Master Ch'en, the head of the family drops the divining blocks over and over again, and then at last Ch'en lights a broom and swats all around the altar with it. Then, with long strings of firecrackers exploding noisily just outside the altar area, he takes up a rolled mat with burning paper cones stuck in either end, whirls it several times, and finally smashes the fortress with it. The family members quickly remove the four paper figures representing the deceased from the table and bring them back to the house.

The description of the conclusion of the ritual which Master Ch'en gave in his 1977 seminar in Paris differed somewhat from what we actually saw at this particular Ritual of Merit. His description follows.

> *Notes:* The officiant, after breaking through the Demon Gate by using the ram gesture, grabs the image of the deceased from inside the fortress, and ties it on the back of the chief mourner. While another family member holds a parasol over the image so that it does not come in contact with or become exposed to the energies of the world of the living, which might bring it back to life and turn it into a roving ghost, the family rushes with the image to the house, where a basin of water and a change of clothing have been prepared. The chief mourner puts on a pair of sandals previously placed under the table, the priest enters just to see that all is in place, and then leaves. Shutting the door to the chapel, the family places the statuette with a burner on the table and then dresses the image with the clothing that had been set out. The priest returns to the altar to perform the exorcism with broom and mat in order to purify the ritual area. He removes the effigies of Kuanyin and the god of the soil from the fortress and brings the latter back to its place at the entrance to the altar. Inside, both image and clothing are burned.
>
> Mediums are often present for this rite. From outside the shut doors of the house, the *chi-t'ung* ("divining youth," the medium) is questioned about the voyage of the deceased: what does he need? Meanwhile, the remains of the fortress are given to an elderly man, who takes them to an isolated spot for burning.

We have already referred to an Attack that ended in essentially this manner in a ritual performed for a girl's early death; we may add here that it was also the chair-bearing mediums who on that occasion destroyed the fortress.

The Attack on Hell is unique in the repertoire of Taoist rituals both for the great variety of ways in which it may be performed and for the fact that some of those variants involve parallel ritual action by the mediums of popular religion. . . .

CHAPTER 7

Three Ways of Ultimate Transformation: (2) Literati Tradition

MOST HOLY MASTER OF ANTIQUITY, THE PHILOSOPHER K'UNG

"Most Holy Master of Antiquity, the Philosopher K'ung," such are the words inscribed on the soul tablet of Confucius that stands above the altar in the Confucian temple. This reader is not the place to attempt a presentation of the life and teachings, much less the influence, of the Master, but we must at least give a few indications. We turn, for the following quotations, to the *Analects (Lun Yü)*, compiled from the personal recollections of the disciples. (Selections are located by chapter and verse. The translation is by the editor [L. G. T.].)

Autobiographical

At fifteen I was determined to study. At thirty I had established [my character]. At forty I was no longer in doubt [about the Way]. At fifty I understood Heaven's will. At sixty when I heard [the Way] I could follow it easily. At seventy what my heart desires does not go beyond the bounds. (II,4)

The Master said, I can be happy even with just simple food to eat and water to drink, and only my bended arm for a pillow. Wealth and honors wrongfully acquired are to me like floating clouds. (VII,15)

The Master said, In a village of ten homes there is bound to be someone as conscientious and sincere as I, but there won't be anyone as fond of learning. (V,27)

The Master said, When three of us walk together, [the others] are bound to be my teachers. I can pick out what is good in them and emulate it, and from what is not good I can learn to change [that same thing] in myself. (VII,21)

The Master said, I have never refused to teach anyone who has come bearing his [tuition fee of] dried meat. (VII,7)

The Master said, If a student is not eager I don't begin, if he won't open up I don't explain. If I hold up one corner and he can't then figure out the other three, I don't repeat the lesson. (VII,8)

The Master said, I wasn't born with wisdom. Being fond of history I diligently seek it through studying the past. (VII,19)

The Master said, How could I dare to claim to be holy and virtuous? You might say with truth that I never give up trying, and I teach without getting tired of it—that's all. A disciple replied. That's just where we disciples are unable to come up to you. (VII,33)

Tzu-kung would judge people. The Master said, You must be a paragon! Personally, I haven't the time for that. (XIV,31)

The Master said, Tz'u, do you think what I'm after is encyclopedic knowledge? The disciple replied, Yes, is it not so? The Master said, No, what I seek is the unifying principles. (XV,2)

The Duke of Shê asked Tzu-lu (a disciple) about Confucius. Tzu-lu had no answer. The Master said, Why didn't you tell him, He is simply a man who is so enthusiastic that he forgets to eat, so happy that he forgets his troubles, and doesn't realize that old age is coming on him. (VII,18)

Through the Eyes of the Disciples

The Master was entirely free from four [faults]: He was not biased, he was not arbitrary, he was not obstinate, and he was not selfish. (IX,4)

The Master said, The Way of the noble man (*chün-tzu*) has three qualities I am not able to claim: He has a perfected moral character (*jen*) and therefore no anxieties; he is wise and therefore has no doubts; he is brave and therefore has no fears. Tzu-kung replied, But that is in fact your own Way, Master. (XIV,30)

[The disciple] Yen Yüan said with a sigh [of admiration] . . . The Master methodically encourages men to become better. He broadened me with culture and disciplined me with the codes of social behavior (*li*). Even if I should want to stop at this point I cannot. Although I've given it all I have, it's as though the goal were still before me, and try though I may to reach it, it still eludes me. (IX,10)

An official once expressed admiration for a disciple of Confucius, saying, Tzu-kung is greater than Confucius. This being reported to Tzu-kung, the latter said, If we use the comparison of a house and its wall, then my wall is only shoulder-high; one may look over it and see whatever is valuable in the house. But the wall around the Master's house is hundreds of feet high. If you don't find the gate by which to enter, you cannot see the beauty of the ancestral temple or the abundance of officials in attendance. But there may be only a few who have found that gate. . . . (XIX,23)

The same official spoke ill of Confucius. Tzu-kung said, That's no use. Confucius cannot be slandered. The greatness of other men is like mounds which can be stepped over, but Confucius is like the sun and moon, and one can never jump over them. Even though you break your neck trying to do so, what harm is done the sun and moon? It only shows your own bad judgment in trying to do so. (XIX,24)

Some Words of Wisdom

The Master said, Study as if the goal were just beyond your grasp and you feared to lose it. (VIII,15)

The Master said, I have tried spending the whole day without eating and the whole night without sleeping in order to think. It was useless. It is better to study. (XV,30)

The Master said, Man is by nature upright. If he lose this character and yet go on living, he's just lucky to avoid [death].

The Master said, the man of moral character (*chün-tzu*) makes demands on himself, the petty man makes demands on others. (XV,20)

The Master said, When it comes to moral character (*jen*) don't yield to your teacher. (XV,35)

The Master said, If a man is not Good (*jen*), what good is it if he goes through the correct social forms? If a man is not Good, what good is it if he has the correct ritual performed [at the sacrifices]? (III,3)

The Master said, Is virtue (*jen*) far off? I have but to wish to be virtuous, and virtue is at hand. (VII,29)

The Master said, The man of moral character (*chün-tzu*) brings out the good in others, and not their bad side. The man of petty character does the opposite. (XII,16)

The Master said, The noble man (*chün-tzu*) hates to think that he will leave no name to posterity. (XV,19)

The Master said, Gentlemen of determination, moral men (*jen jen*), will not seek life at the expense of virtue (*jen*). They will give their lives for their moral principles (*jen*).

Tzu-kung said, Does the man of moral character (*chün-tzu*) also hate? The Master said, He does. He hates those who talk about how bad other people are. He hates moral delinquents who slander those of higher character. He hates men who are bold but have no manners. He hates those who are obstinate but narrow-minded. (XVII,24)

Yen Yüan asked about moral perfection (*jen*). The Master said, To subordinate the self and in all things act according to the codes of social behavior is moral perfection. If one could for a single day subordinate oneself to these codes the whole world would become morally perfect. Now, does moral perfection derive from oneself, or from others? (XII,1.1)

Chung-kung asked about moral perfection. The Master said, When you are in public be as polite as though receiving a distinguished guest. When you are in charge of the people be as scrupulous as though conducting a great sacrifice. What you don't like done to yourself, don't do to others. [Acting in this way] you will arouse no resentment either at home or abroad. (XII,2)

Ssu-ma Niu asked about moral perfection. The Master said, Moral perfection lies in choosing one's words with care. The disciple exclaimed, Choosing one's words with care—this is moral perfection? The Master said, Living a moral life is difficult. Can one be other than careful in talking about it? (XII,3)

Ssu-ma Niu asked about the man of moral character (*chün-tzu*). The Master said, The man of moral character is neither anxious nor afraid. The disciple exclaimed, Neither anxious nor afraid—this is the man of moral character? The Master said, On examining himself he finds no moral fault. So why would he be anxious or afraid? (XII,4)

The Master said, Virtue (*tê*) is not solitary—it is bound to have company. (IV,25)

The Master said, I've never seen anyone who loved virtue as much as he loved women. (IX,7)

The Master said, The goody-goodies are the ones who sabotage virtue (XVII,13)

An officer in power asked Confucius about government. Confucius replied, To govern (*chêng*) is to correct (another *chêng*). If you, Sir, lead them correctly, who will dare not to be correct? (XII,17)

The same official, being concerned about robbery in his state, consulted with Confucius. The latter replied, If you, Sir, were not avaricious, then even if you paid them your people would not steal. (XII,18)

The same official again asked Confucius about government, saying, What do you say to slaying the bad to save the good? Confucius replied, Sir, in governing why use slaying at all? If you, Sir, seek to be good, all your people will be good. The virtue of the nobleman (*chün-tzu*) is like the wind, while the virtue of the common people is like the grass. As the wind blows, the grass must bend. (XII,19)

Tzu-kung asked, What do you say about a man who is liked by all his neighbors? The Master said, We can't judge him by that. Tzu-kung then asked, What if he is hated by all his neighbors? The Master said, We can't judge him by that, either. A better test is if the good people of his neighborhood like him, and the bad people hate him. (XIII,24)

Fan Ch'ih asked about wisdom. The Master said, Do your duty to men, and while paying due respect to spirits keep your distance. This may be called wisdom. [The disciple] asked about virtue (*jen*). The Master said, The victory [of right] in the [moral] struggle [within a man's heart] may be called virtue. (VI,20)

The Master said, Yu, shall I teach you about wisdom? When you know it, know that you know it; when you don't know it, admit you don't know it. That's wisdom. (II,17)

The Master said, Don't worry about not having a position—worry about making yourself fit to hold one. Don't worry that you aren't famous—try to act so you will deserve to be famous. (IV,14)

The Master said, Don't worry that men won't know you—worry about your lack of ability. (XIV,32)

The Master said, If a man does not constantly ask himself, What should be done? What should be done? I really don't know what should be done about him! (XV,15)

[The Master said,] When the Way prevails in a country one should be ashamed of being poor and undistinguished. When the Way does not prevail in a country one should be ashamed of being rich and exalted. (VIII,13.3)

The Master said, Seeing a great man, aspire to equal him; seeing an ignoble man, take a good look at yourself. (IV,17)

[The Master said,] To see what is right but not do it is cowardice. (II,24.2)

The Master said, Make conscientiousness (*chung*) and sincerity (*hsin*) your chief principles. Have no friends not equal to yourself. Don't hesitate to correct your own faults. (IX,24)

Tzu-kung asked, Is there a single word that may serve as the guide for one's whole life? The Master said, Will reciprocity (*shu*) do? What you don't like yourself don't do to others. (XV,23)

Someone asked, What do you think of the principle that one should requite injury with kindness? The Master said, Then with what should one requite kindness? One should requite injury with justice, and kindness with kindness. (XIV,36)

The Master said, Men by nature are similar. Through practice they come to diverge. (XVII,2)

The Master said, It is only the wisest and the stupidest who never change. (XVII,3)

The Master said, Young people should be respected. Who can tell but that they will be as good as we? Only if someone has no reputation by the age of forty or fifty, then he may not merit our respect.

The Master said, It is man who makes the Way greater, not the Way that makes man greater. (XV,28)

The Master said, If a man could realize Tao in the morning, he could die that evening [without regret]. (IV,8)

China's "Herodotus," the great Ssu-ma Ch'ien, eloquently summed up the Chinese feeling about Confucius, in his biography of the Sage (*Shih Chi, Historical Memoirs, K'ung Tzu Shih Chia*):

When I read the writings of Confucius I imagine I can see the man. When I went to [his home state of] Lu I saw the ancestral temple of Chung-ni (his given name), the carriages, robes, and ritual implements. There were students who performed the rites at his home at the proper times. I started to leave, only to return again; I could not tear myself away. There have been many rulers and eminent men in this world, who were honored while they lived, but forgotten when they were dead. [The doctrines of] Confucius, who only wore a common cloth garment, have been transmitted for more than ten generations, and all the scholars honor him. Whenever the Six Arts (i.e. all learning) are discussed in China by anyone—from the Son of Heaven, kings, or lords [on down]—the words of the Master are the final authority. We can say that he is Most Holy!

CONFUCIUS AS PATRON SAINT

The general resistance on the part of the literati to deification of their Master, Confucius, cannot negate his vast importance in Chinese religion. His teachings formed the moral character of the nation. His worship was, at least during the later centuries, most prominent in the state cults throughout the country. His birthplace at Ch'üeh-li and the ancestral home of his clan at Ch'ü–fu (these are in Ch'ü–fu country, southwestern Shantung province) have through the ages been preserved as shrines, visited by countless pilgrims and honored by the inscriptions of emperors.

Following are a brief description of these shrines and a general description of an official Confucian Temple, a discussion of the music and dancing (or posturing) in the ritual, and some visual illustrations. The first item is extracted from a volume by E. H. Parker, entitled *Studies in Chinese Religion,* Chapman and Hall (London, 1910). He is quoting in turn from a report by James Stewart Lockhart, who paid a visit to Ch'ü–fu in 1903, where he was received by the Yen-sheng Kung ("Duke who propagates holiness"—official title of the current head of the K'ung clan; in this instance the seventy-sixth lineal descendant of the Sage). (We have condensed and slightly edited this material, which is found on pages 192–197).

On Sunday, the 10th of May, I went in uniform[1] to the Temple of Confucius to show my respect for China's Great Sage. I was conducted by descendants of the Sage to that portion of the temple where Chinese have to kneel and perform the

---

[1]Lockhart was paying an official call as a British Commissioner. (L. G. T.)

kowtow to their great teacher. Having raised my hat, I read in Chinese a short encomium of Confucius. I then proceeded to the main building of the temple, where the Duke and his suite were waiting to receive me. . . .

On Monday, the 11th of May, we proceeded to the Temple of Confucius, and were met at the entrance by two of the uncles of the Duke and his steward, who conducted us all round the buildings.

The grounds of the temple cover about thirty-five acres, and are well wooded with fine old cypress, yew, and fir trees of great age. Among the trees are one planted by the Sage himself, and two planted during the T'ang (A.D. 618–907) and Sung dynasties (A.D. 960–1126).

The temple is divided into a series of courts, of which there are six, before the main temple is reached. Each court is separated from the other by a gateway, but has steps leading into the court on either side. The main temple is built upon the spot where Confucius . . . lived. In front of the entrance to the main temple are thirteen pavilions covering tablets with inscriptions written by various emperors of China. The main temple itself consists of ten buildings and an altar: Each building has a court to itself.

After passing through the entrance to the main temple, the altar called the Hsing T'an is reached. It is open on four sides, and is so named because Confucius received those who came to seek his instruction at a place so called. Behind the Hsing T'an is the Ya Ch'eng Tien, a great hall containing a statue of Confucius, sixteen feet high, seated on a throne and screened with curtains embroidered with dragons. The hall is supported in front by white marble pillars with deeply carved dragons, and in the north, east, and west by pillars of black marble carved in cameo-work. The floor is lined with black marble, and the roof is covered with yellow tiles. The ceiling consists of 486 panels, square in shape, gilded at the edge, and ornamented with dragons.

In front of the statue is a table on which are displayed enamelled vases and bronze urns and tripods, presented to the temple by the Emperor Yung Chêng (A.D. 1723–1736), and which are said to date back to the second year of Yüan Ho, of the Han Dynasty (A.D. 85). In the hall are suspended four gilded tablets and three pairs of scrolls presented by emperors of the present [Ch'ing] dynasty, and there are also statues of Yen Tzu and Tsêng Tzu, his favorite disciples, of his grandson, of Mencius, and of twelve of his chief disciples. At the east and west of the great hall are two corridors containing the tablets of his disciples and the philosophers who have supported his teaching from the earliest times up to the present dynasty. Behind the grand hall is a building in honor of his wife, and in the rear of it is a building panelled with black marble, in which are depicted scenes in the life of Confucius, and in one of which is a picture of the Sage. On the west are three buildings, the first being the hall in which the music is played at the worship of Confucius, the instruments used being kept in a building still further to the west. The second contains the statue of the father of Confucius; the third is in honor of his mother. On the east are three buildings. The first is in honor of the classics [which Confucius is supposed to have written and edited], and the other two are in honor of his ancestors. In the court in front of these two buildings are a tablet on which is engraved the genealogical tree of the family of Confucius, but which is so affected by age that it is not possible to obtain from it satisfactory rubbings; the well used by Confucius; and a pillar marking the spot where the Confucian classics were found in the wall of the house formerly inhabited by Confucius, having been hidden there to save them from the general burning of Books ordered in 213 B.C. by the first Emperor Shih Huang Ti. . . .

In the afternoon we went to the tomb of Confucius, which is situated to the north of the city and is distant from it about a mile and a half. . . . The approach to the tomb is through a fine avenue lined with cypress trees, symbolical of the immortality of the frame of the Sage, and leads up to the gates of the cemetery, which covers a large area of ground, thickly wooded with trees of large size and great age.

After passing through the entrance, the road, which is lined with pillars inscribed by various emperors, winds to the west until a brook called the Chu Shui, "the Red Water," is reached. This brook is crossed by three bridges, the center one of which leads to an avenue of trees, one of which is the famous tree planted by Tzu Kung, one of the most distinguished of Confucius' disciples. At the end of the avenue are six stone figures, four of animals and two of men, sixteen feet in height, which are immediately in front of a hall, containing an incense table, in which the ceremonies in honor of Confucius are performed. This hall opens by four folding doors into the enclosure, in which are three mounds, marking the last resting-place of the Sage, his son, and his grandson.

The grave of Confucius is a mound about thirty feet in height and one hundred in circumference, covered with trees and brushwood. In front of it are a stone urn and altar, and a tombstone with the following inscription in seal characters: "The most holy ancient Sage, the Prince of Culture."

To the west of the tomb is a small building erected on the spot where Tzu Kung, the beloved disciple of the Sage, mourned for his master six years.

To the east of Confucius's tomb is the grave of his son, and to the southeast that of his grandson. Both are high mounds with stone urns and pillars, and in front of the grave of the grandson are two colossal stone figures. The tombstones bear the following inscriptions in ordinary characters: "The tomb of the Marquis of Ssu Shui" (the title by which the son is known to posterity). "The tomb of the Transmitter of the Sacred Sage, of the State of I" (the title by which the grandson is known to posterity). . . .

The following description of a Confucian Temple is taken from the Introduction (pp. v–vii) to Thomas Watters's book, *A Guide to the Tablets in a Temple of Confucius* (American Presbyterian Mission Press: Shanghai, 1879). The material is given complete with slight editing.

According to the laws of China there must be a Wên-miao or Temple of Confucius attached to every Prefecture, Sub-Prefecture, District, and in every market-town throughout the empire. Consequently not only has each town its temple but all Prefectural cities contain two and some three.

A Wên-miao may be built on any convenient site within the wall of a town but it must in all cases face the South. There are differences of detail from place to place but the essentials of the temple are much the same everywhere, and vary only in size and completeness. It must consist of three Courts which generally follow in a line from South to North. The outermost of these is called the P'an-kung, from the name given to the state College of a feudal principality during the period of the Chou dynasty. It is bounded on the South by a wall called the Hang-ch'iang, a name which recalls that of the Government Colleges during the Han period. The colour of this wall, as of the temple generally, is red, that having been adopted by the Chou rulers as their official colour. It is not provided with a gate until a student of the district to which the temple is attached succeeds in obtaining the title Chuang-yuan, that is, first among the Chin-shih (i.e., the recipients of the highest, or "doctoral" degree, awarded after extremely competitive examinations conducted in the imperial capital) of his year. When this occurs the middle portion of the wall is taken away and a gate substituted, through which, however, only a Chuang-yuan and an Emperor or Prince may pass. A little to the north of this wall is an ornamental arch of wood or stone called the Ling-hsing-mên and beyond this is a pond called the P'an-ch'ih. This pond is of semicircular shape properly, and extends from East by South to West according to the rule established for state colleges during the Chou period. These had "half-ponds" while the Emperor's College had a complete circular pond. . . . The pond is spanned by the Yuan-ch'iao or Arched Bridge, also reserved for the use of a Chuang-yuan or Emperor, and often called the Wang-ch'iao, or Royal Bridge. The chief entrances to the Court are by two gates, one in the east wall and one in the west. At the upper end on the west side is the Tsai-sheng-t'ing, a room in which the animals for sacrifice are kept, and at the opposite corner is a chamber for the private use of the chief worshiper. In this he rests for a short time, on coming to the temple, and it is hence called the Kuan-t'ing or Official Pavilion. It is known also as the Kêng-yi-so because the mandarin here changes his ordinary robes for Court uniform.

The north side of this Court, which is usually planted with trees, is occupied by a large hall in the middle of which is the Ta-ch'êng-mên, opened only for a Chuang-yuan or an Emperor. This is also known as the Chi-mên or Spear Door, because for some time it was adorned by two stands of antique spears. On each side of this is a small door leading into the next or principal Court, on entering which two long narrow buildings are seen extending along the east and west walls. These are called respectively the Tung-wu and Hsi-wu, and they contain the tablets of the Former Worthies and Scholars arranged in chronological order. Between these buildings is an open space called Tan-ch'ih or Vermilion Porch, that having been the name of a corresponding open square in front of a palace during the Chou dynasty. This part of the Court is usually planted with cypresses or in their absence with oleas and other handsome trees. Here all ordinary worshipers kneel and prostrate themselves when celebrating the worship of Confucius. Above the Tan-ch'ih is a stone platform called the Yueh-t'ai or Moon Terrace, also a survival from the Chou times. This adjoins the Ta-ch'êng-tien or Hall of Great Perfection, the Temple proper. In many places this is an imposing structure with massive pillars of wood or stone and embellished with quaint devices in painting. In the middle of the north wall, "superior and alone," sometimes in a large niche and sometimes merely resting on a table, is the Sage's tablet. Before it stands an altar on which are usually a few sacrificial vessels, and overhead are short eulogistic inscriptions. Next below the Sage are the Four Associates,[2] two on his left hand and two on his right. Their tablets are in niches or frames and

---

[2]Yen Hui, favorite disciple of the Master; Tzu Ssu, his grandson, and putative author of *Chung Yung*; Tseng Tzu, another favorite disciple; and Mencius, the Second Sage. (L.G.T.)

have altars before them. Lower in the Hall and arranged along the walls are the tablets of the Twelve "Wise Ones," six on each side, also furnished with altars.

The next Court, which is behind the principal one, or, if space requires, at its east side, contains the Ch'ung-shêng-tz'u, Ancestral Hall of Exalted Sages. In it are the tablets of five ancestors of Confucius, of his half-brother, of the fathers of the Associates and of certain other worthies. With a few exceptions the men worshiped there have been canonized on account of the merits of their posterity and not from any great virtue in themselves.

The official residence of the Director of Studies is in close proximity to the Confucian temple which is under the care of that mandarin. Certain buildings for the use of government students and chambers for the worship of deceased local celebrities, or deserving officials, are also sometimes found either within the temple precincts or immediately outside. The Wên-ch'ang-kung, moreover, or Hall of the God of Literature, is now often found close beside the Temple of Confucius.

"RECOLLECTIONS OF THE TOILS OF LEARNING"

The above descriptions of temples devoted to "The First Teacher" could equally well have been placed in Chapter 5, for the rituals that take place there are state rituals and rituals oriented toward the patron spirits of the civil service system. But these temples were initially created as an alternative to the Taoist temples mentioned in the preceding chapter and to the Buddhist monasteries to be discussed in the following chapter. They had multiple functions. Aside from the rituals carried out there, they often had classrooms for the literati-oriented education, and they served as a clubhouse for the elite, those who had passed at least the first of the three civil service examinations, especially retired officials or those without a government position. It is in these temples, that the civil servants could immerse themselves in a religious milieu oriented toward their own ideology, spirits, and symbols.

There are few studies of the religious dimension of *ju-chia* (the Confucian tradition). Rodney Taylor has pointed to enlightenment experiences within this tradition, never, of course, separate from the other modes of "ultimate transformation." The following autobiography by Kao P'an-lung is from Taylor's *The Religious Dimensions of Confucianism* (Albany: State University of New York Press, 1990), pp. 60–64.

KAO P'AN-LUNG'S K'UN-HSÜEH CHI (RECOLLECTIONS OF THE TOILS OF LEARNING)

At age twenty-five, when I heard Magistrate Li Yüan-ch'ung and Ku Ching-yang discuss learning, I resolved to pursue the quest of sagehood. I considered that there must be a way of becoming a sage, though I was yet unacquainted with the methods. I had read the *Ta-hsüeh huo-wen* and observed that Master Chu said there is nothing to equal reverent seriousness for entering the Way. Therefore, I exerted all my effort toward respecting and concentrating on it, keeping the mind to a square inch of space in my chest. I was aware, however, only of the oppression of my vital forces and restraint upon myself. It was decidedly unsatisfactory to me and so, subsequently, I dropped it, drifting again as before. I could find no remedy.

After quite a length of time I suddenly remembered that Master Ch'eng had said: "The mind must be retained within the bodily frame." I did not know [however], what the bodily frame referred to. Was it really in a square inch of space or not? I searched for an explanation without success, then quite by chance I found it explained in the *Hsiao-hsüeh* in the following manner, "The bodily frame is simply like speaking of the body." I was very happy for the mind was not just a square inch of space, but the entire body was the mind. For a time my life was relaxed and contented. Then Lo Chih-an of Chiang-yu [Kiangsi] came and spoke of Li Chien-lo's self-cultivation as the foundation of learning. It was in line with what I took to be my own guide. I was increasingly happy, having no doubts. During this period, I spent all my effort working on "knowing the root." This caused both body and mind to progress together and word and deed to be without error. After passing the examination of the *Chi-ch'ou* year of *Wan-li* [1589] I was even more aware that these ideas were progressing. When [I found myself] in mourning [I] studied the *[Book] of Rites* and the *[Book] of Changes*.

It was in the *Jen-ch'en* year of *Wan-li* [1592], that I presented myself for appointment as a successful candidate. Since in my daily life the sense of shame was very great, when I received my appointment I took an oath to myself saying, "I have not yet perceived anything of the Way. I shall simply act upon my solitary knowledge. Right and wrong, good and bad: that which follows without [my having] acted, that comes from Heaven." In examining [my life], I found it very near to this. With a little insight into the mind, I vainly thought that whenever I saw what was righteous I would do it.

In the winter I traveled to the Chao-t'ien Temple to practice the rules of ceremony. While quiet-sitting in a monastery seeking for the original substance, I suddenly thought of the sentence, "He does away with what is false and preserves his integrity. I felt that in the immediate response [of the nature] there was nothing false, but that all was sincere and I had no further need for seeking sincerity. In that moment I felt rapturous, as if all fetters were cast off.

In the *Kuei-ssu* year of *Wan-li* [1593], I was banished because I had spoken out on certain affairs. It did not, however, disturb my thoughts. After my return [home] I tasted the ways of the world and my mind became once more agitated. In the *Chia-wu* year of *Wan-li* [1594] during the autumn I headed for Chieh-yang [Kwangtung]. I realized that within myself principle and desire waged battle without peaceful resolution. In Wu-lin [Chekiang] I talked for several days with Lu Ku-ch'iao and Wu Tzu-wang. One day Ku-ch'iao suddenly asked, "What is the original substance like?" What I said was vague though I answered by saying: "Without sound or smell." However this came only from my mouth and ears, not from a true understanding.

The night before I crossed over the river the moonlight was pure and clear. I sat beside the Liu-ho Tower. The river and the mountains were clear and inviting. Good friends urged me to drink more. In this most agreeable of times I suddenly felt unhappy, as if something were constraining me. I exerted myself to rouse my joy, but my spirit did not accompany me. Late in the night when the others had gone I went on board the boat and in a sudden realization said to myself: "How is it that today the scenery was as it was and yet my feelings were like this?" Making a thorough investigation, I realized that being totally ignorant of the Way, my mind and body had nothing on which to draw. Thus, I strongly affirmed: "If I don't penetrate it on this trip, then my life will have been in vain."

The next day in the boat I earnestly arranged the mat and seriously established rules and regulations. For one half of the day I practiced quiet-sitting while for the other half I engaged in study. During quiet-sitting, whenever I felt ill at ease, I would just follow the instructions of Ch'eng [I] and Chu [Hsi], taking up in turn: With sincerity and reverent seriousness consider quietude as fundamental; observe happiness, anger, sorrow, and joy before they arise; sit in silence and purify the mind; realize for oneself the Principle of Heaven. Whether I was standing, sitting, eating, or resting, these thoughts were continuously present. At night I did not undress, and only when I was weary to the bone did I fall asleep. Upon waking I returned to sitting, repeating and alternating these various methods of practice. When the substance of the mind was clear and peaceful there was a sense of filling all Heaven and earth, but it did not last.

The duration of the journey was two months and fortunately there were no normal involvements. The mountains and waters were clear and beautiful; my servant and I supported each other. It was very quiet. One evening I ordered a bit of wine. We stopped the boat before a green mountain and drifted to and from beside a jade green mountain stream. I sat on a large rock for a time. The sound of the stream, the harmonies of the birds, flourishing trees and tall bamboo, all these things pleased my mind and yet it remained unattached.

I passed by T'ing-chou [Fukien] and traveled on by land until I reached an inn. The inn had a small tower; to the front were mountains, to the rear a nearby rushing stream. I climbed the tower and was very much at ease. In my hand, I held a book of the two Ch'eng brothers. Quite by chance I saw a saying by [Ch'eng] Ming-tao, "In the midst of the ten-thousand affairs and the hundred-thousand weapons 'joy still exists though water is my drink and a bent arm[my pillow]. The myriad changes all exist within the person; in reality there is not a single thing." Suddenly I realized this and said, "It really is like this, in reality there is not a single thing!" With this single thought, all entanglements were broken. Suddenly, it was as if a load of a hundred pounds had fallen to the ground in an instant. It was as if a flash of lightening had penetrated the body and pierced the intelligence. Subsequently, I was merged with the Great Transformation until there was no differentiation between Heaven and humanity, exterior and interior. At this point I saw that the six points were all my mind, "frame of the body" was their field and "square inch of space" was their original seat. In terms of their spiritual and luminous character, no location could actually be spoken of. I ordinarily despised scholars who discussed enlightenment with grand display, but now I could see that it was something quite natural and realized that from now on it was suitable to apply my own efforts to this end.

In the spring of the *I-wei* year of *Wan-li* [1595], as I was returning from Chieh-yang [Kwangtung], I took up [the writings] of both Buddhists and Taoists to read them. The differences between the Buddhists and the [Confucian] Sages are very subtle. As for the points in which [the Buddhists] speak so well, Confucian teachings already have them all: they do not go beyond [the concept] expressed in the two words *wu-chi* [Ultimate of Nonbeing].As for their defects, these have already been discussed by earlier Confucians and can be summed up in the words *wu-li* [having no principle]. Having studied the two [heterodox] schools, I appreciated all the more how worthy of respect were the teachings of the [Confucian] Sages.

If the Way of the Sages did not exist, human life could not be sustained. Even the followers of these two schools depend on this Way for food, drink, and clothing without being conscious of the fact.

In the *Wu-hsü* year of *Wan-li* [1958], I built the Water Dwelling with the intention of practicing quiet-sitting and engaging in study there. After the *Ping-shen* year of *Wan-li* [1956] I had lost my parents, moved about, and saw my children getting married. Those years allowed me no peace. In the midst of these activities, I tried to continue my practice of discipline but was only too well aware of the difficulties of transforming one's physical nature.

In the *Chia-ch'en* year of *Wan-li* [1604], the Teacher Ku Ching-yang first established the Tung-lin Academy. I was able to benefit from discussions with my friends. As I came to realize, I could do nothing without making the effort to concentrate on quietude. The maladies of each person are different. The Sages and the Worthies must have great spiritual capacity to enable them to master quietude in their ordinary daily lives. For the scholar whose spirit is deficient and whose physical nature is unstable several tens of years of effort are needed before quietude can be deeply established. The chief defect lies in one's youth, when one is without the benefit of a [proper] education in basic things. Gradually one becomes used to worldly habits that are difficult to root out. One should bury one's head in study, allow the principle of righteousness to flow everywhere, transforming his own worldly flesh and bone. By purifying the spirit and sitting in stillness, one can cause worldly delusions to disperse. It is then possible to strengthen the right mind and the right spirit. With my own inferior endowment, what use could any expansive insight be in the absence of such exertion? Fortunately, ever since I have come into my own, I can take up a plan [to improve myself] and find the "original state" there.

In the *Pin-wu* year of *Wan-li* [1606], I came to truly believe in the principle of Mencius that human nature is good. This nature is neither old nor new, neither sagely nor common, for Heaven, earth, and humanity are one. Only with the highest grade of [nature], pure and clear and with no obscuration, can one begin to believe. The next grade is entirely dependent upon the effort of learning. If a single speck of dust intervenes, it might as well be ten thousand *li*. This is why Mencius spoke of a medicine that causes a reaction.

In the *Ting-wei* year of *Wan-li* [1607], I came to truly believe in [the principle of] Master Ch'eng, "The hawk flies and fish swim" and also the [idea of Mencius], "You must work at it." That which is called nature is entirely spontaneous, not from the effort of man. "A hawk flies and fish swim," who caused this to be? "Do not forget it, but also do not assist it. This is an admonition to students. But in the case of the true primary substance that unceasingly flows and spreads in the past and the present, with no movement or rest, where can it be forgotten or assisted? Therefore, "one must work at it." Consider, for example, plants and trees. The roots, sprouts, flowers, and fruit change and transform of their own, yet they are cared for, watered, and fostered. If in the hard work of learning, one leaves everything to the natural, nothing will get done, no change or transformation will be accomplished and there will not even be anything natural.

In the *Hsin-hai* year of *Wan-li* [1611], I came to truly believe in the *Great Learning* and its principle of "knowing the root." This is fully recorded in another work. In the *Jen-tzu* year of *Wan-li* [1612], I came to truly believe the principle of the *Doctrine of the Mean*. Most surely words cannot describe this Way. Master Ch'eng called it the Principle of Heaven, [Wang] Yang-ming called it innate knowledge. Neither, however, equals the two words *centrality* and *normality*. *Centrality* is what is appropriate and fitting; *normality* is what is ordinary and dependable. If even a slight transgression takes place nothing will be suitable or fitting. If there is only a slight amount of artifice or contrivance, it will not be ordinary or dependable. It is this way with the substance and it is this way with moral effort.

The Sage cannot fathom the limits of Heaven and earth. How much less people like us? How can there be a limit [to our efforts]? We should honor human relations, speak with care, act diligently and be cautious unceasingly until the day of our death. In the toils of study, the years mount up and the months accumulate with only more difficulties. And still there is nothing sufficient to bring a smile to the face of a wise man. For those who are deficient like me, they may find something useful in my account.

Recorded in the *Chia-yin* year of *Wan-li* [1614].

CHAPTER 8

Three Ways of Ultimate Transformation: (3) Buddhist Tradition

BUDDHISM BECOMES CHINESE

As the only foreign religion that ever—at least until the twentieth century—became truly assimilated into the Chinese civilization, Buddhism has a special interest. In order for assimilation to take place, Buddhism had to undergo a process of Sinicization, which resulted in a religion that was quite different from the Indian original. At the same time, it not only yielded to certain Chinese cultural imperatives, but it spread into that culture and colored it. We see the two processes at work most clearly in the early centuries, between Han and T'ang (roughly C.E. 250 to C.E. 600), a period when China was divided between numerous ephemeral states, "barbarian" (i.e., non-Chinese) in the north, and Chinese in the south; when the sway of Confucian orthodoxy was tenuous at best, because the Confucian State had disintegrated; when conditions encouraged escapism of all sorts in thought and behavior; when both "philosophical" and "religious" Taoism were popular. The selection that follows brings out the most salient features of this crucial period of Buddhism's penetration into Chinese culture.

The Conflict of Buddhism with Native Chinese Ideologies by Richard Mather first appeared in the *Review of Religion, XX* (1955–56), pp. 25–37.

Introduction

In the West the notion of conflict is well defined and can be documented from both our political and religious history. The notion can be traced in part, I believe, to a generally assumed world view inherited from the Hebrew-Christian tradition, which, stated in its barest terms, sees the created world set over against a transcendent Creator, and man, who was made in the Creator's image, set in a triple relation of confrontation: (1) to God, in which his reaction is, more often than not, one of anxious rebellion, (2) to nature, against which he is pitted in a life-and-death struggle for mastery, and (3) to other men, among whom his relation is often that of a competitor.

In China conflict is certainly not unknown, but it is less well defined, and, in using the term to describe Buddhism's relation to native ideologies, we should be warned at the start that it is not quite comparable with the conflict, let us say, between the early Christian community and the Roman emperors, in which context the slogan was born that "the blood of the martyrs is the seed of the Church." None of the Chinese religions has, to my knowledge, produced any extensive martyrology, and this illuminates in a striking way their different notion of conflict. If, as their world view describes it, Ultimate Reality is completely contained within the framework of the self-created, self-sustaining natural-social order, with its immanent principle of operation, the Tao, then all conflicts appearing on the periphery, since they cannot originate outside the order of Reality, will, if followed back to the Source or Center, be found to be in harmony.

Most Chinese Buddhists, therefore, clung to the traditional harmonious world view. They saw no real conflict of the new religion with China's best traditions. On the contrary, it represented for them a needed complement, offering a penetrating and consoling analysis of neglected problems like suffering and death, and affording a metaphysical basis for morality without altering accepted standards. A vast number of non-Buddhists as well were willing to accept the new religion as a colorful variation on a familiar theme—the cultivation of goodness.

A few discerning critics, however, saw in the Indian doctrine of Nirvāna a complete negation of the Chinese world view itself, for which no harmonious integration within the system was possible. Nirvāna, the sole Buddhist Reality, lay outside the Chinese order of reality altogether. The empirical world and its inner principle, which the Chinese assumed to be all of Reality, was, according to Indian Buddhism, sheer illusion. Reactions of the critics, therefore, were mostly of two sorts: (1) during the first three or four centuries of our era, while the Buddhist community was predominantly foreign, they ignored it as a mere barbarism which would eventually yield to the civilizing influence of Chinese culture: (2) especially after about A.D. 400, when Chinese Buddhists were a conspicuous segment of the population and even gentry families and members of the imperial household were being attracted to its support, they attempted belatedly to suppress it root and branch. This may seem odd in a system built on harmonious compromise, until we realize that it was precisely because the critics saw this delicately balanced system, which for them was the system of the universe itself, being turned upside down, the catastrophic omens of which were everywhere apparent, that they reacted in alarm.

Though particular criticism arose over many separate issues, the underlying complaint was invariably the same: the adherence of Buddhist monks and nuns to an other-worldly ideal, which caused them to repudiate the actual world with its obligations and to practice principles contrary to nature, was a dangerous threat not only to society and the state, but to the harmony of the universe as well. For every issue raised, however, the Buddhist had a ready answer: Truth is one, but the traditional Chinese view of it is too circumscribed. In the words of the popular *Vimalakīrtī Sūtra*, "The Buddha preachers with one voice, but all beings understand according to their several capacities."[1] Confucius, according to one apologist, accommodated his teaching to a crassly materialistic society and hence addressed himself only to "salvaging abuses in their final stages," while the Buddha "illumined their root causes."[2] Lao-tzu, wrote another, confined his teaching to the "fulfilment of life," while the Buddha "illumined the ideal" beyond the

---

[1] *Taishō* 475 (vol. 14) 538a: quoted by Tao-an (*Kuang hung ming chi* 8.25b) and others.

[2] Sun Ch'o, in *Hung ming chi* (hereafter abbreviated *HMC*) 3.17b.

relativities of life.[3] Thus they felt Buddhism did not contradict any of China's sages. It merely went deeper than they dared to go.

Beginning with the basic conflict in world view, I shall briefly trace the controversy as it centered about particular issues.

Metaphysical Issues

Interestingly enough, the earlier critics of Buddhism, while recognizing in concrete situations conflicts with their own ideology, rarely discussed the underlying metaphysical conflict. The first clear expression of it which I have discovered is by the Neo-Confucianist, Chang Tsai (1020–1077), in his "Western Inscription." "As for those who speak about Nirvāna," he wrote, "they mean by this a *departure* (from the universe) which leads to no return," while the Confucian sage is "one who completely understands the course that lies *within* (the cosmic cycle), who embodies it in himself . . . and who to the highest degree preserves its spirituality."[4] Though Chang Tsai would have quickly rejected the thought, his view of the sage "embodying" the Tao and "preserving its spirituality" was very close to the concept of the monk's relation to Nirvāna held by Chinese Buddhists themselves, and may have owed something to it. Hui-yüan (334–416), the founder of the Pure Land Sect, expressed this relation as the "embodiment of the Ultimate" (*t'i chi*). The Ultimate, or Nirvāna, however world-denying or transcendent it may have been to Indian Buddhists, is clearly identified in Hui-yüan's mind with the immanent principle of the universe, the Tao.[5] Embodying the Ultimate in the world of relativity, the monk is able to transcend mortality and shower benefits on the world. What could be more sagelike than this?

Discussions of the immanence or transcendence of Nirvāna probably made scant impression on the average unlettered Chinese who embraced Buddhism in the early days, but one thing appealed to him mightily, namely, life after death—rebirth in the jeweled splendors of the Western Paradise of the faithful, and amid the unintermittent tortures of Avīcī Hell for the violent and oppressive. All schools of Indian Buddhism denied the survival of a personal entity or "soul" from one incarnation to the next. Only one component of the pseudo-personality survived, namely consciousness, *vijñāna* (Chinese *shih*). Chinese Buddhists, on the other hand, linked this surviving consciousness to the native concept of the departed spirit, or *shèn*, calling it the "conscious spirit" (*shih-shèn*), or "spirit-consciousness" (*shèn-shih*), and from it developed a purely indigenous doctrine of immortality.[6] It was not surprising, however, that Confucian and Taoist intellectuals should view this new departure with disfavor, since the calm acceptance of one's fated span was a measure of one's adjustment to the cosmic cycle. Even Taoist efforts at prolonging the span consisted primarily of a more thorough adjustment to the cycle. Personal survival after death would upset the balance of the universe quite as much as the survival of summer weather into winter.

---

[3]Ming Seng-shao, *HMC* 6.14a.

[4]Fung Yu-lan, *History of Chinese Philosophy* (Princeton, 1953), II.497 (italics mine.)

[5]*HMC* 5.12b–15b; cf. Liebenthal, "Shih Hui-yüan's Buddhism as set forth in his Writings," *JAOS* 70 (1950), 247, 258.

[6]See Bodde, "The Chinese View of Immortality," *Review of Religion* 6 (1942), 371ff.; also Liebenthal, *op. cit.*, p. 252.

The controversy, already alive in the second century,[7] reached its most articulate stage over the publication in the southern capital of Fan Chen's essay on "The Destruction of the Soul (at Death)," *Shèn mièh lùn*, toward the close of the fifth century, to which literally scores of rebuttals were composed, one by the Emperor Liang Wu-ti himself.[8] Recognizing this doctrine as Buddhism's most powerful appeal in China, Fan Chen concentrated his attack on it, marshalling simple logic and homely analogy to demonstrate that the soul is an inseparable function of the body, and that both belong to the natural cycle. "When we come," he wrote, "it is not because we cause it to come, and when we go it is not because we drive it away. We but ride on the principle of Heaven."[9]

Buddhist apologists for the doctrine insisted on the separate and eternal existence of the soul. They discovered dim intimations of immortality in China's own custom of recalling the departed spirit,[10] and in the writings of Lao-tzǔ and Chuang-tzǔ.[11] Far from accepting the charge that they were upsetting the traditionally calm acquiescence to fate, they claimed their approach to the Great Change was even less perturbed than the traditional one. The anonymous author of the "Rectification of False Charges," *Chèng wū lùn*, describes the Buddhist attitude as one of fearless repose in the midst of calamity. Quoting the *Book of Changes* he wrote, " 'Rejoicing in heaven (the Buddhist) knows his fate,' content with the times he dwells in resignation, and that is all." But the others, on the contrary, mourn death and dread its finality, thereby merely aggravating their perturbation over it.[12]

Social Issues

Almost from the beginnings of Chinese monasticism objections were leveled against its obvious upsetting of the family system. Mou-tzǔ's questioner in the late second century raised the issues of abandoning the care of parents and family, disfiguring (by shaving and burning) the body bequeathed whole by one's parents, cutting off the family line, and giving away the family patrimony. Mou-tzǔ's reply was that "if there is a great good (to be gained), one does not hesitate at small (obstacles)." This was for him merely an application of the Confucian principle of "doing what is appropriate to the moment" (*shíh i*).[13]

Later apologists quoted the *Classic of Filial Piety* itself to the effect that the highest form of filial devotion was to achieve the happiness of one's parents and to bring glory to the family name by establishing oneself.[14] Only a slight extension of meaning was required to interpret this as acquiring religious merit for oneself

[7]See Mou-tzu (*HMC* 1.8b–9a): Pelliot, "Meou-tseu ou les doutes levés," *TP* 19 (1920), 301f.

[8]Fan Chen's treatise is found in *Nan shih* 57.20ab, and *Liang shu* 48.5b–10a; most of the rebuttals are in *HMC* 9 and 10. It has been translated by Balasz in *Sinica* 7 (1932), 220–34, and in part by Ch'en in *HJAS* 15 (1952). See note 11 below.

[9]Fung, *op. cit.*, II.291f.

[10]Mou-tzu, *HMC* 1.8b; Pelliot, *op. cit.*, pp. 301f.

[11]See Ch'en, "Anti-Buddhist Propaganda during the Nan-ch'ao," *HJAS* 15 (1952), 174, and Liebenthal, *op. cit.*, pp. 251f.

[12]*HMC* 1.29b; *Chou I* 7-3a (Legge, *SBE* 16.354).

[13]*HMC* 1.7a. The reference seems to be to the *Doctrine of the Mean* 25 (Legge 1.419). See Pelliot, *op. cit.*, p. 298.

[14]*Hsiao ching* 1 (Legge, *SBE* 3.466). The passage was quoted by An-ling-shou to her father (Wright, *HJAS* 15.195) and by Sun Ch'o (*HMC* 3.18a), both of the fourth century.

and one's family. One writer affirmed, moreover, that of the twelve divisions of
the Buddhist canon, the fourth is concerned solely with encouraging filial piety.
"Its solicitude may be said to be unsurpassed," he wrote, "yet the irreligious,
without having investigated the sources or having had any experience (of what
they are talking about), proceed with blind assertions and false statements to
make attacks and raise objections."[15]

While we may regard this as a somewhat sanguine view of the filial solicitude
of the Buddhist scriptures, it is true that both Indian and Chinese texts on monastic discipline mention a requirement of parental consent before young men or
women may be ordained.[16] Legislation in the Toba domain even provided for
monks and nuns to observe mourning rites for their parents.[17] Devout families, of
course, were not averse to offering their sons and daughters to the Church, and in
times of distress, as at the close of the first quarter of the sixth century in the north,
many did so to ease the strain at home and to evade forced labor and the draft.[18]

Economic Issues

The sight of large numbers of able-bodied men and women flocking from their
farms and mulberry groves to the monasteries and convents, the deeding of large
tracts of arable land to tax-free temples, and the investment of huge sums in
bronze images and pagodas could hardly be expected to arouse the enthusiasm
of officials charged with tax-collection and recruitment. Before the fifth century,
when the monastic establishments were comparatively modest, not many overt
attacks were made. But by 405, when Kumārajīva became State Preceptor in the
later Ch'in state, it was estimated by one writer that in the heavily non-Chinese
northwest nine-tenths of the population were Buddhist.[19] And after the early
Toba rulers adopted the foreign religion as a sort of state cult, appointing a Chief
Monk and constructing an official temple at the capital in 398,[20] the rapid expansion of the Church in the north threatened to get out of hand. Urged on by
the Taoist minister, Ts'ui Hao (d. 450), the Toba Emperor, T'ai-wu-ti, published
his repressive edicts of 444 and 446, which were directed not only against the
clergy but against their lay supporters as well. The immediate occasion for the
first edict was the discovery of arms and supplies in a certain monastery near
Ch'ang-an, in the territory of a local chieftain then in revolt against Toba rule,[21]
and the issue of the economic and political role of monasteries was dramatically
raised. Though the edict of 446 called for the virtual annihilation of Buddhist
property and personnel, the intervention of a sympathetic prince, and the will-
ingness of local officials, many of whom doubtless had investments in monastery
property, to turn their backs, enabled most of the monks to return safely to lay

---

[15]*HMC* 3.18a.

[16]*Mahāvagga* 1.55 (Oldenberg, *Vinaya Texts, SBE* 1.210); *Szu fen lü tsang* 34 (*Taishō* 22.810a,
cited in Wright, *ibid.*).

[17]Ware, "Wei Shou on Buddhism," *TP* 33 (1930), 158.

[18]*Ibid.* 178 f.

[19]*Chin shu* 117, 10 b; *Tzu-chih t'ung chien* 114, 1 b.

[20]Eberhard, *Das Toba-reich Nordchinas* (Leiden, 1949), p. 229.

[21]Ware, *op. cit.*, p. 139.

life, while some, like T'an Yao, continued to practice their religion in secret.[22] The proscription was short-lived and was followed by further official patronage.

But the economic loss involved in the dislocation of the normal division of labor, with its primary stress on agriculture, continued, at least until the ninth century, to be a conspicuous source of irritation. Fu I (555–639), in his memorial to T'ang Kao-tsu in 624, recommended that the estimated 100,000 monks and nuns of his day be made to marry and produce sons for the army and silk and food for the empire.[23] When we read that in the devastating proscription under T'ang Wu-tsung in 845, in which 4600 larger and 40,000 smaller monasteries were ordered demolished, 260,500 monks and nuns secularized, 150,000 temple slaves and thousands of acres of temple land redistributed among tax-paying families, tens of thousands of catties in bronze images and bells melted down for coinage, iron images recast into agricultural implements, and gold and silver ornaments returned to the state coffers, we can gain some impression of the sheer material wealth tied up in the Church at that time.[24] After 845 reprisals against the Church were mostly in the form of quota limitation rather than attempted extirpation.[25] The temporal power of the Church had been permanently broken.

I have mentioned the implications of the discovery by the Toba Emperor, T'ai-wu-ti, of a stockpile of bows and arrows and other goods in a Ch'ang-an monastery. While the smaller Buddhist sects shared with their Taoist counterparts a history of guilt by association with rebellion,[26] there was a deeper underlying mistrust of the principle of monasticism itself, with its extraterritorial immunity from Chinese law.[27] The origin of this immunity was undoubtedly the predominantly foreign constituency of the earlier religious communities, but as more and more Chinese joined the Order the problem became more acute.

Controversy began in the south during the reigns of the Eastern Chin Emperors, Ch'eng-ti and K'ang-ti (326–345), when Yü Ping (d. 344) raised the question of *lèse-majesté* over the failure of Buddhist monks to kowtow in the presence of the Emperor. At that time the pro-Buddhist minister, Ho Ch'ung (d. 346), defended the monks on the ground that they should not be forced for the sake of outward ceremonial to compromise their method of cultivating inward goodness, a method which involved severing all wordly ties.[28] Later, in the year 402, the usurper, Huan Hsüan, anxious to buttress his authority, took up the argument with the significant observation that honors paid to the emblems of royalty were by no means an empty gesture, since the ability to "comprehend life and regulate objects" resides in the ruler, and in the role of life-giver he is the embodiment of Heaven and Earth. How could the monks accept his life-giving favors and neglect the honor due to him?[29] Huan Hsüan observed further that in the old

---

[22]*Ibid.*, p. 143.

[23]A. F. Wright, "Fu I and the Rejection of Buddhism," *Journal of the History of Ideas* 12 (1951), 41.

[24]J. J. M. de Groot, *Sectarianism and Religious Persecution in China* (Amsterdam, 1903), pp. 36–40.

[25]E. g., the measures of the first Ming Emperor, *ibid.*, 81f.

[26]E. g., the popular messianic Maitreya Cult in the north during the fifth and sixth centuries, see Eberhard, *History of China* (Berkeley, 1950), p. 156.

[27]Ware, *op. cit.*, p. 158.

[28]HMC 12.112–142.

days the first foreign devotees of Buddhism were permitted to observe their barbaric customs unmolested, but, now that Chinese emperors themselves were believers, they should make Chinese custom standard for all.[30]

It was primarily in answer to Huan Hsüan that Hüi-yuan wrote his treatise, "Why a Śramana does not do Obeisance to Kings," *Shā-mèn pú chìng wáng che lùn*.[31] In it he marks a dualism between the Taoist principle of "conforming to transformations (both of nature and of the sovereign)," *shùn-huà*, and the Buddhist principle of "seeking the Ideal (beyond all transformation)," *ch'iù-tsūng*. The Buddhist layman takes the first course,[32] the monk the latter.[33] But in doing so his nonconformity is not disloyalty; he merely transcends the dualism. For the Ideal he seeks is Ultimate Reality itself (Nirvāna or Tao). During his quest he deviates from accepted patterns which involve him with other beings in endless rebirth and suffering. At the end of his quest he "embodies the Ultimate" (*tǐ–chi*), and is in a better position than kings to bestow favors on other beings. Heaven and Earth can give life, and kings can preserve it, but neither of these can grant immortality or freedom from suffering. The śramana, however, can do both. Therefore he treats kings and commoners with equal compassion and equal ceremony.[34]

Needless to say, this type of argument was lost on many hearers who saw in it a confirmation of their worst suspicions, namely, that the monks were a group of "super-emperors" offering the inducements of heaven and the restraints of hell in full usurpation of the emperor's prerogatives as sole rewarder and punisher. Fu I, in the memorial to T'ang Kao-tsu referred to above, reminded his emperor of a passage in the *Book of Documents* that states, "The sovereign alone creates blessings and intimidations . . . and if his subjects (do the same) . . . they damage his house and bring misfortune on his kingdom."[35] He even hinted darkly that through their connections at court the clergy threatened to seize political control from the gentry.[36] In actuality, however, the struggle seems not to have been altogether one of gentry versus clergy, or Chinese versus foreigners, but the lines were drawn between factions among the gentry themselves, some of whom favored, and some of whom feared the Church.[37]

In the Toba state the monks got neatly around the loyalty issue by declaring the emperor to be an incarnation of Maitreya and publicly venerating him as such.[38]

---

[29]*Ibid.*, 14b–15a.

[30]*Ibid.*, 17b–18a.

[31]*HMC* 5-9b–19a.

[32]*Ibid.*, 10b–11b.

[33]*Ibid.*, 11b–12b.

[34]*Ibid.*, 12b–15b.

[35]*Shang-shu* 7.4b (Legge, *SBE* 3.144); de Groot, *op. cit.*, 38; Wright, "Fu I," p. 41. Fu I's argument had been anticipated a century earlier by Hsün Chi, of the Liang Dynasty, who had written "the most powerful and scathing attack leveled against Buddhism up to this time" (Ch'en, *op. cit.*, p. 191).

[36]See Wright, *op. cit.*, p. 42, and de Groot, *op. cit.*, pp. 40f.

[37]Eberhard, *Toba-reich,* p. 239.

[38]Ware, *op. cit.*, p. 129; Eberhard, *op. cit.*, p. 229.

Cultural and Moral Issues

After the proscription of 845, the sphere in which Buddhist influence was prin-cipally felt was in the culture and mores of ordinary people, among whom it had by now become permanently acclimated, with its impressive artistic monuments, its colorful temple ceremonies and festivals, its masses for the dead, and its con-tributions to folklore and mythology.

From the very beginning the process of acculturation was upsetting to China's intellectuals. Since, until very recent times, China has never exhibited the kind of xenophobia with which we are familiar in the West, the almost chauvin-istic contempt for "barbarian" culture characterizing nearly all critiques of Bud-dhism in China seems paradoxical enough. But it was precisely because the Chinese intellectuals did not champion a nationalistic culture, but insisted instead on maintaining a *universal* one, that divergent practices were rejected, not so much on the grounds that they were Indian or Parthian or Kuchean, as that they rep-resented *no* culture. If the foreign missionaries had accepted this universal cul-ture and lived by its principles, no objections would have been raised. The cultured man (and he is inseparable from the moral man) is one who accepts the pattern of the universe, as it has been perceived and transmitted by sage kings and emperors, and cultivates it within himself. Among other things, this involves developing a proper balance between the physical, mental, and emotional forces of human nature.

Now the Buddhists were making men and women act contrary to their na-ture by living as celibates, and by mutilation and even self-immolation,[39] and were thereby upsetting the universal pattern. It was not simply a matter of cul-tural inferiority, but of cultural nihilism. The argument had appeared already in Mou-tzu, where it was countered by the extraordinary observation that even one of China's own commentators had acknowledged that the pole star is in the mid-dle of the heavens but to the *north* of China, which proves that China is not in the middle of the world. Those, therefore, who honor Buddha are not necessarily moving off center, nor is the gold of India necessarily incompatible with the jade of China.[40]

China's cultural Great Wall, erected over centuries of relative isolation from other major cultures, was not, however, to be breached in a day. During the fourth century, and intermittently on down to the thirteenth, controversy raged between Taoists and Buddhists over the tract, "The Conversion of the Barbarians," *Huà-hú-ching*, which had claimed that Lao-tzu, in his mission to the king of Kashmir, adapted his teaching to people completely lacking in the amenities of life, and hence the doctrine which he developed there (later known as Buddhism) was totally neg-ative. It could not in any sense apply to those who had benefited from the influ-ences of culture. In 467 another Taoist, Ku Huan (390-ca. 483), added fuel to the fire

---

[39]Cf. the case of the monk Hui-i, who drenched himself with oil and burned to death in a public square in Nanking in 463 reciting the story of Bhaisajya-rāja from the *Lotus Sūtra* (Goodrich, *A Short History of the Chinese People,* New York, 1951) p. 106; Hu Shih, "Buddhistic In-fluence on Chinese Religious Life," *Chin. Soc. and Pol. Sci. Rev.* 9, 1925, 148f. It was this aspect of Buddhism which provoked the sharpest attack from Han Yü in his famous memorial to T'ang Hsien-ti in 819 (translated in Giles *Gems of Chinese Literature: Prose,* London, 1926, 127).

[40]*HMC* 1.10ab; Pelliot, *op. cit.,* pp. 303f.

with his "Treatise on Barbarians and Chinese," *I-hsià-lùn*,[41] in which he stated: "Buddhism and Taoism may be equal in aiming at conversion, but there is a difference between the methods of barbarians and Chinese ... Buddhism is a means of destroying evil; Taoism is a device to develop goodness. ..."[42] The implication is unmistakable that one religion is suitable for boors and the other for the cultured.

It is to the credit of the apologists for Buddhism that they were able to extricate themselves from the cultural isolation in which their opponents stood all unaware. In doing so they represented one of the most salutary contributions Buddhism ever made to Chinese culture.

> To Ku Huan's charge, Chu Chao replied: "I beg to inquire, the cruelty of branding (criminals)—is this a Sogdian or Indian form of punishment? The pain of shedding blood—was it not begotten in the (Chinese states of) Ch'i and Chin? The atrocity of ripping up (pregnant women)—did this idea originate with those who button the lapel on the left? ... If we probe their nature and sentiments, Chinese and barbarians are one and the same. I resent the false assumption that the one is civilized and the other boorish."[43]

On the positive side, many of the Buddhist clergy, especially in the south during the period of division (317–589), came from the educated classes and were prominent figures among the intellectual elite at the capital and at K'uai-chi in modern Chekiang.[44] The Buddhist historians Seng-yu (d. 518) and Hui-chiao (d. 554) were at great pains to demonstrate the intellectual respectability of the Buddhist religion and its adaptability to the Chinese scene.[45]

Conclusion

In describing here the *conflict* which Buddhism encountered with China's native ideologies I hope not in any sense to have distorted the normal view of the essential unity of the "Three Religions" held nearly universally in all periods by the educated and illiterate alike in China. While certain vocal critics deplored what they considered the wholesale abandonment of the traditional view of a real, self-contained, and basically good universe, with social, economic, and political responsibilities built into the nature of things, they remained a minority, and their counsels were only sporadically, though sometimes devastatingly, applied against the foreign cult.

What was probably a majority view among non-Buddhist intellectuals was expressed by Liu Tsung-yüan (773–819), who, though a close friend of the implacable foe of Buddhism, Han Yü, did not share the latter's views on the subject. He wrote:

> There is much in Buddhism which could not well be denounced; namely, all those tenets which are based on principles common to our own sacred books. It is pre-

---

[41]Largely preserved in rebuttals (see *HMC* 6 and 7).

[42]Ch'en, *op. cit.*, pp. 170f.

[43]*HMC* 7-5a.

[44]See Wright, "Biography and Hagiography, Hui-chiao's Lives of Eminent Monks," *Silver Jubilee Volume, Zinbun-kagaku-kenkyūsyo*, Kyōto University, 1954, p. 397.

[45]*Ibid.*, p. 392.

cisely to these essentials, at once in perfect harmony with human nature and the teachings of Confucius, that I give my adhesion. . . . Now Han Yü objects to the commandments. He objects to the bald pates of the priests, their dark robes, their renunciation of domestic ties, their idleness, and life generally at the expense of others. So do I. But Han Yü misses the kernel while railing at the husk. He sees the lode but not the ore. I see both; hence my partiality for the faith.

Again, intercourse with men of this religion does not necessarily imply conversion. Even if it did, Buddhism admits no rivalry for place or power. The majority of its adherents love only to lead a simple life of contemplation amid the charms of hill and stream. And when I turn my gaze towards the hurry-scurry of the age, in its daily race for the seals and tassels of office, I ask myself if I am to reject those in order to take my place among the ranks of these. . . .[46]

For Liu Tsung-yüan and scores of other officials similarly caught in the net of political intrigue,[47] this sentiment was expressed out of a burning personal conviction hardly to be matched by any conventional allegiance to Confucian orthodoxy.

BUDDHISM IN T'ANG CHINA

The fortunes of Buddhism are generally conceded to have reached their limits in the China of the T'ang dynasty (618–907). At the same time, in accordance with the ancient Chinese insight that the very height of *yang's* expansion means the beginning of its displacement by *yin,* it was during the mid-ninth century that the great suppression of Buddhism occurred that was to mean the end of its spiritual and temporal predominance. A glimpse of Buddhism in the mid-ninth century will therefore give us some conception both of the glory of the institution and the tragedy of its fall. We are extremely fortunate that such a glimpse has been preserved for us in the diary of a Japanese monk sent by the Court to study and obtain sacred literature, who traveled in China between 838 and 847. This diary is the source of the notes below. The translation is by Edwin O. Reischauer (*Ennin's Diary. The Record of a Pilgrimage to China in Search of the Law,* Ronald Press, New York, 1955); we have condensed and slightly edited the text.

The Lantern Festival (First Moon, Fifteenth Day)[48]

At night they burned lamps in the private homes along the streets[49] to the east and west. It was not unlike New Year's Eve in Japan. In the monastery they burned lamps and offered them to the Buddha. They also paid reverence to the pictures of their teachers. Laymen did likewise.

---

[46]Giles, *op. cit.,* pp. 140f.

[47]On the verge of high political power, Liu Tsung-yüan became involved in an aborted coup d'état and was banished to a distant post at the age of thirty-three, dying fourteen years later in obscurity. Against this background his interest in Buddhism becomes most meaningful. (See Crump, "Lyou Dzūng-ywán," *JAOS* 67 (1947) 166–171.

(Bibliographic note: Chinese references are cited from the Commercial Press *Szu pu ts'ung k'an* edition, unless otherwise indicated.)

[48]This festival marks the end of the many rituals connected with the New Year season. (L.G.T.)

[49]Ennin is in the great city of Yang-chou, on the lower Yangtze River. (L.G.T.)

In this monastery they erected a lamp tower in front of the Buddha Hall. Below the steps, in the courtyard, and along the sides of the galleries they burned oil. The lamp cups were quite beyond count. In the streets men and women did not fear the late hour, but entered the monastery and looked around, and in accordance with their lot cast coppers before the lamps which had been offered. After looking around they went on to other monasteries and looked around and worshiped and cast their coppers.

The halls of the various monasteries and the various cloisters all vie with one another in the burning of lamps. Those who come always give coppers before departing. The Wu-liang-i-ssu (temple name) sets up a "spoon-and-bamboo lamp."[50] I estimated that it has a thousand lamps. The spoon-and-bamboo lamp is constructed like a tree and looks like a pagoda. The way in which it is bound together is most ingenious. It is about seven or eight feet in height. [This festival] lasts for a period of three nights from this night to the night of the seventeenth. (p. 71)

. . . 17th Day . . . After the forenoon meal they spread out in front of the halls of the monastery the treasures [of the establishment], laying out forty-two portraits of sages and saints and all sorts of rare colored silks beyond count. As for the countenances of the sages and saints, some were concentrating with closed eyes, others with faces uplifted were gazing into the distance, others looking to the side seemed to be speaking, and others with lowered visages regarded the ground. The forty-two pictures had forty-two different types of countenances. As for the differences in their sitting postures, some sat in the full cross-legged position and others in the half cross-legged position. Their postures thus differed. Besides the forty-two sages and saints, there were pictures of Fugen and Monju (i.e., the celestial Bodhisattvas Samantabhadra and Mañjuśrī) and of *Gumyō-chō* and *Karyō binga-chō* (mythical Indian birds).

At sunset they lit lamps and offered them to the pictures of the saints. At night they chanted praises and worshipped Buddha and recited Sanskrit hymns of praise. The monks reciting Sanskrit came in together, some of them holding golden lotuses and jeweled banners, and sat in a row in front of [the pictures of] the saints and intoned together Sanskrit hymns of praise. They went through the night without resting, lighting a cup lamp in front of each saint. (pp. 71–73).

Visit to Wu-t'ai Shan

Mt. Wu-t'ai is in the far northern province of Shansi, close to Mongolia. It has for centuries been a center for pilgrimage by both Chinese and Mongol Buddhists. It is the heart of the cult of the Bodhisattva Manjusri—Wen-shu in its Chinese pronunciation, or Monju in the Japanese version of Ennin. For a detailed account of a pilgrimage to Wu-t'ai Shan by a twentieth-century Western Buddhist, see John Blofeld, *The Wheel of Life,* Chapter 6.

(A.D. 840, Fourth Moon) 28th Day. We entered an open valley and went west for thirty *li* (Chinese miles), arriving at the T'ing-tien Common Cloister[51] at 10 A.M. Before entering the cloister we saw toward the northwest the central

---

[50]Translator's note says: Apparently this was a tree-like tower constructed of bamboo, with metal or pottery spoons for burning oil tied to the ends of the bamboo branches.

[51]Translator's note says: [Common cloisters] appear to have been a type of Buddhist inn erected on the approaches to Mt. Wu-t'ai for the convenience of clerical and lay pilgrims.

terrace,[52] and bowing to the ground, we worshipped it. This then is the region of Monjushiri. There are no trees to be seen on the rounded heights of the five summits, and they look like overturned bronze bowls. On looking at them from afar, our tears flowed involuntarily. The trees and strange flowers are unlike those anywhere else, and it is a most unusual region. This then is the gold-colored world of Mt. Ch'ing-liang,[53] where Monjushiri manifested himself for our benefit . . .

Since we entered the mountains at 4 P.M. on the twenty-third day up until today we have been going along mountain valleys for a total of six days and, without getting through the mountains, have reached Wu-t'ai. (pp. 214f)

Fifth Moon: 2nd Day. We went to the Commandments Cloister (referring to Vinaya) [of the Chu-lin-ssu—a temple, still standing, according to the translator, about seven kilometers south of the western terrace] and, ascending to the balcony, worshipped the mandara[54] of seventy-two sages, saints, and deities [made] for the benefit of the nation. The coloring is exquisite. Next they opened up the Wan-sheng ("Myriad Saints") Ordination Platform. It is made of jade and is three feet high and octagonal. . . . The beams, rafters, and pillars are painted exquisitely. We called on the venerable monk in charge of the platform. His Buddhist name is Ling-chüeh, and he is one hundred years old, having been a monk for seventy-two years. His visage is unusual, and he is indeed a Consecrated Reverence. When he saw his guests, he was courteous. I am told that during the sixth moon last year three monks of the Nalanda Monastery in India came to Wu-t'ai and saw a nimbus in the form of a five-colored cloud shining about his person. . . . (pp. 217f)

16th Day. Early in the morning we left the Chu-lin-ssu and, following a valley, went ten *li* east and ten *li* toward the northeast to the Ta-hua-yen-ssu and entered the K'u-yüan ("Living Quarters Cloister") and lodged there. After the forenoon meal we went to the Nieh-p'an-yüan ("Nirvana Cloister") and saw abbot Fa-chien lecturing on the *Mo-ho-chih-kuan* in a fairly high [two]–storied hall. More than forty monks seated in rows were listening to him lecture. . . . It was impressive and beautiful in the hall beyond description. . . .

[Abbot] Chih-yüan Ho-shang of his own accord said, "The Learned Doctor Saichō of Japan went to T'ien-t'ai in the twentieth year of Chen-yüan (804) in search of the Law. Lord Lu, the Prefect of T'ai-chou, himself provided him with paper and scribes, and they copied several hundred scrolls which he gave to the Learned Doctor [Sai]chō. The Learned Doctor, on obtaining the commentaries, returned to his native land." Then he asked about the prosperity of the Tendai [Sect] in Japan, and I related in brief how Nan-yo Ta-shih (considered to be the second patriarch of T'ien t'ai sect) was [re]born in Japan. The congregation rejoiced greatly, and the Abbot [Chih]–yüan, on hearing me tell of the [re]birth of Nan-yo Ta-shih in Japan and the spread of Buddhism there, was extremely happy. . . .

After drinking tea we went to the Nieh-p'an ("Nirvana") Place of Ritual and worshipped the representation of [the Buddha attaining] Nirvana. The sixteen-foot figure [of the Buddha] lying on his right side beneath a pair of trees in the grove,

---

[52]Wu-t'ai literally means Five Terraces; this then refers to the central terrace or peak of the group. (L.G.T.)

[53]Translator's note: Another name for Mt. Wu-t'ai. "Gold-colored world" is a term for the paradise of Monju.

[54]Or *mandala*, a sacred cosmological diagram. (L.G.T.)

the figure of Maya swooning to the ground in anguish, the Four [Heavenly] Kings and the eight classes of demigods, and a crowd of saints, some holding up their hands and weeping bitterly, some with their eyes closed in an attitude of contemplation, everything that was described in the scriptures, was completely portrayed in these figures.

We also saw a picture of Ta-hsieh Ho-shang, who formerly performed Buddhist practices on this mountain. He made fifty pilgrimages around the five terraces and lived on the summit of the central terrace for three years, both winter and summer, without descending. Finally, with the aid of His Holiness [Monju], he was able to put on some large shoes. They were a foot high and a foot and a half long, and the larger pair was twenty-five pounds and the smaller ten pounds. At present they are placed in front of the picture. The Priest formerly made 15,000 robes and gave them to 15,000 monks, and he arranged 75,000 offerings [of food for monks]. Now they have made his picture and put it in a high balcony and make offerings to it.

. . . When one enters this region of His Holiness [Monju], if one sees a very lowly man, one does not dare to feel contemptuous, and if one meets a donkey, one wonders if it might be a manifestation of Monju. Everything before one's eyes raises thoughts of the manifestations of Monju. The holy land makes one have a spontaneous feeling of respect for the region. (pp. 222–225)

17th Day. . . . In the evening I went with several other monks up to the P'u-sa-t'ang-yüan ("Cloister of the Bodhisattva Hall") and saw the Devotions Priest. He is seventy years old, but at first glance could be around forty. They say that his being ripe of age but hale and hearty is because he has the power of "devotion." We opened the hall and worshiped an image of His Holiness the Bodhisattva Monju. Its appearance is solemn and majestic beyond compare. The figure riding on a lion fills the five-bay hall (that is, a building with a length of five bays between six main columns). The lion is supernatural. Its body is majestic, and it seems to be walking, and vapors come from its mouth. We looked at it for quite a while, and it looked just as if it were moving.

The venerable monk told us that, when they first made the Bodhisattva, they would make it and it would crack. Six times they cast it, and six times it cracked to pieces. The master was disappointed and said, "Being of the highest skill, I am known throughout the empire, and all admit my unique ability. My whole life I have cast Buddhist images, and never before have I had them crack. When making the image this time, I observed religious abstinence with my whole heart and used all the finesse of my craft . . . but now I have made it six times and six times it has completely cracked. Clearly it does not meet the desire of His Holiness [Monju]. If this be correct, I humbly pray that His Holiness the Bodhisattva Monju show his true appearance to me in person. If I gaze directly on his golden countenance, then I shall copy it to make [the image]. When he had finished making this prayer, he opened his eyes and saw the Bodhisattva Monju riding on a gold-colored lion right before him. After a little while [Monju] mounted on a cloud of five colors and flew away up into space. . . . After [the master] had made this image, he placed it in the hall, and with tears welling up in his dewy eyes, he said, "Marvelous! What has never been seen before, I have now been able to see. I pray always to be the disciple of Monjushiri, generation after generation and rebirth after rebirth." And so saying, he died.

Later this image emitted light from time to time and continually manifested auspicious signs. Each time there was a sign it was recorded in detail and reported to the throne, and on Imperial command Buddhist scarves were bestowed. . . . Because of this, each year an Imperial Commissioner sends one hundred Buddhist scarves, which are bestowed on the monks of the monastery, and each year the Imperial Commissioner on separate Imperial command sends incense, flowers, precious baldachins, pearl [decorated] banners and baldachins, jades, jewels, precious crowns of the "seven treasures," engraved golden incense burners, large and small mirrors, flowered carpets, white cotton cloth, marvelous imitation flowers and fruits, and the like. . . . The things sent yearly by various other official or private patrons from the provinces, prefectures, or regional commanderies are quite beyond count. . . . (pp. 231–234)

Miracle of Buddhist Relics

At the entrance to the mountain was a small monastery called the Shih-men-ssu . . . in which there was a monk who for many years had been reciting the *Lotus Sutra*. Recently some Buddhist relics were revealed to him, and everybody in the whole city came to make offerings. The monastery was overflowing with monks and laymen . . .

The origin of the discovery of the relics [was as follows]: The scripture-reciting monk was sitting in his room at night, reciting the scriptures, when three beams of light shone in and illumined the whole room and lighted up the whole monastery. Seeking the source of the light, [he discovered that] it came from the foot of the . . . cliff west of the monastery. After several days the monk followed the light to the cliff and dug down into the ground for over ten feet and came upon three jars of relics of the Buddha. . . . He brought them back and placed them in the Buddha Hall and made offerings to them. The noble and lowly, and the men and women of T'ai-yüan city and the various villages, and the officials, both high and low, all came and paid reverence and made offerings. Everyone said, "This has been revealed because of the wondrous strength of the Priest in his devotion to the *Lotus Sutra*." . . . (pp. 271f)

Reverencing Relics, Buddha's Teeth

The Ta-chuang-yen-ssu ([a monastery] in the southwestern corner of the capital, Ch'ang-an) held an offering to the tooth of the Buddha Shakamuni from the eighth day of the third moon until the fifteenth day. The Chien-fu-ssu[55] held an offering to the tooth of Buddha. From the eighth day to the fifteenth day Lan-t'ien-hsien (a county seat to the southeast of Ch'ang-an) had tea and food without restrictions, and monks and laymen came from every direction to eat. T'i-hsü Fa-shih, the Archbishop of the Streets of the Left (a governmental title) served as the head of the festival. The Various monasteries took part, each arranging fine offerings. All sorts of medicines and foods, rare fruits and flowers, and many kinds of incense were carefully prepared and offered to the Buddha's tooth. They were spread out beyond count in the gallery around the storied offering hall. The

---

[55]*ssu* means Buddhist monastery. (L.G.T.)

Buddha's tooth was in the . . . storied hall. All the Reverences of the city were in the storied hall adoring it and making praises. The whole city came to worship and make offerings. . . .

We monks in search of the Law went on the tenth day and performed adoration. We went up into the storied hall of the Buddha's tooth and saw the Buddha's tooth ourselves and reverently held it and worshiped it. . . .

The Hsing-fu-ssu west of the Sung-shu-chieh ("Pine Tree Street") also holds an offering to the Buddha's tooth from the eighth day to the fifteenth day of the second moon, and the Ch'ung-sheng-ssu hold another offering to the Buddha's tooth. In all there are four teeth of the Buddha in the city. The Buddha's tooth at the Ch'ung-sheng-ssu was brought from heaven by Prince Nata and given to the Preceptor [Tao]–hsüan of the Chung-nan Mountains. The Buddha's tooth at the Chuang-yen-ssu was brought from India in the flesh of a [person's] thigh. The Protector of the Law, the deity Kabira, was able to bring it. Another was brought by Fa-chieh Ho-shang from the land of Khotan, and another was brought from Tibet. . . . (pp. 300–302)

Church and State in Harmony: A Maigre Feast

A.D. 838, Twelfth Moon, 8th Day. Today was a national anniversary day, and accordingly fifty strings of cash were given to the K'ai-yüan-ssu (in Yang-chou) to arrange a maigre feast for five hundred monks. Early in the morning the monastic congregations gathered in this monastery and seated themselves in rows in the flanking buildings on the east, north, and west. At 8 A.M. the Minister of State and the General entered the monastery by the great gate. The Minister of State and the General walked in slowly side by side. Soldiers in ranks guarded them on all sides, and all the officials of the prefecture and of the regional commandery followed behind. They came as far as the foot of the steps in front of the lecture hall, and then the Minister of State and the General parted, the Minister of State going to the east and entering behind a curtain on the east side [of the courtyard], and the General going to the west and entering behind a curtain on the west side. They quickly changed their slippers, washed their hands, and came out again. In front of the hall were two bridges. The Minister of State mounted the eastern bridge and the General the western bridge, and thus the two of them circled around from the east and west and met at the center door of the hall. They took their seats and worshiped the Buddha.

After that, several tens of monks lined up in rows at both the east and west doors of the hall. Each one held artificial lotus flowers and green banners. A monk struck a stone triangle and chanted, "All be worshipful and reverence the three eternal treasures."[56] After that the Minister of State and the General arose and took censers, and the prefectural officials all followed after them, taking incense cups. They divided, going to the east and west, with the Minister of State going towards the east. The monks who were carrying flowered banners preceded him, chanting in unison a two-line hymn in Sanskrit, "The wonderful body of the *Nyorai* (i.e., Tathagata—an appellation of the Buddha)," etc. A venerable monk followed first [behind the Minister of State] and then the soldiers

---

[56]Buddha, Dharma, Buddhist community. (L.G.T.)

guarding him. They went along the gallery under the eaves. After all the monks had burned incense, they returned toward the hall by this route, chanting Sanskrit hymns without cease. . . .

During this time, there was beautiful responsive chanting of Sanskrit hymns by [the groups of monks] on the east and west. The leader of the chants, standing alone and motionless, struck a stone triangle, and the Sanskrit [chanting] stopped. Then they again recited, "Honor the three eternal treasures." The Minister of State and the General sat down together in their original seats. When they burned incense, the incense burners in which their incense was placed stood side by side. A venerable monk, Yüan-Ch'eng Ho-shang, read a prayer, after which the leader of the chants intoned hymns in behalf of the eight classes of demi-gods. The purport of the wording was to glorify the spirit of the [late] Emperor (on whose behalf the national holiday was declared). At the end of each verse he recited, "Honor the three eternal treasures." The Minister of State and the officials rose to their feet together and did reverence to the Buddha, chanting three or four times. Then all [were free] to do as they wished.

The Minister of State and the others, taking the soldiers [with them], went into the great hall behind the [lecture] hall and dined. The congregation of five hundred monks dined in the galleries. The numbers of monks invited varied in accordance with the size of the monastery. The large monasteries had thirty, the middle-sized monasteries twenty-five, and the small monasteries twenty. All were seated together as groups in long rows, and managers were dispatched from each monastery to attend to the serving of their respective groups. . . . The maigre feast was not served in a single place, but was served and eaten at the same time [in all places], and then [the monks] arose and dispersed, each one going to his own monastery. (pp. 61–63)

Portents of the Persecution to Come

In 841 a new emperor, known in history as Wu-tsung, ascended the throne. Ennin's diary for 842 contains the following ominous entry:

On the 9th day of the Tenth moon an Imperial edict was issued [to the effect that] all the monks and nuns of the empire who understand alchemy, the art of incantations, and the black arts, who have fled from the army, who have on their bodies the scars of flagellations and tattoo marks [for former offenses], [who have been condemned to] various forms of labor, who have formerly committed sexual offenses or maintain wives, or who do not observe the Buddhist rules, should all be forced to return to lay life. If monks and nuns have money, grains, fields, or estates, these should be surrendered to the government. If they regret [the loss of] their wealth and wish to return to lay life [in order to retain it], in accordance with their wishes, they are to be forced to return to lay life and are to pay the "double tax" and perform the corvee. . . . (pp. 321f)

The manifestations of Imperial displeasure with the Buddhist establishment grew increasingly serious. The edict quoted in the following incident is illustrative of arguments used by anti-Buddhist literati through the ages:

843, Sixth Moon, 11th Day. It was the present Emperor's birthday, and a maigre feast was held in the Palace. Reverences and Taoist priests from the two halves of the capital debated in the Imperial presence. . . . Two Taoist priests were granted purple robes on Imperial decree, but none of the Reverences was allowed to wear the purple.

. . . The General Manager of the Crown Prince's Household, Wei Tsung-ch'ing, compiled a commentary on the *Nirvana Sutra* in twenty scrolls and presented it to the throne. When the Emperor saw the commentary, he burned it and issued a decree, ordering the Imperial Secretariat and Imperial Chancellery to go to [Wei's] house and find the original draft and burn it. The text of this edict is as follows:

'An Imperial Edict.

Wei Tsung-ch'ing . . . stands among those of honorable degree and should conform to the Confucian way of life, but he is drowned in evil doctrines, which stir up depraved customs. He has opened the door to delusions and has gone completely against the doctrines of the sages. How deep is the depravity among those of high office! So much the more should We proscribe that which is not the words of the sages. Why should foreign religions be propagated? . . .

The Buddha was a western barbarian in origin, and his teachings spread the doctrine of "nonbirth." Confucius, however, was a Chinese sage, and the Classics provide words of profit. Wei Tsung-ch'ing, while being an ordinary Confucianist, a scholar, an official, and [a man of] distinguished family, has not been able to spread [the teachings of] Confucius and Mo-tzu, but, on the contrary, believes blindly in Buddhism and has foolishly made compilations from barbarian writings and has rashly presented them. How much more have the common people of China been steeped for long in these ways! In truth, their delusions should all be stopped, and they should be made to return to their pristine simplicity. . . .' (pp. 330–332)

In the tightening of the measures against Buddhism, Taoist rivals played a conspicuous part:

844, Third Moon. In order to destroy Lu-fu (a place in northern China which was in revolt) the Emperor summoned eighty-one Taoist priests [to perform sacrifices]. He also had a "ritual place of the nine heavens" constructed in the open on the Palace grounds. Eighty benches were piled up high and covered with elegantly colored [drapes], and at the twelve hours [of the day] ceremonies were held and sacrifices made to the heavenly deities (of Taoism). Dried meats, wine, and meat were used in the sacrifices to the Huo-lo Heaven. [The ceremony] started on the first Day of the fourth Moon and lasted until the fifteenth day of the seventh moon. . . .

The present Emperor is a biased believer in Taoism and hates Buddhism. He does not like to see monks and does not wish to hear about the "three treasures." Buddhist images and scriptures have been placed since early times in the place of ritual inside the Ch'ang-sheng Hall, and three sets of seven monks who are versed in devotions have been drawn from the monasteries of the two halves of the city and assigned in rotation to perform devotions there each day without cease, both day and night. However, the present Emperor has had the scriptures burned and the Buddhist images smashed. He has routed out the monks and sent them back to their respective monasteries and in the place of ritual has put images of the heavenly deities (Taoist) and of Lao-tzu and has had Taoist monks read Taoist scriptures and practice Taoist arts. . . . (pp. 341f)

844, Seventh Moon. Another Imperial edict was issued ordering that throughout the land the mountain monasteries, the common Buddha halls, and the fasting halls at the public wells and in the villages which were less than two hundred *ken* [in size] and not officially registered, were to be destroyed and their monks and nuns all forced to return to lay life and to perform the local corvee. . . . In the wards within the city of Ch'ang-an there are more than three hundred Buddha halls. . . . But in accordance with the edict they are being destroyed. . . . There [also] was an Imperial edict ordering the destruction of all the revered stone pillars and the grave monuments of monks. [Another] Imperial edict called upon the University for Sons of the State (*Kuo-tzu-chien*), the Scholars (of the National Academy), those who had achieved the status of Accomplished Literati (i.e., received the "doctorate," *chin-shih*) of the land, and those of learning, to take up Taoism, but so far not a single person has done so. (pp. 347f)

The details of the mounting persecution related by Ennin are fascinating and important, but we can only reproduce a few more passages here:

845, Third Moon, entry of Third Day: Several days later an Imperial edict was issued to the effect that monks and nuns of the land under fifty were all to be forced to return to lay life and to be sent back to their places of origin. . . . (p. 357) Fourth Moon: Because it was being carried out on Imperial order, beginning on the first day of the fourth moon the monks and nuns under forty returned to lay life and were sent back to their places of origin. Each day three hundred monks returned to lay life, and on the fifteenth day the monks and nuns under forty had all disappeared. Beginning on the sixteenth day the monks and nuns under fifty returned to lay life, and by the tenth day of the Fifth Moon they had all disappeared. Beginning on the eleventh day those over fifty who lacked documents from the Bureau of Sacrifices returned to lay life. . . . (pp. 361f)

Sixth Moon, 28th Day. We reached Yang-chou and saw the monks and nuns of the city being sent back to their places of origin with their heads wrapped up. The monasteries are to be destroyed, and their money, estates, and bells are being confiscated by the government. Recently a document came on Imperial command saying that the bronze and iron Buddhas of the land were all to be smashed and weighed and handed over to the Salt and Iron Bureau and a record of this made and reported to the throne. (p. 373).

Eighth Moon, 16th Day. We went north for 1,300 *li* at one stretch, going all the way through mountains and waste lands. . . . Teng-chou is the northeastern extremity of China. . . . Although it is a remote place, it has been no different from the capital in the regulation of monks and nuns, the destruction of the monasteries, the banning of the scriptures, the breaking of the images, and the confiscation of the property of the monasteries. Moreover they have peeled off the gold from the Buddhas and smashed the bronze and iron Buddhas and measured their weight. What a pity! What limit was there to the bronze, iron, and gold Buddhas of the land? And yet, in accordance with the Imperial edict, all have been destroyed and have been turned into trash. (p. 382)

Epilogue: The Persecution Terminated

Ennin remained in China long enough to see normalcy return. The emperor Wu-tsung died and was succeeded by Hsüan-tsung in 847. But, although the *Diary* thus ends on a happier note, irreparable damage had been done, damage from which Buddhism as an institution never completely recovered.

846, Fifth Moon, first Day. The new Emperor, whose surname is Li, had a great amnesty in the fifth moon. There also was an Imperial edict that each prefecture of the land was to build two monasteries and that the regional commanderies were permitted to build three, and each monastery was to have fifty monks. The monks over fifty years of age who had been returned to lay life last year were allowed to take Buddhist orders as of old, and on those who had reached eighty years were bestowed five strings of cash by the state. . . . (pp. 391f)

THE LAUGHING BUDDHA

The figure of "the laughing Buddha" is perhaps the most widely known icon, at least among foreigners, of Chinese religion. Even those who have not the slightest notion about Buddhism or Chinese religion are familiar with the fat, grinning monk, who may be found as a "curio," a paperweight or ashtray decoration, or even as an element in an advertisement or trademark. Visitors to Buddhist temples always find this figure facing them in the entrance hall, an incongruous intrusion, it would seem, into the lofty symbols of the religion. But whether debased to the most vulgar artistic and commercial level, or enthroned in a monastery, the laughing Buddha is a figure that arouses our curiosity.

Investigation of the laughing Buddha reveals many significant aspects of the Sinification of Buddhism, and of that most Chinese of Buddhist developments, Ch'an (or Zen, in Japanese pronunciation). The following essay is taken from Ferdinand D. Lessing, *Yung-Ho-Kung. An Iconography of the Lamaist Cathedral in Peking;* the Sino-Swedish Expedition Publications (Stockholm, 1942), Vol. 1, pp. 15–35; we have condensed and edited the text.

When entering [the first Hall] we naturally look first towards the center of the Hall where we hope to encounter some exalted deity of noble bearing whose very appearance would prepare us for greater revelations to come. Instead of this we discover an almost dwarfish image of disproportionate growth, a caricature of a monk, as we should infer from his bald pate, or perhaps a mere court jester to the gods, judging by the broad smile shining over his somewhat coarse features. . . . [This is] a genuine Chinese, man and god in person, the fulfillment of the hopes of the pious Buddhist, Lord Maitreya, the Saviour-Buddha, manifested in the flesh of a humble monk. His most familiar names are: the Pot-bellied Buddha Maitreya, Ta-tu-tzu Mi-lo-fo, and Pu-tai Ho-shang, the "Hemp-bag bonze." His legend abounds in genuine Ch'an features, proving that it was the Ch'an monks who substituted his distinctly Chinese personality for their colourless, outlandish Ch'ieh-lan (the original protective deity derived from Indian Buddhist mythology).

Artistic considerations no longer played a part in these changes. . . . So another step towards the Sinification of Buddhism had been taken: The first god to greet the Chinese worshipper was bone of his bones, and flesh of his flesh, and it was on him that the hope of Buddhism rested. . . .

To understand fully the apocryphal newcomer in the Chinese pantheon occupying this throne and his curious career, we must delve into the interesting legend of the person represented. . . . All the "biographies" agree that Pu-tai was a native of Ssu-ming in the Prefecture of Fêng-hua of the Province of Chêkiang and that he lived in the first half of the tenth century. He had no permanent residence except for a sojourn of three years in the Yüeh-lin-ssu in the Prefecture of Fêng-hua.

His real name was unknown, as were those of so many wandering monks of that time. One source says that he used to call himself Ch'i-tz'u, a truly Ch'an (Zen) name, which might mean: "Congruent with This," "This" meaning either his own person or the inexpressible something, the Buddha within us, the God-head, the Absolute.

It seems that his occasional predictions contributed to his popularity. He gave them by word of mouth or indicated them by his behaviour. They were considered infallible.

We are told that when rain was expected the monk wore wet sandals and hastened on as if seeking shelter. When he was seen wearing wooden sandals with nails under the soles, or sleeping on the market-bridge in a squatting posture with his head resting on his knees (as he is sometimes depicted), the approach of warm weather was indicated. His supposed ability to predict the weather even in this indirect manner probably gained him favour with the farmer.

Almost all sources describe him as obese, with wrinkled forehead, and a white protruding belly which he left uncovered.

There was one feature in his bodily appearance which more than others attracted general attention, although he was not the only person distinguished by it. Wherever he went, he wore a *pu-tai*. This word means literally a hemp (cloth) bag, but at that time it also meant a glutton, just as today we have the *chiu-nang fan-tai* "wine-bag and rice-sack," as an epithet for a person who is immoderate in eating and drinking. The liking of the Chinese for facetious puns and their propensity for nicknames gave our monk the sobriquet Pu-tai Ho-shang, "Hemp-bag Bonze." It is under this name that he has won his country-wide popularity. . . .

Two sources state that he carried his hemp bag on a stick over his shoulder and wandered through the hamlets and markets begging for everything he saw. Whatever he received, pickles, fish and meat, he would promptly taste, putting the remainder in his bag. This bag also served as a container for rubbish, even stones and bricks. At times he even seems to have indulged in barter or trade.

This bag was naturally an object of curiosity with old and young, and particularly with the country urchins who tried to snatch it from him. One source relates that once a crowd of sixteen boys shouted at him . . . chased him, and vied with each other in seizing his bag. Another source speaking of eighteen children adds, mysteriously, that it was not known whence they came.

At times Pu-tai would open the bag, displaying its heterogeneous contents to people, strewing alms, alms-bowl, clogs, bricks, stones—everything on the ground, saying, "Look here, look here." Then he would pick up each article one after the other and ask, "What is this? What is this?"

This scene with the children survives both in art and pantomime. The number sixteen is significant. It corresponds with one of the various groups of the Arhats (Chinese, Lohan), to which Pu-tai and Dharmatāla were added later. . . . Statues representing the reclining Pu-tai surrounded by children show either six or as many as eighteen. In the first case they are explained as the six receptive faculties (*indriya*), in the second as the eighteen *dhātus*: six receptive faculties (*indriya*), six sense-objects (*vishaya*), six resulting "bases" (*dhātus*). . . .

One expects his utterances to shed more light on his character, particularly those connected with events related in the legends about him. They are, however, very brief and for the most part of that enigmatical type characteristic of the masters of Ch'an in which the corresponding sources abound . . . So we find that the ever-recurrent question: "What was the idea of the Patriarch's (i.e., Bodhidharma's) coming from the West?" was also put to Ch'i-tz'u. Instead of answering it directly he put down his bag and stood there, crossing his hands in front of his breast. "Is there nothing else to it?" the interlocutor asked him. Thereupon the master took up his bag "with his fingers," shouldered it and left. He probably intended to indicate that Bodhidharma's aim in coming to China could be stated in definite terms as little as that of Ch'an Buddhism in general.

This method of answering a question by "the great silence," so familiar to the student of Ch'an Buddhism . . . is found in another episode from his life. The bonze Pai-lu, "White Deer," asked him the simple question, "What is it about your bag?" The master placed the bag on the ground. "What do you mean by putting down your bag?" the other asked. Thereupon Pu-tai shouldered it again and went away. The same happened to the bonze Pao-fu who asked him about the gist of Buddhism. Pu-tai sometimes followed this habit of responding to a question by not giving any direct answer, but by breaking off the conversation altogether even when he himself had begun it.

Once he overtook a monk wandering along the road. Tapping him on the back, he begged him, "Give me a cash."[57] These words are . . . a Zenist *kungan* (Japanese, *kōan*), subject for meditation. The source continues: The bonze, turning his back, said, "If the truth (or path, *tao*) is found, I will give you a cash." The master put down his bag and stood there with crossed hands.

His taciturn mood alternated, however, as the sources assure us, with moments when he was more communicative, though he always remained laconic.

Once, when he was wandering in Min (Fukien), a layman of the name of Ch'en, a great worshipper of his, elicited from him the following information: "How old are you?" The master replied: "My bag here is as old as space." When asked for further details, he answered: "My surname is Li (the name legend ascribes to the reputed author of the *Tao-tê-ching*, Lao Tzu). I was born on the eighth day of the second moon." The comparison of space with a bag or more precisely with bellows is found in a frequently quoted passage of the *Tao-te-ching*, Ch. 5: "Heaven and Earth and all that lies between is like a bellows in that it is empty, but gives a supply that never fails." The word in question means a sack which is open at both ends. It may also mean a bellows. . . .

There is another incident related in Pu-tai's legend which has some analogy to a story told about Diogenes. Once he stood on a road . . . When he was asked by a monk, "What are you doing here?" he replied, "I am waiting for a man." The

---

[57]The smallest coin. (L.G.T.)

bonze said, "Here he is." The master took an orange from his robe and offered it to him. As soon as the other reached for it Pu-tai withdrew his hand and said: "You are not that man." But when the monk asked, "What kind of man is it (for whom you are waiting)?" he received the surprising reply, "Give me a cash." . . .

But there are other episodes which give us a different picture of his attitude towards current beliefs, and they refer, characteristically enough, to the Messianic hope of the Buddhists, which is focused around Maitreya [Mi-lo-fo], the Coming Buddha.

The scene with the urchins examining the contents of his bag . . . concludes: "Thereupon he wrapped up some excrements with the words: "This is the ground of the inner court of Maitreya." The inner court is a part of Maitreya's palace that plays some role in the eschatological ideas of the Buddhists. This palace in which the Bodhisattva is believed to reside is made of gold . . . Similar crude comparisons are also found in other writers. We mention e.g. Chuang Tzu's characteristic statement about ubiquitous Tao. Still, we are at a loss how to explain this saying of the monk in this connection. Was it really purported to be iconoclastic, like the sayings and doings of so many of his fellow-monks since the advent of Bodhidharma almost 500 years before? Viewed in the light of another episode . . . we feel inclined to think so. Once, it is said, he pointed to a privy, saying: "Conversion (or: begging alms) does not amount to as much as these excretions." . . .

But how did it happen that a man of this mentality became a god, even Maitreya himself? That he did not escape the fate of other religious characters, more eminent than he . . . of being made into something which he either did not believe to exist at all or considered to be irrelevant to religious thinking. The answer is that he, too, fell a victim to idealization through religious fiction. . . .

One source states: The magistrate Wang Jen of P'u-t'ien saw him . . . The monk gave him a religious poem (*chieh* = *gatha*) which reads:

> Mi-lo (i.e., Maitreya), true Mi-lo,
> Reborn innumerable times,
> From time to time manifested to men,
> The men of the age do not recognize you.

Insignificant as such words may seem to the average unbelieving person, they assume magic suggestiveness when raised above the level of every day affairs and connected with such a momentous event as death. Taken as a swan-song, they are capable of surrounding their author with a glamour of mysticism and winning him a nimbus of immortality. . . .

According to one source Pu-tai entered Nirvana sitting on a rock in the Eastern vestibule of the temple Yüeh-lin-ssu in the second year of Chên-ming of the Later Liang Dynasty (AD. 916). . . . [In the same source we find] miraculous features accompanying his funeral rites. A beadle of that district who formerly had taken offense at the conduct of the idle mendicant, had upon three occasions given him a scolding and deprived him of his bag, which he burned, but, to his surprise, Pu-tai had reappeared each time with that same old bag. After the saint's death, the beadle, repenting of his harshness, bought a coffin for his funeral. But the whole crowd present was unable to move the coffin. Thereupon they substituted a man by the name of T'ung (which means "boy") who had always shown respect to the Master. It appeared that for him the coffin was as light as a feather. . . . Are we justified to . . . assume that "a (virgin) boy" or "(virgin) boys" were the only ones able to carry the coffin of him who is stated in the text to have remained virgin all his life? The "universal" character of this legend is well enough known to be discussed here. The reader may be reminded of the coffin of the Buddha, Shākyamuni, about which a similar legend is on record.

Because of his popularity, the credulous crowd was only too willing to believe the rumours denying his death. The fact that these regions in those times were rich in religious characters of a similar type with whom Pu-tai may have been confounded seems to offer a sufficient explanation for the origin of such stories. So he is reported to have been seen by people in other districts. To one of them he said, "By mistake, I have taken this sandal with me. Take it back with you." When the man returned, he learned that the master had already died. The people inspected his tomb at Feng-shan, and lo! they found only one sandal in it. . . . The circumstance of the single sandal found in the tomb is frequent in Chinese resurrection stories and has its well-known analogies elsewhere.

It is, therefore, apparent that this and similar stories have been borrowed from other legends in order to strengthen the belief aroused by his famous poem that he was a "preincarnation," so to speak, of Maitreya.

One source speaks of the cult of his relics: "And so they took a flask of celadon[58] used for consecrated water and his mendicant's rattlestaff with six rings, which they found near the pagoda marking his tomb, and preserved them as sacred relics in the temple where he had breathed his last." This is evidently the beginning of his deification. . . .

More miracle stories were rife and enhanced his fame. Already looked upon with amazement, because, when lying on the snow (apparently to sleep), his body remained unaffected by it, this amazement grew into real awe when it became known that a man named Chiang Mo-ho, when bathing with him in a brook, had discovered an eye on his back, which could but be the eye of "transcendent wisdom" (*prajñā-cakshus*). Utterly surprised, the layman exclaimed, "You are a Buddha!" The master hushed him: "Don't tell anyone." . . . Another source tells the same story with this variant: Chiang, rubbing (Pu-tai's) back (with a towel) suddenly discovered four eyes shining brightly. Startled he did obeisance to him and exclaimed: "Reverend Sir, you are a Buddha." The Master said, "Don't tell people. That I have been with you three, four years, that may be called a great 'grace.' I must leave you. Don't be sad." The number four is probably introduced here with the intention to outdo the older version. Four eyes in addition to Pu-tai's natural eyes would symbolize the fivefold eye (*pañcacakshus*) of a Buddha.

But two other factors cooperated in raising him above the level of his contemporaries, and even higher than the most illustrious of his predecessors: the poems composed by, or ascribed to him, and the drawings made of him. . . . All [the poems] express that spirit of Ch'an . . .

[A poem in one source] is one of a whole series of parting stanzas with which Pu-tai answers questions of his hospitable friend Ch'en. Here it answers the question about the Buddha-nature.

The first stanza describes the universality of the mind, a favourite subject with the Ch'an mystic; the second develops the state of mind of the wandering monk; the third asserts the futility of cherished scholastic distinctions. The fourth stanza

---

[58]A green porcelain ware. (L.G.T.)

carrying the ideas set forth in the third, describes the state of the "saint" who is fundamentally not different from the profane man, living in the same world with him. The fifth stanza is an exhortation to strive "after that one great aim."

1. This mind, mind, mind is the Buddha,
   The transcendental something in the worlds of the ten quarters.
   In all directions it operates miraculously in the pitiful sentient beings,
   And all the *dharmas* are not real, as the mind is.
2. Ascending, transcending, free and independent, bound for no destination,
   With all-embracing wisdom he moves, the man who left his family.
   If he beholds before his eyes the Real Great Way,
   He does not even regard the tiny (tip of a) hair as real: a miracle indeed.
3. The ten thousand *dharmas*, how are they different, and the mind, how is it distinguishable?
   What is the use of searching the meaning of the *sutras?*
   The mind-king in its original state severs the manifold knowledge.
   Only he is wise who understands (or: by whom is illustrated?) the state of Nonlearning.
4. Since there is neither profane nor saint, what should one do?
   Abstain from differentiation, and there is the state of the saint, which is solitude.
   That priceless pearl of the mind in its original state is round and pure.
   All differences caused by qualities are futile names.
5. It is MAN who makes TAO (the "truth," "way") great, and TAO stands out in clarity.
   Numberless pure and noble (men) praise TAO.
   Dragging (your) pilgrim's staff (feel) like ascending the path leading home.
   Do not worry that nowhere (you) hear a sound.

The same sources give us another poem:

One alms-bowl contains the rice of a thousand families;
A lonely body wanders ten thousand *li.*
(Only) a few people cast friendly looks upon me
For the road I ask the white clouds.

. . . But these poems, even in combination with the legends relating prophecies and miracles, would hardly have been sufficient to secure him a permanent place in tradition and a comparatively high rank in the pantheon, if pictorial art had not come to their aid.

"Thereupon" [says the source] (continuing the story about his reappearance after his burial), "priests and laymen vied with each other in drawing his portrait. Even now in the eastern side hall of the Great Hall of the Yüeh-lin-ssu (where he died) a full portrait of him has been preserved." Another source states expressly that the portraits drawn by the people were worshipped, and our oldest source declares that his poem about Maitreya led to the belief that he had pointed towards himself as the actual Maitreya.

The *Kao-seng-chuan* (*Lives of Eminent Monks*) says that his portrait was frequently painted by people "in the region of the Yang-tzu and the Che-chiang rivers" (modern Che-kiang), the cradle of so many religious innovations. The cult of the Arhats, among whom Pu-tai is a belated guest, spread from there over China. . . .

We omit several extracts from the author's sources, which give a circumstantial and obviously fictional account of the portrait and other matters further illustrating the deification of the monk Pu-tai.

This is apparently all the information we have about the inception of his iconographic portrait. What it resembled we can only vaguely imagine from his literary picture, as nothing genuine seems to have survived of those presumably crude wall-paintings which were originally mere "graffiti" or scribblings of a more or less perishable nature made by novices or visitors. But perhaps it is quite safe to assume that they inspired, indirectly, the oldest real paintings which have come down to us. Such a type, with his grotesque features and his ragged, dirty garb, appealed to the Chinese genius with its leaning for the bizarre, which often enough, for instance in the traditional Arhat type, gives us the erroneous impression of intentional caricature. Intentional caricaturing is doubtless to be found in many more recent reproductions, as the type underwent certain remarkable changes in the course of time.

For the earliest drawings or paintings just mentioned no outside influences need be assumed. It seems, however, quite possible, or even probable, that the statuary was inspired by some squatty *Yaksha* type, as Lucian Scherman was the first to surmise.[59] Certain statues of the sitting Pu-tai show essential similarities to that of the Yaksha Jambhala, and it may be that later images of the monk represent a crossing between the Chinese paintings and some Yaksha. The peach seen in the hand of Pu-tai has very probably been substituted by the Chinese for the lemon held by Jambhala which had less meaning for them. One of the oldest Chinese stone figures in existence, dating from the Sung Dynasty, is found at Yen-hsia-tung in the province of Che-kiang. It shows the type familiar to us.

This short-limbed (*kharva*) Yaksha-type goes back, as Scherman surmises for good reasons, to a popular type of Silenos, the friend of children, who has survived in Buddhist iconography since the age of Gandharan art, though we are not yet able to give an uninterrupted history of his evolution. It may be observed, however, that the broad grin Pu-tai displays in the more recent images is contradictory both to the description of the legend and to the traditional type of Jambhala (who, particularly as *Ucchushma*, is expressly described as frowning, *kṛta-bhṛkuṭin*); whereas it would fit the popular conception of a Silenos. The "winebag" characteristic of Silenos, was often misunderstood and converted into a fold or corner of his garb. That would explain the feature noticeable in images of Pu-tai showing him without his chief attribute, the bag, instead of which he clutches a corner of his "monastic robe" with his left hand.

Statues of him have usually neither nimbus nor aureola, nor the ornaments of Maitreya either. There are, however, statues where the solemn combines with the grotesque: the fat, half-nude monk wears a crown, much in the same way as the "real" Maitreya as "crownprince" (*yuva-rāja*, i.e., as designated successor of Gautama or Shākyamuni).

. . . Summing up, it seems that Pu-tai Ho-shang was a figurehead representing a whole category of similar characters of the Ch'an school, posing as religious

---

[59]"Die Dickbauchtypen," in *Jahrbuch der asiatischen Kunst*, Vol. I, pp. 120–136.

eccentrics, commanding a deep respect with the populace willing to worship them and to credit them with superhuman qualities. As a matter of fact one Chinese text enumerates four Pu-tais:

1. Ch'i-tz'u, in the T'ang dynasty.
2. Liao-ming, a fat monk, Sung dynasty.
3. Pu-tai, Yüan dynasty (considered to be a reincarnation of Nos. 1 and 2).
4. Chang's son of Tsao-yang, said to resemble a painted Pu-tai.

This statement, if correct . . . would be another proof of the undoubtable fact that the popularity of the fat monk grew rapidly. He eclipsed the entire crowd of older, nobler, and more famous colleagues, among whom were quite a few very popular figures, for he was Maitreya, the Buddha-to-Come, who, temporarily in a humble guise and in an unpretentious manner, preached the message of Ch'an Buddhism in the language of the people. Ch'an, as Dr. Hu Shih has justly pointed out, is the Chinese version of the Buddhist gospel, and Pu-tai, or the Pu-tais, were the last of its apostles, the Messiahs of the Latter Days. Systematic mythology required a definite place and rank for this preincarnation in the pantheon, and so he became not only one of the last Arhats, but also the first saint to greet the worshipper visiting the temple.

This then is Pu-tai Ho-shang, the Hemp-bag Monk, alias the Pot-bellied Maitreya, mendicant, friar, philosopher, poet, hero of legends, guardian of the temple, saint and saviour in disguise, one of those Eulenspiegels in which Chinese folklore is so rich and who lived up to Lao-Tzu's saying: "The highest wisdom is like foolishness, the greatest eloquence like stuttering."

In China he is still one of the most favourite figures of popular religion, known everywhere and to everyone. A thousand years have not dimmed his popularity, on the contrary, they have increased it. This appears even in commonplace sayings of everyday life. If a mother proudly refers to her fat baby as a *Tz'u-wa-wa,* "a porcelain doll," she has in mind the numerous ugly porcelain figures of the monk.

ZEN AND AMIDISM IN CHINESE BUDDHISM

The syncretistic character of Chinese Buddhism is something that has been noted by many writers. In recent centuries the dominant forms have been the pietistic Pure Land (*ching-t'u*), or what is often called Amidism because recitation of the name of Amitabha Buddha is the heart of this form, and Ch'an, which we shall call by the better-known Japanese pronunciation Zen. To Westerners, with their experience of dogmatic sectarianism, nothing would seem more unlikely than the easy ecumenical relationship of these utterly different practices. Even in Japan, where both Amidism and Zen flourish—as well as various other sects—there is a clear-cut separation between the different sects. So we may consider that the Chinese way is indeed uniquely Chinese.

The following material is extracted from an autobiography by the English Buddhist John Blofeld, entitled *The Wheel of Life* (London: Rider and Co. 1959), pp. 87–90. His conversation with the Venerable Hsü Yün, no doubt the most eminent Buddhist monk of this century, will illustrate the Chinese attitude better than any abstract discussion.

The present Abbott [of the Nan Hua Monastery in North Kwangtung province] was no other than the Venerable Hsü Yün, who was believed to be well over a hundred years old, though still able to walk as much as thirty miles a day. He was renowned all over China as the greatest living Master of Zen; so I was delighted to hear the unexpected news that he had just returned after an absence of several months spent in a distant province. Not long after my arrival, I excitedly followed the Reverend Receiver of Guests to pay my respects to this almost mythical personage. I beheld a middle-sized man with a short, wispy beard and remarkably penetrating eyes. He was not precisely youthful-looking as I had been led to expect, but had one of those ageless faces not uncommon in China. Nobody could have guessed that he was already a centenarian. Finding myself in his presence, I became virtually tongue-tied and had to rack my brains for something to say, although there was so much that I could profitably have asked him. At last, I managed to ask:

'Is this famous monastery *purely* Zen, Your Reverence?'

'Oh yes,' he answered in a surprisingly vigorous voice. 'It is a great center of Zen.'

'So you do not worship Amida Buddha or keep his statue here?'

The question seemed to puzzle him; for he took some time to reply.

'But certainly we keep his statue here. Every morning and evening we perform rites before it and repeat the sacred name while circumambulating the altar.'

'Then the monastery is not *purely* Zen,' I persisted, puzzled in my turn.

'Why not? It is like every other Zen monastery in China. Why should it be different? Hundreds of years ago there were many sects, but the teachings have long been synthesized—which is as it should be. If by Zen you mean the practice of Zen meditation, why, that is the very essence of Buddhism. It leads to a direct perception of Reality in *this* life, enabling us to transcend duality and go straight to the One Mind. This One Mind, otherwise known as our Original Nature, belongs to everybody and everything. But the method is very hard—hard even for those who practice it night and day for years on end. How many people are prepared or even able to do that? The monastery also has to serve the needs of simple people, illiterate people. How many of them would understand if we taught only the highest method? I speak of the farmers on our own land here and of the simple pilgrims who come for the great annual festivals. To them we offer that other way—repetition of the sacred name—which is yet the same way adapted for simple minds. They believe that by such repetition they will gain the Western Paradise and there receive divine teaching from Amida Buddha himself—teaching which will lead them directly to *Nirvana*.'

At once reluctantly and somewhat daringly I answered: 'I see. But isn't that a kind of—well, a sort of—of—er—deception? Good, no doubt, but—'

I broke off, not so much in confusion as because the Venerable Hsü Yün was roaring with laughter.

'Deception? Deception? Ha, ha, ha, ha-ha! Not at all. Not a bit. No, of course not.'

'Then, Your Reverence, if you too believe in the Western Heaven and so on, why do you trouble to teach the much harder road to Zen?'

'I do not understand the distinction you are making. They are identical.'

'But—,'

'Listen, Mr. P'u, Zen manifests self-strength; Amidism manifests other-strength. You rely on your own efforts, or you rely on the saving power of Amida. Is that right?'

'Yes. But they are—I mean, they seem—entirely different from each other.'

I became aware that some of the other monks were beginning to look at me coldly, as though I were showing unpardonable rudeness in pertinaciously arguing with this renowned scholar and saint; but the Master, who was quite unperturbed, seemed to be enjoying himself.

'Why insist so much on this difference?' he asked. 'You know that in reality there is nought but the One Mind. You may choose to regard it as *in* you or *out* of you, but "in" and "out" have no ultimate significance whatever—just as you, Mr. P'u, and I and Amida Buddha have no *real* separateness. In ordinary life, self is self and other is other; in reality they are the same. Take Bodhidharma who sat for nine years in front of a blank wall. What did he contemplate? What did he see? Nothing but his Original Self, the true Self beyond duality. Thus he saw Reality face to face. He was thereby freed from the Wheel and entered *Nirvana*, never to be reborn—unless voluntarily as a Bodhisattva.'

'Yet, Reverence, I do not think that Bodhidharma spoke of Amida. Or am I wrong?'

'True, true. He did not. But when Farmer Wang comes to me for teaching, am I to speak to him of his Original Self or of Reality and so on? What do such terms mean to him? Morning and evening, he repeats the sacred name, concentrating on it until he grows oblivious of all else. Even in the fields, as he stoops to tend the rice, he repeats the name. In time, after a month, a year, a decade, a lifetime or several lifetimes, he achieves such a state of perfect concentration that duality is transcended and he, too, comes face to face with Reality. He calls the power by which he hopes to achieve this Amida; you call it Zen; I may call it Original Mind. What is the difference? The power he thought was outside himself was inside all the time.'

Deeply struck by this argument and anxious, perhaps, to display my acquaintance with the Zen way of putting things, I exclaimed:

'I see, I see. Bodhidharma entered the shrine-room from the sitting-room. Farmer Wang entered it through the kitchen, but they both arrived at the same place. I see.'

'No,' answered the Zen Master, 'you do not see. They didn't arrive at any place. They just discovered that there is no place for them to reach.'

This reply made me feel proud of myself. It seemed I *had* grasped the point correctly, for the Master had condescended to answer with one of those Zen paradoxes which force the hearer into even deeper understanding. His broad smile was enough to show that he was really satisfied with my reply.

'After all,' I added complacently, 'it's all a matter of *words*.'

Instead of nodding approvingly, the Venerable Hsü Yün turned away from me suddenly and began speaking on quite a different subject to one of his disciples.

His withdrawal was so pointed that, for a moment, I felt hurt as by a harsh snub. Then I saw the point and almost laughed aloud. 'Of course that's it,' I said to myself. 'The significance of that turning away is as clear as clear can be. It means, "On the contrary, it is all a matter of no words—*silence*." Of course that was it.' I prostrated myself and walked out to find the room allotted to me for the night.

THE RELIGIOUS VOCATION

Many observers have expressed their opinions about the caliber of the Buddhist Sangha in China in modern times, and many reasons have been advanced to explain why its members choose this career. There is no need to doubt that in such a large and ancient institution there will be found persons of all sorts, and that their reasons for having joined the Order will be varied.

What we mean to emphasize, by including the following selection here, is that one should not underestimate the importance of a true vocation for some among the Sangha. If we accept the universality, the humanness of religious needs, the fact that humans are by nature *homo religiosus,* then we will not be surprised to find those in every culture who turn to the religious life simply because that part of their nature is dominant.

This brief testament, *Diary of a Chinese Buddhist Nun: T'ze Kuang,* appeared originally in Chinese in the prominent Buddhist periodical *Hai Ch'ao Yin* (Sound of the Tide), II, 11–12 (February 1923). The translation by Y. Y. Tsu was published in *The Journal of Religion,* VII, 5–6 (October 1927), pp. 612–618.

---

[60]*26th Day of 10th Moon.*—Today is the one hundredth day after brother Wen's death; we held a memorial service for him in the "Paradise Nunnery." Just three years ago this day, brother started on his honeymoon trip with his bride. . . . alas, what a dream life is! This morning I accompanied sister-in-law to the nunnery, we lunched with the nuns, sharing their meager meal (because we asked them not to prepare specially for us), and afterward joined them in their devotional service amid the music of the bells and the fragrance of the burning incense. On our way home my heart felt the longing for the quiet and serene life of the nunnery, and wondered whether it could be mine also. . . .

---

[60]TRANSLATOR'S NOTE.—The diary covers seventeen days within three months in the life of a young woman that led to her "taking the veil" of a nun. The Chinese equivalent for taking the veil is "shaving the head," or "discarding the hair," the hair being looked upon as symbol of wordly vanity. There is no reason to doubt that the document is genuine. The Chinese terms for family relations, such as Wen Ku for elder brother Wen, and Wen Sao for sister-in-law or wife of elder brother Wen, have a charm untranslatable in English. The term for addressing a Buddhist monk or nun is Fa Shih, which means "teacher of law," so "Chin Kuang Fa Shih" will be Teacher of Law Chin Kuang; for brevity it is usually shortened into "Chin Shih," Teacher Chin. In the translation, Fa Shih, for a nun, is given as "Sister" for convenience. Excepting for one small portion omitted in the entry for 29th of 11th Moon, the Chinese text has been faithfully followed in the translation. The *Hai Ch'ao Yin* is the official organ of the modern Buddhist movement in China, and under the powerful editorship of Tai Hsu, the St. Paul of Chinese Buddhism, it has a high standing in Buddhist and literary circles. It contains valuable material for a student of comparative religion and psychology of religion.

4th Day of 11th Moon.—Morning: read prayers with mother and sister-in-law for two hours. Since brother's death sister-in-law has been fasting, reading prayers, and constantly talking with me about the Buddhist life. When the great sorrow came to her, she almost wanted to give up living; now she seems determined to follow Buddha's way. Afternoon: Sister Chin Kuang called, and we urged her to spend the night with us. Sister Chin Kuang has a beautiful personality, sympathetic and serene, is of the same age with sister-in-law, and literary. We find much in common and are good friends. Often we would ask her about her past, but she kept it to herself. This evening she told us that she was the daughter of Li family, a high official in the Manchu Dynasty, married at seventeen to Mr. Shen, but finding no happiness in her husband's house, she secured the consent of her family and entered the nunnery on the first day of the tenth moon in the fourth year of the Republic [1915], five months after her wedding! We talked together until midnight.

7th Day of 11th Moon.—Sister-in-law and I got mother's consent to invite Sister Chin Kuang to our house to teach us the sutras, and so in the afternoon we went to the nunnery and explained our errand to her. She spoke to the Abbess, who gladly agreed. It began to rain, and so we were asked to pass the night there. In the evening Sister Chin Kuang showed us two photographs. One was of herself before she shaved off her hair—such refined presence and elegant bearing—and on the margin was written, "Taken three days before initiation. From now on, my wordly self remains in the picture only." The second photograph shows her with the shaven head and dress of a nun, and on the margin was written: "Taken two days after initiation; almost a different person from the one in the other picture." I shared a room with another nun, Hui Kuang. She is fifteen only, bright and pretty, early lost her mother, was ill-treated by her stepmother, and now finds her happiness in a nun's life.

8th Day of 11th Moon.—Rose at 4 A.M. Watched the nuns at their early matins. After breakfast, sat in meditation before Buddha with the others until 10 A.M. At that time a Mrs. Wang called, and seeing sister-in-law and myself, inquired whether we were there preparing for initiation. I replied, "I hope that such may be my good fortune some day." Sister-in-law was delighted to know that I had the same desire as she. Sister Chin Kuang had her head shaved preparatory to coming to our house, and as we watched the procedure, she showed us a box in which her beautiful original hair was kept, which she said would be burnt with her body after death. We came home and arranged an altar for Buddha.

12th Day of 11th Moon.—Rose at 4:30 A.M. Sister-in-law has already formed the practice of spending an early morning hour in silent meditation and prayer. At six, breakfast. Afterward had our morning service with Sister Chin Kuang. I can repeat a number of sutras, only the rhythm is not so smooth. Afternoon, Mr. Chen came to say that brother Wen's grave was prepared and that the burial would take place on the twenty-fifth, etc. It was a hard day for sister-in-law, but she felt much comforted by our saying the prayers.

21st Day of 11th Moon.—We spent the day with our regular services. In the evening sister-in-law asked me to help her dress her hair. I protested that it was already late, but she insisted, and so I gave in and helped her. Then she explained: "I have long wanted to enter the Buddhist life; I am glad that I have met Sister Chin Kuang, for you have strengthened my decision. When my husband was here he admired my hair greatly. I am going to cut it off and have it buried with him in his grave. There is no time to wait for a regular initiation, and so I am going to ask Sister Chin Kuang to shave my head this evening. I have not told my father and mother, for they might not agree to this, but they will understand afterward." Sister Chin Kuang gladly consented. I watched the procedure in silence. Sister-in-law put the cut braids in a blackwood box and retired to her own room.

22nd Day of 11th Moon.—This morning the servants were greatly surprised to see sister-in-law's shaven head, but she remained wonderfully calm. When our parents were up, we three went in and sister-in-law knelt before them and explained her conduct. Our parents could not but accept the *fait accompli,* and suggested that sister-in-law should give up her ordinary dress and put on nun's robes. As we had none ready, Sister Chin Kuang lent her a few pieces of her own. Afternoon we went to the nunnery and informed the Abbess. It was agreed that the initiation ceremony be held on the eighth of next Moon.

25th Day of 11th Moon.—At 7 A.M. brother Wen was buried. Sister-in-law put the blackwood box into the grave. Before doing so, she opened the box and showed the farmers who were watching the burial the contents, so as to disarm any suspicion that it might contain jewelry. We returned to the city by boat.

28th Day of 11th Moon.—Sister-in-law completed her arrangements to leave home. She turned over all her possessions to mother. Mother proposed to sell her things and let her have the money for use in the nunnery. But father suggested keeping her things and giving her $1,500 and donating 30 mao of land to the nunnery. Sister-in-law was very happy and grateful. For days I felt unhappy; I wished that I could join sister-in-law in her initiation. We talked the whole night without sleep.

29th Day of 11th Moon.—We overslept this morning. Got up at 9 A.M. and commenced my meditation, but other thoughts came in and I could not exclude them. Afternoon, sister-in-law left home with Sister Chin Kuang, never to return again. My spirit was despondent, as if having lost someone. I retired early.

8th Day of 12th Moon.—7 A.M., accompanied mother to Paradise Nunnery, 10 A.M., sister-in-law was initiated and given the name of Chih Kuang. Henceforth I do not address her as sister-in-law, but as Sister Chih Kuang. About twenty friends attended the service. Sister-in-law looked radiant and happy.

9th Day of 12th Moon.—Last night I dreamed that Sister Chih shaved my head and I was happy, but on waking I felt my head and was greatly disappointed. Got up at 5:30 A.M., had my usual morning devotion, but felt very lonely. Helped mother in home work, but my heart was heavy. Retired early to my own room but could not sleep.

14th Day of 12th Moon.—Today is my uncle's birthday, and also the completion of the first moon of a little girl cousin. Mother, Sister Chih, and myself called to offer our congratulations. Sister Chih Kuang at first would not go, but grandmother insisted that though she had entered the Buddhist life she was still a member of the family. A number of female guests were there, and there was naturally much whispered talk about Sister Chih. It was wonderful to see how calm and self-possessed she was. When others addressed her by her family name, she suggested that she be called Sister Chih Kuang. Sister Chih spent the night with me at home, the first time after initiation. We talked late into the night. I told her that lately I had been thinking of the mystery of life—birth, reproduction, death, in endless rotation—and was oppressed by the sense of the vanity of all things.

15th Day of 12th Moon.—The talk last evening had helped me to make up my mind. Rose at 6:30 A.M., morning devotion. Saw parents and told them my wish, but they would not consent. I was told that it was natural for sister-in-law, widowed and alone, to seek the Buddhist life, but I was in my young womanhood with a glorious future before me. I went into my room and cried out my heart. Sister Chih said to hold on to my purpose and she would do her best for me to realize it.

6th Day of 1st Moon.—Morning: when I was fixing my hair, our maid Ch'ung Hsiang told me that father had selected the 18th of next moon to engage me to a certain young man of well-to-do family and a college graduate, and congratulated me. I was horrified and decided to act before it was too late. Afternoon: went hurriedly to the nunnery and told Sister Chih Kuang and Sister Chin Kuang. We agreed that there was no time to waste, and so decided upon an early initiation, provided the Abbess would agree to it. Fortunately the Abbess consented and chose the fifteenth as the day of initiation, and said that I was to go to the nunnery on the fourteenth. I returned home but said nothing to my parents.

14th Day of 1st Moon.—Afternoon: went to a photographer and had my picture taken as a memento for mother. To the nunnery: Sister Chih Kuang had prepared some nun's dresses for me and I put them on. My clothes were given away to a poor girl. Evening: Sister Chih dressed my hair into six braids, preparing for the ceremony next morning.

15th Day of 1st Moon.—Today is the day I shave off my hair and leave this wordly life to enter the "gate of law," the most memorable, most precious day of my whole life. After this day, I shall be a new person.

Rose at 4 A.M., joined morning devotion; breakfast, beans and bean curd only, but they tasted sweet in my mouth. The nuns filed into the big hall with musical accompaniment, each wearing the rubrical mantle. Sister Chih Kuang put a red mantle over me, and Sister Chin Kuang led me into a hall. Excepting the members of the nunnery, none was present, and even the outer gate was locked to prevent any outsiders from coming in (precaution against possible interruption on the part of my family).

After doing homage to "the Three Precious" and saluting the Abbess, I knelt before Buddha. Sister Chin Kuang took scissors and cut the six braids near the roots and put them in the tray held by little Sister Hui Kuang, who gave me a smile in her eyes. I was asked to prostrate myself three times and stand up. My head was washed and then shaven smooth. Some medicated stuff was put on my forehead, and six short sticks of incense (half an inch long) were stuck into it and lighted. Two nuns held my head tightly. I closed my eyes and repeated the name of Buddha; just felt slightly warm on the head and the sticks of incense were already burnt into the skin. Henceforth six scars will remain forever on my forehead. After receiving the "Five Obligations" I prostrated myself in thanksgiving before Buddha and also thanked the Abbess and Sister Chin. The service finished, all the nuns offered congratulation and I thanked them with the usual salute of "joined palms" (palms together, fingers upward). Sister Hui, with a smile, gave back the braids and shaven hair for me to keep. Sister Chin produced a mirror and asked me to look into it and see whether I could recognize myself. I could not. The head looks clean and smooth; the scars are still sore; I feel somewhat cold without wearing a hat. Afternoon: I went home with the Abbess and Sisters Chin and Chih to call on father and mother. They were visibly surprised and even angry. I knelt before them and explained. Father and mother gave me $1,000 as an endowment for my life in the nunnery. Toward evening we returned to our nunnery. . . . Henceforth with peace in my heart I follow Buddha's way, undisturbed by worldly anxieties and regrets!

T'ZE KUANG (RADIANT BENEVOLENCE)

RELIGIOUS ACTIVITIES IN THE BUDDHIST MONASTERY

The following description of the daily life in a typical Buddhist monastery is from the pen of Karl L. Reichelt, a Christian missionary who spent many years during the first half of the twentieth century working among Chinese Buddhists. Reichelt belonged to the small but distinguished group of missionaries who did not allow their Christian and Western biases to blind them to what was admirable and valuable in the Chinese culture. In the selection presented here from his book, *Truth and Tradition in Chinese Buddhism* (translated from the Norwegian by Kathrina van Wagenen Bugge; Shanghai, 1928), we see his wide acquaintance with the subject, and his warm empathy. (Selection is from pp. 272–282.)

The fixed daily services begin very early in the morning, especially in the summer. Even in the winter one can hear the first signal for the morning mass at three o'clock in the morning. The monks then get out of bed and gather, quiet and solemn, in the big temple hall. Each knows his place, either in the East party or the West party.[61] The instructor stands by the altar on the right side. He plays one of the instruments and leads the chanting in a full, clear voice. . . . Farther to the right stands the drummer and the man who beats the well-known hollow "wooden fish" (*mu-yü*). Farther out in the congregation stands the one of the East party who beats the time by striking a little bell (*ch'ing-tzu*). In some places, cymbals and other kinds of strange instruments are in use, for the "time" is very difficult. It is remarkable to hear what they can achieve with these instruments in the chants, which may last for hours. The well-known daily masses are sung without any book of ritual, but during the long extra masses the inspector and the main leaders have the books in front of them. . . .

The service begins with a "prelude," the time being given by striking the different instruments. A signal is then given on the bell, and the whole congregation bows in silence on the praying stools or praying mats, not merely on their knees, but all the way down, so that the forehead lightly touches the floor. This is done in unison, and when several hundred monks in the same dress are seen doing this the effect is quite striking. They get up and then bend again, nine times in all. This is the holy greeting, three repeated three times (3 × 3). When bowing, they must remember to let the right knee touch the floor first, for the right side is the clean one, while the left is unclean. Therefore the cloak, which is the garment used during the mass, is only worn on the left shoulder. The kneeling rug is spread out neatly during the first prostration.

---

[61]The two groups into which the monks are divided for administrative convenience. (L.G.T.)

Meanwhile, the abbot, accompanied by his acolytes, has come in. He also begins with the nine-fold prostration. He may be recognized by a red patch on his gown. As soon as he has finished his silent prayer, a signal is given on the bell and the instructor introduces the mass by singing, in very low chanting tones, the first words of the sutra used. As a rule, it is the formula of greeting "Nan-mo," then comes the name of the Buddha or bodhisattva concerned, and finally "fo" [Buddha] or "p'u-sa" [bodhisattva]. After "Nan-mo," all join in, supported by the beating on the instruments, and a rushing volume of chanting rises to the high temple ceilings. The first sections of praise and the holy vows which are daily renewed offer the greatest variety. Here the alternating instruments and song are most effective. Besides facing the altar, the worshipers turn several times to one side so that the parties of the West and East face each other.

Special parts of the mass are sung by the abbot. He genuflects and bends in a rather interesting way. It is when one comes to the sutra itself that the greatest demands are made upon the monks who take part. In order to get through it all within reasonable time the speed has to be increased enormously. The chant rushes along breathlessly so that everybody feels great relief when the last section is reached, where they can rest in the long tones of praise. This last part of the mass, chanted in kneeling position, is the most touching.

The chanting tones have a pronouncedly mournful character. The music and the tunes of Buddhism are known as "pei-t'iao" (tunes of woe). And yet, at times, during the great festivals, a cheerful hymn of praise may arise. To those who hear such masses for the first time the effect may be strange and eerie. But one need not have been present many times at mass in one of the larger monasteries or heard a well-drilled monk choir, before one is struck by the devotion and religious intensity of the singing. This is doubtless true of the most serious and devout of the monks, while on the other hand many only take part in a mechanical way. More than once I have spoken with monks who have talked with enthusiasm of their longing to get to certain monasteries where the singing is especially cultivated, as for instance, to Chiao Shan, the remarkable little island in the lower part of the Yangtze, where some of the best singers of Buddhism gather. I have been present with them at several of their masses and I shall never forget the impression of noble singing and religious devotion which I there received. . . .

If it be asked: "Why do we not see larger ethical results from all this religious emotion?" I will answer with my hand on my heart: "The Chinese have the same difficulty in exchanging religious rapture and emotion for a well-directed holy life as we Westerners have. But that these masses are often ethically helpful I am quite convinced." Several Buddhists have told me: "It was not till I took part in these solemn masses that I understood what Buddhism was. I felt regenerated."

The mass often closes with a quiet procession round the great temple hall. The participants walk in long rows between the stools or out into the corridors, with hands folded (*ho-chang*) and eyes half-closed, pronouncing a greeting to the different Buddhas and bodhisattvas by prefixing every name with the well-known "Nan-mo." Or all may be united in a five-hundred- or one-thousand-fold greeting to Amitabha. The final act takes place before the high altar, the abbot after the nine prostrations returning to his apartment followed by the acolytes, and the instructor singing the last hymns and making the last genuflections, after which everybody retires.

In some monasteries there are as many as three such services every day, but two are the usual rule, for there are many other things to be attended to, and such a service may last one or two hours.

After morning mass there is a chance to complete one's toilet, after which comes breakfast. This is often followed by the ordered masses for the dead, when a band of monks must serve again in the temple hall. Then guests come who have to be entertained, the daily business must be attended to, etc. In some places, there are special schools for the young monks and novices. All too soon it is eleven o'-clock and the dinner bell calls the monks to the refectory. In the afternoon there is, as a rule, less to do, so it is easy then to get a talk with the monks. The evening mass is about five o'clock and is quite impressive. It differs from the morning mass only in including, as a rule, a part of the confession litany. The beautiful prayer of the "Pure Land" . . . is also chanted. The sutra used is often the little Amitabha scripture (the "O-mi-t'o Ching").

When there are no novices being educated in the monastery and all is quiet, it is considered a meritorious undertaking to have a law scholar (Fashih) connected with the monastery giving regular lectures or expositions of different classical writings. If the abbot himself is a law scholar he may do it, but as a rule some famous expositor from another place is engaged. This serves to bring fame to the monastery. It is announced a long time ahead, by big posters, that such and such a master is going to give lectures on some of the scriptures. "All who are devoted to Buddhism are welcomed." The master is received and treated with veneration. . . . The lecture usually takes place in the afternoon. It has fallen to my lot to be present on many such occasions.

The master comes in, accompanied by the abbot, and takes his seat on a stage beside the image of Vairocana or Maitreya. When he enters, everybody stands up. A short mass is read as an introduction to the lecture. The master sits with his feet crossed under him like a living Buddha, and the choir boys arrange the folds of his gown neatly around him. In addition to the monks there gradually assemble a group of interested laymen, old pensioned officials, scholars, or even a group of venerable matrons. The young monks distribute copies of the scripture that is to be read, to every one present. First the master reads a passage. Then he begins to explain sentence by sentence, while he gives a general survey later. He sometimes launches out into the deep so that it is difficult for the "unlearned" to follow him, but often he gives out real pearls. His theme carries him away, one feels his deep emotion, but he controls himself and forces himself back to the usual academic style.

Without doubt these lectures do much good, especially among the monks who are led deeper into the great religious thoughts. They act as an antidote to the mechanical routine which constantly tends to blunt the mind. . . .

It remains now to say something further about meditation. This can be done either privately in the different cells or unitedly in the meditation hall. At the latter place, regular courses in meditation are given under the leadership of the "wei-na" [instructor] or the "t'ang-chu" [assistant instructor]. These are meant to assist the newly ordained monks to become familiar with this holy art, but one often sees older monks also, both from among the casual visitors and those who have definite occupations in the monastery, joining in voluntarily. These older monks have their seats on the left side as one enters. Here, also, the "lord of the hall" (*t'ang-chu*) sits. The instructor sits on the right side near the group of young monks.

He has the "fragrant beating boards" (*hsiang-pan*) on his side, and is placed on a separate raised seat. He keeps a close watch on all, and if irregularities occur, he gives his reprimand when the period is over, at which time the "fragrant boards" may be used. By his side he has two young assistants, who help in his work.

Special beating of the big drum calls the monks together for meditation. In order to benefit fully from the holy exercise it is the rule first to take two or three quick marches to get the blood moving. The whole group makes a round of the corridors and then re-enter and take their places. At a given signal everybody gets up again, and the quick march is resumed, this time round the hall, going a certain number of times round in circles, the leader at the side of the group with a long bamboo pole in his hand. "Right about face" is ordered by a heavy stroke of the bamboo pole on the floor, after which the quick step goes in the opposite direction. This is done as many as three times. Then the big drum is again sounded, the door is shut, the participants resume their seats, and the meditation proper commences. Meanwhile, a long incense stick has been lighted in one of the outer halls. This is looked after by an attendant (*hsiang-têng*). Three quarters of an hour may elapse before it has burned down. When it does, the fact is announced by renewed drum beating. A new stick is then lighted, burns out, and another three quarters of an hour has passed. If the meditation is to take "three incense sticks," still another is lighted, and in this way they mark altogether two and a quarter hours. The periods in the meditation are thus divided according to the burning down of the incense sticks. This, too, expresses the thought that meditation should assist a person to concentrate his mind so that it ascends in a fine, straight line, as one sees the incense smoke rise from a stick in a closed room. . . .

It is of first importance in meditation to get the correct posture. Without this, it is difficult to attain to the right condition of mind. The posture is the same as that of the historic Buddha when he sat under the Bodhi-tree and had his great inner experience: the legs crossed under him, the eyes half shut, the hands loosely crossed in front. If one sits quietly and immovably like this, and breathes deeply and regularly, one will have bound or chained that part of the body which mostly hinders man in the free expansion of the mind. But more is required, for though it is difficult to get accustomed to the rather uncomfortable position, this is gradually learned, particularly if one begins in youth. A thousand times more difficult is the next step: to become calm and acquire concentration. To help toward this the instructor repeatedly enjoins: "Away with all unnecessary and vain thoughts," "the heart must get to rest" (*hsin kuei-i*). Here it is that many fight a desperate inner battle, and worst of all, one is not allowed to ask Buddha for help. No, here in the meditation hall, Buddha must in no form be invoked for mercy. Here one must "yung kung" oneself, labor on to the goal. Many have given up the effort at this, the second step, and allowed it to become a merely mechanical performance.

Where, then, shall those who would attain to this calm of mind begin? The answer is: You must begin with yourself. Think of where you have come from; what you were before you were born into the world as a man. Think until you see your original face (*pen-lai-ti mien-mu*). Then think of what you may attain to if all the illusions of the world, all the wordly and carnal desires, are annihilated. (Here drastic directions are given of how to see through the emptiness and ugliness of everything connected with the body and the senses.) Think of being delivered from all this! Think what it means to get behind all feelings of pleasure and displeasure, to be raised above the vicissitudes of life, to see clearly, to see "emptily," and face the future as one who has already conquered it. At this stage one may begin thinking of Buddha, not the historical Buddha, but the Buddha idea. And from this elevation he is seen in a new light: Buddha is not a distant personality, he is myself in my final redemption, which I now perceive from the midst of the white mist in which I am sitting. The few elect who attain to this feel as if their seats have been changed into a flowery bed of the most brilliant and fragrant lotus. Personally, I have met such persons. They long for the hour of meditation, and even continue their meditation in their own chambers until late at night.

From this it will be understood why the Buddhists call meditating "tso kung-fu" or "yung-kung"; namely, work. They often measure the spiritual worth and character of a monk by the extent to which he finds his enjoyment in meditation. . . .

A CONDEMNATION OF BUDDHISM

Buddhism was a major factor in Chinese religion from the chaotic time following the loss of northern China to non-Chinese invaders and the consequent migration of many of the elite to the south in the early fourth century, to the time of the major suppression that took place in the ninth century. Jacques Gernet has made the point that Buddhist institutions became so involved with economic interests that when the economic footing was pulled out in the suppression, Buddhism never recovered its previous domination. From that time until a resurgence beginning in the early twentieth century, again in a period of cultural chaos, Buddhism was held in askance by many, perhaps the majority, of Chinese, its assimilated elements notwithstanding. A summation of the attitude toward Buddhism as a foreign religion beneath contempt was forcefully stated by the highly influential scholar-official and essayist Han Yü (768–824). His memorial to the throne was instigated by the planning of a ceremony in which the Emperor was to receive a relic, a finger bone supposedly of the Buddha. The expected punishment of execution for such an attack on the Emperor was commuted to banishment because of the groundswell of support for the memorial by the literati. Han Yü's memorial was in part responsible for the shift in opinion that led to the suppression of the mid-ninth century. These attitudes can still be found today among many Chinese who hold to traditional values. The translation is by the editor (J.P.).

HAN YÜ: MEMORIAL TO THE THRONE ON THE BONE OF THE BUDDHA

Your servant humbly submits that Buddhism is merely a barbarian mode of behaving. Only during the later part of the Han dynasty did it gradually enter China; it was not present in remote antiquity.

In ancient times, the Yellow Emperor reigned for a century and lived to be 110; Shao Hao reigned for eighty years and lived to be 100; Chuan Hsü reigned for seventy-nine years and lived to be 98; Emperor Yao reigned for ninety-eight years and lived to be 118; and Emperors Shun and Yao both lived to be 100. During these times, the world was peaceful, and the people were happy and enjoyed long lives because China did not yet have Buddhism.

Afterward T'ang of Yin lived to be a hundred, and his descendants T'ai-mou reigned for seventy-five years and Wu-ting for fifty-nine years. While the histories do not record how long they lived, surely it was not less than a hundred years. In the Chou dynasty, King Wen lived to be ninety-seven and King Wu ninety-three, and King Mu reigned for a century. In those times, Buddhist doctrines has still not entered China. It was not due to worshiping Buddha that these kings achieved such longevity.

It was during the reign of Emperor Ming of the Han dynasty that Buddhist doctrines first appeared; Emperor Ming reigned but eighteen years. Afterward, disaster followed upon disaster, and the reigns were all short. From the Sung, Ch'i, Liang, Ch'en and Northern Wei dynasties onward, the worship of Buddhism increased and the reign spans decreased, excepting Emperor Wu of the Liang dynasty, who reigned for forty-eight years. During his reign, he thrice consecrated himself to the Buddha [as a monk]; in his ancestral temple, he did not sacrifice animals; and he daily ate but a single vegetarian meal. But in the end, he was conquered by Hou Ching and starved to death in the T'ai-ch'eng palace, and his state was destroyed. Hence, the worship of Buddha in the search for prosperity but resulted in disaster. It should be obvious that Buddha is not worthy of worship.

When Kao-tsu (the first emperor of the T'ang dynasty) first succeeded the Sui dynasty, he considered doing away with Buddhism, but the ministers at the time were lacking in ability and foresight, and they had a weak understanding of the ancient kings' way and of what was suitable for the past and the present. Thus they were incapable of giving sagely advice in order to save the country from this evil. Your obedient servant has always regretted that the attempt [to get rid of Buddhism] was stopped short.

Your Majesty is sagacious, supreme in the arts of war and peace, a divine sage and great hero, as has not appeared for a thousand years. When you ascended the throne, you forbade the ordination of monks, nuns, and Taoist priests; you did not allow the construction of new temples and monasteries. I was certain the Kao-tsu's intentions would be carried out by Your Majesty's hand. Or if this could not be accomplished, at least [Buddhism and Taoism] would not be permitted to spread and flourish.

Now one hears that Your Majesty has ordered monks to welcome a bone of the Buddha at Feng-hsiang and is preparing to watch from a tower its entry into the palace. Moreover, every monastery [as the relic passes through China] has been ordered to reverence it in turn. Although your servant is most ignorant, even he certainly knows Your Majesty is not so deluded about Buddhism that you would worship this relic to seek blessings. Rather, because this is a year of prosperity and happiness, you accord with the people's wishes in allowing the population of the capital this weird and perverse spectacle. For how could a sage intelligence as yours believe in this?

The minds of ordinary people, however, are easy to mislead but difficult to enlighten. If they see Your Majesty acting in this manner, they will think you are really worshiping the Buddha. All will say, "If the Son of Heaven, a great sage, believes with all his heart, then how can we ordinary people begrudge our bodies and our lives?" Thus, they will cauterize their scalps and burn off their fingers [in being initiated as monks and nuns], by the tens and the hundreds they will throw off their [ordinary] clothes and disperse their wealth [in joining the Buddhist clergy], and from dawn to dusk they will follow each other in fear of being left behind. Old and young in restless waves will discard their trades and professions and if they are not immediately stopped, will go from monastery to monastery cutting off their arms and mutilating their bodies as a form of sacrifice! Such immoral behavior, which will make us a laughing stock to the world, is not a trifling matter.

The Buddha was a barbarian: he did not understand Chinese; his clothing was of a different cut. He did not speak of matters pertaining to the ancient kings, nor did he wear clothing as prescribed by the former kings. He did not know the deportment suitable to ruler and minister nor the affection between father and son. Should he be alive and come to court as an envoy of his country, Your Majesty would have admitted him and granted a single audience in the reception hall, a single banquet, and a single suit of clothing. He would then be escorted to the border and not be allowed to delude the multitudes. [Since this is all you would do were he alive,] given that he has been dead for such a long time, how is it possible that this rotten and decayed bone, this evil and filthy relic, is allowed to enter the private apartments of the palace?

Kung-fu-tzu (Confucius) said: "Respect the spirits (the dead of other families) but keep your distance from them." In antiquity, when a feudal lord went on a visit of condolence, even were it in their own state, they ordered an exorcist to recite incantations and precede them with a peachwood wand to remove all possibility of misfortune. Only then did they proceed to go and offer their condolences [to the bereaved].

But now with no reason, you will personally observe this decayed and unclean thing without being preceded by an exorcist, and the peachwood wand will not be used. Your officers do not speak of this error, and your censors do not raise this mistake. I am deeply ashamed. I entreat you to hand this bone over to the proper authorities so it can be thrown into fire and water so that it be destroyed forever, ending the world's confusion and halting the delusions of future generations. This will cause all of the people of the world to know how a great sage's actions are vastly beyond those of ordinary people. How could this not lead to success! How could this not lead to rejoicing!

If the Buddha actually has spiritual power and is able to bring about misfortune, then let all the calamities befall your servant. Heaven will witness that your servant will not complain nor regret it. With the deepest emotion and profound sincerity, your servant humbly presents this memorial.

CHAPTER 9

Their Separate Ways: Cults and Sects

THE LUNG-HUA SECT: SECRET RELIGIOUS SOCIETY

How much of the true religious life of the Chinese has been carried on in sects or societies popular among the masses we shall never be able to determine because all sectarian organizations of this sort being illegal in the Chinese polity, their membership, beliefs, and practices have usually not been documented. Certain of the secret societies have indeed played a prominent role in history, but there must have been countless others that came into existence and eventually ended without any historical notice. It has been remarkably difficult to obtain detailed information even about those known by name. Nevertheless, we believe that the need for religious life, felt by the Chinese as by every other people and unsatisfied by any other institution of the traditional civilization, must most commonly have found its expression through participation in these clandestine groups.

One of the most circumstantial accounts available to us is that of two closely related sects, the Sien-t'ien [Hsien-t'ien] and the Lung-hwa [Lung-hua], which came under the expert scrutiny of J. J. M. de Groot in Amoy in 1887. Through great good luck Dr. de Groot was made privy to all the details concerning these sects, which he then included in his book, *Sectarianism and Religious Persecution in China*, E. J. Brill (Leiden, 1901; reprinted in Taipei, 1963, Literature House, Ltd.). The second of the two sects seems likely to be the more representative of the type, and we therefore extract from de Groot's account some particulars about the religious character of the group. This condensation comes from Chapter 7, pp. 197–241.

[The Lung-Hwa sect] worships a great number of gods and goddesses, and makes painted or carved likenesses of them. At the head of the Pantheon are the three Apexes of the Hsien-t'ien sect,[1] mostly represented in watercolors on large scrolls,

---

[1]These have earlier been described by the author as the Wu-chi, the T'ai-chi, and the Huang-chi; they are abstract philosophical concepts rather than personalities—the first means Limitless (or in de Groot's interpretation, Apex of Nothingness), the second Extreme Limit (or in de Groot's translation, Grand Apex), and the third Omnipotence (or what de Groot calls Apex of Imperiality). The first two terms have a long and complicated history in Chinese philosophy; but here they are deified and anthropomorphized. (L.G.T.)

as three old men, each holding in his hands the eight trigrams, arranged in a circle . . . In some meeting places I saw these pictures suspended on the wall for worship during the religious exercises. The Wu-chi or Apex of Nothingness is the principal person of this Triad, and thus the chief god of the sect. He is the sovereign ruler of the Nirvana-Paradise, and regulates the admission thereto. . . . As in the Hsien-t'ien sect, we find among the deities of the Lung-hwa society the Triratna of Buddhism [i.e. the Three Jewels: Buddha, Dharma, Sangha], and moreover, all kinds of Buddhist, Confucian and Taoist saints. The chief of these dii minores [minor deities] are the God of Heaven (T'ien-kung) and the Goddess of Earth (Hou-t'u), the sun, the moon, Avalokiteśvara, Amitabha, Śakyamuni, Dharmapala. In some meetingplaces I also saw a tablet inscribed with the name of the tutelary god of the City-walls and Moats (Ch'eng-huang Yeh), . . . Besides, I also saw a similar tablet dedicated to the far more ancient, homebred god of the Domestic Fireplace (Tsao-shen), and also tablets of four generals of an imaginary army by means of which the God of Heaven maintains order and peace in the Universe, which is incessantly disturbed and harassed by evil demons. . . .

For their common services in honour of these deities, and for their religious meetings in general, the sectaries use the principal apartment or hall *(t'ang* or *miao)* in ordinary dwelling-houses, with the full consent, of course, of the owner, often himself a leader. Such places they call at Amoy, *ts'ai-tug (ts'ai-t'ang)*, "vegetarian halls," because the Buddhist command against the killing of living beings makes the sectaries altogether vegetarians. [There follows here an explanation of the hierarchy of the organization, which we omit.]

Looking upon each other as brothers and sisters [the members of the sect] generally denominate one another familiarly as *ts'ài-iú (ts'ai-yu)* or "vegetarian friends," the men as *ts'ài-kong (ts'ai-kung)* or "gentlemen vegetarians," the women as *ts'ai-ko (ts'ai-ku)* or "lady vegetarians"; the leaders they simply call *ts'ài-t'âo (ts'ai-t'ou)* or "vegetarian chiefs." Each parish or hall has a leader, who most often is the master of the house. He has charge of the altar which bears the images of the Triratna, Avalokiteśvara, and whatever other Saints the brotherhood may worship, as also a tablet inscribed with the names of the seven latest deceased leaders, and held to be inhabited by their souls. . . . All communities of the Lung-hwa society are zealous in enlisting new members. A chief encouragement to this work is the great reward held out to all who bring in neophytes, namely, promotion to a higher religious rank. . . .

[The author next describes in detail the initiation ceremonies, whose overall character is summed up thus:] As a matter of fact it is nothing else than a subdivision of the consecration-ritual of Buddhist monks. . . . Besides the intrinsically Buddhistic character of the sect, the ritual of the initiation shows us the syncretic spirit of it. The five fundamental Commandments of Buddha [against killing, theft, sexual immorality, lying, drinking alcohol] are, indeed, brought in connection with the five Constant Matters *(wu ch'ang)* or Confucian fundamental virtues: benevolence, righteousness, ceremonies and rites, knowledge, and trustworthiness, which from time immemorial have played an important part in classical ethics. Following Mencius, who boldly declared that the first four of these virtues are innate, philosophers have always identified them with man's character, his *hsing*, bestowed by heaven, and therefore intrinsically good. Hence they are, like this natural character, emanations from the Way of heaven, the Tao . . . The ground theme of Confucian ethics being thus essentially Taoistic, the Lung-hwa sect by adopting it gives itself a Taoistic character. Its syncretism goes further still, for novices are admonished by the Initiator to identify themselves with the five Elements [*wu hsing*][2] of which the universe is composed. . . . And finally, the syncretism of the sect is evident from the compulsion laid upon the neophytes to obey six precepts of the Sage Edict [promulgated by the first emperor of the Ming dynasty]. . . . The initiation or first consecration in reality changes the recipients into Devas [divine powers], unless they break their vow, renounce the Triratna, and sin against the commandments. . . .

As already noticed, the members of the Lung-hwa sect at Amoy, in order to promote their individual and mutual Salvation, hold quiet meetings for the worship of their Saints and Buddhas, and for the reciting of Sutras,[3] liturgical prayers, and powerful Tantrani [magical utterances]. These meetings do not generally take place on fixed dates, but at the convenience of the participators . . . Moreover, the sect has a number of so-called *pài-kìng jít* (*pai-ching jih*) or "days of worship," being calendar days devoted to the worship of special Saints. These are:

1. Fifth of first month, in commemoration of the Patriarch Lo, the founder of the sect.
2. Ninth of first month, in honor of the God of Heaven.
3. Fifteenth of first month, in honor of the Rulers of the three Worlds.
4. Nineteenth of second month, in honor of Kwan-yin.
5. Nineteenth of third month, in honor of the Lord of the Great Light (*t'ai-yang kung*), the Sun.
6. Eighth of fourth month, birthday of the Buddha Śakyamuni.
7. Sixth of sixth month, the opening of Heaven.
8. Nineteenth of sixth month, in honor of Kwan-yin.
9. Last of seventh month, birthday of the Lord of Hell, Ti-tsang Wang.
10. Fifteenth of eighth month, chief festival of the Moon.
11. Nineteenth of ninth month, in honor of Kwan-yin.
12. Seventeenth of eleventh month, birthday of the Buddha Amitabha.
13. Twenty-third of twelfth month, on which the gods ascend to heaven.

In this list the syncretic character of the sect is especially conspicuous. No less than five of these thirteen days are . . . calendrical festivals of the people in general, viz. the second, third, seventh, tenth and thirteenth . . . Buddhistic yearly feasts of the laity are the fourth, eighth, and eleventh; and the sixth, ninth and twelfth days are taken from the calendar of Buddhist monastic life. The first alone is the special property of the sect. The list shows that the principal Saints of the sect are the same as those of the Chinese Mahayana church in general. . . .

In the early morning of the feastdays cups of tea are placed upon the altar of the hall, to refresh the Saints residing there. . . . Successively more members make

---

[2]Water, fire, wood, metal, earth. (L. G. T.)

[3]Discourses, or sections of discourses, by the Buddha. (L. G.T.)

their appearance, until the male or female leader is of the opinion that enough of them are present to commence the great service. Rice, vegetables, fruit and tea are now placed upon a table in front of the altar, together with fragrant incense, for the benefit of the Saint whose festival is being celebrated. A smaller portion is in like manner allotted to each of the other principal Saints of the hall, and the members range themselves in one or more long rows along the sidewalls of the apartment, the men, attired in the long ceremonial robe and with a conical straw hat overlaid with red fringe, to the left of the saints, and the women to the right. In both rows the highest graduates are nearest to the altar. With closed eyes, and the palms of the hands pressed together before their breasts, all mumble unanimously a series of formulas and extracts from the Sutras, one of them tapping with a wooden knocker on a hollow wooden bowl at every syllable pronounced. And the first word of every strophe is marked by a stroke on a metal bell. When this pious work has been continued for some little time, the men come forward, two by two, and kneel in front of the sacrifice, respectfully saluting the Buddhas and Saints on the altar by touching the ground nine times with their foreheads. After them the women do the same, only at a somewhat greater distance from the altar. This act of devotion ended, the dishes with food are removed from the altar, and converted into a vegetarian meal, of which all the brethren and sisters may partake. . . . When the meal is over, each member takes leave of the head of the parish with a courteous bow, thanks him, and departs.

On the four annual days specially devoted to Kwan-yin and Amitabha, and, if desired, on any other festival, either immediately after this first meeting, or later on in the day, the fraternity assembles again. This second meeting is called that of the *pan-jo ch'uan*, "the Ship of Prajna or Wisdom," i.e., the highest of the Parami or perfections by which Nirvana is reached.

A small barge or boat of bamboo and paper, intended to convey departed souls to the Paradise of the West, is placed in the open court in front of the hall. The sails, flags or pennons, and other parts of the rigging are decorated with inscriptions bearing upon this spirit-journey. At the rudder is a paper effigy of Kwan-yin, the high patroness of the Mahayana church, and as such, supreme guide of its members on the road to Salvation. Her satellite Hwan-shen-tsai holds the sheet, her female attendant, called the Dragon's Daughter, stands on the foreship, holding up a streamer on which is written *chieh-yin hsi-fang*, "be admitted and introduced into the West (the Paradise)." Several other Buddhist saints, such as Brahma, and Wei-t'o-shen or Indra, do duty as sailors. Round this Bark of Mercy (*tz'u-hang*) the members of the sect range themselves, and under the guidance or not, as the case may be, of one or more of their number, who are consecrated monks, they hold a series of Sutra readings, interspersed with invocations and Tantrani, to induce the holy Kwan-yin to take souls on board and convey them to the land of bliss. And finally, under the should of *O-bî-tô (O-mi-tó)* repeated many hundred times, the ship with all its contents is burned on the spot. Thus, through fire and flame, the Bark of Wisdom plies right across the sea of transmigration to the promised Nirvana, where the highest Intelligence prevails. If the seashore is near, the bark is sometimes launched there on a plank, and allowed to drift away with the tide. . . .

Another solemnity, performed on many of those festivals, is called *pài ts'ien hút (pai ch'ien fo)*, "Veneration of the thousand Buddhas." All present stand in rows, with the palms of their hands pressed together before their breasts. Some who can read have a small table in front of them, on which the Sutra lies. They mumble an All-saints litany, every sentence of which is, "Namah Buddha So and So" followed by a slow semigenuflexion. In this manner, at least a thousand names are recited, even two or three times successively; but as it is impossible to keep up the knee-drill long, the litany is now and again broken off, and the interlude filled up with a piece of another Sutra, or with invocations without genuflexions. The object of this litany is to obtain pardon of sins by exciting internally, at the invocation of each name, a feeling of deep repentance. It is therefore called "The Sutra of Repentance of the Names of a thousand Buddhas." The members who cannot read the litany and do not know it by heart, only mumble in their mind. This act of repentance plays an important part in monastic life, and is performed in many different forms. . . .

As in the meetinghalls, so in private houses Sutra readings form as essential part of the great practice of Salvation. These readings are performed either standing or kneeling, and often the worshiper accompanies himself by tapping rapidly on a hollow wooden bowl, and at intervals on a metal bell, as the monks in Buddhist convents are wont to do. Very few sectaries understand what they recite. Most of them have only learned by heart the sound of the characters. . . . The understanding has nothing to do with the meritoriousness of this pious work. For the Sutras are the sacred books which make known the roads that lead to Salvation, and to proclaim them at all times, together with the Vinayas or religious rescripts which serve to keep mankind in those roads, is the highest duty imposed upon the sons and daughters of Buddah. . . . He who fulfils this duty is deserving in the highest degree. What then does it matter whether he understands what he recites? The mighty salvation power contained in the Sutra or Vinaya loses nothing by it, and moreover—who can tell?—perchance there are myriads of unseen spirits on the spot listening to the recital, and obtaining Salvation thereby. . . . It is the quantity of the recited matter that is of chief importance. . . .

If the members of the sect are asked for the reason why Kwan-yin occupies so prominent a place among their patron saints, the ready answer is to the effect that she has constantly proved herself a faithful deliverer of all victims of misfortune and oppression who invoke her. . . . The stories about deliverance brought by Kwan-yin, most of them centuries old, generally represent her appearances to have been called forth by the reading of Sutras dedicated to her.

Very zealous sectaries recite at least once a day; many do so twice, in the morning and in the evening, not counting the extra readings on calendar feast-days and sundry special occasions. When a sick man or woman is to be comforted or cured by means of Sutras, the reading of these is benevolently performed at the bedside by one or more brethren, who, in conclusion, burn a written prayer on behalf of the patient, addressed to Kwan-yin.

For those who cannot read, or cannot learn Sutras by heart, there exists an easy, and therefore very popular method of obtaining Salvation. This consists in repeating hundreds and thousands of times one and the same Saint's name, with the prefix *lam-bû* (Namah). And here the name of Amitabha (Amit'o), the Lord of Paradise, is of paramount efficacy. [On the sail of the Bark of Mercy and Wisdom previously described, which is depicted on woodcut prints used in keeping track of the number of times one recites the formula, the following is written:] "The mere word Amit'o is a precious sword cutting down all heresies. It is a brave general who defeats hell. It is a bright torch shedding its light in the blackest darkness. It is a bark of mercy into Paradise; the shortest path to lead us out of the wheel of transmigration; a salutary means to help us out of existence. It is a mysterious, magic word which makes us immortal, a remedy imbued with spiritual power, which renovates our bones. The 84,000 schools of the Dharma are contained in those six words (Na-mah A-mi-t'o-fo); those words are one sword-stroke which cuts through 1700 dolichos stalks. If one mutters nothing but the word Amit'o, one need not even trouble to clap one's fingers, in order to reach the West."

Other prints of this kind . . . bear similar inscriptions, but represent Salvation somewhat differently. Here Amit'o stands in the ship, which sails in a shower of flowers, while several devotees, recognizable as people of either sex and of various social position and age, in kneeling attitude, and with hands folded as in prayer, crowd a strip of light which emanates from his hand. Thus the bark in full sail draws them along by this Buddha's light of Salvation towards Paradise.

The foregoing pages have shown, that the pious work of saving the dead by prevailing upon Kwan-yin to convey them into the Western Paradise of Amit'o, forms one of the chief items in the religious program of the Lung-hwa sect. Doubtless this work is its vital point, as the prospect of being piloted by brethren and sisters in Buddha to those regions of supreme felicity must be the strongest motive for most neophytes to join the sect. What will become of my soul and body after death? is the great question which occupies the minds of the whole Chinese people, and *a fortiori* of those who strive after ideals, the realization of which lies in a future world. Is it to be wondered at that so many childless concubines and widows take refuge with the sect? They know well, that in the human society in which they live, where begetting sons is one of the highest moral duties, they are looked upon as worthless creatures, only deserving of being buried in a poor style by indifferent relations, or even by public charity; they know well that, but for the religious community to which they entrust themselves, only a trifling sum will be spent on religious ceremonies on behalf of their souls.

[The author now describes the washing and dressing of the corpse, which is clad in what is essentially a Buddhist clerical garb. This being done by the sectarian brothers (for males) or sisters (for females),] the saving process of the dead begins. Candles are lighted in the apartment, and particularly near the body; incense is burnt in considerable quantities, and some sectaries recite together various sanctifying Sutras, repeating the name of Amit'o hundreds and hundreds of times. The death of a Buddhist who walked in the path of Salvation is called deliverance from the ocean of earthly woe, transition from an existence of imperfection and misery to one of perfection and felicity, therefore a most joyful event. Hence—unless they do not share the views of the sect—the relatives of the deceased do not spend the day in loud wailing and weeping, as the old and orthodox Confucian doctrine urgently prescribes; none of the inscriptions on red paper, adorning the outer and inner doors, are pasted over with white as sign of mourning; no furniture is removed from the apartment where the corpse lies, not even the domestic altar is taken away, to save the Saints whose animated images stand thereon, the spectacle of death, which might possibly bring them disaster. Mock paper money, which no true Confucian will omit to burn in large quantities to enrich his departed in the other world, is not used by the sect. The Buddhist, who forsakes the world and keeps the Commandments, ought to loathe riches, and shall he mar the felicity of his dead co-religionists by forcing treasures upon them? . . .

With the body in the coffin there are deposited three letters, or certificates, to facilitate the reception of the deceased into the Western Paradise. We give some excerpts from one of these documents, in de Groot's translation:

> Most humbly we hope that the defunct, on going home (to Nirvana), may be exempted from entering again any terrestrial wombs, and may enter into the womb of sanctity.
>
> This is to certify about an inhabitant of the place Amoy ... By worshipping the Buddhas, and by abstinence from forbidden food he has been drawn up to Salvation and carried to a higher condition ... He was born in this life on [such and such a year, month, day, hour]. Humbly bowed down to the ground, he saw the gates of the Dharma opened wide for him by the Highest Apex of Nothingness, the Sage Patriarch; he took refuge in the orthodox doctrine, and accepted the excellent laws of the Tathagatas, which lead to the nine religious degrees ... and so having accepted the Religion, he earnestly applied himself to this day to the keeping of the five Commandments; and the ten Commandments too he steadfastly kept. Now he has gone home. . . . His great destiny is herewith settled, and the years of his life in this world of light are accomplished; so we turn towards Thee, most high Apex of Nothingness, Sage Patriarch, to declare all together before Thy Lotus-throne that he, an offspring of the beautiful Religion, has followed the instruction of his teachers and thus obtained degrees; that he has burnt no (paper) money (for the spirits and gods) on high, nor (paper) horses for (the souls in) the infernal regions; that he has promulgated the admirable principles come to us from the West [India], and has felt sorrow and remorse over the iniquities of the East (China). . . .
>
> We give this good certificate to the wise soul of [so-and-so], graduated in our Religion. He will travel with it first to the Mountain of the Souls (i.e., T'ai Shan), and have it examined there for determination of the share of felicity to be allotted to him; and then he will return to his origin (Nirvana), to be rooted and grounded therein for everlasting kalpas, to sorrow over the sins and vices of the present life, and to gather inexhaustible blessing. . . .

Under the guidance of members who are consecrated Buddhist priests, a service is now celebrated which has for its object to convey the soul into Paradise. It is called *téng se-hong (chuan hsi-fang)*, "going or sending home to the West." ... The altar erected for the occasion, is adorned with portraits in watercolors of some principal Saints of the sect. Those of the three Apexes may on no account be absent. The chief of this triad, the Apex of Nothingness, the personification of the Nirvana-Paradise into which the deceased is expected to be received, hangs in the middle. . . .

On the way to the grave the following verse is recited at intervals:

> For several dozen years thou hast kept the fast unbroken,
> And now thou travellest home, and returnest to thine origin.
> At the assembly on the Mountain of Souls [T'ai Shan] mayest thou have
>   pleasant meetings;
> We hope that in the West thou mayest be seated on a precious lotus.
> Today, on this journey homeward, all things cease for thee to exist,
> Thou hast nothing further to do with springs and autumns of human life;
> Depart then to-day quickly to the West,
> There take thy stand on a lotus-throne, to ascend step by step ever higher
>   thereon.
> Namah, Buddha Amit'o. . . .

HUNG HSIU-CH'UAN AND A CHINESE UNDERSTANDING OF CHRISTIANITY

The government's suspicion of sectarian movements was not without cause. In periods of dynastic collapse and resultant social chaos, Chinese millenarian movements sought to create a paradise in the here and now, and some such movements have led to rebellion. A ready ideological basis was the notion of the "Mandate of Heaven." When interpreted by any movement as having been lost by the government in power, the mandate descended on the movement itself. In the mid-nineteenth century, following the *de facto* near collapse of the government consequent to its acquiescing to Britain and other European powers after the short-lived first "Opium War," a Chinese mode of Christianity adopted a militaristic revolutionary stance and conquered all of central China. Had European armies and generals not bolstered the weak Ch'ing regime, it surely would have fallen. The following analysis of the religious understanding of the movement's visionary leader is taken from Jordan Paper's *The Spirits Are Drunk: Comparative Approaches to Chinese Religion*, pp. 247–259, with unessential references removed.

Since the formation of the first Chinese empire over two millennia ago, there have been three major heterodox, communal revolutionary movements instigated by foreign ideas. The first was the Yellow Turban movement of the second century, probably inspired in part by awareness of Buddhism. The second, the Taiping movement of the nineteenth century, whose name coincides with the name of the first movement's major text, was inspired by Christianity. The last, the Chinese Communist party of the twentieth century, was inspired by Marxist–Leninism. The first two movements swept over much of China before being destroyed by the existing dynasty, which in each case subsequently collapsed after several decades. The last movement ultimately succeeded in unifying and establishing control over China.

Each movement's understanding of the foreign inspiring ideas was partial at best. Buddhism was still a religion of foreign traders in the second century, and Indian ideas were not fully understood in China for another several hundred years when a few Chinese became experts in Sanskrit. Neither Stalin nor Kruschev thought Mao Zedong understood Marxist–Leninism. The understanding of Christianity by the founder of the Taiping movement, Hong Xiuquan, is the subject of this section.

Biography

Hong Xiuquan (1814–1864) was brought up in a southern Chinese farming family but studied for the civil service examinations. Although he passed the preliminary examination, he repeatedly failed the first examination, as did all but a small percentage of those who sat for it.

Following one of these failures in 1837, Hong became seriously ill and in delirium had a vision that was subsequently to form the basis of the Taiping movement. After his last failed attempt at the examinations in 1843, a cousin called his attention to a book he had been given seven years previous in Canton but to which he had paid little attention. This book, the *Quanshi liangyan* (English title: *Good Words to Admonish the Age: Being Nine Miscellaneous Christian Tracts*) provided Hong with an ideological basis for understanding his earlier vision.

> Consequently, in the words of one of his followers, He exhorted everyone to worship God and cultivate virtue, saying that people willing to worship God would avoid disasters and suffering. Those who did not worship God would be injured by serpents and tigers. Those who worshipped God must not worship other deities: those who worshipped other deities would be committing a crime.[4]

Hong converted friends and relatives, and within a year a friend founded the Bai Shangdi hui (God Worshippers Society).

The *Quanshi liangyan* by Liang Afa, published in 1832, includes in English: "printed at the expense of the Religious Tract Society, Canton, China." An eclectic but primarily Christian work, it is the basic source for Hong's limited understanding of Christianity. In it we find the origin for Hong's terminology, including *shen* (spirit), as well as *shangdi* God), *tianguo* (heavenly kingdom) meaning both Paradise and a kingdom on earth of Christian believers, and *taiping* (great peace), a perfect God-worshipping kingdom. Hence, the title for Hong's nearly successful state, *Taiping tianguo*, derives from Liang's book.

Hong, however, did not slavishly follow the *Quanshi liangyan*. His movement adopted many Chinese religious practices specially forbidden by the text. These practices included offering food and wine to God as well as burning paper money and interpreting dreams and omens. By 1848, two of Hong's followers began to function as mediums for God, the Heavenly Father, and Jesus, the Heavenly Elder Brother. Their descents and messages, especially preceding military crises, continued the revelation of Hong's initial vision.

Hong's awareness of Christianity was further increased during the month or so he spent in 1847 with the Reverend Issachar T. Roberts, an American Southern Baptist, in Canton. However, Hong left or was forced leave before becoming formally baptized.

Between 1847 and 1849, the economic and political situation in southern China continued to deteriorate. The God Worshippers Society began to arm and begin military training for its followers. By 1850, military clashes occurred between the Manchu government and the Society. Following a successful repulse of a major Manchu attack on the Society's forces at the end of 1850, at the beginning of 1851, Hong ceremoniously proclaimed himself the Tianwang (heavenly king) and declared the Taiping tianguo (heavenly kingdom of great peace). The Taiping armies continued on the whole to be successful, and in 1853 captured Nanjing. The old capital in central China was declared the Taiping capital.

Biblical Text

Hong probably encountered his first Bible during his stay with Roberts. Prior to being assigned to Canton, Roberts served as an assistant to Charles Gützlaff, one of the early Protestant translators of the Bible. Undoubtedly, Roberts was using

---

[4]C. A. Curwin, *Taiping Rebel, The Deposition of Li Hsiu-ch'eng* (Cambridge: Cambridge University Press, 1977), 79.

the Medhurst-Gützlaff Chinese text version, the New Testament having been printed in 1835 and the Old Testament in 1838.

It is this version of the Bible that the Taiping began to print in 1853 soon after capturing Nanjing and making it their capital. The first six books of the Old Testament (Genesis through Joshua) were published under the title *The Holy Book of the Old Testament Promulgated by Royal Order,* and the complete New Testament under the title, *The Holy Book of the Former Testament Promulgated by Royal Order.* That this Bible became important to Hong is evident in that it was substituted for the Classics as the text for the civil service examinations within the Taiping state.

The British Museum possesses a copy of the 1853 Taiping edition of the Bible, complete but for the fourth gospel (John), that must have been Hong's personal copy, for it has his hand-written annotations on the upper margins (the usual place for annotating Chinese books). These comments form the basis for the following analysis. Being marginalia, they are difficult to read and not always readily coherent to other than the writer. However, these difficulties are not likely to lead to any major errors in our understanding of Hong's thoughts since the commentary tends to be repetitive.

There have been two publications of these notes: a partial one by Xiao (1936:folio 1), and a complete text in Jin and Tian (1955:75–88).

Understanding the New Testament

Hong's comments on the New Testament fall into three recurring major themes and five minor points. The three major themes may be labelled (1) "Mediumism," (2) "The Trinity," and (3) "The Kingdom."

MEDIUMISM

Hong understood the biblical Jesus as Christ mediumistically descended into Jesus rather than Jesus as Christ being an incarnation of God. Hence, the descent of the spirit of God in Matthew 3:16–17 is understood as a mediumistic experience. More important, he indicates that God and Christ have now also mediumistically descended to the earth:

> The Holy Ghost is God. Moreover, the Great Elder Brother [Christ] is God's Primary Son. So they came [into the world when Jesus was baptized by John]. Now in the present, God and Christ have descended into the ordinary world. Respect this [phrase used to conclude imperial documents].

The immediate presence of God and Christ is repeatedly emphasized:

> [Matthew 5:19—at the end of the commentary] Today, the Heavenly Father and Heavenly Elder Brother have descended into the ordinary world to begin the Heavenly Kingdom. Respect this.
>   [The commentaries to both Matthew 10:32–33 and 13:30 contain this passage:] Now the Father and Elder Brother have descended into the ordinary world to destroy evil and preserve the righteous.

That the above passages can only be understood as referring to mediumistic descent is certain from the commentary to 1 John 5:7, where in the midst of one of the longest commentaries is found explicit reference to the two individuals who are understood as the mediums for God and Christ:

> It is in the present time that God has descended into the ordinary world, descended from the spirit world into the Eastern King [Yang Xiuqing], descended from the spirit world into the person of the Eastern King as the Holy Spirit. . . . The Father knows the New Testament has erroneous records. Therefore, he descended into the Eastern King to proclaim and certify that the Holy Spirit is God. . . . Also, He knows that ordinary people mistakenly understand Christ as God. Therefore, God descended into the Eastern King in order to make clear that the Divine Father indeed exists. Christ descended into the Western king [Xiao Chaoguei] in order to make clear that the Primary Son indeed exists.

The concept is repeated in the commentary to Revelations 11:19.

Mediumistic descent is understood according to the usual functions of mediumism, such as divine direction from above, healing, and divination. Jesus's healing in Matthew 8:3, 9:29–30, and Mark 2:12 are commented upon by Hong as mediumistic possession:

> [Matthew 8:3] God spiritually descended to reside in the head of the Great Elder Brother. A word from the Great Elder Brother was a word from God. Therefore, the leper was cleansed. Respect this.

Mediumistic guidance is referred to in Hong's comments to Romans 10:10 and Revelations 12:13–16 and 21:1–2.

THE TRINITY

More commentary is devoted to explicitly arguing that the Christian understanding of the Trinity is mistaken more often than any other theme. As in the comment to Matthew 3:17 quoted above and repeated in Mark 1:11 and Corinthians 2:10–16, the Holy Ghost is God.

Even more important is the point that God and Christ are two different spiritual entities; father and son cannot be the same person. Indeed, both are present in two different possessed mediums as quoted in the commentary to 1 John 5:7 above. Hong's understanding of monotheism in some respects is closer to Judaism and Islam than to normative Christianity:

> [Mark 12:29 where Jesus speaks the "Shema"] The Great Elder Brother clearly proclaimed a single Supreme Lord. Why did later disciples erroneously consider Christ to be God? If this were true, then there would be two Gods. Respect this.

In the comment to the following passage concerning Jesus teaching in the temple, Hong continues the argument and points out the evidence of his vision:

> Furthermore, how can it be that at the same time I ascended into Heaven, I met in Heaven God the Heavenly Father, Mom the Heavenly Mother, as well as the Great Elder Brother Christ and the Heavenly Elder Sister-in-law. Now [I] have descended into the ordinary world and there is still the Heavenly Father, the Heavenly Mother, the Heavenly Elder Brother and the Heavenly Sister-in-law! Respect this.

Further arguments that God and Christ are two different deities are to be found in Hong's comments to Luke 4:12, 7:16, and 12:8–10; Acts 4:24 and 7:55; Romans 1:4 and 9:5; and Corinthians 1:9 and 8:6.

Different from the Semitic understanding of monotheism is Hong's Chinese understanding of God as having a family; hence, we have in effect a single God-family. The vision described in the preceding quotation is repeated in the comments to 1 John 5:7 and Revelations 12:1–17.

Hong considered himself a member of this divine family, a younger brother of Christ:

> [Hebrews 7:1] This Melchizedek is myself [Hong uses the Chinese term for self used only by the emperor]. Previously in Heaven, Mom gave birth to the Great Elder Brother, myself and others of my generation. [Here follows a story of Hong blessing Abraham and a statement of Yang Xiuqing speaking as God that is understood as referring to Hong.] This statement is evidence that today I have descended to the ordinary world to be Lord. Respect this.

This commentary is repeated in but slightly different words in Hong's comments to Revelations 12:13–16. His "descent into the world as a human" is the subject of his commentary to Acts 2:22. In the first line of his commentary to Revelations 6:12–17, Hong writes, "I am the Taiyang; my wife is the Taiyin." Taiyang [Great *yang*] means the sun, but the sun as masculine, celestial power, humanized in the Chinese emperor, and Taiyin [Great *yin*] means the moon, but the moon as feminine, celestial power, humanized in the wife of the emperor.

That Hong is the Taiyang, in the sense of both the sun and the emperor, is reiterated in several commentaries to passages in Matthew:

> [Matthew 4:16–17] God is flame; the Taiyang is also flame. Therefore, God and the Taiyang have arrived together. Respect this . . . God is flame; therefore, he is Spiritual Light. The Great Elder Brother is flame; therefore, he is Great Light. I am the Taiyang; therefore, I am also light. Respect this.

In Matthew 24:27–29, Hong found reference to both himself and his wife:

> The Great Elder Brother feared to divulge it; therefore, he issued a secret proclamation that I am the Taiyang and have descended to the world to become a human. Hence, it [the sun] "darkened." My wife, the Taiyin, has descended to the world to become a human. Hence, it [moon] "does not give its light."

In this regard, Hong also plays a Chinese word game:

> [Matthew 27:40] Three dots is Hong [referring to the first three strokes in the written character]. "Three days" is Hong/sun [day and sun are the same Chinese character]. The Great Elder Brother secretly proclaiming Hong/sun will become Lord and rebuild the temple which God destroyed. Respect this.

THE KINGDOM

From a Chinese standpoint, Heaven and Earth are equal; they are, respectively, the male and female procreative forces. Both were sacrificed to by the emperor:

[Matthew 5:19] The unitary Great Kingdom includes Heaven above and Earth below, and one speaks of Heaven above as including the Heavenly Kingdom and Earth below as including the Earthly Kingdom. Heaven above and Earth below together compose the Divine Father's Heavenly Kingdom. Do not mistakenly assume it only refers to the Heavenly Kingdom in Heaven above. Therefore, the Great Elder Brother issued a proclamation stating "the Heavenly Kingdom is almost at hand," meaning the Heavenly Kingdom will come on the ordinary world. Today, the Heavenly Father and Heavenly Elder Brother descend to the ordinary world to establish the Heavenly Kingdom. Respect this.

The capture of Nanjing by Hong's movement was understood as the fulfillment of the promise of the second coming; hence, the establishment of the Taiping tianguo (heavenly kingdom of great peace). Hong understands the New Testament to be referring to future events that have now actually occurred:

[Matthew 24:38–39] Now the Father and Elder Brother ascend to Heaven on clouds [see Chapters 3 and 6] and gather all the people, who come from the four quarters, from the boundaries of the sky [the horizon]. All has been fulfilled. Respect this.

[Acts 15:15–16] Now God and Christ have descended to the ordinary world to rebuild God's temple in the Heavenly Capital. All the realm is united and seeks the Supreme Lord. Respect this.

Nanjing was declared the Taiping capital, the Heavenly Capital, and was understood as the New Jerusalem:

[Revelations 3:12] The Heavenly Father, God, sent down from Heaven the New Jerusalem which is now our Heavenly Capital. It is fulfilled. Respect this.

[Revelations 21:1–2] On Earth as it is in Heaven, what John saw was the Great Heavenly Palace. Heaven above and Earth below are the same. The New Jerusalem is now our Heavenly Capital.

MINOR POINTS

(1) *Sacrifice*   The practice of sacrificial meals has been central to Chinese religious practices since the Neolithic period (see Chapter 2) although denied to Chinese Christians by missionaries since the end of the Rites Controversy. Hong disagreed with the Christian missionaries and allowed a shift of the normative sacrifices from ancestral spirits to God:

[Matthew 9:12–13] The Great Elder Brother proclaimed his desire for mercy rather than sacrifice. This means people must have a good heart before sacrificing to God [a concept stressed in the *Lunyu* (Analects) of Kongfuzi (Confucius)]. [Christ] did not proclaim people should not sacrifice to God. Respect this.

This point is reiterated in Hong's commentary to Hebrews 10:8.

(2) *Confronting God and Christ*   Now that the Heavenly Kingdom is established, God and Christ are to be confronted as the emperor at an imperial audience:

The character *hui* [to assemble] . . . now changed to the character *jin* [an inferior presenting himself to his superior]. Before the Father and Elder Brother descended to the ordinary world to reign, it was appropriate to gather and *hui*. Now that the Father and Elder Brother have descended to the world to reign, it is appropriate to *jin* at court. Respect this.

(3) *Mary*   Mary becomes understood as the mother of God from a mediumistic standpoint rather than from the normative Christian position:

[Luke 1:35] It is said that the Holy Spirit, God, spiritually descended to her. It is not said that the Holy Spirit, God, entered her womb, was conceived and became a human. It is essential to understand [this]. Respect this.

(4) *Polygamy*   Contrary to the rulings of Christian missionaries in regard to common Chinese practices of the wealthy in the nineteenth century, Hong allowed the practice of polygamy, at least for the high officials:

[Titus 1:6] Now God's holy directive is that high officials' wives are not limited [Hong's language here is unclear].

(5) *Chinese Buddhist influence*   In Hong's commentaries there are a few examples of minor influence from popular Chinese religion. For example, in Hong's commentary to 1 Corinthians 15:49, he mentions "thirty-three Heavens."

In Revelations, Abaddon is equated by Hong (e.g., 9:11) with Yenlo (Sanskrit: Yama), who in Chinese Buddhism is ruler of one or all of the Hells (there are regional variations). In Revelations 12:13–16, in the midst of a long commentary, Yenlo is conflated with the "dragon" of the New Testament text as Satan: "serpent Yenlo," "serpent-demon Yenlo," and "the great red dragon is Abaddon Yenlo supernatural creature." Hong saw his role in this regard as follows:

Therefore, now the Father and Elder Brother have descended into the ordinary world making me the sovereign to especially destroy this serpent. Now the serpents and beasts have been destroyed and there is great peace [*taiping*] in the realm. Respect this.

Analysis

The analysis in this section is specific to Hong's commentary to the New Testament. Hence, the presentation of Hong's thought is limited and accordingly simplistic. Such a restricted presentation has the advantage of accentuating those points specific to biblical interpretation. A more general and thorough analysis of Hong's thought and Taiping ideology, and one that is relatively similar to my own, will be found in Shih (1967).[5]

For the typical mid-nineteenth-century missionary in China, usually fundamentalist, Hong and his movement was anathema. Robert Forrest, who translated a number of the above commentaries in the 1860s, wrote: "Considering the life of Hong-tsiu-tsuen [Hong Xiuquan], I am in no wise astonished at the grotesque monstrosity of his belief."[6]

---

[5]Vincent Y. C. Shih, *The Taiping Ideology, Its Sources, Interpretations, and Influences* (Seattle: University of Washington Press, 1967).

[6]Robert J. Forrest, "The Christianity of Hung Tsiu Tsuen, A Review of Taiping Books," *Journal of the North Branch of the Royal Asiatic Society* N. S. 4 (1867), 204.

However Europeans more aware and understanding of Chinese culture, and of the fact that there are and have been many kinds of Christianity, took a more equable view. Thomas Taylor Meadows, writing during the early part of the movement, noted:

> That a number of adult converts of a nation like the Chinese, which so long entertained, and is thoroughly imbued with, a particular set of fundamental beliefs, would, with or without express intention, considerably modify the Christianity which had attracted them was not simply probable—it was, humanly speaking, a certainty.[7]

An analysis of Hong's commentaries to the New Testament but serve to confirm Meadows' initial insight into Taiping Christianity. All of the foci of Hong's remarks—mediumism, the Trinity, and the Kingdom—reflect basic aspects of Chinese religious ideology and practice with a longstanding history.

Both shamanism and mediumism can be traced back at least as far as protohistoric Chinese religion, and they continue in Chinese culture to the present. Hence, it is to be expected that Hong understood the healing of Jesus from the standpoint of mediumism. Nor for that mater is such an interpretation uniquely Chinese. Morton Smith (1978) has analyzed the early Christian understanding of Jesus's healing within the context of Near Eastern magic, similar to but not identical with shamanism and mediumism.[8]

Furthermore, local Chinese deities develop out of specific individuals' mediumistic experiences. Illnesses, especially those in which the person experienced visions, are often understood as deities summoning individuals to become their mediums, a phenomenon virtually universal to mediumism, from Africa through Indonesia. This is, of course, how Hong eventually understood his initial vision which occurred during an illness. That two other persons became mediums for the Holy Spirit and Jesus confirmed Hong's understanding that he had become the medium for, that is, he himself was, the deity, Jesus's younger brother.

Monotheism is alien to the Chinese concept of the numinous, outside of the mystic or union trance experience of the Dao found in Daoist thought (see Chapter 5). Hence, the Christian struggle to maintain a monotheistic concept as a primary value, leading to the development of the idea of the Trinity, is incomprehensible within Chinese ideology.

The Christian terminology of Father and Son, however, is perfectly comprehensible within Chinese thought from two regards. Within elite ideology, the emperor, of semidivine status, is conceived of as the Son of Heaven. In popular Chinese religion, local deities are understood as related to other deities, the relationship of deities reflecting the overwhelming family concept of Chinese society and culture. Hence, Hong's understanding of himself as younger brother within a divine family is congruous with the Chinese ideological pattern.

Finally, the understanding of the Kingdom as taking place on earth reflects Chinese messianism and is virtually identical with Israelite and probably early Christian concepts. Messianism has a history in China as long as it does in the

---

[7]Thomas Taylor Meadows, *The Chinese and Their Rebellions* (London: Smith Elder 1856 [Stanford: Academic Reprints, 1953], 412.

[8]Morton Smith, *Jesus the Magician* (San Francisco: Harper and Row, 1978).

Near East. Even the term, *taiping,* can be found as describing the ideal state in Chinese texts dating from the third century B.C.E. For example, in *Zhuangzi* 13, we find the phrase, "This is called Da[=Tai]ping, the most perfect form of government."

Max Kaltenmark (1979:24), in discussing the *Taiping jing* of the late Han period (first to second century C.E.) points out the messianism of the period, which is indistinguishable from that of Hong nearly two millennia later:

> The Celestial Master presents himself as a "divine man" *(shen-jen)* sent by Heaven to save mankind [from the accumulated inheritance of sins *(ch'eng-fu)*] by means of a celestial scripture *(t'ien-shu),* which teaches how one can return to a method of ideal government and assist the immanent arrival of the "Breath of T'ai-p'ing."[9]

In the *Taiping jing,* as well, Earth is explicitly the equal of Heaven:

> Father and mother are equally human beings, and Heaven and Earth are both "Celestial" (Kaltenmark 1979:37).[10]

Hence, Hong's understanding of the Kingdom as the establishment of ideal government, of the millennium, on earth, and Earth as the equivalent of Heaven is the Chinese common understanding. Furthermore, the Chinese concept of the Mandate of Heaven, a concept which in its early form dates to at least the eleventh century B.C.E., assumes that the successful establishment of a new regime is one of ideal peace under a Son of Heaven. The Taiping capture of Nanjing was understood to signify that the millennium had actually begun.

Overall, Hong's religious understanding is closer to that of popular Chinese religion than that of the elite, especially in regard to mediumism, which came to be frowned upon in elite culture. This, combined with the Taiping communistic economic program, led to disfavor among the elite, one of the factors leading to their eventual collapse, as Meadows presciently observed.[11]

---

[9]Max Kaltenmark, "The Ideology of the T'ai-p'ing ching," *Facets of Taoism,* ed. by Holmes Welch and Anna Seidel (New Haven: Yale University Press, 1979), 24.

[10]Kaltenmark 37.

[11]"Meadows, 456–457, 463.

CHAPTER 10

The Festival Year

THE CHINESE NEW YEAR CELEBRATIONS

Given continuous development over several thousand years and the incorporation of aspects of Buddhism, the Chinese have a rich festival tradition. The most complex is the Spring (New Year's) Festival, which takes place over the course of a full month. The following depiction of the many aspects of this festival is from Michael Saso's *Blue Dragon White Tiger: Daoist Rites of Passage,* pp. 165–174. As pointed out in Chapter 6, Saso has had long experience with the practice of Chinese religion and is associated with the Taoist church. He adheres to a contemporary Taoist position that all indigenous Chinese religion is Taoist, a position with which the editors do not agree. But that position barely nuances his excellent encapsulation of the festival. Readers should also note that the month references by number are to the Chinese lunar calendar; the festival takes place between late January to late February of the Western solar calendar, depending on the particular year.

The Winter Solstice; Beginning of Rebirth in the Cosmos

The celebration of Chinese new year extends from the period following the tenth month fifteenth day's festival of water through the Dragon Dance and Lantern Parade of the first lunar month, fifteenth day. The period preceding the lunar new year is a time for paying debts, house cleaning, marriage, and worker's annual bonuses. The actual day for celebrating the New Year festival has varied from ancient China until the present. The Winter Solstice, i.e., the solar new year, is technically speaking the true cosmic new year, while the first day of the first lunar month is a celebration of the beginning of spring. The rituals of the Winter Solstice festival are therefore properly associated with the birth of yang in the cosmos, that day when the sun sets earliest and the night is longest. After the winter solstice (except in some parts of the tropics) the days begin to lengthen, even though the weather continues cold through the twelfth and first lunar months.

There are three basic rituals celebrated at the Winter Solstice. The first is the offering of round glutinous rice balls, with red bean paste in the center, to symbolize the rebirth of yang in the cosmos. These round rice balls, called mochi cakes in Japanese, are pasted or placed around the household in the various places where blessing has accrued to the family. Sweet rice cakes or rounded balls (with the consistency of thick marshmallow) are put on the lintels, the altar of the main room, the kitchen, the well or water faucet, the parent's bedroom, and the toilet (n.b., night soil is used as fertilizer). In modern times the rice cakes are also placed on the television set, to give thanks for the entertainment provided the family on the electronic screen. In some parts of China and in Japan at the New Year festival, the branch of a tree is placed in the main room by the altar, and decorated (rather like a Christmas tree in the west) with various symbols of blessing. Paper money, rice balls and ornaments, paper flowers, and so forth, symbolize blessings sought for the new year.

The second part of the feast consists in a ritual sacrifice offered to the ancestors. The rite described in the previous chapter for ancestor memorial can be used at this time. The rounded rice cakes, in pink and white colors, are made into a sweet soup (a sugar flavored syrup, warmed, with pink and white rice balls) and placed on the ancestor altar as an offering. The round rice cakes symbolize the rebirth of yang, seen as a bright pearl found in the depths of the ocean, where life is annually regenerated by the powers of the Tao in nature. The rice cakes are first offered to the ancestors and the household spirits, then eaten by the living members of the family at the banquet.

The third stage of the festival is the banquet. The table set for the banquet is often pushed up against the ancestor shrine, to show that the deceased members of the family are also present. (Note that the ritual north, that is, the seat which is placed directly in front of the family altar, back to north and face to south, is the seat of honor at a Chinese banquet). The rice balls are served in the sweetened soup as a part of the banquet. The Winter Solstice is a family festival, and is not usually celebrated in public. The rituals prescribed for the emperor and the imperial court on the Winter Solstice are of course no longer observed.

12/15: The Last Festival of the Guardian Spirit of the Soil

The Duke or Marquis of the Soil, T'u-ti Kung, is one of the most popular patron spirits of China. Folk legends abound concerning his origins, and shrines dedicated to him and sometimes his wife (T'u-ti Ma) are found on every street and in every household in China. Local Cantonese and other dialects may change the name, but the function of this sometimes benign and sometimes angry soil spirit are analogous. Temples and households of China, whether Buddhist, Taoist, or folk religion oriented offer sacrifice to the soil spirit on the first and fifteenth day of each month. Temples always offer special services on these days, and many trades such as barbers and butchers take the day off.

The last day of the lunar year on which the Marquis of the Soil is fêted is the twelfth month, fifteenth day. Custom decrees that on this day employers give a banquet for all of their employees, and present a bonus to each worker, from the lowest kitchen help to the vice-president of the company. Foreigners residing in China who do not give a bonus on this day will be bothered later by occult compensation in the form of servants or cooks stealing from the kitchen and household supplies. Work does not go well in companies which do not provide the twelfth month bonus. The custom is also observed in Japan in the form of the *Bo-nen-kai* (end of the year party) where the giving of a bonus is strictly observed.

From the end-of-the-year party until the new year festival, all families pre-pare for the rituals and banquets of new year. Fancy foods, new clothes, and a re-newed life express the changes soon to be celebrated in nature. (Chinese New Year, it must be remembered, falls at the end of January or the beginning of Feb-ruary in the western solar calendar). Lion dance teams begin to practice for the lion dances to be performed in the market places and merchant districts at New Year. The route of each lion dance team or kung-fu club must be determined ahead of time. Competition between teams for the "best" (wealthiest) stores which give the largest stipend in the red envelope (li-hsi or hung-pao) is keen be-tween the lion dance clubs. To avoid street battles and bad feelings in the com-munity, the lion dance teams and their kung-fu club sponsors agree amicably among themselves to trade off streets and shops each year, so as to share the prof-its. Sometime immediately preceding the New Year festival in Canton, or imme-diately following the festival in Fukien and other parts of China, the lion dancers perform in front of each store and pray for blessing. A stipend is hidden in each shop, and a puzzle given to the lion to solve, before receiving the money.

12/24: House-Cleaning day. The Patron Spirits of the House are Sent Off to Heaven

The day for cleaning the home and sending off the household spirits varies throughout China, Japan, Korea, Okinawa, and those nations influenced by Chi-nese culture. The entire house must be cleaned from top to bottom, windows washed, bedding aired out, and dust scrupulously swept away. The family altar especially must be cleaned, the brass incense burner and candle holders pol-ished, and the ritual utensils made to shine anew. In many parts of China the custom still exists to send off the spirit of the hearth, *Tsao-shen,* to report to the heavens on the good and bad bad deeds of the family during the past year. The spirit of the hearth is the *szu-ming,* the spirit official who controls fate in the man-darinate of the heavenly rulers. Since the entire family tend to gossip in the kitchen, the hearth spirit hears and records all of the good and bad deeds of the village community. A paper effigy of the spirit is put atop a small paper horse, and (in some areas) sweet glutinous rice or honey smeared across the lips, so that he can say "sweet" things when he reports to the Emperor of the heavens. The effigy is then burned, thus "sending off" the hearth spirit to the heavens by fire and wind.

With the hearth spirit go all of the household guardians, to spend the new year holiday in the heavens. Since the spirits are away and cannot object to any changes made in the family, the best time to marry a bride is said to be between 12/24 and 1/4, when the spirits return to take up their household duties. The practicality of such a custom is obvious. The huge wedding banquet can be com-bined with the new year celebration. The buying of new furniture for the family, painting the rooms of the house, and other changes necessary at the time of mar-riage fit in well with the spirit of the new year and home improvements. Myth and ritual confirm the practicality of the Chinese farmer and merchant.

12/31: The New Year Eve Banquet

Since cooking, cleaning, and other chores are forbidden for the first three days of the new year, the entire new year eve is spent preparing food, setting out new clothes, and performing ritual duties at the family altar. The stores in Chinatown of Honolulu, San Francisco, and the other communities of the diaspora are especially busy during the last few days before the New Year. *Tui-lien* scrolls must be purchased to hang on either side of the door, *nien-kao* sweet rice cake must be prepared for the New Year feast, and *hung-pao* or *li-hsi* red envelopes with money gifts inside presented to every member of the family. The various events and duties of new year's eve are listed as follows:

1. Buying and preparing the foods for the new year banquet.
In bygone days the rice grains (glutinous rice) were pounded by hand or ground by a foot-powered machine, whereas nowadays glutinous rice powder is found in supermarkets throughout Hongkong, Taiwan, Honolulu, and the mainland United States. The *nien-kao* glutinous rice cake is made of rice flower, brown sugar, and sometimes coconut juice, poured into a *ti* (liliaceaous plant) or banana leaf, and steamed until cooked. When cooled and hardened, a piece of the *nien-kao* is sliced off the large cake, and deep fried or steamed to softness, before eating. Puffed glutinous rice is also deep-fried into a sweet round ball, called jin-dui in Cantonese, by mixing with sugar and water syrup, peanuts, and sesame seeds. Boxes of sweet puffed-rice rice cakes are given to close friends and relatives (Mandarin: t'ung-mi; Cantonese: tung-mai). Candied fruit peels, winter squash, lotus roots, and other delicacies are prepared in sets of five (for the five elements) to present to guests who come after new year's day to visit. Since material culture decides what foods are to be prepared and eaten at the new year eve banquet and for the first three days of the new year, it is impossible to describe the abundant variety of good dishes prepared for the banquets. Kwangtung province, especially in the Chung-shan and T'ai-shan area, eat only chai or vegetarian food for the new year banquet; Taiwan, Fukien, and most of north China eat the five meats (pork, chicken, goat, duck, fish, but never beef, since the water buffalo helps plough the fields, and so is taboo as a dinner food at New year banquets) along with the abundant variety of vegetables, legumes, bean-curds, and sweets.

2. *Tui-lien:* hanging paired scrolls with felicitous Chinese characters to bring good fortune.
One of the most important ritual duties of the new year is the hanging of good fortune scrolls on either side of the main door, and in propitious places around the home. In scholarly families the father of the household usually composes his own scrolls, from a great variety of felicitous phrases. In modern China, Taiwan, Honolulu, and southeast Asia the scrolls are found in supermarkets, temples, and even youth clubs as money raising projects for charitable organizations. Each family have their own favorites, which might include:

> *Kung-hsi fa-ts'ai:* Blessing and wealth for the new year.
>
> *Yang ch'un chieh fu:* Welcome spring and have blessing.
>
> *Szu-chi p'ing-an:* Peace, blessing for the four seasons.

Wu-fu lin men: May the five blessings enter these doors.

Hsin ch'un ta-chi: The new spring brings great blessing.

In some areas of China the hanging of a character for blessing upside down over the door post is a sign of blessing. The word for upside down (tao) is a homonym for "arrived"! (tao-le).

3. New clothes, hair ornaments, and flowers.
Children are given new clothes, and must bathe in herbs on new year's eve. Young girls and elderly women wear flowers in their hair, since flower (hua) sounds like change (hua) for blessing and good fortune. Since it is not allowed to sweep on the new year, comb the hair, or do anything such as bathe (wash away) which might sweep out or wash away the new blessing, all care is given to personal and household cleanliness on new year's eve. Brooms are put away after the final cleaning, lest the taboo be broken by a forgetful person new year's day.

4. The New Year Eve meal.
The last meal of the old year is a very important and moving occasion, celebrated by the entire family and a few chosen friends. To be invited to a Chinese new year eve banquet is indeed a rare and fortuitous honor. No evil or scolding word can be spoken on this evening, and all must dress in their newest and prettiest clothes. A small fire pot (hibachi) is put under the main banquet table, (or a fire pot with red paper inside, symbolically representing fire, if the banquet takes place in a warm climate) to represent the new fire of yang enkindled by the transcendent Tao in the center of the cosmos. Before the banquet begins, a sampling of each dish is presented to the ancestors on a special table laid out before the main altar. The dishes are laid out in sevens, i.e., with seven rice bowls, wine cups, and chopsticks. After the incense is lit, and a few minutes of quiet prayer spent by the ancestor shrine, the dishes are laid on the banquet table and the celebration begins.

In many parts of China the doors of the household are sealed or closed at this time, until the new year opens. In other parts, the doors are left open, and the banquet begins with family members and friends coming in throughout the evening. Toasts are made to each member of the family. Foreigners are warned to sip at each toast (sui-i) and not drain the cup (kan-pei). Riotous and boisterous talk would destroy the rapport of the new year banquet; if one drains the cup (kan-pei) to one member of the family, it is necessary to "bottoms up" with each adult male member. Discretion at Chinese banquets is the better part of valor. At least 24 dishes are served; a sweet dish, often mistaken for dessert, is presented half way through the evening. The more enjoyment during the banquet, the greater the blessings won for the coming year.

5. Items offered on the family altar.
Even though material culture determines for each part of China what foods are to be offered at new year's on the family altar, there are certain rules and items observed almost universally throughout China. Fruit, especially oranges stacked in sets of five (five elements, five blessings) must be on the new year altar. The orange is sweet (t'ien), a homonym for heaven (t'ien). So too the candied fruits

and peels are sweetened, as is the new year cake (nien-kao) and the various cookies and candies. Sweets and fruits are laid out on plates in sets of five, on the family altar. Also de rigeur are cakes made of baking powder or yeast, which have swollen out and broken open at the top. The swelling cake (fa-kao) symbolizes abundant good fortune and blessing. Into each cake is inserted a paper flower made of red and gold cut-outs. On the flower is pasted in gold the Chinese character for spring (ch'un), which is a homonym for ts'un abundance. Sweet, pure foods are offered to the heavens. Cooked and chopped foods are offered to earth spirits and to the living. Raw foods (never seen at new year banquets) are for the dead, and for exorcism.

A special offering is made at new year's for those members of the family who may have died young, who are not commemorated in an ancestor tablet, and for the original owners of the land on which the household is constructed. This lesser sacrifice is called the offering to the spirit for the foundations, and the orphan souls. In Hawaii on such occasions poi (pounded taro root) and Primo (local) beer are often laid out for the Hawaiians of long ago. Paper money with silver trim is offered to these spirits, while paper money with gold decoration is offered to the heavenly spirits and the ancestors at new year's.

6. Computing the beginning of the new year.
Some families still observe the old Taoist custom of computing the exact beginning of the new year. Fire crackers must be burned at the moment the new year begins, the doors and windows opened, and sometimes a model ship hung over the front door to symbolically represent the coming of the new year and heaven's blessing. The new year is computed by watching the tail of the Big Dipper (Ursa Major) in the heavens. When the tail of the dipper points to the east (the cyclical character mao), the new year's blessing is thought to arrive. It is at this moment that firecrackers are exploded. People who hate the sound of firecrackers are said to be demonic, while those not frightened will receive blessing. Firecrackers exorcise evil and welcome good, telling the entire neighborhood of the festive ritual.

New Year's day: 1/1, Ch'un-chieh

On the first day of the new year the family arises early, and begins to visit local temples, relatives, and friends. The li-hsi or hung-pao with money gifts are given to the children of the family at this time. Red (black) tea with sugar can be served to guests, with dishes of five kinds of candy, fruit, and cookies. Food offerings are placed on the family altar, incense burned, and guests served a bowl of chai, a gourmet vegetarian dish prepared on the first day of the new year.

Chai is made of the most luxurious vegetarian ingredients. These can include a variety of bean curds made to look like meat, the so called "long rice" or "spring rain" noodles, a translucent pasta made from bean flour, rice flour, or sweet potato starch. "Cracked seed," dried red plums (salted), ginko nuts, a variety of dried mushrooms, fresh mushrooms, water chestnuts, bamboo shoots, and so forth, are used in these exquisitely prepared dishes. Children bow before their parents and grandparents, and receive presents from visitors.

The second day after new years, called k'ai-nien (year is open) allows the family to eat meat again, and continue the holiday festivities. No work is allowed until the fourth day after new year, when the patron spirits "come down" and resume their duties in the household. If a wedding took place during the new year period, the young bride is allowed to return home for her first visit only on the fifth day after new year, that is, after the three days of rest, and the fourth day when the household spirits return from their vacation in heaven.

Other festivals occur during the week or so immediately following the new year, according to local custom and provincial norms. In old China the seventh day after new year is thought to be the occasion on which one year is added to each person's age; thus no matter on what day the birthday is celebrated, each person in the family is counted a year older on the occasion of the new year celebration. The ninth day after new year is the festival of the Jade Emperor, *Yü-huang Ta-ti*, the heavenly emperor who controls the spirits of the cosmos much as the visible emperor acts as head of the Chinese state. The Jade Emperor's festival is celebrated by raising a banquet table off the ground on stilts, offering sugar Cane (t'ien for sugar is homonym for t'ien, heaven), and burning large sheets of gold coated paper money. The sheets of paper money are rolled into large cylindrical tubes, standing for *ting*, the male organ, and fertility in bearing children. It is taboo to carry washing through the room in which the Jade Emperor is being honored. Menstruating women, or mothers "sitting the month" after birth are also forbidden to take part in this ceremony.

1/15: Dragon Dance and Lantern Parade; Shang-yüan Chieh

The first full moon of the first lunar month is called *Shang-Yüan Chieh*, the festival of the principle of heaven. Technically, the first full moon of the new year is seen as a sign of the strengthening power of yang, and the working of primordial breath (yüan-ch'i) in the cosmos. Like a bright red pearl flaming with the power of new life, the transcendent Tao has implanted a new charge of primordial breath in the center of the cosmos. This charge of pure yang or primordial breath is seen atop the Chinese temple as a bright red ball of flames, and atop the Taoist priest's crown as a *hua-yang* flame pin representing the presence of the Tao within the center of the microcosmic body.

The festival of 1/15, *Shang-yüan chieh* celebrates the awareness of this principle of life-breath within the macro and microcosm. Two customs are observed almost universally throughout China to celebrate new light. The first is the dragon dance, in which young men (and sometimes women) dance through the streets carrying a huge 150 foot long dragon, sewn in elaborate embroidered cloth. The dragon attempts to catch a bright red ball of flame carried by another youth, which symbolizes the "primordial breath" (yüan-ch'i) principle of new life. The second custom, called *Hua-teng Chieh* or lantern festival, calls for the carrying of ornate lanterns around the city, and hanging more elaborate artistic lanterns in temples, to celebrate the renewed presence of the immanent Tao in nature.

The dragon dance is a strenuous and entertaining event. Youths from the kung-fu marital arts clubs usually carry the dragon, and perform a series of intricate dances, twists, and patterned drills while moving the 150 long effigy in graceful swirls. In front of the procession is carried the lighted circular lantern, shaped like the round ball of flames seen atop temples or atop the Taoist's ceremonial crown. The dragon chases the red ball through the streets until finally the ball is caught and swallowed. Then sitting contentedly in the middle of the city plaza, the dragon allows the people of the village or urban community to pass in and out under the Tao-laden belly. Humans who pass under the belly of the dragon which has swallowed the Tao (the alchemical pill of longevity) are filled with blessings.

While the dragon dance is proceeding through the streets, and throughout the evening of 1/15, children and adults carry lighted lanterns in procession, representing the rebirth of Yang and the presence of the Tao in nature. Children especially love to walk in the lantern parade, and are warned to keep their colorful lamp lit no matter how strong the wind. If the lantern goes out, it is immediately lighted by an observant adult. To lose the light of renewal through the winds of ill-fortune or slander is considered a sign of bad luck. Fortune therefore smiles on those who keep their lanterns lit, i.e., always aware of the workings of the transcendent Tao in nature.

CHAPTER 11

Traditional Chinese Religion as Means of Coping

THE GARDEN FOR PLEASURE IN SOLITUDE

For most traditionally oriented Chinese, a spell of misfortune will lead to seeking succor from the many available religious means. These include seeking information as to the cause of the problems and assistance in clearing up these causes from ancestral spirits and deities through mediums, rituals to exorcise in various ways bad luck from the family or individual, and rituals to simply change one's luck. The intelligentsia, however, tended to avoid some of these rituals as slightly demeaning. They also sought surcease in aesthetic activities following from their education in literature and brushwork, writing traditionally having utilized the brush and ink since the earliest evidence we have for writing in China, approximately thirty-five hundred years ago. These activities were termed the "Three Treasures": poetry, calligraphy and painting.[1]

As the Chinese civil service system developed, political leaders out of favor with the Emperor were less likely to be executed and instead suffered forced retirement, often temporary, or banishment to the frontiers. Ssu-Ma Kuang (1009–1086) was twice prime minister of China and a noted essayist. In between his stints as prime minister, when on the political outings, he retired to his estate, had a garden constructed, and in it wrote one of China's major histories, still read as the definitive history for the period prior to his own time. During this period in his life, he wrote an essay, "The Garden for Pleasure in Solitude," which continues to be one of the models of Chinese prose (a quality not observed in the translation, of course) and a perfect example of the synthesis between *ju-chia* (Confucian) and *tao-chia* (Taoist) thought that so influenced the lives of the literati. In office, they adhered to the *ju-chia* tradition with its focus on service to humanity through government office. Out of office, they found the *tao-chia* tradition, with its orientation toward individualistic religious experience more relevant. It was *tao-chia* thought that gave the literati a means of coping with the vicissitudes of political life. The translation is by the editor (J.P.).

---

[1]For a treatise on the religious aspects of these activities, see Jordan Paper, *The Spirits Are Drunk*, chapters 6 and 7.

SSU-MA KUANG: THE GARDEN FOR PLEASURE IN SOLITUDE

Mencius said: "Enjoying music by oneself is less desirable than enjoying music with others" and "enjoying music with a few is less desirable than enjoying music with the multitudes."[2] This is how kings, lords, and great men can take their pleasure; it is not for the humble and poor. Confucius said: "Having but rice and vegetables to eat, but water to drink, and but my bent arm for a pillow, I can still enjoy myself in the midst of these circumstances." And it is recorded: "Yen-tzu had but a single, small bowlful to eat, but a single ladleful to drink . . . yet this had no effect on his enjoyment."[3] This is how the great sages take their pleasure; ordinary people cannot attain to this level. For "when the little tailor-bird builds her nest in the deep wood, she used no more than one branch; when the mole drinks from the river, he takes no more than a bellyful."[4] Each fully utilized their share and were content. This then is how I take my pleasure.

In 1072,[5] I moved to Loyang. In 1074, I purchased ten acres in the north part of Tsun-hsien and enclosed it to create a garden. Within I had a building constructed and filled it with more than five thousand volumes. I named it "Studying Hall."

On the south side of the hall, there is a small room with water channeled to flow under its eaves. In the midst of this stream, a fishpond was constructed more than a meter in depth into which water was made to flow in five streams resembling a tiger's claws. From the pond, the water flowed northward through a concealed channel, exiting by the north stairs into a courtyard, shooting forth as a stream from an elephant's trunk. From the waterfall, the water was diverted into two channels flowing around the border of the courtyard, meeting in the northwest corner and then flowing out. I called this the "Playing With Water Pavilion."

North of the hall, a pond was constructed with an island in its center. Bamboo were planted in a circle on the island in the shape of a jade bracelet, more than ten meters in circumference. The tops of the bamboo were tied together, giving the appearance of a fisherman's thatched hut. I called it "Gone Fishing Hut."[6]

North of the pond a house of six columns was built,[7] its walls enclosed with woven reeds to ward off the burning sun. The door was placed on its east side, and the south and north sides of the house had tall windows to catch the cool

---

[2]The book of dialogues by Meng-tzu (Mencius) of the third century B.C.E. became, by the time of Ssu-Ma Kuang, the major basis of *ju-chia* (Confucian) ideology. The point of the quotation in this context is that communal values override individualistic ones.

[3]These two quotations are from the *Lun-yü* (Analects) of K'ung-fu-tzu (Confucius).

[4]This quotation is from the *Chuang-tzu*, the primary *tao-chia* text. It is important to note that in his introductory paragraph, Ssu-Ma Kuang, a political conservative and the foremost *ju-chia* theorist of his time, downplays the primary *ju-chia* texts and promotes the *tao-chia* one.

[5]The year Wang An-shih, Ssu-Ma Kuang's political rival, came to power, and Ssu-Ma Kuang was forced into retirement. It is at this time that he wrote his monumental history.

[6]Fishermen and woodcutters symbolize the ideal *tao-chia* rustic existence in Chinese literati poetry and painting.

[7]Traditional Chinese architecture is of curtain-wall construction (non-load-bearing). The supporting columns are usually the same distance apart. Hence, the size of structures was given by the number of supporting column

breezes. Ornamental bamboo were planted to the front and rear; the whole becoming a retreat from the heat of summer. I named it "The Study with Potted Bamboo."

East of the pond is a garden with 120 miscellaneous medicinal plants and herbs, all carefully recorded and labeled. North of this garden, I had bamboo planted in a square, as a chessboard, the diagonal of each section being four meters. The branches of the bamboo were bent and interwoven so that each section became a separate room. More bamboo was planted so that the footpath became a maze, and the whole was covered over with vines. Trees and shrubs were planted along the borders to form a secure hedge. This I named "The Garden for Gathering Herbs."

South of the garden, a railing with six balusters formed from peony trees, peonies, and various flowers was built. Each plant had its double; for each variety of plant there were but two roots. I had no need for more as I was but studying their appearances and recording my observations. North of this balustrade, a *t'ing*[8] was built. I called it, "Water Blossom *T'ing*."

It is not a great distance from the city wall of Loyang to the mountains, but the forest in between was dense and thick, and I was continuously annoyed that I could not see the mountains. So I raised a tower in the middle of the garden and built a room on the top from which I could gaze at Wan-an, Huan-yüan and even T'ai-shan.[9] I named it "The Tower for Viewing the Mountains."

I spent much of my time each day studying. First, I followed [the writings of] the great sages; then I befriended the multitude of worthies [through their works]. I sought out the source of *jen* and *yi* and examined the clues [to understanding] ritual and music.[10] Before the beginning of things, there were their forms; at the extremes of the four directions, there can be nothing beyond infinity. All affairs and things have their underlying principles. With all the writings of the past available to my eyes, I was distressed that my studies were incomplete. Yet can I seek the final results from someone else? Can I await the completion of my work to come from the outside world?[11]

When my will becomes weary and my body tired, I grab my rod and fish, or catch up my gown and gather herbs, or open the irrigation ditches and water the flowers, or grasp a hatchet and trim the bamboo. I cool off by plunging my hands in the stream and rest my eyes by gazing off toward the heights. Wandering about here and there, I only let my mind dwell on pleasant things. The full moon arrives in its own time; the cool breeze comes of itself. My strolling is not due to any need; I do not stop from any necessity.[12] My eyes, ears, lungs and bowels are

---

[8]The *t'ing* is a roofed but open-sided pavilion, omnipresent in Chinese gardens and scenic places.

[9]The latter is the most important sacred mountain in China, located in its eastern part. Of course, it could not possibly be actually seen from the tower. The statement is metaphorical.

[10]The two major *ju-chia* virtues together with their major modes of formal expression.

[11]Ssu-Ma Kuang was engaged in writing the first comprehensive historical overview of China's past since Ssu-Ma Ch'ien's writings of more than a millennium previous. The point of studying history was to understand the principles of change, of the universe itself as it applies to human lives.

[12]These statements all refer to the concept of *tzu-jan*: "that which arises of itself;" i.e., spontaneity—the basic principle of *tao-chia* theory and Chinese religio-aesthetics.

all my own personal possessions—I utterly follow my will, am utterly un-
bounded in scope! [Previously,] I had not known what it meant to be an inhabitant between Heaven and Earth.[13] What pleasure can be greater than this!
Therefore, I named the whole concept, "The Garden for Pleasure in Solitude."

Some censure me by saying: "We have learned that a gentleman takes his pleasure communally with others. Now how can it be that you, sir, find sufficiency in
yourself alone rather than in extending yourself to others?" I confess to them: "I am
a simple person; how can I be compared to a gentlemen? I fear that my pleasures
are second-rate; how can I extend them to others? Moreover, my pleasures are poor,
vulgar, despicable and rustic—those that the whole world rejects. Even were I to extend them to others, no one would take them. How could I force them to do so? Certainly, if others were willing to share these pleasures, I would repeatedly pay my
respects and offer them. How could I dare monopolize these pleasures!"[14]

RED CLIFF FU I

Su Shih lived a generation after Ssu-Ma Kuang and was in many respects his pro-
tégé. Not only a leader of his political party, he was the founder, along with his
friend Mi Fu, of literati aesthetics from his time to the present. He remains one of
China's best known poets, essayists, and calligraphers and was a noted painter in
his time (none of his paintings have survived).

The first of Su Shih's two "Red Cliff *Fu* (prose poems)" captures, as perhaps no
other writing, the essence of *tao-chia* ideology. Although we agree with several contemporary scholars of Chinese religion that in the past Western scholars have ex-
aggerated a difference between *tao-chia* and *tao-chiao* (institutionalized Taoism),
there still remains a degree of difference. For example, the "Red Cliff *Fu*" advocates
an acceptance of life as it is in lieu of the arts of longevity, a major orientation of
institutional Taoism. The following translation by the editor (J.P.) emphasizes ideological clarity over literary expression and precision.

SU SHIH: RED CLIFF FU I

On the sixteenth day of the seventh month (lunar calendar) of 1082, I took some
friends on a boat trip to the Red Cliff.[15] The wind was gentle, with not a ripple
to be seen. I raised my cup and toasted my friends. We chanted the "Bright Moon"
ode from the *Shih,* with the verse about the demure woman. Soon the moon rose
above the hills to the east, and meandered between the Dipper and the Herdboy

---

[13]Associated with the duality of Heaven and Earth, is the three-fold Heaven, Earth and Humans, the latter existing between the two cosmic beings. In other words, "to be a human being."

[14]This, of course, is written tongue-in-cheek. In essence, Ssu-Ma Kuang, the arch-*ju-chia* conservative in office (as prime minister of China and head of his political party) is a rampant *tao-
chia* individualist when in (temporary) retirement.

[15]The Red Cliff is on the upper Yangtze River, where a major river battle took place in the
third century. According to modern scholarship, Su Shih and his friends were actually at the
wrong place on the river.

Star. A white mist hovered above the river, blending the light on the water with the sky. We let our little boat drift about the vast water, which merged into the horizon. It was as if we were drifting up into the void borne by the wind, to we knew not where, or as if we had sprouted wings and risen as *hsien*[16] leaving the human realm behind.[17]

We drank until merry, we sang a verse beating out the rhythm on the gunwales with our hands . . .

One of my friends accompanied our singing with his flute. His notes were like sobs; at times complaining and longing, at other times weeping and imploring. When our singing was done, the flute's sound did not cease, but lingered on as an unbroken thread. The dragons underwater must have been moved to dance in the dark depths; it was as if a widow were weeping in our solitary boat.

I solemnly sat up, straightened my garments, and asked my friend: "Why did you play so?"

My friend replied:

A full moon, the stars few
Crows and magpies fly southward . . .

"Did not Ts'ao Ts'ao[18] write this verse?[19] Between Hsia-k'ou to the west and Wu-ch'ang in the east, with mountains and the river all about him in between, is this not the spot [the Red Cliff] that Ts'ao Ts'ao was surrounded by Chou Yü? When Ts'ao Ts'ao conquered Ching-chou and sailed downstream to Chiang-ling, his ships were lined up for hundreds of miles and his flags hid the sky. Looking at the river, drinking [wine] deeply while holding his spear, he composed this poem [the first two lines above]. He was the great hero of his time, but where is he now?[20] And how can we be compared with him? We are but fishermen and woodcutters[21] by the river's edge, with fish, shrimps, and deer[22] for companions, riding a boat as flat as a leaf, and drinking from bottlegourds.[23] We are but mayflies[24] briefly visiting between Heaven and Earth,[25] but flecks in this vast sea, mourning

---

[16]A word that originally meant a shaman over twenty-five hundred years ago and subsequently came to mean both (a) one who succeeds in the Taoist endeavor to attain longevity by making the body ethereal and (b) a winged humanoid spirit.

[17]Note the number of allusions to trance-flight experiences, which also became a metaphor for freedom from the normative constraints of family, clan, and state obligations on the literati/scholar-officials.

[18]Ts'ao Ts'ao (second century) was the chief general at the end of the Han dynasty, who put down the rebellion that led to the formation of the Taoist churches. The effort led to the collapse of the Han, and his son became the first emperor of the Wei dynasty of the Three Kingdoms period. He was also a noted poet, and his second son was one of the most important poets in Chinese history. Ts'ao Ts'ao led the forces on one side of the battle fought below the Red Cliff.

[19]This is one of the best known poems in China.

[20]I.e., he is dead! Death does not evoke a pleasant image in the Chinese mind, but it is recognized as inevitable.

[21]Fishermen and woodcutters are metaphors for the ideal *tao-chia* rustic existence.

[22]All of these are symbols to be found in Taoist imagery.

[23]Another common Taoist image.

[24]Mayflies live but one day.

[25]The three realms: Heaven (Sky), humans, and Earth (the first and last are divinized).

the passing of our short lives, envying the never-ending long river.[26] To roam far off with a flying *hsien* and forever clasp the moon in one's arms are arts[27] difficult to attain. This is why my music coalesced with the sobbing wind."

"My friend, do you understood the water and the moon?" I responded. "The first streams past yet is never gone; the second waxes and wanes eternally yet finally never increases nor diminishes. If you look from the standpoint of change,[28] Heaven and Earth do not last for even a blink of the eye, but if you look from the standpoint of changelessness, that within and without ourselves are inexhaustible. So why should we envy anything?

"Moreover, each thing between Heaven and Earth has its owner; even a single hair that is not mine can never be a part of me. Only the cool breeze on the river and the full moon over the mountains caught by the ear becomes sound and, encountered by the eye, becomes color. No one can prevent us from having them, and there is no limit to our use of it. These are the limitless reserves of all that is created, and you and I can share in the joy of it."

My friend smiled, consoled. We washed the cups and poured more wine. When the food was all gone and the wine cups and dishes lay scattered about, we lounged against each other in the boat, and did not even notice the sky turning white in the east.

ASCENDING MOUNT LU

The above mode of encountering the vicissitudes of life is not archaic, it remained a persistent pattern for those who received a partial traditional education even in the twentieth century. When Mao Tse-tung encountered political difficulties after his disastrous "Great Leap Forward," he wrote a poem in the traditional formal mode that flows from the same ideology as expressed by Ssu-Ma Kuang and Su Shih. The following translation and analysis is from Jordan Paper's *The Spirits Are Drunk*, pp. 159–162 (with unessential references removed).

Mao Zedong (Mao Tse-tung) hardly requires an introduction. Although of peasant background, Mao received a traditional education (against his father's will). Even when attending normal school (1913–18), he received training in classical prose, a skill which he continued to maintain. Throughout his life, he practiced calligraphy and wrote poetry in the classical style. Although it is unlikely he would have used the term to describe himself, he was a *wenren*. In inclination and occupation, he fully maintained the dominant elite ideal, service to others (*ren*): "party" and "people" replacing "clan" and "state" as objects of service.

---

[26]The Long River is the common Chinese name for the Yangtze, the river on which they are presently drifting.

[27]The arts for attaining longevity: inner and outer alchemy—special gymnastic, dietary, sexual, breathing, and meditation practices.

[28]The *I* (Book of Changes) is the oldest of the Classics. The concept of change is of major importance to Chinese ideology of all aspects: The one constant is change itself.

Among Mao's published poems, one is exceptional in regard to the sentiments expressed. The following translation is overly literal in order to indicate the parallel structure of the middle lines.

Ascending Mount Lu

Single mountain peak floats beside Great River [Yangtze];
Briskly ascend four hundred verdant switchbacks.
Coldly look toward ocean, see world—
Warm wind blowing rain from sky to river.
Clouds hang over Nine Tributaries, yellow crane hovers;
Waves descend toward Three Wu, white mist rises.
Magistrate Tao not know what place gone—
Perhaps at Peach Blossom Spring ploughing a field?

The poem is in the Tang (seventh to tenth centuries) eight-line regulated verse form, a highly structured poetic genre, little of which can be indicated in translation. In this genre, the poem is divided into two quatrains with the import of the entire poem in the last couplet. The first quatrain provides the setting; the second, the meaning. The fifth and sixth lines oppose rising to descending.

The "yellow crane" here has two closely related meanings, each well known through a number of poems, including those of China's most famous poet, Li Bo (701–762). In one, Li Bo mentions a Yellow Crane Tower by the Yangtze, a name derived from its primary meaning as a familiar of the *xian* (see Chapter 3). This sense of "yellow crane" is found in another poem by Li Bo. In turn, Li Bo's use of the term derives from the poetry of Ruan Ji (210–263). The Yellow Crane Tower was built to commemorate the place where, according to legend, a person attained *xian*hood, flying off on a yellow crane. Mao referred to the tower in an early (1927) poem, "Tower of the Yellow Crane."

"White mist" has been a variant of "white cloud," a symbol of shamanic ascent, since it is first found in the *Zhuangzi*. From the time of the *Chuci*, it has come to serve as a poetic (or visual in painting) metaphor for a euphoric state, ranging from the mystic experience to the simple ecstasy of freedom. Although the two lines could be read somewhat differently, its meaning is certain when we realize that Bao Zhao (421–465), one of China's most important medieval poets, wrote a poem with the same title which contains the following lines:

We will mount the road of feathered men
And merge forever with smoke and mist.[29]

By using Bao Zhao's title, Mao is clearly referring to the older poem, especially the two lines on which he writes a variation.

"Magistrate Tao" refers to the famous poet, Tao Qian (Yuanming, 365–427), who is the traditional epitome of a Daoist poet, an individual who rejects the dominant social ideals to live a life of wine, rusticity, nature, and mystic experience. His home was a village at the south foot of Mount Lu. The key word here is *magistrate*, because it is unusual to refer to him in that manner. Tao only held

---

[29]Wai-lim Yip, *Chinese Poetry: Major Modes and Genres* (Berkeley: University of California Press, 1976), p. 199.

that position once for a brief period, and he gave up the position and refused to hold others. "Peach Blossom Spring" is the title of his well-known allegory which describes the social ideal of the *Zhuangzi:* an isolated egalitarian village where food, shelter, and leisure time are in sufficiency but not excess.

I have discussed the meaning of the poem in some detail, because scholars have gone to great lengths to find exclusively political meaning in the poem. The poem was written on 1 July 1959 when Mao was sixty-five. He had to a degree retired, giving up (or forced to give up) chairmanship of the government half a year previously (while retaining chairmanship of the party) following growing dissatisfaction with his "Great Leap Forward." In August, a plenum of the Central Committee was to be held at Mount Lu, where Mao maintained his summer retreat, reversing many of his policies. Also, serious difficulties were brewing with the Soviets, leading to the rupture soon to follow.

In his poem, Mao is expressing a longing for freedom; freedom from responsibility, from cares, from office. He does so through the traditional mode, through a literary expression of the Daoist ideal. For Mao, Daoism (as a set of *daojia* concepts, not a *daojiao* system of doctrines) meant an alternative to the dominant ideology. This Daoism was understood as an aesthetic sensibility expressed through poetry and painting, as well as a mode of living (retirement). Wolfgang Bauer has related Mao's famous Yangtze swims, interpreting swimming as a variation of the flying metaphor, to the association of Daoism with "the idea of renewal, mobility and revolution."[30]

---

[30]Wolfgang Bauer, *China and the Search for Happiness,* translated by M. Shaw (New York: Seabury Press), pp. 411–418.

CHAPTER 12

The Disruption of Tradition

In many respects it is easier to analyze the past than the present, for we cannot speak from hindsight with regard to the present, and predictions for the future with regard to religion in retrospect are seldom found to have been reliable. Hence, the many predictions earlier in this century that Chinese religion would not survive communism or modernity outside of the Mainland in Hong Kong, Singapore, and Taiwan have proved to be most inaccurate. Even more, the analyses by scholars who were not specialists on Chinese religion that the Cultural Revolution would lead to a long-lived religion of Maoism have turned out to be hollow. The depth of Chinese religion within Chinese culture and society lies at its very roots and is not readily displaced.

Although the destruction of religious sites and paraphernalia during the Cultural Revolution, as all aspects of Chinese tradition, was immense, and sporadic attempts by the government to eradicate Chinese religion outside of controllable institutional aspects continues, an enormous resurgence of religious practices has taken place since the relaxation that slowly began in the early 1980s. Rampant capitalism since the early 1990s has but accelerated the pace. By this time, shops were openly selling religious paraphernalia not only in outlying regions but in Beijing itself. Most startling of all, by 1993, the deceased Mao Tse-tung had become the new God of Wealth for the new capitalist milieu. Talismans with his photograph combined with a replica of a gold ingot were ubiquitous, even hanging from the rear-view mirrors of government automobiles.

CELEBRATING A DEITY'S BIRTHDAY IN CHINA TODAY

In Chapter 4, there was reference to renewed pilgrimages to T'ai-shan and Kuan-yin temples, as well as a reading concerning the revitalization of the Jen-tsu Festival. The following extract from Kenneth Dean's *Taoist Ritual and Popular Cults of Southeast China,* pp. 62–69, documents one of the many revivals that has taken place in the 1980s and 1990s.

The Setting

The village of Baijiao today has perhaps twenty-five hundred residents. Most families divide up the labor, with one son involved in farming, another in fishing; and if there are more, they try to find work as laborers in Xiamen. The majority are surnamed Wang, and they worship their clan ancestor and namesake, the Kaimin Shengwang (Saintly King who Developed Fujian) Wang Shengzhi (r. 909–925). A statue of the god and his consort stands behind a statue of Baosheng Dadi as a little boy, in the back hall of the Ciji gong (Temple of Merciful Salvation). This god is paraded about the streets of the village on the fifteenth of the first month.

The village is situated near the northern side of the long mouth of the Nine Dragon River, which passes next to Zhangzhou. The river has silted up and is no longer navigable all the way to Zhangzhou. The process of reclaiming land from the sea to expand the four coastal plains of Fujian has gone on for centuries, aided by the silting in of the major rivers. The silting has led to the rise and fall of major harbors in the area—first Quanzhou from the twelfth century to the fifteenth, then Haicheng, across the broad mouth of the river from Baijiao in the sixteenth and seventeenth centuries, and finally Xiamen, which from the mid seventeenth century on would eventually supersede all these central Minnan ports (Ng, 1983). To reach Baijiao from Xiamen now, one must rely on the tides. A passenger boat takes over an hour to reach Haicang. From there one can walk forty-five minutes into the village, passing first Hongluo, then Qingjiao. A ten-minute walk between Qingjiao and Baijiao proceeds on a raised dirt road above rice fields and vegetable gardens. One enters the village and walks toward its center along a narrow lane between brick and wood houses. Suddenly one emerges onto a vast square; immediately on one's right is an enormous temple with five entranceways and a two-story front hall with an inner balcony with drum and bell in the left and right inner wings. To the left across the square is a large concrete stage facing the temple. Inside the temple there are two side courtyards with front and back halls, and a central courtyard with a well and a protruding open stone altar. Behind it one sees the central hall, with statues of Baosheng Dadi at the center. To his left and right are cases holding statues of thirty-six generals, representing the thirty-six *tiangang* (stellar spirits of the Polar Star constellation). Two side altars house images of the god as a young boy. Behind the central hall and up a flight of stairs is the back hall. There are six altars to other divinities, including one for Guanyin.

The open stone altar is the oldest part of the building, very likely dating to the Song. The altar was no doubt used for Taoist rituals, and the rituals would have been viewed from the balcony. . . . Relief carvings of flying devas playing flutes adorn the sides of the altar, and on top at the front sits a stone lion with a seal in its paw, held face outward. Upstairs, Qing frescoes cover the walls. A bell cast in 1873 hangs in the second-story balcony opposite a large, recently made drum. There are five doors into the temple, a sign of the high status of the god. The walls of the entrance hall and the central hall are covered with fifteen steles, which describe the temples that had branched off from this temple and that were, at that time, sponsoring renovations of the ancestral temple. These stelae begin in the Qing Jiaqing period and continue up to 1984. With their assistance, and drawing on local gazetteers, it is possible to chart the spread of the cult first from the Song to 1799, and then in greater detail on to the present day.

This temple is known as the Western temple. In a recent redrawing of county boundaries, the village has been assigned to Longhai xian (county seat, Shima, across the mouth of the river). Originally Baijiao belonged to Tongan xian, and the temples that have branched off from it come almost exclusively from the greater Quanzhou region to the north. Xiamen also belonged to Tongan, although it was fought over by Quanzhou and Zhangzhou bureaucrats over the centuries. Many affiliated temples of this ancestral temple are on Taiwan. This may partially explain the good condition of the temple. The support offered by overseas Chinese encourages government support and interest in the Baijiao temple. The impressive carved stone dragon pillars in front of this temple were reputedly shipped over from Taiwan in the 1930s.

A half-mile's walk northwest across the spine of the peninsula takes one to the Eastern temple in Qingjiao. This temple was once even larger and more impressive than the Western temple, but it is now in much worse repair. When I first visited in 1985, the roof of the back hall had collapsed, and the side halls were in ruins. The floor of the second-story balcony threatened to collapse. Fortunately, major restorations were sponsored in 1989 by an affiliated Taiwanese temple from Taizhong. In their prime, both temples originally housed *shuyuan* (Confucian academies). Both temples have altars to Guanyin, originally established in the right wing of each temple. The Qingjiao temple is across the county line into the Xiamen City expanded limits. Originally, the temple belonged to Longxi District, and served the greater Zhangzhou region, especially Haicheng. Five steles in this temple, beginning with one from 1697 in the Kangxi period and continuing to 1923, give the names of affiliated temples from Haicheng to Zhangpu. The names of the affiliated temples that visited the temples in 1987 were also posted.

Contemporary Observances

I attended the celebrations surrounding the birthday of the god on lunar 3/15 (1987). A vast number of temples sent groups of young men and older men to pay homage at the temple. Groups arrived by tractor-trailer, truck, chartered bus, or boat. Visiting groups of overseas Chinese were greeted with tea and pleas for aid in reconstruction. Most local temple groups were led by a man holding a banner giving the name of their temple and its location. Behind him came two or three sona players, and a few drum and gong men. Then came a group of four to eight men shouldering a god's palanquin. Many of the groups also brought a medium, usually an older man, who would direct the gathering of incense from the temple burners and the placement of offerings on the altar (sometimes by climbing on top of the altar and placing them himself). Upon entering the great temple, he would go into a trance and lead the group in a mad clockwise dash around the temple. Finally, he would lead the god chair to the open stone altar in the courtyard before the main altar. The god would be set down facing the original god statue (actually a 1982 duplicate of the original destroyed in the Cultural Revolution). After sufficient time had passed for the incense of the offerings to communicate the sincere intentions of the group to the god, the medium would signal the departure, and the sedan chair would race, counterclockwise, out of the temple. Out in the courtyard the chair would dart about seemingly under the power of the god as vast numbers of firecrackers exploded all about it. Finally, they would load the god onto a truck and drive off in yet another burst of firecrackers.

There were many variations on this pattern. Interestingly, a number of groups came without a god because they belong to temples that have not yet been rebuilt. This was the case for four or five groups from Xiamen. Newly built temple groups making their first visit to the temple were filled with exuberance and put on a good show. Many groups from Tongan were led by young mediums in traditional yellow medium's aprons, who worked with four young men dressed in aprons of four different colors. These troupes represent the five spirit soldier camps that protect many villages in this region. They would chant long rhythmic passages to a pounding drum, then assist the medium as he went into a trance. A god's silk umbrella was lowered over the medium's head as a skewer was stuck through his cheek. Then the medium would continue dancing and leaping wildly about as the chanting went on. At each drum beat all five men would hop. The medium would begin beating himself with a sword or a mace of nails. Some of the men would try to protect him from inflicting too much damage by blocking his blows with whisk brooms. Finally, the medium would cry out and leap into the air. The others rushed to catch him and lowered the umbrella over his head and removed the skewer.

Some of the men in the aprons of the five camps were much older and were probably Ritual Masters responsible for the training of this young generation. At least one Taoist priest dared to don his robes briefly at the entrance of one large group. The mediums were fitted out with swords, flags with the dipper star design, and whips of hempen rope. They took scoops of incense on the end of their swords and placed them in incense burners from the home temple carefully transported in sealed wooden boxes shaped like miniature temples.

The most spectacular showing was made by a group of villages from Tongan, all belonging to the same higher-order lineage, who arrived in thirty large boats. They numbered almost fifteen hundred, as virtually every male in the five or six villages was taking part. They marched up the road from Haicang, pausing to paste printed strips of paper announcing the passage of the god onto doorways along the way. When they were out of view of the town, ten mediums, varying in age from early twenties to mid-sixties, climbed atop ten god's palanquins and were carried through the fields to the temple. The group then fanned out across the courtyard before the temple, and the mediums dismounted. They began leaping about, possessed, flailing at themselves with an assortment of weapons. Drums, gongs, oboes, and firecrackers combined with the roar of excited onlookers. Then they charged into the temple, first pausing to rush forward and then back three times by way of saluting the god. Great clouds of incense smoke filled the air of the temple. Several mediums climbed atop the altar and passed a forest of glowing incense sticks into the huge burner, which was now a bonfire. Bands of mediums and chanters set to chanting. The temple committee was frantically struggling to record the names of all the donations and to pass out talismans and souvenirs with photos of the god. The entire episode lasted less than an hour, and soon everyone was outside again, regrouping according to their villages and their gods. They marched back in high spirits to the dock, loaded the heavy sedan chairs with their god statues aboard their boats, and sailed back into the setting sun.

All these visits from temples that had branched off occurred before the actual birthdate of the god, for local custom reserves the worship of the god on that day for the residents of the village of Baijiao. The night before, elaborate preparations were made for all the young men in the village to go barefoot and carry the newly carved, thirty-six attendant generals over a pile of red-hot coals into the temple. This is called *guohuo*, and De Groot again provides a glowing description of the rites involving a barefoot Taoist priest, the barefoot lads, and the male members of the temple community. De Groot feels that these rites are closely connected to the cult of Baosheng Dadi. But he does note that similar rituals were performed on the fifteenth of the first month before many temples. At that time the Taoist wears a tiger's mask when he leaps across the bonfire. Such rituals are always performed at the consecration of a new temple, and so have been very common in Southeast China in the last few years. I observed one medium in Tongan throw himself back-first into a bonfire at the conclusion of a long, entranced dance. Unfortunately, the Taoist priest who had been summoned some time before did not appear by the chosen hour on the dawn of the god's birthday and so the ritual had to be postponed.

Photographs in the Qingjiao temple show large processions with marching bands, singing troupes (*huagu* or *yaogu*) in uniforms, men in traditional long blue gowns, and god chairs carried by enthusiastic young men. Interestingly, De Groot's description focuses on the absence of literati and the filthiness of the "dirty coolies" who carry the god chairs. Nowadays, by contrast, in most villages in Taiwan and increasingly in the Fujian countryside as well, it is considered an honor to carry the god.

The Baijiao temple committee told me that one of the most important Baosheng Dadi temples in Jinjiang was planning to make a major pilgrimage that year (1988) or the next. They planned to have all the men in the village follow the traditional route in the customary manner, walking the entire way in traditional costume and carrying the gods. They estimated the trip would take a week. They hoped to stop along the way in villages with other Baosheng Dadi temples with which the village had connections. They would sponsor theatrical performances each evening. What they have in mind sounds very much like the Dajia pilgrimage to Beigang in Taiwan in honor of Mazu. One does occasionally see processions with mediums in god chairs along the major highway connecting Chaozhou (and Guangzhou) with Fuzhou. But something of this scope has yet to be attempted.

The temple committee informed me that, during the year, the donations usually came to about two thousand yuan a month, but that, during the fortnight around the god's birthday, they collected at least that much each day. They pointed out quite accurately that these funds were still not adequate for the extensive repairs that needed to be made to preserve the building and to maintain the Chinese and Western clinic in the temple. They complained that it was difficult to persuade Cultural Officials to assign the temple the status of a provincial cultural relic, which would free up some government money for repairs.

MATRIFOCAL RITUALS IN PATRIARCHAL CHINA

Traditional Chinese religion in China is far from moribund, and major issues have arisen as the tradition encounters contemporary concerns. China has embarked on a massive change in social culture to resolve its most pressing problem: population growth. China has but a small part of the arable land of this planet but nearly a quarter of its human population. To enable economic growth and social improvement, a one-child policy has been in place since the early 1980s, a policy that on the whole is supported by the population, else it would have no chance of succeeding. But this policy is antithetical to the religious basis of Chinese culture and society: the patrilineal family. Consequently, the abortion of female fetuses is rampant and female infanticide not uncommon. The government has sought to stop both practices but with little success. If both Chinese religion is to continue and there is to be population control (the basis of environmental renewal), then a shift in Chinese religion is mandatory. There are hints that the religious basis of the family may shift under the new circumstances to bilateral lineage rituals, but it would be foolish to make any predictions. The following are excerpts from an article by the editor (J.P.) and Li Chuang Paper, "Matrifocal Rituals in Patrilineal Chinese Religion: The Variability of Patriarchality," *International Journal of Comparative Philosophy and Religion* 1/2 (1995), pp. 22–39, on a contemporary family oriented toward matrilineal rituals.

Introduction

In an earlier article concerned with gender aspects of Chinese religion, "The Persistence of Female Spirits in Patriarchal China,"[1] a co-author of this article mentioned an example of matrilineal rituals in lieu of the patrilineal norm in an aside. The daughters of a deceased female made offerings at the grave of their mother when, in theory and normative practice, they should have made these offerings at the grave sites of their husband's parents. Moreover, in sacrificing to their mother her favorite foods, they placed emphasis on offerings of strong liquor, which they threw on the grave, and lit cigarettes, which they stuck upright in the grave. This was another notable feature of the sacrifice.

These women did not offer sacrifices to their husband's ancestors, the usual procedure, and their children identified with their maternal lineage, rather than that of their fathers, contrary to the Chinese patrilineal pattern. The author noted that this phenomenon, observed in 1986, was worth further exploration. In 1992, an opportunity arose for us to return to the same area and gather information on the life of the woman to whom her daughters offered sacrifice.

Biography

The subject of this article, whom we shall refer to as Laolao (Grandmother), was born in 1902 and died in 1969 . . .

Prior to the success of the Communist party, there was the normative name plaque for sacrifices in Laolao's home with the surnames of both spouses' families, as well as an image of the customary Manchurian fox deity [the family lived in Liaoning Province, but she was of Han parentage and culture]. At the lunar New Year, Ch'ing-ming (the festival for sacrificing at the grave site), and probably other appropriate occasions, Laolao made the traditional offerings to these spirits and to her dead daughter. The latter behavior was unusual, since, by tradition, an unmarried female could not receive sacrifices (hence, the custom of spirit marriages), as she was not ritually a part of her natal family.

In spite of being strictly raised by her conservative, traditional mother, Laolao always spoke positively about her mother and praised her for being able to

---

[1]Jordan Paper, "The Persistence of Female Deities in Patriarchal China," *Journal of Feminist Studies in Religion* 6 (1990), pp. 26–40.

handle money. After the death of her mother, Laolao sacrificed to her, but not to her husband's parents.

These sacrifices were carried out in the traditional mode of far northern China. According to custom, a circle with a break in it is drawn during the night at a neighborhood crossroad. The circle is to exclude unwanted spirits; the break is to allow the offering to reach the desired spirits. The crossroad symbolizes the offering being able to reach the spirits no matter where they are. In the circle, the traditional spirit money is burnt and an offering is made of the deceased's favorite foods. For her mother, Laolao offered steamed bread, eggs, apples, and tangerines, the latter being an expensive luxury in northern China. Every Ch'ing-ming, she went by herself to offer sacrifice to her mother and dead children and came back with eyes red from crying, but kept what she was doing from her children (probably because of the Chinese Communist Party [CCP] policy against "superstition").

After the CCP succeeded in uniting China in the late 1940s, Laolao and her children became ardent communists, except for her eldest surviving daughter (the mother of one of the authors), who left for Taiwan with her husband, an officer with the Kuo-min-tang and a fervent anticommunist. Save for the youngest surviving child, the rest of Laolao's children became Party members. One daughter joined the People's Liberation Army, and two others and her son became local government administrators. Laoyeh also became an administrator in the transportation sector.

When Laolao was upset with her daughters, she would tell them how lucky they were because of the CCP. If it was not for the Party, they would have been married when young and sent off to live with their husband's family, Chinese culture being patrilocal as well as patrilineal.

Laolao herself was in charge of the neighborhood committee, the neighborhood populated by approximately four hundred families. She was responsible for their safety and for family affairs (family squabbles, children fighting, relations between children and parents, etc.), a position that required considerable tact and an ability to work with people. Unusual for Chinese females, Laolao was quite outspoken at meetings and expressed her views forcefully. She had a reputation for being incorruptible and was greatly respected and trusted. She even used her own meager resources to help people. Her house was always full of people seeking her assistance or mediation. People frequently stopped Laolao on the street to talk to her about their problems.

Although around the age of fifty at this time, Laolao was still seeking to improve her written vocabulary. Her position on the neighborhood committee required a fair degree of literacy, and, of course, she had no formal education. She would learn ten new words every day from the granddaughter, then in primary school, who lived with her. With her excellent memory, Laolao never needed to have them repeated.

During the Cultural Revolution, which began in 1966, Laolao was the neighborhood *kan-pu* (cadre). During that time, if one had relatives outside of China (she had a daughter in Taiwan) or connections with the Kuo-min-tang (her husband had been a Kuo-min-tang military officer and her son-in-law in Taiwan still was), one would be in dire straights. However, because of her reputation, members of Laolao's family did not suffer as much as they might have.

Still, Laolao died in the early years of the Cultural Revolution of a heart attack . . .

Analysis

. . . in attempting to understand the 1986 observation of the earlier article, the author first gave consideration to the possibility that, as the family was Manchurian, Manchurian customs had predominated over Han Chinese ones. Manchurian culture has, or at least had, matrifocal aspects. For example, often the eldest daughter did not marry and leave her natal home but became the family "shaman," a religious function passed on through the maternal line. Manchurian women, on the whole, took stronger social and political roles than did Han Chinese women. One need but think of Tzu Hsi, the notorious regent at the end of the Manchu dynasty. However, after investigation it was clear that not only was the subject not technically Manchurian, but her mother had been culturally Han Chinese. Moreover, the fact that there was an attempt to bind her feet was conclusive in this regard, since Manchurian women, to distinguish themselves from Chinese, did not do so. (Instead, they wore shoes on a small platform, approximating the size of a bound foot.)

A second possibility, as mentioned in the previous article, was that the changed socioeconomic status of women, who now are not only wage earners but hold professional and administrative positions, led to matrifocal rituals. It seems that matrifocal sacrifices are no longer considered uncommon, but it is not possible to know if this was also the case prior to the twentieth century. One of the daughter's husbands explained that the current practice was the result of both the (theoretical) equality of males and females under communism and the one-child policy. Hence, it was important to determine the ritual activities of Laolao herself, since not only did she live most of her life before the success of the Chinese Communist Party, but her childhood took place prior to the 1911 Revolution. Although information on her religious practices was sparse, there was no doubt that she offered sacrifices to her mother as we delineated above, but not after the late 1940s to her father nor to her husband's parents.

Although she was unusual, surely Laolao was not unique. All the husbands of the daughters, save one, seem to accept the situation with equanimity. At the Ch'ing-ming sacrifice at Laolao's grave site in 1992 were all five surviving children, including the daughter who resides in Taiwan; three grandchildren (and one of their spouses), including one who resides in Canada; several great-grandchildren; and the spouse of one of the daughters, who took a very active role. All offered lit cigarettes, liquor and food to her; all toasted her with *pai-chiu* [clear, very strong liquor—she both smoked and drank] . . .

The matrifocal religious practices of this unusual, matrilineally oriented family continue unabated into the third generation. No doubt the influence of Laolao, the subject of this biographical study, will continue not only through the generations of her descendants, but also through the hundreds of neighbors she encountered during her life.

As an afterword to the above reading, further research since the article was written has indicated that a shift to bilateral sacrifices is not as far-fetched as it might seem. First, there is precedence for it in the Canons of Ritual and Protocol, which date to the Han dynasty and earlier. The reading in Chapter 5, "Female Spirituality in Traditional Chinese Religion," mentions that a daughter would take the son's role in funeral ceremonies and subsequent sacrifices if there were no son. Moreover, in contemporary Taiwan, with considerable change in the status of females due to the changing socioeconomic situation, it is becoming normative for the name plaques of both husband and wife to be on the family altar. Alternatively, the wife may go to her parent's home, if her parents are alive and do not live too far for a reasonable journey by automobile in order to join in the periodic sacrifices in her natal home.

THE INSTITUTIONALIZATION OF ECSTATIC RELIGIOUS FUNCTIONARIES IN CHINA

Many scholars had assumed that popular Chinese religion, often termed "folk religion" in the literature would disappear with widespread education and modernity. The opposite has occurred. Since the end of the 1980s, Hong Kong, Singapore, and Taiwan have become some of the most modern and technologically advanced societies in the world. Simultaneously, traditional religion has flourished. New temples of all types are being constructed everywhere, and old temples are being refurbished and expanded. Home shrines are increasing in size, and often an entire room in middle-class and upper-class homes are exclusively dedicated to functioning as the family's temple. Stores selling ritual paraphernalia for homes are ubiquitous and thriving. Aside from the geometric growth of manifestations of religious practice, traditional aspects of popular religions are rapidly adjusting to the contemporary milieu. One example is that a group of mediums in Taiwan have formed a modern professional association with a publishing house, a "college," and standards for the certification of practitioners. The following is extracted from an article, "Mediums and Modernity: the Institutionalization of Ecstatic Religious Functionaries in Taiwan," by the editor (J.P.) and published in *The Journal of Chinese Religions* 24(1996): 105–129 (unessential references and other notes have been removed).

THE REPUBLIC OF CHINA ASSOCIATION OF MEDIUMS

Origin and Purpose

The Association originally began in 1987, after the organizers received divine inspiration that those working for the deities should unite to improve the moral tone of a disintegrating society and world. The Association was first called Meihua Lienmeng Tungxin Hui (Plum Flower United With One Heart Society). Given that practitioners of popular religion were officially held in disrepute, it was felt than an association with an explicit title could not receive the requisite government recognition. (The plum flower has many Chinese cultural associations, but one major aspect of the Society's choice of symbol was that it is also the symbol of the Republic of China, emphasizing the Society's strong patriotic bent.)

Martial law ended shortly afterward, and in May 1989, the organizers applied to the government to register the Society. Tentative permission was received in two weeks under the more explicit name of the Zhonghua Minguo Lingji Xiehui (Republic of China Association of Mediums), which the organizers considered a miracle, given both the approval and the quick response of the normally leaden bureaucracy. The qualification for full registration required an organizing meeting within six months. In September of that year, the Association held its first meeting; present was a representative from the Ministry of the Interior. The purpose of the Association was articulated at that meeting. The following is a free rendition of the statement written in the florid prose of formal statements:

> The religious functionaries of the people urgently need assistance and guidance. Hence, for several years, such people have gathered to explore and study the spirit realm, leading to an enhancement of their understanding. Therefore, they have been able to raise the character of the religious practitioners, particularly to increase their empathy, sincerity and willingness to sacrifice themselves for the good of society. This will allow the improvement of society, the reversal of the weakening morality, and the continuation of the traditional lineage of *rujia* thought.
>
> The symbolism of the Association's flag is indicative of its intentions: The twelve plume-flower stars on the field of blue represent the national soul and the Chinese people, symbolize perseverance in spite of diversity and eternal continuity, and also represent the spirit of East Asia and the original mother of humans. The blue sky and the sun represent the light of the spirits on the world. The five petals of each plum flower represent the five nationalities of the Republic of China all united with one heart, the interdependence of the five agents, and that all humans are siblings. [Twelve and five are the most important numbers in Chinese ideology.]
>
> The society is for all religious practitioners, without concern for sect (etc.). The ensuing dialogue among the practitioners of the Association will have many benefits: The spirits [of the dead] will be pacified and the nation protected. People's spirits and bodies will be united and contending groups will be harmonized. The tensions causing unhappiness in dead spirits [leading to problems among the living] will be dissolved. Guidance will be received from mountain spirits and the energy of Earth. . . .
>
> (In summary,) the purpose of the Association is to mediate with the spirit realm to assist the country and the people, so that nature will cooperate with the crops, the country and people will be in peace, and society will achieve *datung* (Great Universality). A voluntary association of *lingji* will raise each others' bodies and spirits, and the spirit realm will work cooperatively with the people. The soul of the organization is based on the understanding that every entity in the spirit realm is equal and false differentiations into higher or lower spirits will not be made, that no differentiation will be made among the members nor among the different religious sects, and that members will not work from personal desires. The Association will abide by the natural method of the Dao and not work for self-aggrandizement nor engage with any political party or other interest groups. In this way, the path of the Dao can be established among the descendants of the Chinese people, in order that their lineage can continue and to enhance the direction of the world.

In ordinary conversation with the leading members, new members and non-member religious practitioners, I repeatedly heard the above simplified into a single statement: Their goal is "to save the world." Toward this end, it is understood that all healings of individuals works toward this goal, as well as their large ritual-meetings when they collectively seek to remedy the ills of the world as a whole (discussed below). It is further understood that the goal will involve all the various methods that the members use in their spiritual work, and it will take a long time to accomplish.

A second major purpose of the Association is to raise the public image of ecstatic religious functionaries. Because of the impact of Western values, particularly Christian sectarian interests, educated Chinese—education in China now Westernized—have come to view traditional practitioners as uneducated charlatans practicing superstition. This was reinforced by the Nationalist Party, which until the end of martial law in 1987 enforced a one-party rule on Taiwan and had maintained loose relationships with Christianity since the 1930s to garner and continue American support. For example, a Taoist priest conducting a funeral ceremony was considered practicing superstition (*mixin*), while a Christian priest or minister doing the same was considered to be practicing religion (*zongjiao*). The Association hopes, through its educational activities for mediums, to change the image of its members among the educated public. Of course, the vast majority of Chinese, of every class, have always gone to such practitioners for succor.

The change in government, with a shift both toward Taiwanese in place of Mainland officials and toward popular Chinese culture, was reflected in the speech of the Ministry of the Interior's representative at the organizing meeting of the Association. She noted that there was a Chinese Buddhist Association and a Chinese Taoist Association, but hitherto none for those who work with Chinese spirits, the major aspect of Chinese religion. Hence, she pointed out that the Ministry was pleased that such an association was forming, with its intention to bring together all the practitioners involved with the spirits, as well as to raise the standards of the practitioners and encourage relevant studies. Indeed, it was the Ministry that suggested the change in the Association's name from the original which avoided mentioning mediums to the more directly denominated present name.

Membership and the Varieties of Religious Functioning

The Association began with a membership of about 1900; at present the Association has well over 2000 individual members and several hundred member temples, a minor portion of functioning mediums and related temples in Taiwan. Almost all of the members are mediums, but non-functioning members are not turned away. Occasionally university students join to take the classes discussed below, and there are some members who may not themselves function mediumistically, but are active in supporting the work of the Association and the temple with which they are associated. None of their members or other mediums they associate with accept money for their work; of course, if they wish, grateful patients and clients are free to make donations to the temples with which the mediums are associated.

Member temples are of many types, but most seem to be those which have developed around a particularly effective medium. Some are predominantly Buddhist in their focus, some Taoist, but most are not linked to any specific *jiao* (doctrine). In the case of those oriented toward Buddhism or Taoism, no Buddhist monks or nuns nor ordained Taoist priests seem to be associated with the temples, but they will have a relationship with either the Buddhist or the Taoist associations.

There are many terms for mediums both in the past, for the last 2500 years or more, and in the present. The most frequent term used in the early literature is *wu*, and the very early dictionary, *Shuowen*, equates *ling* with *wu*. The most common term in southeastern Chinese culture, at least for the last century, is *jitung* (to divine + child), the words reversed in Fujianese (*tâng-ki*). The term the Association uses, and perhaps created, is *lingji*, which seems to be a conflation of the colloquial generic term for mediums, *lingmei* (spirit + go-between/marriage-broker) and *jitung*. The Association has adopted it in order to distinguish its members from non-member mediums, who are denoted by the common term. The focus of the Association is to bring *jitung* into the Association. In particular, the Association considers both the self-torture aspects of common *jitung* practices, as well as their rehearsed dances and posturings, to be unnecessary for effective healing by the spirits. But Association members do associate comfortably with *jitung* who do not utilize these methods; that is, *jitung* who, except for not being members of the Association, are otherwise indistinguishable from Association members. For example, Association members took me to non-member temples with healing *jitung* so that I could see a variety of mediums at work.

I am translating *jitung* and *lingji* as "medium," as the word describes a large majority of the members. As discussed in the section below, "Shamans and Mediums in Chinese Culture," however, some *lingji* actually function as shamans. Moreover, at least a few do not seem to use trance but counsel from the strength of their *ling* (meaning their own spirit and the power of the spirits[s] with which they have a relationship). Indeed, many mediums seem to test each other by asking their colleagues to look at them with their *ling* and tell what they see.

In an article by the foremost theoretician of the Association, Lai Zongxian, "What I Know of *Lingji* Phenomena," *lingji* is first equated with *lingmei* and then further explained:[2]

> *Lingji* signifies someone whose body is available to the *ling* (spirit) realm to communicate to humans, which may be special messages, songs or poems to advise, wake up or save the world, or answers to questions asked by people. *Lingji* are selected by the spirits primarily from those who have inherited the ability through their family lineage or, secondarily, from those who in their previous life developed a relationship with spirits due to a number of reasons. One can recognize that one is potentially a *lingmei* if one begins to have visions with the eyes closed, if one has special dreams, if one hears voices, if one sees written characters while the eyes are open, if one begins to do automatic writing of literary Chinese (not having studied it) or if one spontaneously speaks or sings (Chinese) opera, etc.
>
> For someone without relatives or friends who are mediums, these experiences can be frightening; it could lead to believing one is going mad. Most people who have these experiences will visit a temple to ask a deity about them, but few really understand the spirit realm. So most of the *lingji* experience a long, painful process in understanding the reason for what they are experiencing: that the person prior to coming to this world had promised that their body could be possessed in this world by the spirit realm to fulfill certain missions.
>
> Students of mediumism first have to understand that their mission is unavoidable, and the must face certain tests as they move from one level to mediumship to another (there are three levels). The first test then for the *lingji* is that they must face and know themselves (especially barriers from their past life known by particular problems happening in their present life).

---

[2]A photocopy of the article from an issue of their journal was given to me by the Association, without the bibliographic data. The following is a free translation of the first part of the article.

While carrying out the research for this report, I had the opportunity to observe a number of different modes of ecstatic functioning in addition to those I had observed on previous research trips to Taiwan. In all cases, mediums go into trance almost instantly with no observable preparation, although the planchette[3] (described below) mediums meditate in a room next to where they work prior to functioning. Among many but not all mediums, various physiological indicators of trance are observable: tremors and/or rigidity of the extremities, distended neck and face, a complete change of expression and voice, uncontrollable loud belching, etc.

None of the *lingji* mediums or the similar *jitung* use costumes to indicate the divinity possessing them nor the traditional child's apron worn by the normative *jitung*. But in one non-Association temple, all the functionaries and those assisting them wore simple, yellow robes; others may wear traditionally cut clothing in white; and during the major ceremonials to be discussed below, the leaders wear purple robes and the other members wear yellow garments.

Some mediums were possessed by different spirits in succession, with discernable changes in voice and behavior. One exorcised evil influences by waving incense sticks in patterns about the patient. Another placed the patient in a chair and, sitting on a chair behind the patient, healed with motions of the hand. In one temple, a medium healed up to eight hundred patients a day every Wednesday and Sunday. There were so many patients waiting their turn that a volunteer orchestra of traditional instruments played for them, and a television set showing videos of temple-sponsored pilgrimages was placed in front of rows of folding chairs. A free multi-course lunch was also provided. At that same temple, healing and counseling were carried out with the planchette (*ji* as in *lingji*).

The planchette is a forked stick with a vertical appendage at the apex. The stick is held with one or two hands and traces Chinese characters either on a plain flat surface or a sandbox on a table. In the healing I observed, the patients write their problem on a modern multi-copy form. This problem is then communicated to a deity via the medium, whose hand is then moved by the divinity possessing her or him to trace out the characters of the response. Two or three readers, placed on opposite sides of the table, together call out the character to ensure that the word is read correctly A scribe then records the response on the lower part of the form filled out by the patient. One copy is returned to the patient, one copy is burned to return it to the spirit realm, and a third copy is kept for the temple records, collections of which are occasionally published. Another assistant may take the patient aside to explain the deity's response. The planchette is struck on a table with a leather surface for each stroke of every character. At times, the planchette is struck on a special red-ink pad and then struck, leaving a red impression, on one of three types of paper: one that can be burned and the ashes drunk with water as medication, one that can be hung in the home as a continual blessing, and one that can be worn around the neck in a pouch as an amulet. Throughout the session, the medium appeared to be continuously in trance; slight tremors of the hand persisted between patients.

This method is also used for writing messages to people in general by deities, and some temples publish multi-volume books based on the received messages.

---

[3]Of course, this is not the planchette of Western Spiritualism, but the term is borrowed for lack of any other.

This is a mediumistic method utilized by the literati for at least the last thousand years. Contrary to the bias of the Western educated Chinese that only the uneducated are involved with mediumistic activities, the medium's assistants included a dean of studies at an institution of higher education, a bank manager, the head of a large corporation and several government officials.

Lingji themselves stressed to me that a patient's belief was essential for the mediums to be effective in their work; hence, the curing would seem to be one of faith healing. However, from my limited observations, there is more involved than faith healing alone, and healing can take place even if the patient has no faith in the process. For example, my Chinese father-in-law drove my wife and me to the temples on the fringes of a city, as they were otherwise difficult for us to reach. He is oriented toward Western culture, having twice studied at military institutes in the United States, and is nominally a Catholic. He is elderly and has several medical problems. After observing a number of healings by the medium described above who sits behind the patient, he was offered an opportunity to be healed.

Throughout the diagnosis and healing, the medium never touched my father-in-law who, of course, could not see what the medium was doing. My wife and I observed from slightly to the rear, so that neither I nor anyone else could be seen by my father-in-law. During the diagnosis part of the session, done by moving the hands over the patient's back without any direct touch, the medium appeared to be in a light trance. The diagnosis completed, the medium went into an observably deeper trance: First his head moved in circles with his eyes closed, and then his neck nearly doubled in circumference; the hands and arms became rigid. The fingers sought a point along the patient's back and then focused on a single spot, again without any direct touch, while the other hand made symbolic gestures. My father-in-law noticeably jerked at that moment and afterwards expressed feeling considerable heat. He also expressed feeling markedly better. In this case, the patient was very skeptical about the healing prior to the session; clearly faith played no part. The method does relate to a standard Chinese healing practice with qi (life-force or energy), but here it was understood that it was a deity that was healing through the body of the possessed medium.

Institutional Structure

The structure of the Association is complex; the following general data are extracted from the detailed 36 page "Member's Manual," which is the equivalent of the Association's constitution. Membership both for individuals and temples requires completing an application which is reviewed by the Executive. Disqualifying factors include being a convicted felon or in a state of bankruptcy. Membership can be removed for those who seriously violate the Association's rules or fail to pay dues for two consecutive years.

The administration includes a provincial (Taiwan) administration, plus five district administrations with eight regional offices. Officers are elected by a meeting of 100 delegates who are elected by district for a four-year term. The officers include provincial and regional executives, advisory boards, and so on.

The Association's finances are based on membership dues: in 1995, the equivalent of approximately U.S. $25 per year for individuals and $50 for institutions. Initiation fees are the same. This is relatively modest amount, given that professional salaries are on a par with the United States, if not higher, although it is to be understood that most members are not well educated and would be lower middle-class at best. Some members—owners of export companies, bank managers, etc.—however, are quite well off. Other sources of income include grants from the government for specific activities (I am uncertain of the details), donations (the Association is a registered non-profit organization), and interest on savings.

Publications

The publication activities of this relatively small society are impressive. In addition to a newsletter printed in newspaper format, various reports, directories, and handbooks, until the early 1990s, the Association published a journal. Called the *Zhonghua Dadao* (Great Way of Chinese Culture) in Chinese and *Natural Law* in English, the journal was printed in large magazine format with numerous illustrations, including full color plates on the outside and inside of the covers. Articles were quite diverse and include learned papers from their seminars, as well as reports on interesting Association activities, such as pilgrimages to major Mainland religious sites. Publication of the journal faded with a shift toward producing textbooks for their college.

As of 1995, three books have been published by the Association. The only textbook published at that time was an elementary one, a paperback of 285 pages, *Zhonghua Daotung Congshu* (1994). It begins with three brief major texts from each of the *sanjiao* (Three Doctrines):[4] The *Heart Sutra*, the shortest and most commonly recited of the Buddhist sutras; the *Qingjing Classic*, a short recitation piece attributed to Laozi; and the *Xueyungsheng Classic*, from the writings of Zhu Xi, the foremost Rujia interpreter. Each is presented with a brief preface and is printed with the phonetic system used in the Taiwan elementary schools beside the Chinese characters to enable recitation by those not well versed in the vocabulary of literary Chinese. These three brief works are followed by two longer works, printed with the same format: the *Daodejing*, well known to Western readers, and the *Diamond Sutra*, the second most popular of the Prajñaparamita scriptures. These texts are followed by various treatises one that relates Chinese metaphysics to Western general science; another that provides detailed, diagrammatic analyses of the *taiji*, the eight trigrams, the 64 hexagrams, geomancy, etc., including parallels to Euclidean geometry; various permutations of the Five Agents; etc.

The other two works, both published in 1995, are handsomely printed, substantial hard-bound books by Huang Haide, the Vice-Director of the Philosophy Research Section of the Siquan Social Science Academy, and Li Gang, a professor at the Religious Studies Institute of Siquan University. One book is *Zhonghua Daojiao Paodian*, a one-volume encyclopedia of Taoism; the second is *Taishang Daozu (Laozi) jing, shih, lun*, the text of the *Daodejing*, together with a history of the book and a detailed commentary.

The Association is presently working on more advanced textbooks. It will probably also publish other books by Mainland scholars on topics considered of importance to its members.

---

[4]The presentation of these texts in this volume illustrate the Chinese meaning of *sanjiao*, rather than the continuing Western misreading of the term as "Three Chinese Religions." The Chinese use of the term is for three sets of doctrines that form a unified ideology that underlies Chinese religion in the singular.

Educational Activities

You Meiling, the Association's Executive Director and one of the lead instructors in the Association's college, understands that a true *lingji* requires no explicit training; the spirits will teach the person how to function. Hence, the purpose of the Association's educational endeavors is "to raise the standards" of the *lingji*, rather than to instruct them on how to be a medium. There are two types of educational programs: one-day seminars and a "college."

The one-day seminars meet on the twelfth day of each lunar month in the Association's headquarters in a temple outside of Taipei,[5] which has a large meeting hall, classrooms, and a dormitory for the students of the college. Topics vary, depending on the speaker; learned members of the Association, sympathetic academics, and leaders of other congenial religious movements (e.g., Taoist and Confucian associations) speak on diverse topics relevant to the mediums. Seminars are also used for discussing various activities and goals of the Association.

The main educational enterprise is named the Chinese Ling College (*Zhonghua ling xueyuan*). Tuition, as well as room and board, are free. There are four courses leading to certificates. The first is the "Introductory Course," which has no requirements for enrollment. The course is taught in a single 12-day session at the main temple and in four three-day courses spread over four months in other parts of Taiwan. Both modes are offered twice a year. Lectures include various aspects of the *sanjiao*, at night there are sessions to "adjust" the students *ling* (healing sessions to harmonize the student's spirit and the spirits with whom they work).

The "Beginners' Course" requires completion of the "Introductory Course" and membership in the Association. It meets for ten days in each of three consecutive months for a total of thirty days. It is held at various places in the countryside to facilitate an environment helpful for the students to purify their *ling*.

The "Intermediate Course" requires completion of the "Beginners' Course" and meets for ten days per month for a total of 120 days. Classes include those on unifying the *ling* and the body, uniting the deity and the body, and understanding the way of Sky-Earth (explained as nature) through studying *yinyang* (the essential energies) and *wuxing* (the Five Agents) as well as meditation.

The fourth certificate course is on "Taoist Studies"[6] and meets for three days each week for four months over two terms, for a total of approximately a hundred days. Enrollment requires completion of the "Beginners' Course." Classes include Taoist studies, civics, *ling* studies, *taijiquan*, *qigung*, and adjusting *ling*.

Association Rituals

The Association has sponsored a variety of occasional pilgrimages. These comprised traveling around the island of Taiwan from one member temple to another and to smaller islands such as Penghu, as well as trips to mainland China. In the latter 140 members took part in a Qingming (Tomb Sweeping) Festival pilgrimage that involved 15,000 people, according to Chinese newspapers, to the tomb of the

---

[5]28-1, Wan-t'an Lu, Hsin-tien, Taipei County, Taiwan, Republic of China.

[6]The leading theoretician of the Association, Lai Zongxian, at the time of the research was studying at a university in Siquan Province on the Mainland for a doctorate in Daoist studies.

mythic founder of Chinese civilization, the Yellow Emperor, in Shanxi Province. Other pilgrimages included trips to the primary Mazu (the most important deity in Taiwan) temple in Fujian Province, and to Mount Tai in Shandung Province, the paramount sacred mountain throughout the history of Chinese religion.

The principal Association ritual is called a *fahui*, an elaborate ritual offering to spirits. The Association holds at least two each year, spring and fall, and others when divinely inspired to do so. The ritual meetings rotate among the Association's districts; and the precise dates, focus, and sponsoring temples are chosen via divination. Several thousand people may take part, and invited guests may include politicians, who will need to stand respectfully for many hours at a time during the several days, usually three, of the ritual. At a late 1995 *fahui*, one of the four candidates for the early 1996 presidential elections was conspicuous.[7] The *fahui* are funded through donations; donors are listed in writing and announced several times during the ritual (for the spirits to hear their names).

Fahui is a Buddhist term, literally meaning Dharma-meeting, but the Association's ritual is predominantly Taoist. The Association provides a history of *fahui*, noting that it is normally called by the Taoist term, *jiao* (renewal ritual). They trace the ritual from the "Five Pecks of Rice" movement of the second century through Chinese history to the present, as would most scholars, and point out that it was carried out in the court for every emperor. The Association theorists understand that their ritual follows both those of the court and the normative Taoist *jiao*. As the *daoshi* (ordained Taoist priests—the only "Taoists" in Chinese culture) replaced the *fangshi* (court exorcists) of the early period, so they see their own members as *lingshi* replacing the *daoshi*.

The following statement of purpose is translated from one of the Association's announcements for a *fahui*.

> The main purpose of a *fahui* is to respectfully invite the sages (*sheng*), deities (*shen*), realized adepts (*xian*), and masters (*shi*) to [mediumistically] descend to the *fa* altar to make peaceful the spirit (*ling*) realm, and harmonize the source of *ling*, in order to serve the needs of the public. The meaning of *fahui* is to seek help from the upper realm to save the spirits of the dead from purgatory, to transpose the spirits of the dead to a better place and raise their status, to protect the country and the people, and create unity through a peaceful reconciliation of both sides of the Taiwan Straight. All of this is to fulfill the wish of Mazu: that we, her descendants, all return to her.

Hence, the main purposes are for "mortuary rituals, to prevent disasters, to help the nation, and to pacify ghosts."

Other stated purposes include harmonizing the participants' minds and natures and purifying their hearts, minds, and mouths, so they can interrelate with spirits and deities to gain blessings and prevent calamities. A secondary set of purposes is for the members to come together and socialize, as well as spread religious teachings. Auxiliary purposes include gaining blessings for the country and the people, collecting charitable contributions for social welfare, cultural

---

[7]Ch'en Li-an was one of the independent candidates for President (the candidates from the two parties are both Christians). He holds a Ph.D. and held many high government positions, including President of the Control Yuan (the equivalent of a cabinet) from 1993 until the election campaign began in 1995.

exchanges between Taiwan and the Mainland, and the spread and enhancement of public morality.

The ritual follows the standard *jiao* procedures: "setting up the altar, putting out the offerings [food which can fill many large tables], burning incense, writing out petitions to the spirits, reading the petitions, reciting sacred texts, all accompanied by candles, music, and ritual dance-steps." However, the above is but an outline, the details of any particular *fahui* ritual are based on the divine inspiration of the ritual leader as the ritual progresses. This is probably how the *jiao* rituals originated.